World Intellectual Property Indicators 2018

WIPO
WORLD
INTELLECTUAL PROPERTY
ORGANIZATION

© WIPO, 2018

World Intellectual Property Organization
34, chemin des Colombettes, P.O. Box 18
CH-1211 Geneva 20, Switzerland

ISBN: 978-92-805-2984-5

Attribution 3.0 IGO
(CC BY 3.0 IGO)

Cover image: monsitj / Getty Images

Printed in Switzerland

Table of contents

Special theme

Patents

Trademarks

Industrial designs

Plant varieties

Geographical indications

Creative economy

Additional information

Foreword

Against the backdrop of solid economic growth worldwide, global intellectual property (IP) filing activity set new records in 2017. Patent filings around the world reached 3.17 million, representing a 5.8% growth on 2016 figures. Trademark filing activity totaled 12.39 million, up 26.8% on 2016. Industrial design filing activity exceeded 1.24 million. China remained the main driver of global growth in IP filings. From already high levels, patent filings in China grew by 14.2% and trademark filing activity in China by 55.2%. These high growth rates propelled China's shares of global patent filings and trademarks filing activity to reach 43.6% and 46.3%, respectively.

Japan (+24.2%) and the United States of America (+12.6%) also saw strong growth in trademark filing activity. However, both of those countries recorded almost no growth in patent filings. The Republic of Korea saw a decline in filing activity for patents and trademarks for the second consecutive year. Other notable trends include large increases in trademark filing activity in the Islamic Republic of Iran (+87.9%), the United Kingdom (+24.1%) and Canada (+19.5%). With regard to industrial design filing activity, the United Kingdom (+92.1%), Spain (+23.5%) and Switzerland (+17.9%) saw double-digit growth in 2017.

The special theme of this year's edition of WIPO's *World Intellectual Property Indicators* explores how one might statistically capture patent litigation activity. It compares patent litigation systems across jurisdictions and documents the challenges associated with collecting comprehensive and comparable patent litigation data. It also presents selected statistics available for the United Kingdom and the United States of America.

For the first time, this year's edition includes statistics on the creative economy. In particular, on the basis of an original survey jointly conducted with the International Publishers Association, we report key performance data on publishing activity covering 28 countries. We recognize that these statistics are in many ways still incomplete, but view them as a first step toward establishing a more complete and comparable picture of global publishing activity worldwide. In the longer term, we also hope to include other parts of the creative economy in our statistical reporting.

Readers wishing to go beyond the statistics presented in this report can use the statistical tools on WIPO's website (*www.wipo.int/ipstats*), notably the IP Statistics Data Center and the Statistical Country Profiles.

Finally, I would like to thank our member states, as well as national and regional IP authorities, for sharing their annual statistics with WIPO. Their invaluable cooperation makes the *World Intellectual Property Indicators* possible.

Francis GURRY
Director General

Acknowledgements

World Intellectual Property Indicators 2018 was prepared under the direction of Francis Gurry (Director General) and supervised by Carsten Fink (Chief Economist). The report was prepared by a team led by Mosahid Khan and comprising Kyle Bergquist, Ryan Lamb, Bruno Le Feuvre and Hao Zhou, all from the Economics and Statistics Division. The geographical indications section was prepared by Matteo Gragnani and benefited greatly from the inputs contributed by Alexandra Grazioli, from the Brands and Designs Sector. Peter Button of the International Union for the Protection of New Varieties of Plants (UPOV) provided comments and suggestions for the plant varieties section. The special theme on patent litigation is based on a background paper prepared by Professor Christian Helmers of Santa Clara University. It also draws on helpful input received from Andrew Toole, Chief Economist of the USPTO.

Samiah Do Carmo Figueiredo and Caterina Valles Galmes provided administrative support. Gratitude is also due to the Communications Division for the editing and design and to staff in the Printing Plant for their services.

Further information

Online resources

The electronic version of the report and the underlying data can be downloaded at *www.wipo.int/ipstats*. This webpage also provides a link to the IP Statistics Data Center, offering access to WIPO's statistical data.

Contact information

Economics and Statistics Division
Website: *www.wipo.int/ipstats*
e-mail: *ipstats.mail@wipo.int*

Key numbers

Patents	2016	2017	Growth rate (%)	Share of world total (%)
Applications worldwide	**3,125,100**	**3,168,900**	..	**100.0**
China	1,338,503	1,381,594	..	43.6
U.S.	605,571	606,956	0.2	19.2
Japan	318,381	318,479	0.0	10.1

Utility models				
Applications worldwide	**1,553,280**	**1,761,200**	..	**100.0**
China	1,475,977	1,687,593	..	95.8
Germany	14,030	13,301	−5.2	0.8
Russian Federation	11,112	10,643	−4.2	0.6

Trademarks				
Application class counts worldwide	**9,771,400**	**12,387,600**	**26.8**	**100.0**
China	3,697,731	5,739,823	55.2	46.3
U.S.	545,279	613,921	12.6	5.0
Japan	451,144	560,269	24.2	4.5

Industrial designs				
Applications design counts worldwide	**1,240,600**	**1,242,100**	..	**100.0**
China	650,344	628,658	..	50.6
EUIPO (EU Office)	104,522	111,021	6.2	8.9
Republic of Korea	69,120	67,357	−2.6	5.4

Plant varieties				
Applications worldwide	**16,560**	**18,490**	**11.7**	**100.0**
China	2,923	4,465	52.8	24.1
Community Plant Variety Office (EU)	3,299	3,422	3.7	18.5
U.S.	1,604	1,557	−2.9	8.4

.. indicates not available.

Note: Due to the new way in which the intellectual property (IP) office of China counts its IP applications received in 2017, the 2016 and 2017 patent, industrial design and utility model application data for China are not comparable. Prior to 2017, it included all applications received in its totals; however, starting in 2017, all China's application counts include only those applications for which the office has received the necessary application fees.

Source: WIPO Statistics Database, September 2018.

Overview of IP filing activity

Table 1. Ranking of total (resident and abroad) IP filing activity by origin, 2017

Origin	Patents	Marks	Designs	Origin	Patents	Marks	Designs
China	1	1	1	Morocco	71	48	22
U.S.	2	2	4	Colombia	48	36	69
Germany	5	4	2	Chile	47	30	82
Japan	3	3	6	Greece (b)	46	74	43
Republic of Korea	4	11	3	Slovakia	57	51	56
France	6	5	8	Liechtenstein (a)	45	62	58
U.K.	7	8	9	Cyprus (b)	59	53	55
Italy	10	12	5	Pakistan	72	33	63
India	11	9	13	Belarus	41	63	72
Switzerland	8	14	11	United Arab Emirates (c)	50	50	79
Iran (Islamic Republic of)	16	6	12	Croatia	69	65	47
Russian Federation	12	7	18	Saudi Arabia (b)	29	95	57
Turkey	22	10	7	Slovenia (a, b, c)	61	73	54
Netherlands	9	19	14	Bangladesh	102	55	36
Spain	23	16	10	Serbia	66	69	59
Sweden	14	21	19	Malta (a, c)	54	68	73
Australia	21	17	17	Mongolia	87	56	52
Canada	13	15	27	Uzbekistan	62	66	68
Brazil	24	13	21	Venezuela (Bolivarian Republic of)	88	46	..
Poland (c)	26	25	16	Lithuania	73	67	64
Austria (c)	17	27	24	Syrian Arab Republic	86	59	60
Ukraine	32	23	15	Estonia	68	75	65
Belgium	18	28	32	Peru	81	42	88
Denmark	19	38	25	Kazakhstan (b)	39	96	86
China, Hong Kong SAR	34	26	23	Monaco	74	76	74
Mexico	33	18	33	Latvia	80	70	76
Indonesia	35	24	28	Sudan	67	97	62
Thailand	40	29	20	Egypt (a, b)	85	115	30
Finland	20	40	35	Kenya	75	72	84
Singapore	25	32	38	Barbados (a)	56	113	67
Czech Republic	36	34	26	Republic of Moldova	89	82	66
Israel	15	52	31	Georgia	94	84	60
Portugal	42	31	29	China, Macao SAR	76	91	77
Viet Nam	51	22	34	Armenia	78	79	91
Norway	27	41	42	Iceland	64	86	100
Argentina	49	20	44	Côte d'Ivoire (a, b, c)	63	108	83
New Zealand	31	37	46	Ecuador	123	57	75
South Africa	37	47	39	Sri Lanka (b)	65	123	69
Romania	43	43	40	Uruguay	89	77	92
Luxembourg	30	44	53	Panama	92	61	106
Malaysia	38	39	50	Costa Rica	100	58	103
Ireland (b)	28	54	50	Jordan	96	81	89
Hungary	44	49	45	Qatar (c)	84	93	90
Philippines	55	35	48	Dominican Republic	113	60	97
Bulgaria	58	45	37	Tunisia (b)	77	112	81

Origin	Patents	Marks	Designs
Cameroon (a, b, c)	53	122	99
Senegal (a, b, c)	60	119	95
Bosnia and Herzegovina	95	104	80
Iraq (b, c)	52	106	122
Guatemala	105	64	112

Origin	Patents	Marks	Designs
San Marino (a, b, c)	115	125	41
Ghana	126	109	49
Jamaica	125	87	85
Bolivia (Plurinational State of)	108	83	107
Azerbaijan (a, b)	70	129	..

.. indicates not available.

Note: Rankings are based on the total numbers of applications filed by origin. Patent data refer to numbers of equivalent patent applications. Trademark data refer to numbers of equivalent trademark applications based on class counts – the number of classes specified in applications. Industrial design data refer to numbers of equivalent industrial design applications based on design counts – the number of designs contained in applications. This table lists origins for which at least two types of IP filing data are available.

(a) Data on patent applications at the national IP office are not available.

(b) Data on trademark applications at the national IP office are not available.

(c) Data on industrial design applications at the national IP office are not available.

Source: WIPO Statistics Database, September 2018.

Table 2. Ranking of resident IP activity by origin, 2017

Origin	Patents	Marks	Designs
China	1	1	1
Japan	3	2	7
Germany	5	6	2
U.S.	2	3	8
Republic of Korea	4	10	3
France	6	5	10
Iran (Islamic Republic of)	9	4	11
Turkey	13	9	4
U.K.	8	11	9
India	10	7	12
Italy	11	13	5
Russian Federation	7	8	15
Spain	20	16	6
Brazil	16	12	19
Netherlands	12	21	18
Switzerland	14	24	14
Poland	17	23	..
Ukraine	25	22	13
Australia	24	17	20
Indonesia	26	20	22
Sweden	15	30	24
Mexico	30	14	28
Canada	19	15	40
Austria	18	34	..
Thailand	37	26	17

Origin	Patents	Marks	Designs
Belgium	23	32	30
Portugal	38	27	23
Czech Republic	36	35	21
Denmark	21	45	26
Viet Nam	46	19	27
Romania	33	37	32
Argentina	49	18	37
Finland	22	47	38
China, Hong Kong SAR	52	29	33
Morocco	58	41	16
Norway	27	44	45
Greece	43	..	35
Malaysia	32	38	47
South Africa	40	42	36
Singapore	28	48	44
Saudi Arabia	31	..	52
Philippines	53	31	41
Bulgaria	56	43	31
Hungary	45	46	39
New Zealand	35	40	55
Ireland	39	..	48
Israel	29	68	34
Colombia	44	33	63
Pakistan	59	28	54
Chile	48	25	79

Origin	Patents	Marks	Designs
Slovakia	57	49	46
Bangladesh	78	50	29
Luxembourg	41	57	60
Mongolia	65	51	43
Uzbekistan	51	56	56
Kazakhstan	34	..	75
Venezuela (Bolivarian Republic of)	71	39	..
Syrian Arab Republic	66	53	53
Sri Lanka	55	..	60
Croatia	62	63	49
Belarus	47	64	67
Peru	70	36	77
Lithuania	68	62	57
Sudan	54	87	50
Kenya	64	60	71

Origin	Patents	Marks	Designs
Tunisia	61	..	69
Serbia	60	74	64
Latvia	68	67	66
United Arab Emirates	75	59	..
Georgia	76	78	51
Estonia	73	72	62
Ecuador	93	52	65
Republic of Moldova	77	75	59
Armenia	67	79	81
Cyprus	79	..	73
Ghana	94	93	42
Dominican Republic	90	54	86
Trinidad and Tobago	..	98	58
Liechtenstein (a)	50	103	83
Uruguay	87	69	82

.. indicates not available.

Note: Rankings are based on the numbers of resident applications filed by origin. Patent data refer to numbers of equivalent patent applications. Trademark data refer to numbers of equivalent trademark applications based on class counts – the number of classes specified in applications. Industrial design data refer to numbers of equivalent industrial design applications based on design counts – the number of designs contained in applications. This table lists origins for which at least two types of IP filing data are available.

(a) Data on patent applications at the national IP office are not available.

Source: WIPO Statistics Database, September 2018.

Special theme

An overview of patent litigation systems across jurisdictions

Introduction

The ability of patent right holders to enforce their intangible property rights when those rights are infringed is an important aspect of the patent system. The value of patents will diminish if right holders are unable to enforce their patent rights. During the past decade, patent disputes have generated news headlines, and attracted considerable attention from both practitioners and policymakers. This is partly due to widely publicized, protracted litigation between well-known technology companies; most notably litigation involving Apple, Huawei, Samsung and Qualcomm. For example, after seven years of litigation, Apple and Samsung settled their patent disputes in 2018.[1] Furthermore, patent litigation has also involved patent assertion entities (PAEs), and there have been a number of litigations involving standard essential patents, all of which have put the functioning of the patent litigation systems in the spotlight.

Apart from the high-profile cases reported in the media, many jurisdictions lack systematic data on patent litigations. Enhancing data availability by effectively monitoring the functioning of the patent litigation system would facilitate evidence-based policymaking. The rise in patent litigation in the United States of America (U.S.) over the past years is well-documented (Cook, 2007; Meurer and Bessen, 2013).[2] However, for other jurisdictions, data on patent litigation activity is either incomplete or unavailable. For example, in the U.S., comprehensive data on court cases are available through both public and private sources, allowing detailed analysis of litigation; while in Germany and the Republic of Korea, only incomplete data are available.

While the patent system in general makes enormous amounts of information and data available to the public, patent litigation has occurred largely out of sight, in the privacy of the court system. As a result, it is often difficult to gauge the magnitude of patent litigation in the various jurisdictions. There have been individual efforts by researchers to compile and analyze litigation data, but these efforts were conducted on an ad hoc basis (Cremers et al., 2016a; Helmers and McDonagh, 2013).

There have been a number of attempts to address this issue outside of the U.S. and substantial progress has been made in some jurisdictions, notably in China where all decisions by courts are supposed to be made publicly available online. However, in practice, coverage is below 100 percent and the data cover infringement decisions only. Commercial data providers have, nevertheless, tapped into this market and made significant investments to improve the existing data infrastructure covering many jurisdictions.

The objective of this section is to explore how one might statistically capture patent litigation activity.[3] It compares patent litigation systems across jurisdictions and documents the challenges involved in collecting comprehensive and comparable patent litigation data. It also presents selected statistics available within the United Kingdom (U.K.) and the U.S.[4]

An overview of patent litigation systems

The main objective of patent litigation is to allow patent owners to enforce their patent claims against potential infringers. As in any type of litigation, the judicial system deals with disputes that could not be settled by the parties out of court and which therefore require adjudication. While the structure of patent litigation proceedings in court is similar across jurisdictions, there are nevertheless important differences. It is therefore useful to review the basic structure common to all patent litigation systems and highlight some of the ways in which systems differ around the world.

One of the most important differences in the various jurisdictions of patent litigation systems is whether they follow a unified or a bifurcated system. In a unified system, infringement and invalidity are dealt with within the same proceedings, where invalidity is usually raised as a defense by the defendant to the infringement claim by the plaintiff. The judge will assess both claims simultaneously, which implies that a patent that is found to be invalid cannot be infringed. In a bifurcated system, there are separate proceedings in different venues to establish infringement and invalidity. In this system, invalidity is not usually an admissible defense to an infringement claim. The defendant will concentrate on a non-infringement defense while potentially attempting to invalidate the patent in parallel at the competent venue. Since the question of validity has a direct effect on infringement proceedings, courts have the option to stay infringement proceedings until validity has been decided.

In most jurisdictions, validity is decided not only by the courts but also administratively by the intellectual property (IP) office. Such administrative validity challenges can take the form of a post-grant opposition that allows third parties to challenge validity within a certain period after the grant. For example, at the European Patent Office (EPO), opposition to the granting of a patent can be filed within nine months of the mention of the grant in the *European Patent Bulletin*. Whether infringement and validity are dealt with in a unified or bifurcated system has a number of important effects on patent litigation behavior and outcomes. For example, depending on the design of the bifurcated system, it is possible for the infringement decision to be made before the invalidity decision. This implies that a patent may be found to be infringed that is eventually invalidated (Cremers *et al.*, 2016b). Bifurcation may also have a direct effect on litigation behavior. Evidence from Germany and the U.K. suggests that a bifurcated system, in which infringement is usually decided first, leads to fewer validity challenges than a unified system. Moreover, infringement actions are more likely to be settled (Cremers *et al.*, 2016b).

The number of courts which are competent to hear patent cases differs significantly across jurisdictions. In the U.S., 94 federal district courts are competent to hear patent cases. Patent infringement claims can also be brought before the International Trade Commission (ITC), but the ITC cannot award monetary damages. In Germany, 12 regional courts are competent to hear first-instance patent infringement claims. In other jurisdictions, such as France or the Netherlands, there is only a single court competent to hear patent cases. In the U.K., there are two courts that hear patent cases,

with one (the Intellectual Property Enterprise Court – IPEC) hearing cases that are less complex and of a lower value than the other (the Patents Court – PHC). In Germany, some regional courts have specialist chambers that hear patent cases. In the U.S., the Court of Appeals for the Federal Circuit (CAFC) is a specialized court, while first-instance district courts are not. The availability of different courts in which to file a claim may provide the opportunity to engage in forum shopping; that is, to make a strategic choice of court venue. This type of behavior may have an impact on the litigation statistics.

The costs associated with patent litigation vary significantly between jurisdictions. For example, in France, cost estimates for each party range between USD 60,000 and USD 250,000 while in Germany they range from USD 90,000 to USD 250,000 (Cremers *et al.*, 2016a). These costs are low in comparison to other jurisdictions, such as the U.K. or the U.S. where costs are commonly well over USD 1 million (Helmers and McDonagh, 2013; AIPLA, 2017). Such large disparities are explained by a number of factors, including the extent of pre-trial discovery and the role of expert witnesses, as well as the length and complexity of the trials themselves.

Table S1 provides an overview of the main characteristics of patent litigation systems for selected jurisdictions.

S1. Overview of the main characteristics of major patent litigation systems

Characteristics	Jurisdiction							
	China	France	Germany	Japan	Netherlands	Republic of Korea	U.K.	U.S.
Bifurcated	Yes	No	Yes	Yes	No	Yes	No	No
Administrative post-grant review	No	Yes (EPO)	Yes (EPO, DPMA)	Yes	Yes (EPO)	Yes	Yes (EPO)	Yes
Jury trial	No	No	No	No	No	No	No	Yes
Preliminary injunction	Yes	Yes	Yes	Yes	Yes	Yes	Yes	Yes
Criminal liability	No	Yes	Yes	Yes	Yes	Yes	Yes	No
Average duration in first instance (months)	6–18	18–24	14	12–15	12	10–18	24–36	18–42
Level of damages	Low	Average	Average	Low	Low	Low	High	High
Punitive damages	No	No	No	No	No	No	No	Yes
Fee shifting	Limited	Limited	Limited	Limited	Full	Limited	Full (item-based)	Limited
Average costs in first instance ('000' USD)	20–150	60–250	90–250	300–500	70–250	150–400	1,000–2,000	1,000–6,000*
Number of courts first instance	18 specialized + regular courts	1	12 (+1 validity)	2	1	5	2	94
Specialized court/ judges first instance	Partly	Yes	Yes	Yes	Yes	Partly	Yes	No
Specialized court of appeal	Yes	No	No	Yes	No	Yes	No	Yes
Separate trial for damages	No	No	Yes	Yes	No	No	Yes	No
Utility models	Yes	No	Yes	Yes	No	Yes	No	No
Design patents	Yes	No	No	No	No	No	No	Yes

* indicates median.

Note: EPO is the European Patent Office. DPMA is the Deutsche Patent- und Markenamt.

Source: AIPLA (2017), Clark (2011), Cremers *et al.* (2016a), Graham and van Zeebroeck (2014) and Thomson Reuters Practical Law.

Challenges associated with compiling and analyzing patent litigation data

Compiling and analyzing patent litigation data is an extremely difficult task for the following reasons:
(a) patent litigation is considered one of the most complex forms of civil litigation,
(b) litigation settled before reaching the court system is not publicly documented,
(c) private information exchanged between parties is not revealed to the court or, even if revealed, it is not recorded,
(d) information on cases is not centrally collated in many jurisdictions (i.e., information has to be accessed from individual courts), and
(e) there are also substantial differences between jurisdictions that affect the interpretation of observed litigation data and make any direct comparison of litigation across jurisdictions challenging.

In most jurisdictions, no official aggregate statistics of patent litigation activity are available. Consequently, it is difficult to verify the completeness of any case-level data set unless the data were collected directly from court records. Collecting court records and converting them into a statistical database of patent litigation is a resource-intensive task.

One of the most frequently used patent litigation indicators is the number of cases. However, there is enormous heterogeneity in court cases, as well as in administrative post-grant reviews, even within the same jurisdiction. This creates challenges when constructing case counts and comparing those counts between jurisdictions. For example, in a bifurcated jurisdiction, court cases will be predominantly infringement claims. Invalidity challenges are recorded as separate cases, even when the validity challenge occurred as a direct response to an infringement action. In a unified system, an infringement action with an invalidity defense would show up only as a single case. One way to account for such heterogeneity is to count cases by type of claim.

Another source of heterogeneity is the number of asserted patents. Plaintiffs may assert claims relating to a single patent or to multiple patents in a case, and courts may decide either to split a case that involves several patents into separate actions or to consolidate separate actions into a single proceeding. A similar problem also arises in post-grant reviews. Multiple parties can file a post-grant administrative validity challenge on the same patent. At the EPO, for example, if several parties oppose a given patent, these multiple oppositions are consolidated into a single proceeding at the end of the nine-month opposition period. In the U.S., in contrast, multiple challenges in the form of an *inter partes* review (IPR) at the Patent Trial and Appeal Board (PTAB) start off as separate petitions that may be joined at some point in the process. This means that a simple count of IPR petitions and a direct comparison with EPO oppositions might be misleading.

Court cases may involve different patent types. For example, court cases in China, Germany or the Republic of Korea may involve utility models; in China or the U.S. they may involve design patents. To facilitate comparability across time, courts, and jurisdictions, it is important to distinguish cases according to the type of patent involved.

The number of patent case counts is often not particularly informative, especially when compared over time or across jurisdictions. To facilitate comparison, litigation rates are often used. The main challenge in constructing these rates is determining their denominator; that is, the measure that is used to weigh the litigation case count. Cremers *et al.* (2016a), for example, use the following:
(a) annual patent filings in a given jurisdiction,
(b) the total number of patents in force in a given jurisdiction,
(c) gross domestic product in a given jurisdiction, and
(d) gross domestic research and development (R&D) spending in a given jurisdiction.

A problem common to these different ways of constructing litigation rates is that their interpretation is unclear. If a rate is low, does that mean that there are fewer underlying disputes, or does it mean that a smaller share of disputes makes it to court, either because they are settled before reaching court or because patent owners decide not to enforce their rights?

Interpreting the outcome of a court case is not straightforward either. In a validity challenge, often only a subset of claims is challenged and invalidated. Depending on the jurisdiction, it may also be possible for the patent owner to amend the claims of the patent during the proceedings and thereby keep the patent alive, albeit with a narrower scope. During infringement proceedings, it is equally possible that infringement is found only with respect to a subset of asserted claims. This means that often the outcome of a case is not as clear cut as is required for a binary coding (win or loss) of the outcome. This situation is further complicated by the appeals process. Depending on the jurisdiction, appeals that could result in first-instance decisions being overturned can be relatively common. Moreover, first-instance decisions may be only partly overturned, further adding to the complexity of the overall case outcome.

Only court cases are observed. Any disputes that are resolved or dropped before the plaintiff files the complaint with a court remain undocumented.[5] This poses a challenge for empirical work as it is practically impossible to account for this type of selection since no information on the underlying set of all patent disputes is available. Some cases are dropped or settled immediately following the filing of the complaint. For these disputes, often the only information available in the case docket is the information provided in the complaint together with the fact that the case did not proceed. If the case is pursued further, more information will be recorded, for example documenting a motion. Parties have the opportunity to settle at any point in the proceedings. This means that the amount of information available regarding a specific case depends on whether and when the parties settled the case. Only in the event that a case proceeds sufficiently for a summary judgment to be available, or if the judge or jury hands down a verdict, is the actual outcome of the case observed. It is important to emphasize that the set of cases decided by a court represents highly selected subsets of cases and is not representative of all the patent disputes filed with the court, and even less so of all the patent disputes that never reach a court. Cases that are decided on appeal are even more highly selected subsets of patent cases and are clearly not representative of patent disputes more generally.

The analysis of litigation data is also challenging due to frequent changes in the law and its application. The U.S., for example, has seen a number of landmark Supreme Court decisions in the past few years that have had a significant impact on litigation behavior.[6] In addition, institutional changes, such as the introduction of opposition procedures in Japan and the Republic of Korea in 2015 and 2017, respectively, or the comprehensive reform of the Patents County Court and its reconstitution as IPEC in the U.K. between 2010 and 2013, are likely to have impacted litigation behavior. The same is true for sweeping legislative changes, such as the one brought about by the America Invents Act (AIA) in the U.S. in 2011. From a policy perspective, studying the effect of such changes on litigation behavior and outcomes is worthwhile in its own right. However, it also means that any analysis of litigation data will have to take the impact of those changes on litigation behavior into account. This is of particular concern with regard to court decisions and institutional changes that, at first glance, may not affect litigation directly, such as changes to post-grant review systems.

Data availability

The main challenge in the analysis of patent litigation lies in the limited availability of case-level information from the courts. However, even when detailed records are available, transforming these records into a sta-

tistical database is fraught with difficulties. Data on administrative post-grant validity challenges are more easily accessible and, to some degree, less complex, as only validity is at issue.

In the U.S., court data are made available by the Administrative Office of the Courts on the Public Access to Court Electronic Records (PACER) system to any registered user. PACER offers access to all cases heard by district courts, the CAFC and the Supreme Court. The data provided through PACER are considered to provide complete coverage of all patent cases in the U.S. from the mid-2000s onward (Schwartz and Sichelman, forthcoming). However, PACER is not designed to generate data that lend themselves easily to statistical analysis. The United States Patent and Trademark Office (USPTO) has recently made the PACER data available for download (Marco et al., 2017). The resulting USPTO Patent Litigation Docket Reports Data cover the period from 1963 to 2015, although the coverage of the pre-2000 data is probably incomplete as not all records are available in electronic format. Data on PTAB proceedings are also publicly available from the USPTO website. While all documents can be downloaded free of charge, the data are not made available for download in a format that facilitates statistical analysis. Unified Patents also offers free access to the data in a more user-friendly format, but there is no bulk download functionality.[7]

In Germany, case-level data are available from official court websites. However, there are a number of problems associated with these publicly available data. There is no court diary or case index that allows verification that all cases filed with a given court are recorded. Moreover, case documents may be redacted; for example, patent numbers or the names of litigating parties are frequently missing from the publicly available documents. Despite the limitations, publicly available data for Germany have been used in research (e.g., Elsner and Zingg, 2018).

In the U.K., basic information on cases listed for a hearing is available from the official court diary. The diary lists all cases for which a claim form has been filed by the plaintiff and the court has scheduled some type of hearing or application. The diary contains basic information on the case, including the case number, the names of the plaintiff and defendant, and the date of the hearing. The diary may also include information on the status of a case – for example, if it has been discontinued due to a settlement. The website of the British and Irish Legal Information Institute (BAILII) contains court records, including published judgments, where court documents for cases listed in the court dairy can be found. Alternative online resources are Lexis Nexis and the Thomson Reuters Westlaw database. In the U.K., these documents usually contain

Special theme

unredacted information on court cases. However, often only a single document on a case is available online, which may not provide all of the relevant information for a given case. The fact that usually not all court records for a given case are observed when the data are assembled from publicly accessible online sources means that the analysis will necessarily be limited. For example, it may not be possible to determine whether specific motions (e.g., for a stay or summary judgment) were filed during proceedings, especially in the event that they were unsuccessful. Such motions may have impacted the parties' litigation behavior, but it is not possible to determine the extent of their effect from the data. Moreover, BAILII does not publish every court record; decisions that are deemed to be more important are more likely to be posted online, creating selection bias in any data set constructed solely from records available on BAILII.

Data on EPO oppositions are available in EPO's Patent Register, which is offered as a data set designed for the purposes of statistical analysis. The ready availability of these data has led to a relatively large amount of research on EPO oppositions.

Since 2014, all decisions by courts in China are publicly available on the China Judgments Online website. In practice, coverage is still well below 100 percent. Moreover, the data only cover infringement decisions as invalidity challenges are decided exclusively by the China National Intellectual Property Administration (CNIPA).

In the case of Japan, the IP High Court provides an online database of court decisions for all courts competent to hear patent cases in Japan.

There have been a number of efforts by academic researchers to collect data directly from the courts. For example, Cremers et al. (2016a) collected data directly from the three most important German regional courts (Landgerichte – LG) for the period 2000 to 2008. For France, Dumont (2015) collected data from the first-instance court in Paris for the period between 2008 and 2013. Helmers et al. (2016) collected case-level data from the two courts competent to hear IP cases in the U.K. – the IPEC and the PHC – for the period from 2007 to 2013.

A large number of commercial data providers and law firms offer access to patent litigation data covering different jurisdictions. However, access to those databases is generally expensive. In addition, information on data coverage and methodology is not always clear.

The USPTO post-grant review statistics

Since the introduction of the AIA in the U.S. in 2011, it has been possible to challenge the validity of patents granted by the USPTO through four different avenues: post-grant review, inter partes review, covered business method and ex parte reexamination. There has been a dramatic increase in PTAB trials since the implementation of the AIA (see figure S2). In contrast, ex parte reexamination has declined. However, the decrease in ex parte reexamination has been far less substantial than the increase in PTAB trials. This implies that the total number of post-grant challenges at the USPTO has risen substantially.

As mentioned above, not all IPRs are reviewed by PTAB. Only those IPRs that have a reasonable likelihood of success are instituted and reviewed by PTAB. Figure S3 shows both the total number of petitions and the number of petitions instituted, which follows a similar trend. However, starting in the third quarter of 2014, the share of instituted petitions dropped and continued to hover around 55 percent of total petitions for the remaining period. On average, PTAB made decisions on approximately 75 percent of all petitions instituted between 2012 and 2015. The decrease in the number of decisions since 2015 is due to data truncation.

Figure S4 shows a breakdown of petitions and institution decisions by technology area for the period from 2012 to 2016.[8] The largest number of petitions was in the field of computer technology (670), followed by telecommunications (308) and digital communication (248). The share of petitions instituted varied from 94.4 percent in surface technology to 38 percent in other consumer goods. Among the top five technologies with the largest number of petitions, telecommunications has the highest institution rate (61.7 percent), followed by computer technology (55.2 percent), medical technology (52.9 percent), digital communication (51.6 percent) and audio-visual (51.2 percent).

Figure S5 shows the PTAB decisions for all IPRs instituted for the period from 2012 to 2016. For the majority of the fields of technology, the invalidation rate was over 80 percent. Among the top five fields of technology with the largest number of decisions, electrical machinery (84 percent) had the highest invalidation rate, followed by transport (81.3 percent), telecommunications (80.2 percent) and computer technology (79.2 percent).

S2. Post-grant PTAB trials and *ex parte* reexaminations, 1999–2017

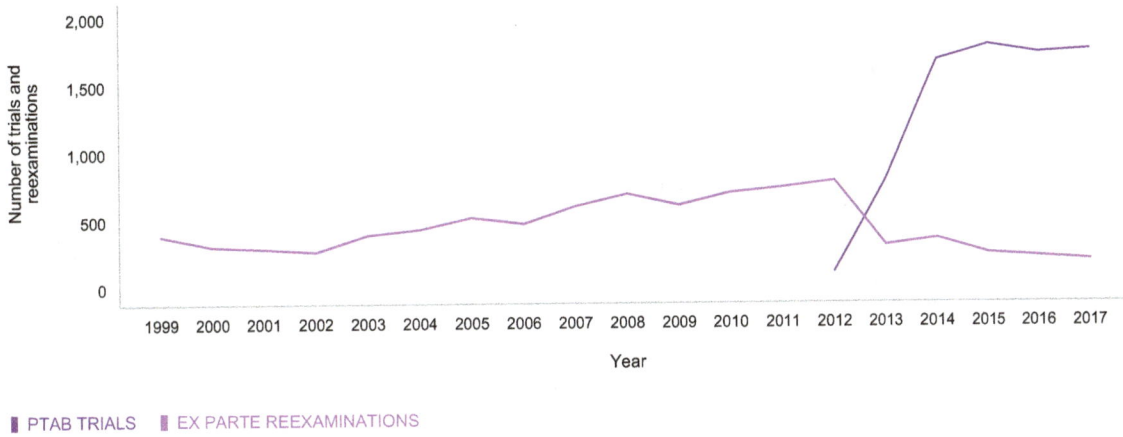

PTAB TRIALS   **EX PARTE REEXAMINATIONS**

Source: *https://ptabdataui.uspto.gov/#/documents.*

S3. Total number of IPR petitions

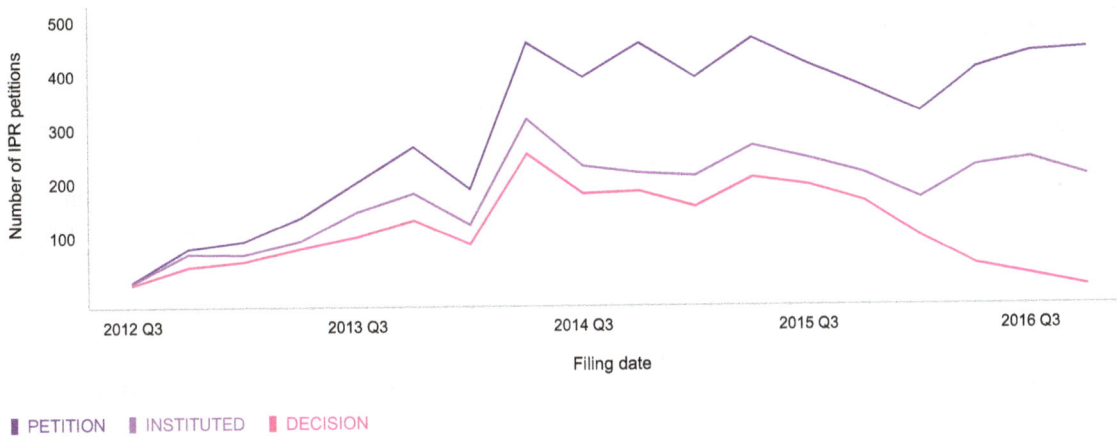

PETITION   **INSTITUTED**   **DECISION**

Source: Helmers (2018).

S4. IPR petition decisions by field of technology, 2012–2016

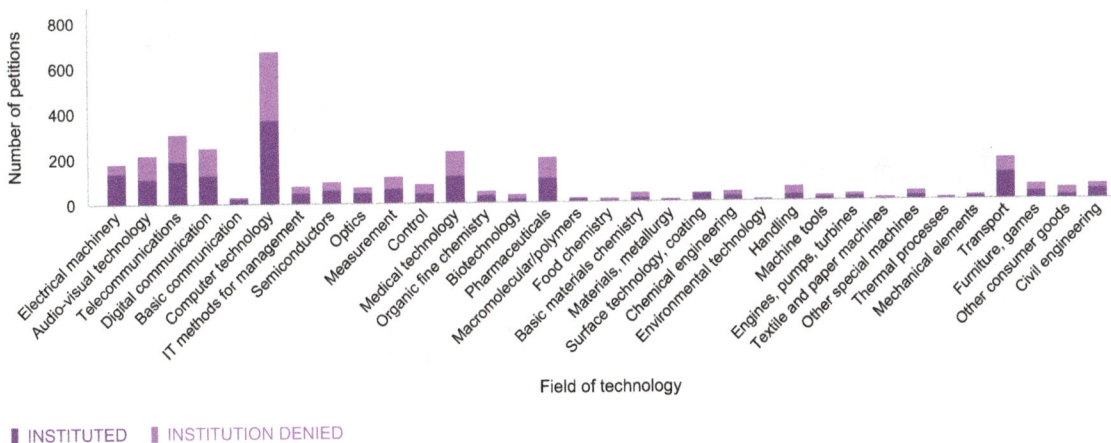

INSTITUTED   **INSTITUTION DENIED**

Source: Helmers (2018).

Special theme

S5. IPR institution decisions by field of technology, 2012–2016

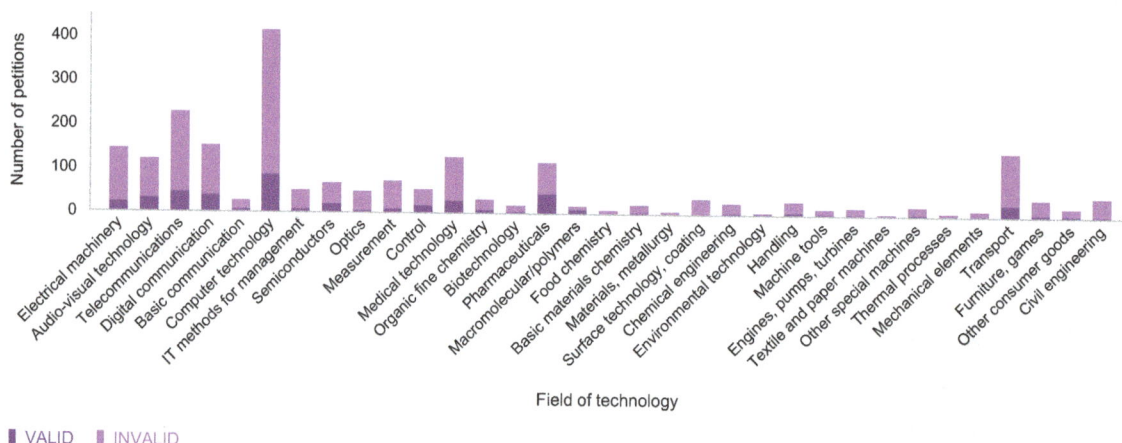

■ VALID   ■ INVALID

Source: Helmers (2018).

The EPO post-grant opposition statistics

At the EPO, oppositions can be filed within nine months of the mention of the grant in the *European Patent Bulletin*. All oppositions that are filed during that time period are combined at the end of the nine-month period before oppositions proceedings begin. This means that the number of oppositions is not directly comparable to the number of IPRs because separate petitions for IPR for the same patent can be filed but are not necessarily combined into a single proceeding. Figure S6 shows that the number of oppositions held relatively steady, at around 3,000 per year, between 2012 and 2014. The decline during 2015 and 2016 is due to truncation of the available data.

S6. Total number of EPO oppositions, 2012–2016

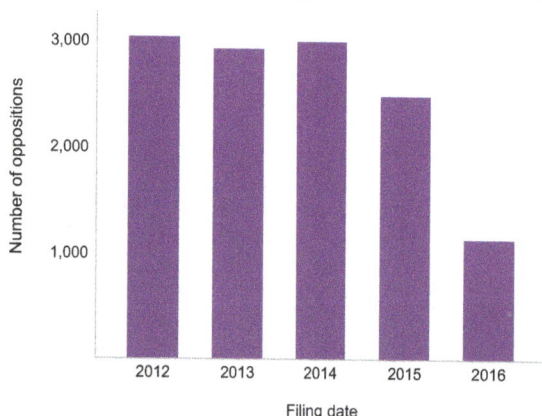

Source: Helmers (2018).

The outcome of the EPO opposition proceedings by field of technology is presented in figure S7. Opposition to the granting of an EPO patent can result in the pat-

ent being invalidated, maintained in its current form or maintained in amended form. Patents related to medical technology attracted the largest number of oppositions (1,029), followed by pharmaceuticals (974), transport (689) and basic materials chemistry (660). In contrast, there were relatively few oppositions in computer technology, telecommunications and digital communication, which is probably explained by differences in the granting practices of software-related patents between the USPTO and the EPO. The distribution of outcomes is fairly even across technology areas; on average around 32 percent of opposed patents were invalidated, 32 percent were upheld and 36 percent were upheld in amended form.

U.K. and U.S. patent litigation statistics

The number of patent litigation cases filed in the U.S. grew gradually between 1999 and 2009. However, between 2009 and 2013 there was a period of considerable growth in the number of cases filed (see figure S8). A similar trend is observed for the U.K., where significant growth in the number of cases filed occurred between 2010 and 2012 (see figure S10). The strong growth in the number of cases filed in both the U.K. and the U.S. occurred during the so-called "global patent wars."

As mentioned above, cases count data are often normalized using the number of filings, patents in force, gross domestic product, etc. Figure S9 presents data on the number of cases filed in the U.S. district courts normalized by patent grants and patents in force. Normalized cases count data follow the same overall trend – significant growth between 2009 and 2013 with a decline thereafter.

S7. EPO opposition outcomes by field of technology, 2012–2016

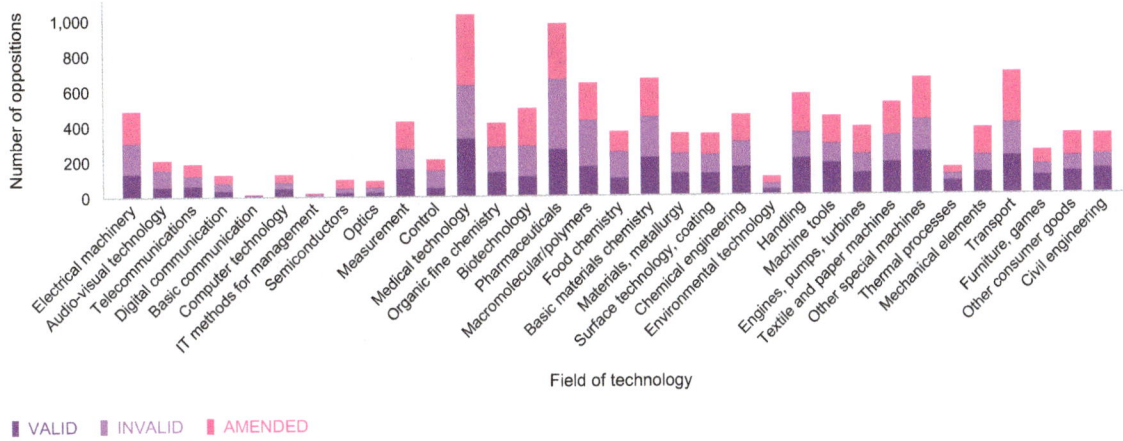

Number of oppositions

VALID   INVALID   AMENDED

Field of technology

Source: Helmers (2018).

S8. Number of patent infringement cases filed in the U.S. district courts, 1999–2016

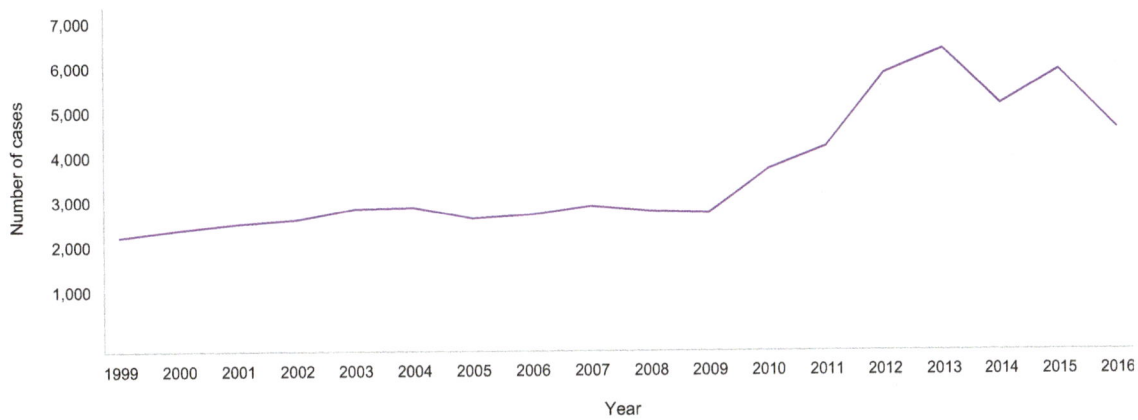

Number of cases

Year

Source: USPTO Patent Litigation Docket Reports Data.

S9. Number of patent cases filed in the U.S. district courts per 100 patent grants and 1,000 patents in force, 1999–2016

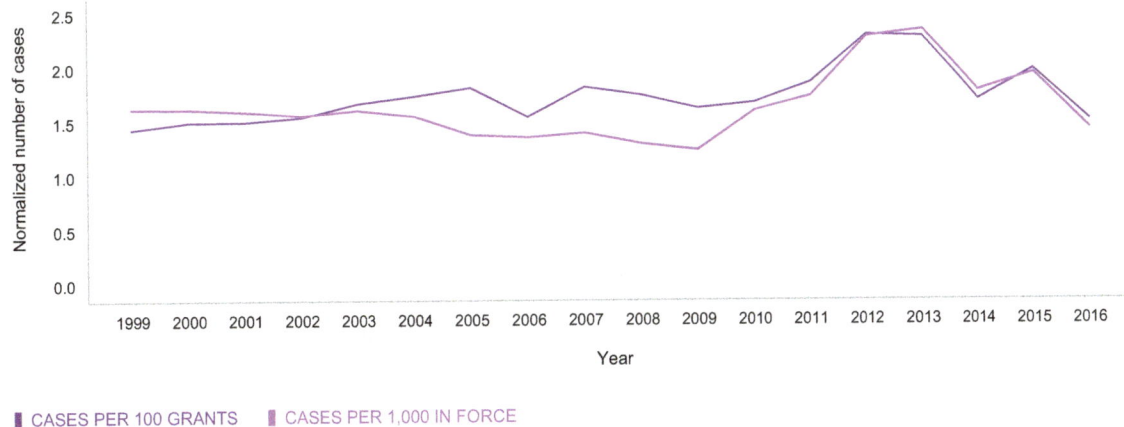

Normalized number of cases

Year

CASES PER 100 GRANTS   CASES PER 1,000 IN FORCE

Source: USPTO Patent Litigation Docket Reports Data and Historical Patent Data Files.

Special theme

S10. Number of patent cases filed in the U.K. patents court and IPEC, 2007–2013

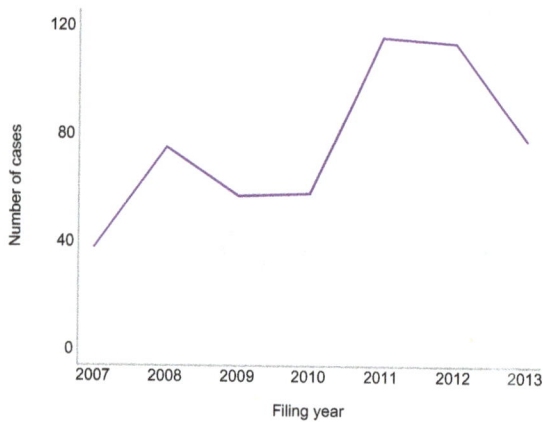

Source: Helmers (2018).

S11. Outcome of cases filed in the U.K. and the U.S.

U.K. patents court and IPEC, 2007–2013

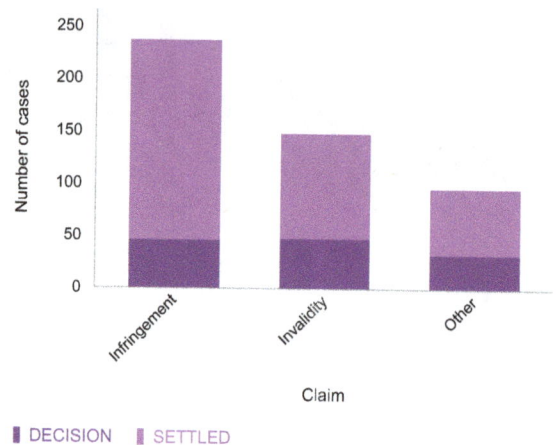

■ DECISION   ■ SETTLED

Figure S11 provides data on cases broken down by types of complaint: infringement, invalidity and other. The "other" category contains a range of patent-related claims, such as disputes regarding inventor- or ownership, false patent marking, licensing contracts, etc. The figure also distinguishes between cases that ended with a decision by the court or a settlement/dismissal. In both jurisdictions, the share of cases determined by court decision is very small. For example, in the U.S. around 10 percent of cases were decided in some way by the courts, while in the U.K. the figure was around 26 percent. Complaints in the U.S. almost all allege infringement of a patent, while a small share of total cases relates to an allegation of invalidity. In contrast, around 30 percent of cases in the U.K. start with a validity challenge. The share of cases decided by the courts in the U.K. is larger for validity challenges (32 percent) than for infringement claims (20 percent).

Figure S12 presents data on the interaction between litigation in court and administrative post-grant reviews. Interaction occurs when a patent that is litigated in court is challenged through an IPR in the U.S. or an opposition at the EPO. The figure shows the number of court cases that have a parallel administrative validity challenge at the EPO for U.K. patents and at the USPTO for U.S. patents. In the U.S., parallel IPRs are filed mainly in infringement cases by the defendant in an attempt to invalidate the patent administratively and thereby achieve a dismissal of the infringement case in court. In the U.K., a relatively large number of cases that challenge a patent's validity in court also challenge the patent's validity administratively at the EPO. Because courts in the U.K. often do not stay proceedings if an opposition is pending at the EPO, this strategy allows the plaintiffs to use all available venues to invalidate a patent.

U.S. district courts, 2010–2016

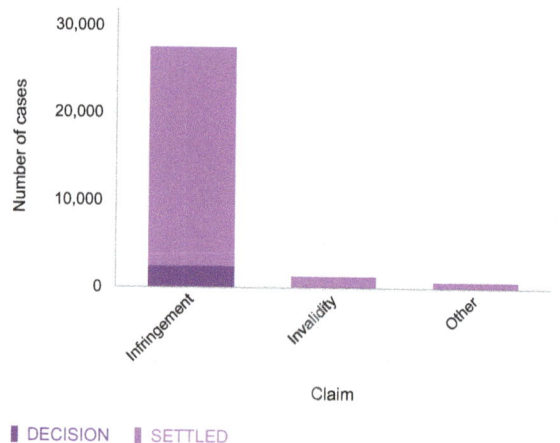

■ DECISION   ■ SETTLED

Source: Helmers (2018).

Conclusions

This chapter has provided an overview of patent litigation systems across jurisdictions. It has documented common aspects applicable to court proceedings in different jurisdictions and outlined how the patent litigation systems differ. It has also outlined the challenges involved in collecting comprehensive and comparable patent litigation data from the various jurisdictions. It is important to understand the litigation system in order to properly interpret the data.

To monitor the functioning of the patent litigation system, data availability is crucial for evidence-based policymaking. However, data availability and access remain a major obstacle to the analysis of the patent litigation system. The U.S. has made significant efforts

S12. Parallel IPRs (U.S.) and EPO oppositions (U.K.)

U.K. patents court/IPEC and EPO oppositions, 2007–2013

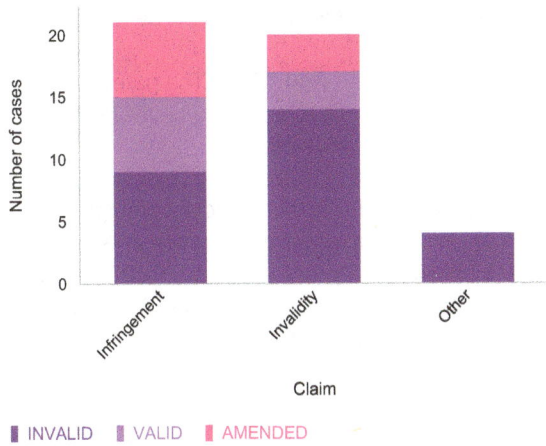

INVALID   VALID   AMENDED

U.S. district courts and PTAB IPRs, 2012–2016

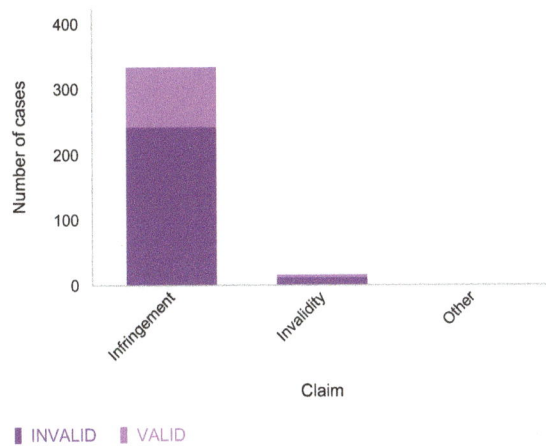

INVALID   VALID

Source: Helmers (2018).

to make patent litigation data available to researchers and policymakers. For example, the efforts of the USPTO (Marco *et al.*, 2017) provide a useful illustration of how to make patent litigation data available for statistical analysis. Beyond the U.S., there is a lack of publicly available official data. As an initial step, patent offices could develop statistical databases of administrative procedural information (e.g., detailed information on oppositions, invalidation, reexamination, etc.). With regard to court records, developing infrastructure to maintain a register of all patent-related cases could be a worthwhile route to take.

1 See *www.nytimes.com/2018/06/27/technology/apple-samsung-smartphone-patent.html* for more details.
2 See *https://obamawhitehouse.archives.gov/sites/default/files/page/files/201603_patent_litigation_issue_brief_cea.pdf* and *https://bits.blogs.nytimes.com/2010/03/04/an-explosion-of-mobile-patent-lawsuits/* for examples.
3 This section is based on a paper prepared by Professor Christian Helmers of Santa Clara University. For further details, see WIPO's *Economic Research Working Paper No. 48.*
4 The U.K. consists of three distinct jurisdictions: England and Wales, Northern Ireland and Scotland. Throughout the remainder of this chapter, we refer to the jurisdiction of England and Wales as the U.K.
5 Lemly *et al.* (2017) estimate, based on survey results for the U.S., that approximately 70 percent of patent infringement claims are resolved out of court.
6 For an overview, see *https://writtendescription.blogspot.com/p/patents-scotus.html*
7 See *https://portal.unifiedpatents.com.*
8 See *www.wipo.int/export/sites/www/ipstats/en/statistics/patents/pdf/wipo_ipc_technology.pdf* for details on technology classification.

References

AIPLA (2017). *AIPLA Report of the Economic Survey 2017*. Arlington, VA: American Intellectual Property Law Association.

Clark, D. (2011). *Patent Litigation in China*. New York: Oxford University Press.

Cook, J. (2007). On understanding the increase in U.S. patent litigation. *American Law and Economics Review*, 9(1), 48–71.

Cremers, K., M. Ernicke, F. Gaessler, D. Harhoff, C. Helmers, L. Donagh, P. Schliessler and N. Van Zeebroeck (2016a). Patent litigation in Europe. *European Journal of Law and Economics*, 44(1), 1–44.

Cremers, K., F. Gaessler, D. Harhoff, C. Helmers and Y. Lefouili (2016b). Invalid but infringed? An analysis of the bifurcated patent litigation system. *Journal of Economic Behavior & Organization*, 131, 218–242.

Dumont, B. (2015). Does patent quality drive damages in patent lawsuits? Lessons from the French judicial system. *Review of Law and Economics*, 11(2), 355–383.

Elsner, E. and R. Zingg (2018). "Protection heterogeneity in a harmonized European system," mimeo.

Graham, S. and N. van Zeebroeck (2014). Comparing patent litigation across Europe: A first look. *Stanford Technology Law Review*, 17, 655–708.

Helmers, C. (2018). The Economic Analysis of Patent Litigation Data. *WIPO Economic Research Working Paper No. 48*. Geneva: WIPO.

Helmers, C., Y. Lefouili, B. Love and L. McDonagh (2016). The Effect of Fee Shifting on Litigation: Evidence from a Court Reform in the UK. *TSE Working Paper 16-740*.

Helmers, C. and L. McDonagh (2013). Patent litigation in England and Wales and the issue-based approach to costs. *Civil Justice Quarterly*, 32(3), 369–384.

Lemley M., K. Richardson and E. Oliver (2017). The Patent Enforcement Iceberg. Stanford Public Law Working Paper.

Marco, A., A. Tesfayesus and A. Toole (2017). Patent Litigation Data from US District Court Electronic Records (1963–2015). *USPTO Economic Working Paper No. 2017-06*. Alexandria, VA: USPTO.

Meurer, M. and J. Bessen (2013). The patent litigation explosion. *Loyola University of Chicago Law Journal*, 45(2), 401–440.

Schwartz, D. and T. Sichelman (forthcoming). Data sources on patents, copyrights, trademarks, and other intellectual property. In Menell, P., D. Schwartz and B. Depoorter (eds), *Research Handbook on the Law and Economics of Intellectual Property*. Cheltenham, U.K.: Edgar Elgar.

Patents

Highlights

Patent applications filed worldwide reached 3.17 million in 2017

Applicants around the world filed almost 3.17 million patent applications in 2017 – a record number (see figure 1.1). Applications grew by an estimated 5.8% on 2016. It is important to note that the intellectual property (IP) office of China revised its method of compiling patent applications statistics in 2017. Prior to 2017, it included all applications received; however, starting in 2017, China's application count data include only those applications for which the office has received the necessary application fees. At the same time, applying the new counting method retroactively, the IP office of China was able to report a growth rate of 14.2% in the number of patent applications filed in 2017 (see the data description section). This 14.2% growth rate for China was then used to calculate the estimated worldwide growth rate of 5.8%.

The long-term trend shows that patent applications worldwide have grown every year since 2003, with the exception of 2009 when they decreased by 3.8% due to the financial crisis.

Patent applications worldwide grew by 5.8%

1.1. Patent applications worldwide, 2001–2017

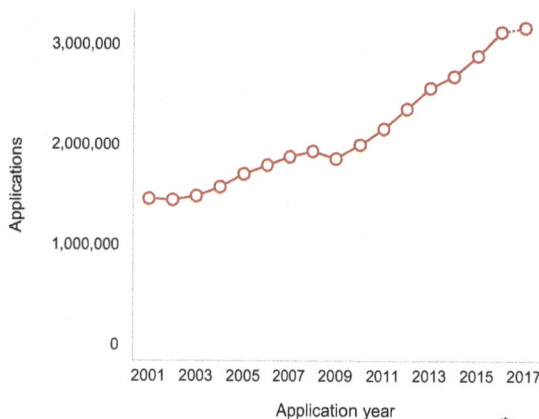

Source: Figure A1.

China received 1.38 million patent applications, double the number received by the United States of America (U.S.)

The National Intellectual Property Administration of the People's Republic of China received 1.38 million patent applications in 2017, which is more than double the number received by the United States Patent and Trademark Office (USPTO), which totaled 606,956. The Japan Patent Office was ranked third, with 318,479 applications. It was followed by the Korean Intellectual Property Office with 204,775 applications and the European Patent Office (EPO) with 166,585. Together, these top five offices accounted for 84.5% of the world total in 2017, which is much higher than their combined 2007 share (75.2%). China's share of the world total increased considerably between 2007 and 2017, while that of the remaining four offices declined over the same period.

The list of top 10 offices in 2017 is identical to the 2016 list. The ranking of top offices is relatively stable – any change in ranking has been gradual over the past 15 years, with the exception of the rapid rise of China. Figure 1.2 shows patent applications received by the top 10 offices, broken down by resident and non-resident filings. The IP offices of China, Japan and the Republic of Korea received the bulk of their applications from resident applicants. In contrast, Australia, Canada, India and the U.S. reported a high share of non-resident filings.

Looking beyond the top 10 offices to the top 20 list, 12 offices were located in high-income, six in upper middle-income and two in lower middle-income countries. In terms of geographical distribution, nine offices were located in Asia, six in Europe, two each in North America and Latin America and the Caribbean (LAC), and one in Oceania. South Africa is the highest ranked African office, in 22nd place.

Of the top 20 offices, 11 received a greater number of applications in 2017 than in 2016, while nine received fewer. China (+14.2%) and Turkey (+24.9%) are the only two offices to have experienced double-digit growth. Note that China's growth rate was reported by the IP office of China and is based on the new method of counting patent applications recently implemented by that office. China has experienced double-digit growth each year since 2010. Turkey has reported double-digit growth for the past three years and, as a result, its ranking has moved from 25th position in 2014 to 20th in 2017. The increases in number of applications filed in China and Turkey were both driven mainly by growth in resident applications.

IP office of China received 1.38 million applications

1.2. Patent applications at the top 10 offices, 2017

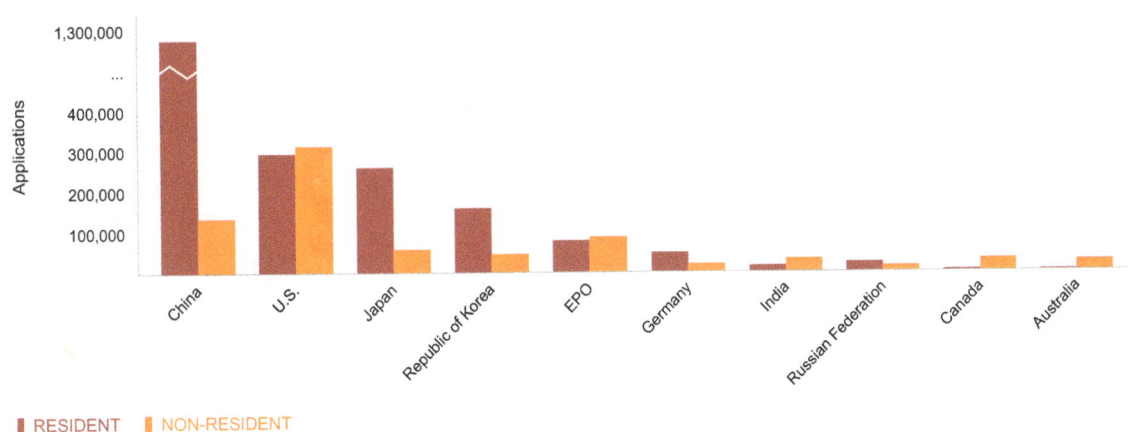

RESIDENT ■ NON-RESIDENT

Source: Figure A8.

Of the nine offices among the top 20 that received fewer applications in 2017 than in 2016, the Russian Federation (–11.3%); Brazil (–8.4%); China, Hong Kong SAR (–5.6%); and Indonesia (–3.5%) reported the most substantial declines. Applications in Brazil fell for a fourth consecutive year, while the Russian Federation reported a second successive year of declining numbers of applications. A decline in resident applications was the primary reason for the decrease in total applications for the Russian Federation in 2017, whereas a decline in non-resident applications was the main driver for Brazil; China, Hong Kong SAR; and Indonesia.

Among the top five offices, the Republic of Korea is the only one to report a small drop in applications in 2017 (–1.9%). China (+14.2%) and the EPO (+4.5%) reported strong growth in the number of applications. The IP offices of Japan (+0.03%) and the U.S. (+0.2%) saw negligible growth. The long-term trend shows that the office of China has recorded year-on-year growth for the past 21 years, while the U.S. office has enjoyed eight consecutive years of growth. The Republic of Korea's office enjoyed solid growth in applications for each year from 2010 to 2015, but filings declined by 2.4% in 2016 and by 1.9% in 2017. The patent office of Japan has experienced either a fall in applications or negligible growth since 2005, mainly reflecting a persistent fall in resident applications. Since 2010, the EPO has experienced fluctuation in the number of applications received – growth in filings in one year is followed by a drop in applications the next year.

Among the offices of low- and middle-income countries, Ecuador (+11.5%), Romania (+10.8%) and Colombia (+7.7%) recorded particularly rapid growth in 2017. Growth in non-resident applications was the main driver

of total growth in Colombia and Ecuador, while resident applications were the main driver in Romania (see figure A11). Two of the three regional offices – the African Intellectual Property Organization (OAPI), the African Regional Intellectual Property Organization (ARIPO) and the Eurasian Patent Organization (EAPO) – have seen applications return to growth following a fall during two successive years. Applications filed at ARIPO grew by 7.2% in 2017, while OAPI reported a 2.6% increase. In contrast, EAPO saw three consecutive years of declines in filings. At most offices of low- and middle-income countries, the bulk of applications are filed by non-residents. As a result, overall increases or decreases in applications received by these offices are determined mainly by the filing behavior of non-resident applicants.

Offices located in Asia received 65% of all applications filed worldwide in 2017

Offices located in Asia received around 2.1 million applications in 2017, representing 65.1% of the world total (see figure 1.3). The combined total of Europe and North America was just below the 1 million mark. Asia's share of all applications filed worldwide increased from 49.7% in 2007 to 65.1% in 2017, primarily driven by strong growth in filings in China, which accounted for around two-thirds of all applications filed in the region. Offices in North America accounted for just over one-fifth of the 2017 world total, while those in Europe accounted for just over one-tenth. The combined share for Africa, LAC and Oceania was 3.4%. The shares of all world regions except Asia have gradually declined over the past decade due to the rapid growth in applications filed in China.

Patents

Offices located in Asia received 65.1% of all patent applications filed worldwide
1.3. Patent applications by region, 2007 and 2017

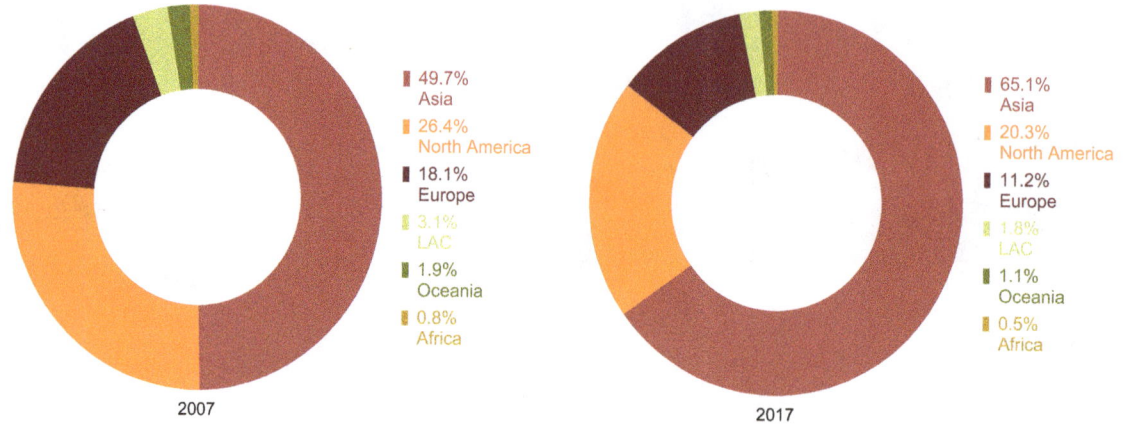

2007
- 49.7% Asia
- 26.4% North America
- 18.1% Europe
- 3.1% LAC
- 1.9% Oceania
- 0.8% Africa

2017
- 65.1% Asia
- 20.3% North America
- 11.2% Europe
- 1.8% LAC
- 1.1% Oceania
- 0.5% Africa

Source: Table A6.

Patent filings since 1883

From 1883 to 1963, the patent office of the U.S. was the leading office for world filings. Application numbers in Japan and the U.S. were stable until the early 1970s, when Japan began to see rapid growth – a pattern also observed for the U.S. from the 1980s onward. Among the top five offices, Japan surpassed the U.S. in 1968 and maintained the top position until 2005. Since the early 2000s, however, the number of applications filed in Japan has followed a downward trend. Both the EPO and the Republic of Korea have seen increases each year since the early 1980s, as has China since 1995. China surpassed the EPO and the Republic of Korea in 2005, Japan in 2010 and the U.S. in 2011 – and it now receives the largest number of applications worldwide. There has been a gradual upward trend in the combined share of the top five offices in the world total – from 75.2% in 2007 to 84.5% in 2017.

Trend in patent applications for the top five offices, 1883–2017

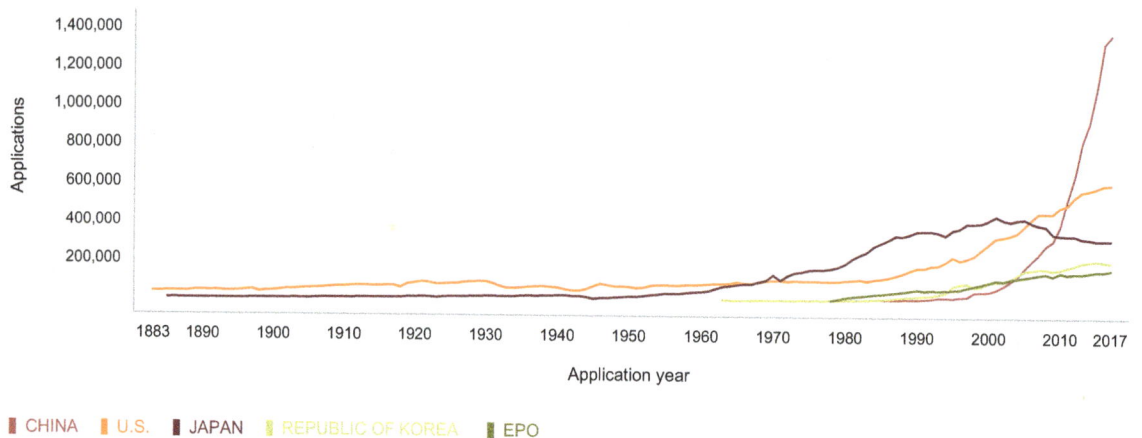

Legend: CHINA   U.S.   JAPAN   REPUBLIC OF KOREA   EPO

Note: The IP office of the Soviet Union, not represented in this figure, was the leading office in the world in terms of filings from 1964 to 1969. Like Japan and the U.S., the office of the Soviet Union saw stable application numbers until the early 1960s, after which it recorded rapid growth in the number of applications filed.

Source: Figure A7.

The distribution of applications by income group shows that offices of high-income countries received 49.1% of all applications filed worldwide in 2017, which is one percentage point above the share received by offices of upper middle-income countries (48.1%) (see table A5). However, there has been a sizeable shift in distribution of applications toward the upper middle-income group, which is largely explained by the strong growth in filings in China and the decline in Japan. The share for offices of upper middle-income countries rose from 19.9% in 2007 to 48.1% in 2017, while that of the high-income group declined from 76.4% to 49.1% over the same period. The combined share of the low- and lower middle-income groups was 2.8% in 2017, which is identical to their share in 2016.

Equivalent application count

Applications at regional IP offices are equivalent to multiple applications in the countries that are members of the organizations establishing those offices. In particular, to calculate the number of equivalent applications for the African Intellectual Property Organization (OAPI), the Eurasian Patent Organization (EAPO) and the Patent Office of the Cooperation Council for the Arab States of the Gulf (GCC Patent Office), each application is multiplied by the corresponding number of member states. For African Regional Intellectual Property Organization (ARIPO) and the European Patent Office (EPO) data, each application is counted as one application abroad if the applicant does not reside in a member state or as one resident application and one application abroad if the applicant resides in a member state. The equivalent application concept is used for reporting data by origin.

Residents of the U.S. filed more than 230,000 patent applications abroad

Applications received by offices from resident and non-resident applicants are referred to as office data, whereas applications filed by applicants at a national/regional office (resident applications) or at foreign offices (applications abroad) are referred to as origin data. Here, patent statistics based on the origin of residence of the first named applicant are reported in order to complement the picture of patent activity worldwide.

Applicants from China filed around 1.31 million equivalent patent applications in 2017, which is more than the combined total for applicants from Japan (460,660), the Republic of Korea (226,568) and the U.S. (524,835). Those four origins, plus Germany (176,235), accounted for the bulk of the global total (see map 1.4). China has been the largest source of patent applications since 2012, when it surpassed Japan. However, it should be noted that only 4.6% of all applications from China are filed abroad, while 95.4% are filed in China. In contrast, filings abroad constitute 43.5% of total applications from Japan and 44% from the U.S.

Twelve of the top 20 origins are located in Europe. Their combined total (518,480 equivalent applications) is slightly lower than that from U.S.-based applicants. All top 20 origins, with the exception of China, India, the Islamic Republic of Iran and the Russian Federation, are high-income countries. Among the top 20 origins, Denmark (+9.6%), India (+8.3%) and Belgium (+6.1%) recorded the fastest growth in 2017 (see figure A18). For both Belgium and Denmark, growth in applications abroad was the main source of overall growth, while for India growth in resident applications was the main driver of overall growth.

Among the large middle-income origins, Indonesia (+101%) and Turkey (+33%) saw the fastest growth in filings in 2017. Malaysia (+9.4%), South Africa (+8.3%), Mexico (+5%) and Brazil (+4%) also saw relatively strong growth in 2017. The overall growth in Brazil, Indonesia, South Africa and Turkey was due to increases in resident applications, while growth in equivalent applications abroad drove overall growth in Malaysia and Mexico.

Filing abroad reflects the globalization of IP protection and a desire to commercialize technology in foreign markets. The costs of filing abroad can be substantial, so the patents for which applicants seek international protection are likely to confer higher values. Among the top 20 origins, applications filed abroad made up for more than three-quarters of the totals for Belgium (77%), Canada (83.1%), Israel (90.7%), the Netherlands (75.3%), Sweden (75.3%) and Switzerland (80.6%). However, in absolute numbers, the U.S. had the most, with 230,931, followed by Japan (200,370), Germany (102,890), the Republic of Korea (67,484) and China (60,310). China, the Republic of Korea and the U.S. saw growth in applications abroad over the past five years, whereas the trend in applications abroad for Germany and Japan was stable over the same period.

High-income origins, such as Ireland (85.2%), Liechtenstein (69%), Luxembourg (79.3%), Norway (71.7%) and Singapore (76.8%), have a high proportion of applications abroad as a share of total applications. Applications abroad accounted for a small percentage of total applications for Brazil (27%), Colombia (24.1%) and Turkey (18.5%).

U.S. applicants accounted for more than half of all non-resident applications filed in Canada (52.8%), Israel (51%), Mexico (52.8%) and Norway (75.3%). Applicants residing in Japan accounted for at least a third of all non-resident applications filed in Germany (36.5%), Indonesia (34.2%), the Republic of Korea (32.9%) and

Patents

China, Germany, Japan, the Republic of Korea and the U.S. were the five largest sources of patent applications
1.4 Equivalent patent applications by origin, 2017

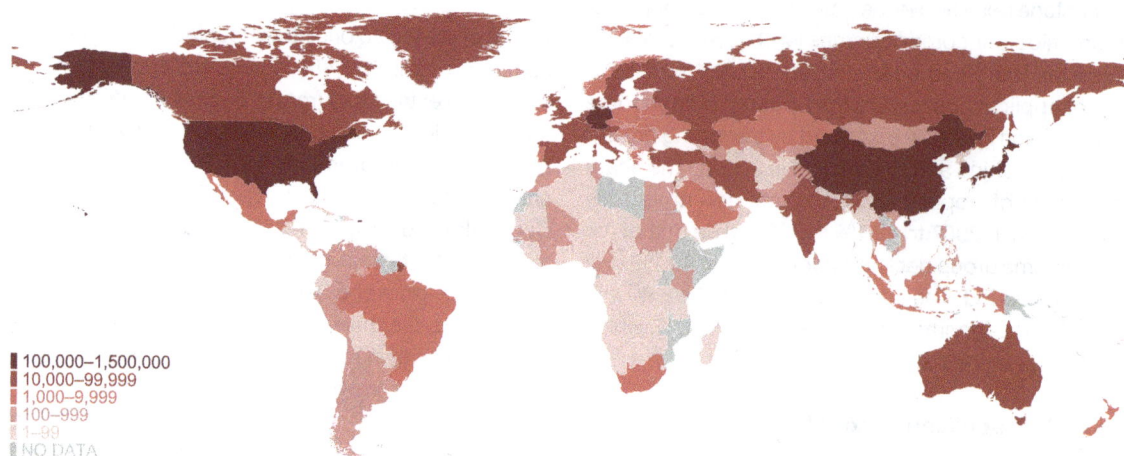

- 100,000–1,500,000
- 10,000–99,999
- 1,000–9,999
- 100–999
- 1–99
- NO DATA

Source: Map A17.

Thailand (49%). German applicants accounted for a high share in France (24.7%) and Italy (31%), while applicants from China accounted for a high proportion of non-resident filings in Luxembourg (66.8%) and the United Kingdom (U.K.) (12.3%).

Patent applications for unique inventions grew by 9.7% to reach 1.56 million worldwide

Patent applicants traditionally file at their national offices and then subsequently abroad. This means that some inventions are recorded more than once. To take this into account, WIPO has developed indicators for patent families, and the trend in patent families mirrors that for patent applications. The total number of patent families worldwide increased from around 780,000 in 2001 to around 1.56 million in 2015 (see figure 1.5). Applicants from China accounted for more than half of all patent families (52.2%) in 2015, followed by Japan (14.6%), the U.S. (10.4%) and the Republic of Korea (8.9%). China's share of the world total more than doubled between 2010 (25.2%) and 2015 (52.2%), while the share of Japan, the Republic of Korea and the U.S. declined over the same period – with Japan seeing the sharpest drop from 26.2% in 2010 to 14.6% in 2015.

Half of all applications were first filing, the other half repeat filings, mostly at foreign offices
1.5. Patent applications and patent families worldwide, 2001–2017

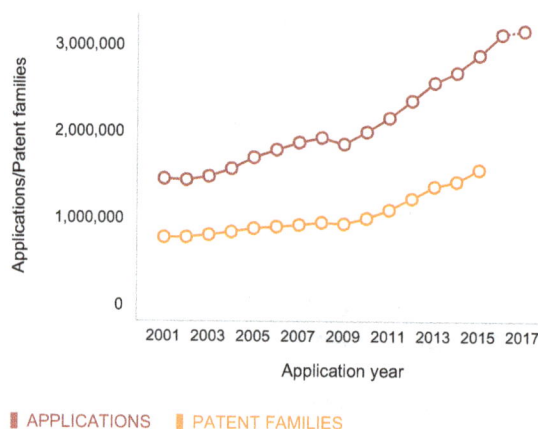

■ APPLICATIONS ■ PATENT FAMILIES

Sources: Figures A1 and A23.

For the past two decades (1995–2015), the ratio of families to applications has remained more or less stable at around 0.54. This means that just over half of all applications are initial filings and the others repetitive filings, mostly at foreign offices. Belgium (0.17), Denmark (0.18), Norway (0.19) and Switzerland (0.16) have low family-to-application ratios for the period from 2012 to 2014 – indicating substantial duplication due to high numbers of cross-border filings. Conversely, China (0.8), Poland (0.7) and the Russian Federation (0.8) have high ratios, indicating less duplication due to low numbers of cross-border filings.

Patent families

A patent family is a set of interrelated patent applications filed in one or more offices to protect the same invention. The patent applications in a family are interlinked by one or more of the following: priority claim, Patent Cooperation Treaty (PCT) national phase entry, continuation, continuation-in-part, internal priority and addition or division. A special subset comprises foreign-oriented patent families – that is, those patent families that have at least one filing office which differs from the office of the applicant's country of origin.

Some foreign-related patent families include only one filing office because applicants may choose to file only with a foreign office. For example, if a Canadian applicant files a patent application directly with the United States Patent and Trademark Office (USPTO) without having previously filed with the patent office of Canada, that patent family will constitute a foreign-oriented patent family with just one office.

The size of patent families (i.e., the number of offices) reflects their geographical coverage. Around 83% of patent families created worldwide between 2013 and 2015 were filed in a single office. There is considerable variation among top origins, however. For example, around two-fifths of all patent families originating from the Netherlands, Sweden and Switzerland cover a single office, whereas single-office patent families account for around 98% of all families for China and the Russian Federation (see figure A24). Focusing exclusively on foreign-oriented patent families shows that the U.S. (154,216) created the largest number of such families between 2013 and 2014, followed by Japan (144,512), the Republic of Korea (58,537), Germany (57,007) and China (35,084) (see figure A26).

Canon Inc. of Japan created the largest number of patent families worldwide

Canon Inc. of Japan created 24,006 patent families between 2013 and 2015, followed by Samsung Electronics (21,836) of the Republic of Korea and the State Grid Corporation of China (21,635). Eight of the top 10 companies are located in Asia. International Business Machines of the U.S. (14,972), ranked fifth, and Robert Bosch of Germany (12,598), ranked 10th, are the only two non-Asian applicants in the top 10 list (see table A27).

The highest shares of Canon's patent families created during this period relate to optics technology (27.5%), audio-visual technology (16.6%) and computer technology (14.7%). Computer technology (26.1%) accounted for the highest share of families belonging to

Samsung Electronics, followed by digital communication (15.9%) and semiconductors (11.9%). For the State Grid Corporation of China, electrical machinery (31.2%) was the most important technology field, followed by measurement (21.3%) and IT methods for management (8.1%).

The top 50 list is comprised of applicants located in just five countries. Japan heads the list with 20 companies, followed by China (13), the Republic of Korea (7), the U.S. (6) and Germany (4). The top 50 list mainly comprises multinational companies. However, five Chinese universities – Harbin Institute of Technology (7,274), Shanghai Jiao Tong University (5,058), Southeast University (6,074), Tsinghua University (5,363) and Zhejiang University (8,108) – also feature.

Three Asian countries – the Republic of Korea, China and Japan – filed the highest number of patents per unit of GDP

Variations in patenting activity across countries reflect differences in their levels of economic growth and development. It is therefore informative to examine resident patent activity with regard to population, R&D spending, GDP and other variables. These are commonly referred to as "patent activity intensity" indicators.

Since 2004, the Republic of Korea has had the highest number of patent applications per unit of USD 100 billion GDP. However, its ratio of resident applications to GDP for the past four years shows a year-on-year decrease. China has the second highest ratio, followed by Japan, Germany and Switzerland (see figure 1.6). Over the past 10 years, the gap between China and the Republic of Korea has narrowed. Reflecting strong growth in resident applications, China's resident applications per unit of GDP increased from 1,594 in 2007 to 5,869 in 2017. In contrast, Japan's ratio fell from 7,100 in 2007 to 5,264 in 2017. Germany's ratio declined slightly, from 2,194 to 1,961, while that of Switzerland remained stable at around 1,774.

The list of the top 20 origins is predominantly comprised of high-income countries. However, four middle-income countries – China, the Islamic Republic of Iran, the Russian Federation and Ukraine – also feature (see figure A39). The rank of the top 20 origins has been stable for the past 10 years, with little movement in country rankings, except in the case of China.

Among the large middle-income origins, Turkey's resident patent application to GDP ratio (448) is far above that of Brazil (186), India (174) and South Africa (104), all of which, with the exception of South Africa, reported a higher ratio for 2017 compared to 2007.

Patents

The Republic of Korea had the highest number of patent applications per unit of GDP

1.6. Resident patent applications per USD 100 billion GDP for the top 10 origins, 2007 and 2017

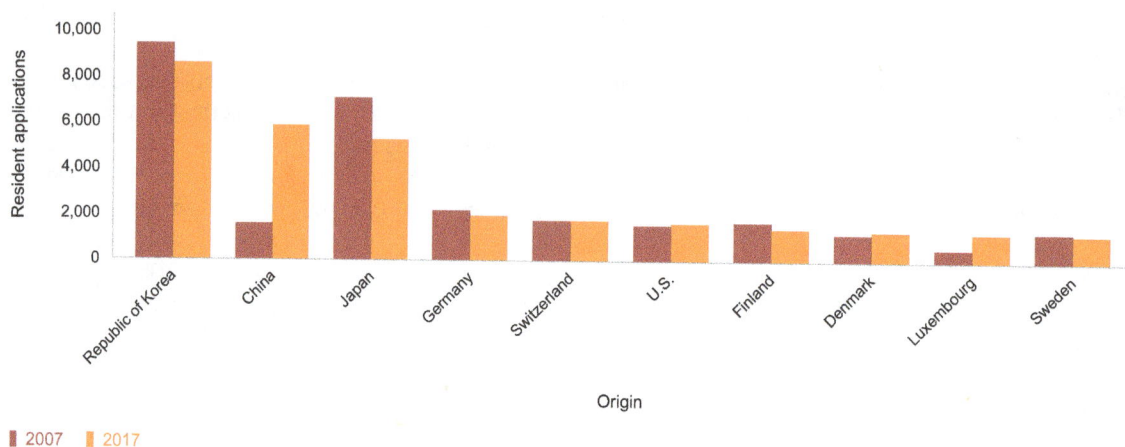

■ 2007 ■ 2017

Source: Figure A39.

The profile of resident applications per million population is similar to that adjusted by GDP, but shows some subtle differences. The Republic of Korea retains its lead, Japan ranks second and Switzerland is ranked third, ahead of the U.S., China and Germany (see figure A40).

Small high-income countries of origin, such as Denmark, Finland, Norway and Singapore, rank highly when resident patent applications are adjusted by population or GDP. Most of the top origins have improved their resident patent application to GDP and population ratios between 2007 and 2017; however, there are a few exceptions, notably Finland, Japan and the U.K., whose ratios have declined.

Computer technology remains the most frequently featured technology field in applications

In 2016 – the latest year for which complete data are available due to the delay between application and publication – computer technology was the most frequently featured technology in published patent applications worldwide with around 198,400 published applications (see table A31). It was followed by electrical machinery (185,600), digital communication (134,000), measurement (129,400) and medical technology (118,700). These five fields accounted for 28.9% of all published applications worldwide.

Among the top 20 technology fields, food chemistry (+12.5%), materials and metallurgy (+8.8%) and digital communication (+8.5%) witnessed the fastest average annual growth between 2006 and 2016. All of the top 20 technology fields saw growth in published applica-

tions between 2006 and 2016, with the exceptions of audio-visual technology (–2.0%) and optics (–1.1%), both of which saw a slight decline.

Among the top 10 origins in the period from 2014 to 2016, China and the Republic of Korea filed most heavily in electrical machinery and computer technology (see figure A32); Japan in electrical machinery; France and Germany in transport; Switzerland and the U.K. in pharmaceuticals; the Netherlands in medical technology; the Russian Federation in food chemistry; and the U.S. in computer technology. The combined share of the top three technologies for the top 10 origins ranged from 19.3% for the U.K. to 29% for the Russian Federation.

Among the large middle-income countries in the period from 2014 to 2016, applicants residing in India (15.7% of total published applications) and Mexico (11.1%) filed most heavily in pharmaceuticals; Brazil (6.5%) in other special machines; Malaysia (8.9%) in computer technology; South Africa (6.3%) in civil engineering and Turkey (11.4%) in other consumer goods. Bermuda (15%) and Singapore (11.5%) – two high-income countries – filed mainly in computer technologies.

The following four areas are categorized as energy-related technologies: solar energy, fuel cell technology, wind energy technology and geothermal energy. The number of published patent applications worldwide for energy-related technologies underwent a substantial increase – from around 14,500 in 2002 to around 42,800 in 2012. However, since then there has been a marked downward trend in energy-related published patent applications, which decreased from 42,800 in 2012 to 32,700 in 2016 (see figure A33).

The office of India granted 50% more patents in 2017 than in 2016

Offices carry out a formal and substantive examination to decide whether or not to issue a patent. The procedure for granting a patent varies between offices, and differences in the numbers of granted patents among offices depend on factors such as examination capacity and procedural delays. For this reason, application data for a given year should not be compared with grant data from the same year.

In 2017, an estimated 1.4 million patents were granted worldwide, up 3.9% on 2016 figures, and represent 17 consecutive years of growth (see figure 1.7). China (420,144) issued the largest number of patents in 2017, followed by the U.S. (318,829), Japan (199,577), the Republic of Korea (120,662) and the EPO (105,645). These five offices issued more than 1.16 million patents between them – 83% of the world total.

Among the top 10 offices, India granted 50.2% more patents in 2017 than in 2016, with grants increasing from 8,248 in 2016 to 12,387 in 2017. Non-resident grants accounted for 85% of the total increase. The EPO (+10.1%) and the Republic of Korea (+10.8%) also exhibited double-digit growth in 2017. For the EPO, this is the second successive year of double-digit growth. The office of the U.S. (+5.2%) also saw strong growth in 2017. Following three successive years of strong growth, China reported modest growth of 3.9% in 2017.

Beyond the top 10 list, Mexico granted 8,510 patents in 2017. Brazil (5,450), Malaysia (5,063) and South Africa (5,535) each issued more than 5,000 patents. Thailand issued 3,080 patents in 2017, which is 67.6% higher than the total for the previous year. All these offices, except Mexico, saw strong annual growth in patent grants.

Asia's share of worldwide patent grants was 57.2% in 2017, which is similar to its 2016 share. However, its share of grants has gradually followed an upward trend over the past 10 years – increasing from 53.5% in 2007 to 57.2% in 2017. Offices located in North America accounted for 24.4% of patent grants worldwide in 2017, while offices in Europe accounted for 14.5% of the world total. The combined share for Africa, LAC and Oceania was 3.9%.

The number of patents in force in the U.S. amounted to 2.98 million in 2017

Patent rights generally last for up to 20 years from the date the application was filed. The estimated number of patents in force worldwide rose from 8.5 million in 2008 to 13.7 million in 2017. In 2017, the largest

Patent granted worldwide grew by 3.9%

1.7. Patent grants worldwide, 2001–2017

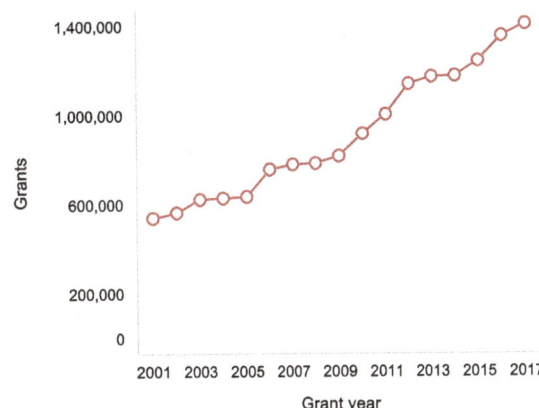

Source: Figure A3.

number of patents in force was recorded in the U.S. (2.98 million). China (2.09 million) and Japan (2.01 million) each had around 2 million patents and the U.K. (1.24 million) and Republic of Korea (970,889); these countries make up the top five jurisdictions (see figure 1.8). Among the top five offices, China recorded the fastest growth between 2010 and 2017, with 20.5% average annual growth. The Republic of Korea (+6.1%), the U.S. (+5.8%) and Japan (+5.1%) exhibited similar growth rates, while the U.K. had close to zero growth (+0.1%). The top 20 list includes 17 offices from high-income countries and three from upper middle-income countries, namely China, Mexico and the Russian Federation (see figure A42).

Holders must pay maintenance/renewal fees to maintain the validity of their patents, and may opt to let a patent lapse before the end of its full term. For the 65 offices that reported their in-force data broken down by year of filing, between 40% and 43% of patents granted remained in force for at least 6 to 10 years after the filing date, and about one-fifth lasted for the full 20 years (see figure A43).

Although patents can be maintained for 20 years, the average age of patents varied across offices. For example, the average age of all patents in force in 2017 in Thailand was 14.2 years, while in China it was 7.2 years. Along with Thailand, India (13 years), Viet Nam (12.2 years) and Chile (12 years) also have high average ages of patents in force (see figure A44).

Half of all patents in force in the U.S. originated from non-resident applicants

1.8. Patents in force at the top 10 offices, 2017

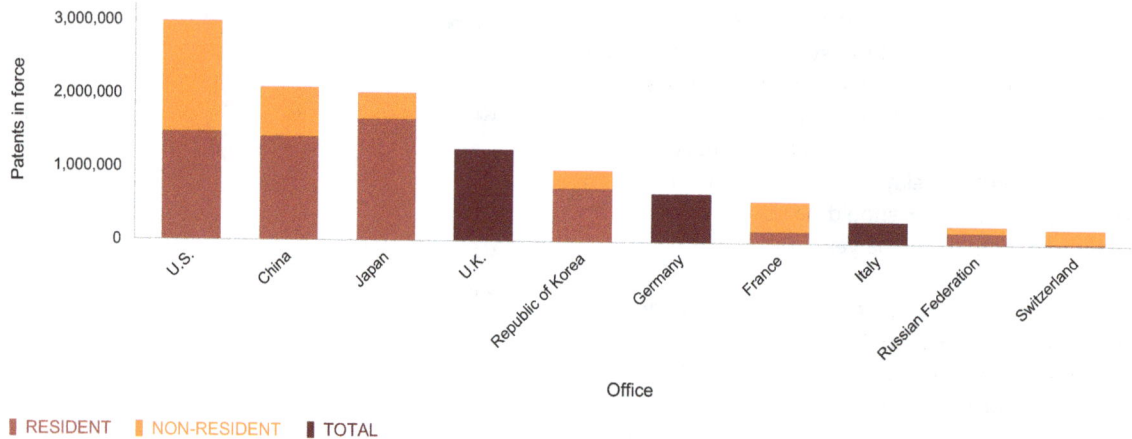

RESIDENT   NON-RESIDENT   TOTAL

Source: Figure A42.

More than 75% of applications examined in 2017 resulted in patents being granted at the offices of Australia and the Russian Federation

Patent offices examine applications and decide whether or not to grant patent rights. Examination processes differ across offices, which makes cross-country comparisons difficult. However, every effort has been made to compile examination outcome data based on common definitions and concepts. More than 75% of applications examined in 2017 resulted in patents being granted at the patent offices of Australia and the Russian Federation. Japan also had a high share of patents granted for applications processed. Among the 10 selected offices, Germany, India, the U.K. and the U.S. granted patents for fewer than half of all applications processed in 2017 (see figure 1.9). The shares of rejected applications were the highest in the U.K. and the U.S., while India reported the highest share of those withdrawn.

The offices of China and the U.S. each had more than one million potentially pending patent applications in 2017

Patent offices must assess whether the claims in applications meet the standards of novelty, non-obviousness and industrial applicability defined in national laws. Processing patents therefore consumes time and resources. The total number of potentially pending applications worldwide stood at 5.7 million in 2017. This estimate is based on data from 108 offices. For the first time, pending applications data is available from the IP office of China.

The IP office of China had the largest number of potentially pending applications (1.11 million) in 2017 (see figure A46). It was followed by the U.S. (1.08 million), Japan (815,295) and the EPO (652,427). Most of those offices had fewer potentially pending applications in 2017 compared to 2016. For China, no data prior to 2017 are available. Among selected middle-income countries, Brazil and India each reported more than 200,000 potentially pending applications in 2017. However, Brazil had 7.2% fewer pending applications in 2017 compared to the previous year, while India saw a 6.7% drop.

Potentially pending applications

Potentially pending applications include all patent applications, at any stage in the process, awaiting a final decision by a patent office, including those applications for which applicants have not filed a request for examination (where applicable).

China and Japan drive PCT international patent application filings to record heights

An international treaty administered by WIPO, the Patent Cooperation Treaty (PCT), allows applicants to seek patent protection for an invention simultaneously in a large number of countries by filing a single PCT international application. The granting of patents remains under the control of national and regional patent offices and is carried out in what is called the "national phase" or "regional phase."

The shares of rejected applications were highest in the U.K. and the U.S.

1.9. Distribution of patent examination outcomes for selected offices, 2017

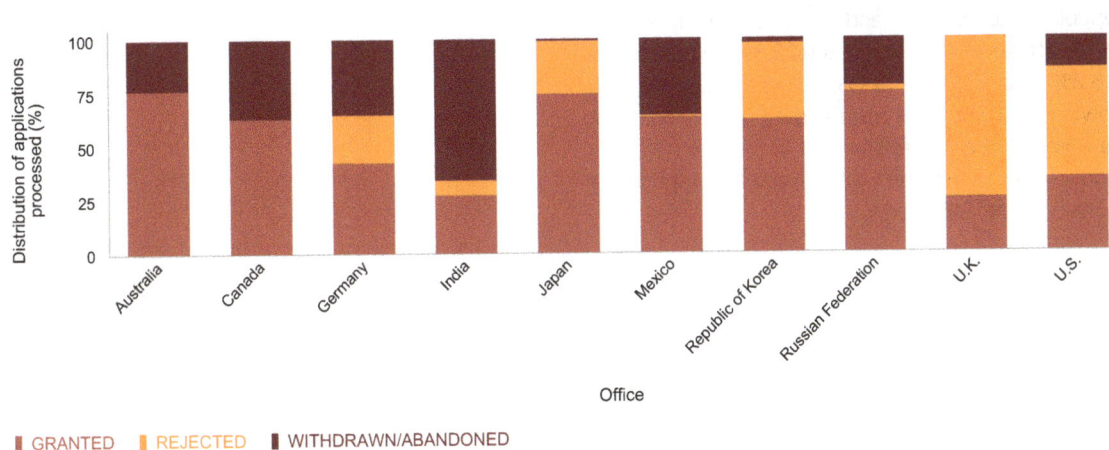

GRANTED ■ REJECTED ■ WITHDRAWN/ABANDONED

Source: Figure A45.

Overall, inventors from around the world filed around 243,500 PCT applications in 2017 – 4.5% more than the previous year, driven by strong growth from China and Japan. China, with 48,900 PCT applications, became the second largest source of PCT applications, closing in on the long-time leader – the U.S. (56,680). Japan (48,206) ranked third, followed by Germany (18,948) and the Republic of Korea (15,752) (see figure A51).

Among the top 20 origins, Belgium (+11.1%) and China (+13.5%) were the only two countries to have recorded double-digit annual growth in 2017. China has now posted growth higher than 10% every year since 2003. Sweden (+6.9%), Japan (+6.6%) and Denmark (+5.4%) also saw strong growth. In contrast, Spain (–5.9%), the Netherlands (–5.3%) and Italy (–4.1%) each saw a decrease in filings.

The share of PCT applications with women inventors is rising

In 2017, 31.2% of PCT applications contained at least one woman inventor, which is a considerably higher figure than the 22.1% recorded in 2003. In terms of volume, the total number of PCT applications with at least one woman inventor has almost tripled, from 24,004 in 2003 to 68,270 in 2017.

Women's participation rate varied across countries. Among the top 20 origins, the Republic of Korea (50.3%) and China (47.9%) had the highest women's participation rates (see figure A36). Belgium (35.7%), Spain (35.4%), the U.S. (32.8%) and France (32.5%) also had relatively high shares of PCT applications

by women inventors. However, the share of women inventors in total inventors is low, ranging from 28.9% in China to 9.1% in Japan (see figure A37).

Fields of technology related to life sciences had comparatively high shares of PCT applications with women inventors in 2017. More than half of PCT applications in the fields of biotechnology (58.3%), pharmaceuticals (56.3%), organic fine chemistry (55.1%), food chemistry (50.7%) and analysis of biological materials (50.6%) included at least one women inventor (see figure A38).

Around 1.76 million utility model applications were filed worldwide in 2017

A utility model is a special form of patent right granted by a state or jurisdiction to an inventor or the inventor's assignee for a fixed period of time. The terms and conditions for granting a utility model differ slightly from those for normal patents, including a shorter term of protection and less stringent eligibility requirements.

In 2017, the total number of utility model applications worldwide reached 1.76 million. The IP office of China received 95.8% of the world total – the remaining 74 offices accounted for just 4.2%. As with invention patents, the IP office of China revised its method of compiling utility model applications statistics in 2017, now counting only those applications for which the office has received the necessary application fees. Due to this break in the data series and to the large number of filings in China, it is not possible to calculate the growth rate for the world total and China.

The IP office of China received 1.69 million applications in 2017 (see figure A55), followed by Germany (13,301), the Russian Federation (10,643), Ukraine (9,108), the Republic of Korea (6,811) and Japan (6,105). Among the top 20 offices, the Philippines (+22.8%), Kazakhstan (+16.3%) and Finland (+13.1%) witnessed double-digit growth in 2017 – albeit from a low base. In contrast, the number of applications filed in Mexico (−12.9%), Austria (−12.4%), Poland (−12.4%) and the Republic of Korea (−12.3%) fell sharply in 2017.

Patent statistics

Patents

Patent applications and grants worldwide

A1. Trend in patent applications worldwide, 2003–2017

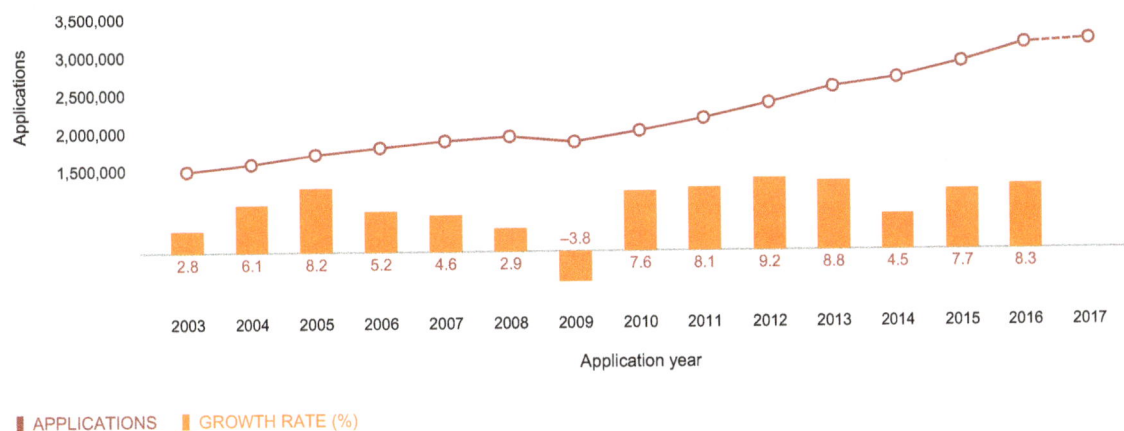

APPLICATIONS ▮ GROWTH RATE (%)

Note: China's 2017 data are not comparable with its previous years' data due to the new way in which the IP office of China now counts its applications data. Prior to 2017, it included all applications received; however, starting in 2017, China's application count data include only those applications for which the office has received the necessary application fees. Due to this break in the data series and to the large number of filings in China, it is not possible to report an accurate 2017 growth rate at world level (see the data description section). World totals are WIPO estimates using data covering 156 patent offices. These totals include applications filed directly with national and regional offices and applications entering offices through the Patent Cooperation Treaty national phase (where applicable).

Source: WIPO Statistics Database, September 2018.

A2. Resident and non-resident patent applications worldwide, 2003–2017

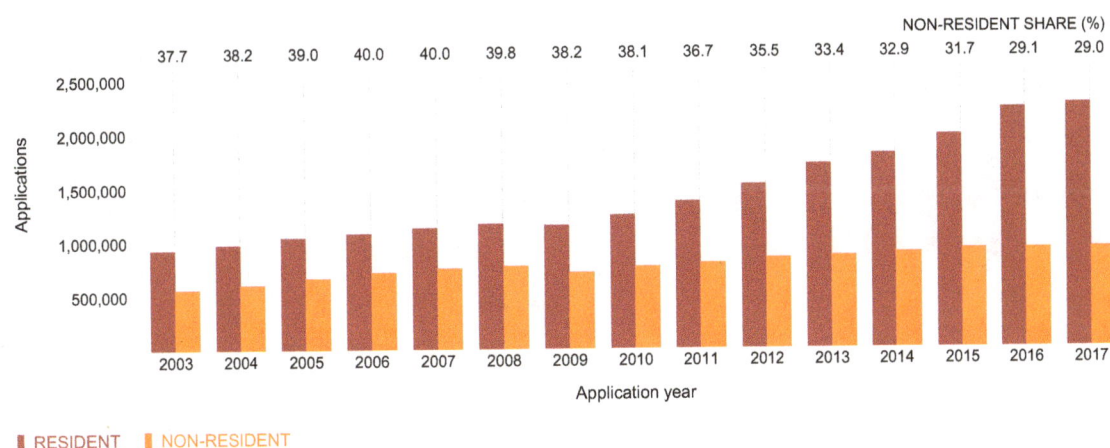

RESIDENT ▮ NON-RESIDENT

Note: World totals are WIPO estimates using data covering 156 patent offices. These totals include applications filed directly with national and regional offices and applications entering offices through the Patent Cooperation Treaty national phase (where applicable). See the glossary for definitions of resident and non-resident.

Source: WIPO Statistics Database, September 2018.

Patents

A3. Trend in patent grants worldwide, 2003–2017

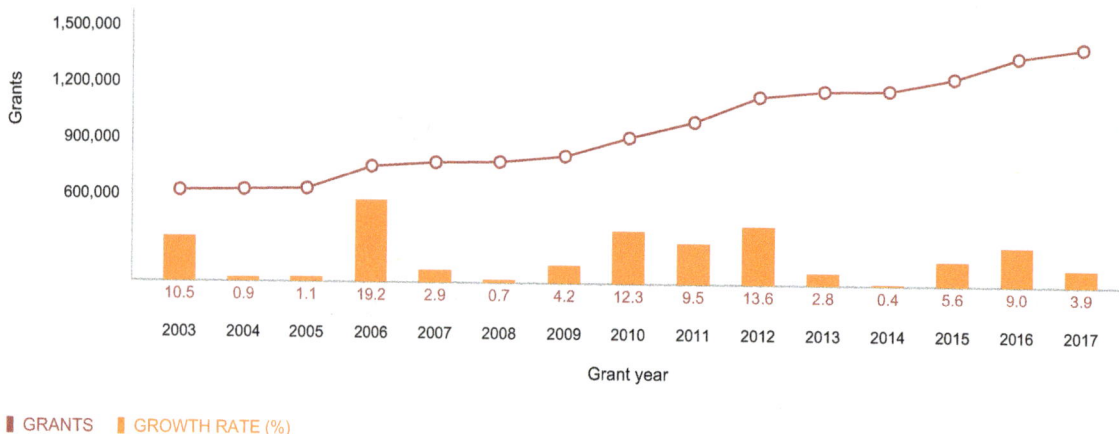

Year	2003	2004	2005	2006	2007	2008	2009	2010	2011	2012	2013	2014	2015	2016	2017
Growth rate	10.5	0.9	1.1	19.2	2.9	0.7	4.2	12.3	9.5	13.6	2.8	0.4	5.6	9.0	3.9

Grant year

GRANTS   GROWTH RATE (%)

Note: World totals are WIPO estimates using data covering 155 patent offices. These totals include patent grants based on applications filed directly with national and regional offices and patents granted by offices on the basis of the Patent Cooperation Treaty national phase (where applicable).

Source: WIPO Statistics Database, September 2018.

A4. Resident and non-resident patent grants worldwide, 2003–2017

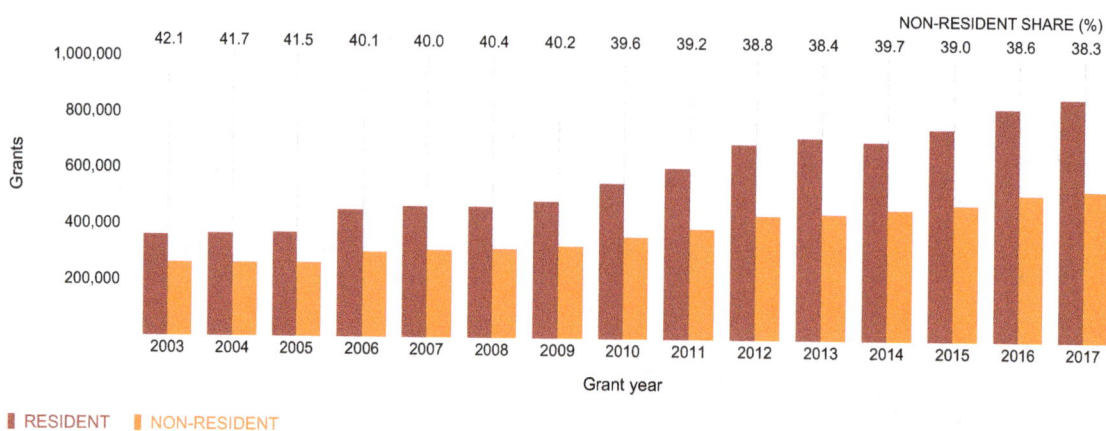

NON-RESIDENT SHARE (%)

Year	2003	2004	2005	2006	2007	2008	2009	2010	2011	2012	2013	2014	2015	2016	2017
Non-resident share	42.1	41.7	41.5	40.1	40.0	40.4	40.2	39.6	39.2	38.8	38.4	39.7	39.0	38.6	38.3

Grant year

RESIDENT   NON-RESIDENT

Note: World totals are WIPO estimates using data covering 155 patent offices. These totals include patent grants based on applications filed directly with national and regional offices and patents granted by offices on the basis of the Patent Cooperation Treaty national phase (where applicable). See the glossary for definitions of resident and non-resident.

Source: WIPO Statistics Database, September 2018.

Patent applications and grants by office

A5. Patent applications by income group, 2007 and 2017

Income group	Number of applications		Resident share (%)		Share of world total (%)		Average growth (%)
	2007	2017	2007	2017	2007	2017	2007–2017
High-income	1,433,000	1,555,600	62.7	58.6	76.4	49.1	0.8
Upper middle-income	372,300	1,524,400	55.4	85.8	19.9	48.1	15.1
Lower middle-income	61,300	78,900	20.8	30.0	3.3	2.5	2.6
Low-income	8,400	10,000	86.5	83.1	0.4	0.3	1.8
World	**1,875,000**	**3,168,900**	**60.0**	**71.0**	**100.0**	**100.0**	**5.4**

Note: China's 2017 data are not comparable with its previous years' data due to the new way in which the IP office of China now counts its applications data. Prior to 2017, it included all applications received; however, starting in 2017, China's application count data include only those applications for which the office has received the necessary application fees (see the data description section). Although there is a break in the data series, the average growth rate for 2007–2017 is reported because this change in method has a limited impact on the long-term growth rate. Totals by income group are WIPO estimates using data covering 156 offices. Each category includes the following number of offices: high-income countries/economies (58), upper middle-income (47), lower middle-income (32) and low-income (19). European Patent Office data are allocated to the high-income group because most of its member states are high-income countries. For similar reasons, data for the African Regional Intellectual Property Organization and the African Intellectual Property Organization are allocated to the low-income group, while those for the Eurasian Patent Organization are allocated to the lower middle-income group. For information on income group classification, see the data description section.

Source: WIPO Statistics Database, September 2018.

A6. Patent applications by region, 2007 and 2017

Region	Number of applications		Resident share (%)		Share of world total (%)		Average growth (%)
	2007	2017	2007	2017	2007	2017	2007–2017
Africa	14,100	16,000	13.9	17.6	0.8	0.5	1.3
Asia	932,500	2,062,500	69.6	83.7	49.7	65.1	8.3
Europe	339,300	355,700	63.7	59.9	18.1	11.2	0.5
Latin America and the Caribbean	58,100	57,600	11.4	15.1	3.1	1.8	−0.1
North America	496,300	642,000	49.6	46.4	26.4	20.3	2.6
Oceania	34,700	35,100	13.3	10.0	1.9	1.1	0.1
World	**1,875,000**	**3,168,900**	**60.0**	**71.0**	**100.0**	**100.0**	**5.4**

Note: China's 2017 data are not comparable with its previous years' data due to the new way in which the IP office of China now counts its applications data. Prior to 2017, it included all applications received; however, starting in 2017, China's application count data include only those applications for which the office has received the necessary application fees (see the data description section). Although there is a break in the data series, the average growth rate for 2007–2017 is reported because this change in method has a limited impact on the long-term growth rate. Totals by geographic region are WIPO estimates using data covering 156 offices. Each region includes the following number of offices: Africa (31), Asia (43), Europe (45), Latin America and the Caribbean (31), North America (2) and Oceania (4).

Source: WIPO Statistics Database, September 2018.

Patents

A7. Trend in patent applications for the top five offices, 1883–2017

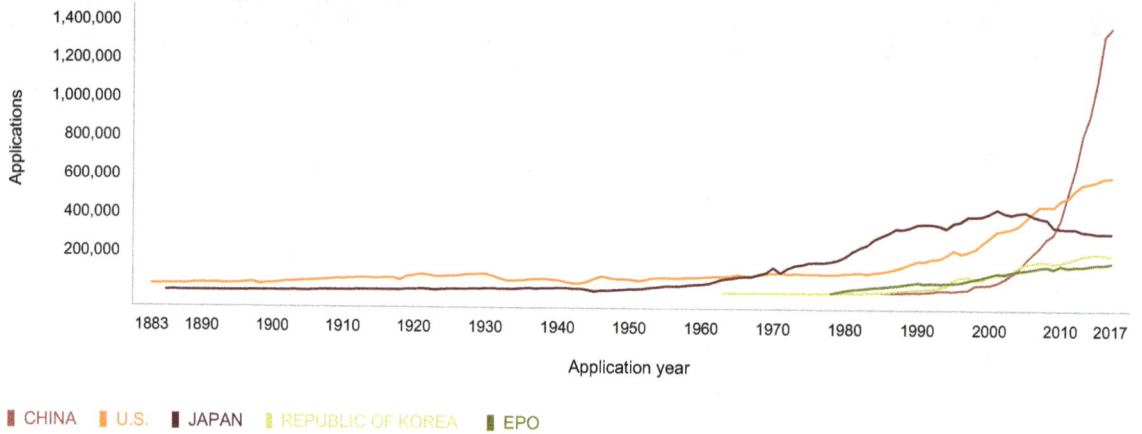

■ CHINA ■ U.S. ■ JAPAN ▓ REPUBLIC OF KOREA ■ EPO

Note: China's 2017 data are not comparable with its previous years' data due to the new way in which the IP office of China now counts its applications data. Prior to 2017, it included all applications received; however, starting in 2017, China's application count data include only those applications for which the office has received the necessary application fees. EPO is the European Patent Office. The top five offices were selected based on their 2017 totals.

Source: WIPO Statistics Database, September 2018.

A8. Patent applications at the top 20 offices, 2017

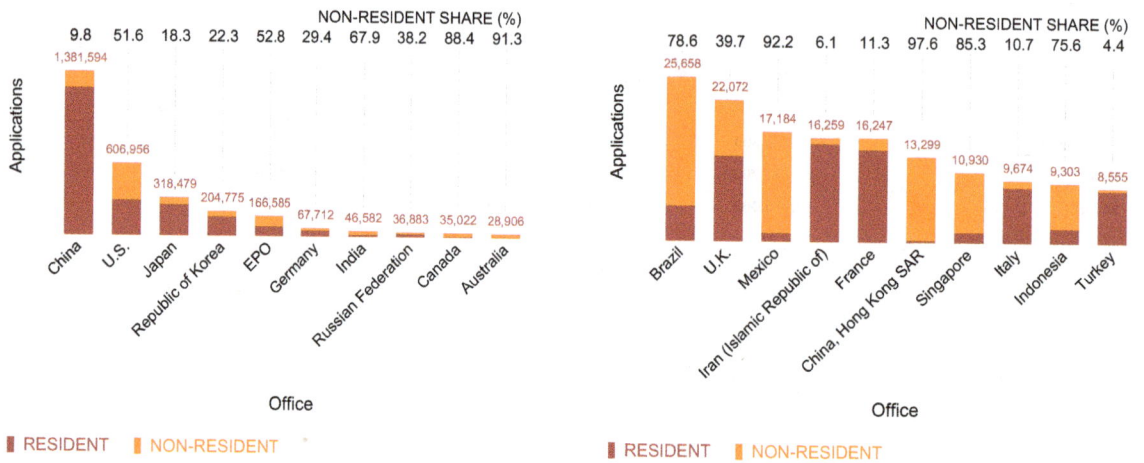

■ RESIDENT ■ NON-RESIDENT

Note: EPO is the European Patent Office. In general, national offices of the EPO member states receive lower volumes of applications because applicants may apply via the EPO to seek protection within any EPO member state.

Source: WIPO Statistics Database, September 2018.

A9. Contribution of resident and non-resident applications to total growth for the top 20 offices, 2016–2017

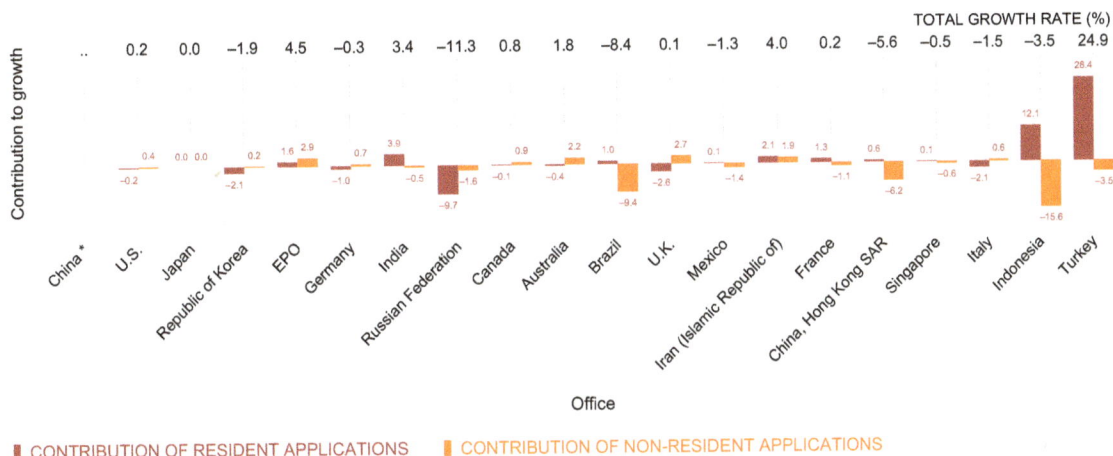

TOTAL GROWTH RATE (%)
.. 0.2 0.0 −1.9 4.5 −0.3 3.4 −11.3 0.8 1.8 −8.4 0.1 −1.3 4.0 0.2 −5.6 −0.5 −1.5 −3.5 24.9

■ CONTRIBUTION OF RESIDENT APPLICATIONS   ■ CONTRIBUTION OF NON-RESIDENT APPLICATIONS

.. indicates not available.

Note: * indicates China's 2017 data are not comparable with its previous years' data due to the new way in which the IP office of China now counts its applications data. Prior to 2017, it included all applications received; however, starting in 2017, China's application count data include only those applications for which the office has received the necessary application fees (see the data description section). Due to this break in the data series, it is not possible to report an accurate 2017 growth rate. EPO is the European Patent Office. This figure shows total growth or decrease in applications at each office, broken down by the respective contributions of resident and non-resident applications. For example, applications filed at the EPO grew by 4.5%. Growth in resident applications accounted for 1.6 percentage points of this increase, whereas the remaining 2.9 percentage points reflected growth in non-resident applications.

Source: WIPO Statistics Database, September 2018.

A10. Patent applications at offices of selected low- and middle-income countries, 2017

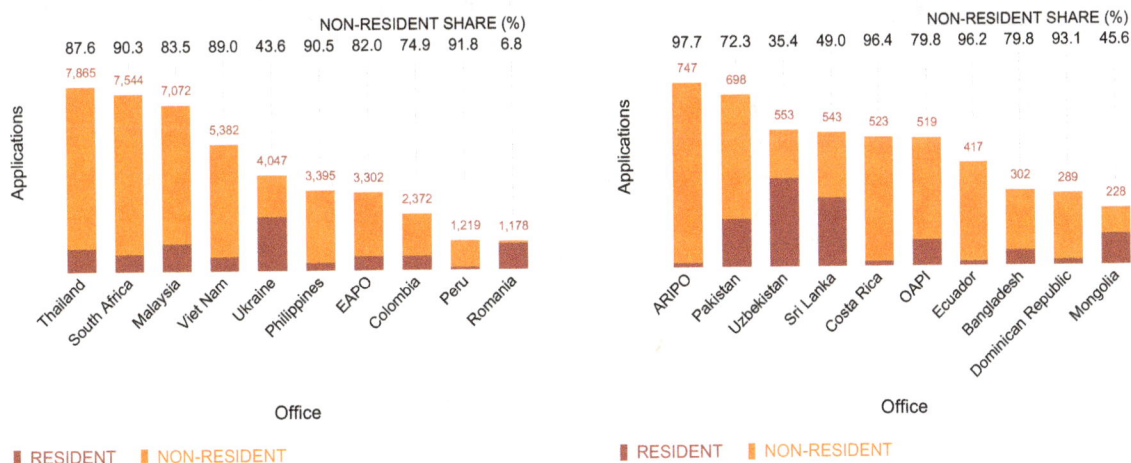

NON-RESIDENT SHARE (%)
87.6 90.3 83.5 89.0 43.6 90.5 82.0 74.9 91.8 6.8

■ RESIDENT   ■ NON-RESIDENT

NON-RESIDENT SHARE (%)
97.7 72.3 35.4 49.0 96.4 79.8 96.2 79.8 93.1 45.6

■ RESIDENT   ■ NON-RESIDENT

Note: ARIPO is the African Regional Intellectual Property Organization, EAPO is the Eurasian Patent Organization and OAPI is the African Intellectual Property Organization. The selected offices are from different world regions and income groups (low-income, lower middle-income and upper middle-income). Where available, data for all offices are presented in table A59.

Source: WIPO Statistics Database, September 2018.

A11. Contribution of resident and non-resident applications to total growth for offices of selected low- and middle-income countries, 2016–2017

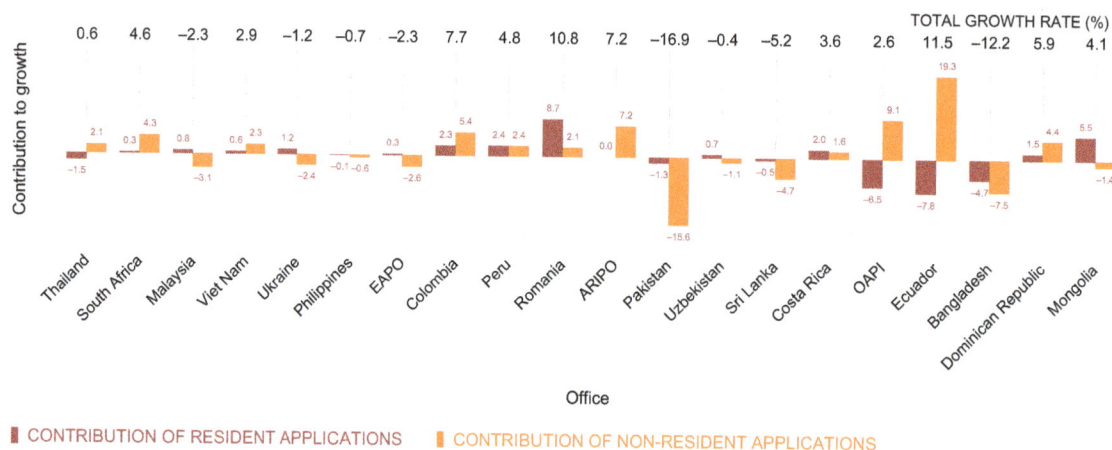

CONTRIBUTION OF RESIDENT APPLICATIONS   CONTRIBUTION OF NON-RESIDENT APPLICATIONS

Note: ARIPO is the African Regional Intellectual Property Organization, EAPO is the Eurasian Patent Organization and OAPI is the African Intellectual Property Organization. The selected offices are from different world regions and income groups (low-income, lower middle-income and upper middle-income). Data for all available offices are presented in the statistical table at the end of this section. This figure shows total growth or decrease in applications at each office, broken down by the respective contributions of resident and non-resident applications. For example, applications filed in South Africa grew by 4.6%. Growth in resident applications accounted for 0.3 percentage points of this increase, whereas the remaining 4.3 percentage points came from growth in non-resident applications.

Source: WIPO Statistics Database, September 2018.

A12. Patent grants by income group, 2007 and 2017

Income group	Number of grants		Resident share (%)		Share of world total (%)		Average growth (%)
	2007	2017	2007	2017	2007	2017	2007–2017
High-income	615,200	874,800	63.5	56.8	79.2	62.3	3.6
Upper middle-income	128,700	497,700	49.5	72.2	16.6	35.4	14.5
Lower middle-income	27,300	24,500	25.5	17.7	3.5	1.7	−1.1
Low-income	5,100	7,600	87.2	86.2	0.7	0.5	4.1
World	**776,300**	**1,404,600**	**60.0**	**61.7**	**100.0**	**100.0**	**6.1**

Note: Totals by income group are WIPO estimates using data covering 155 offices. Each category includes the following number of offices: high-income countries/economies (59), upper middle-income (45), lower middle-income (32) and low-income (19). European Patent Office data are allocated to the high-income group because most of its member states are high-income countries. For similar reasons, data for the African Regional Intellectual Property Organization and the African Intellectual Property Organization are allocated to the low-income group, while those for the Eurasian Patent Organization are allocated to the lower middle-income group. For information on income group classification, see the data description section.

Source: WIPO Statistics Database, September 2018.

A13. Patent grants by region, 2007 and 2017

Region	Number of grants		Resident share (%)		Share of world total (%)		Average growth (%)
	2007	2017	2007	2017	2007	2017	2007–2017
Africa	4,600	9,400	32.0	14.1	0.6	0.7	7.4
Asia	415,200	803,100	69.1	73.8	53.5	57.2	6.8
Europe	149,300	203,600	62.6	57.2	19.2	14.5	3.2
Latin America and the Caribbean	16,600	20,300	6.1	8.3	2.1	1.4	2.0
North America	175,800	342,900	46.3	44.7	22.6	24.4	6.9
Oceania	14,800	25,300	10.6	5.4	1.9	1.8	5.5
World	**776,300**	**1,404,600**	**60.0**	**61.7**	**100.0**	**100.0**	**6.1**

Note: Totals by geographic region are WIPO estimates using data covering 155 offices. Each region includes the following number of offices: Africa (30), Asia (43), Europe (45), Latin America and the Caribbean (30), North America (2) and Oceania (5).

Source: WIPO Statistics Database, September 2018.

A14. Trend in patent grants for the top five offices, 1883–2017

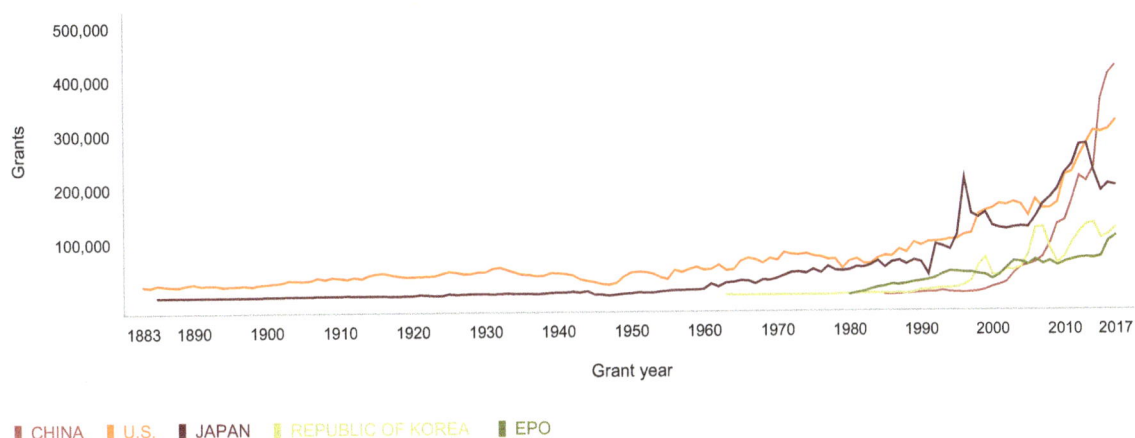

Note: EPO is the European Patent Office. The top five offices were selected based on their 2017 totals.

Source: WIPO Statistics Database, September 2018.

Patents

A15. Patent grants for the top 20 offices, 2017

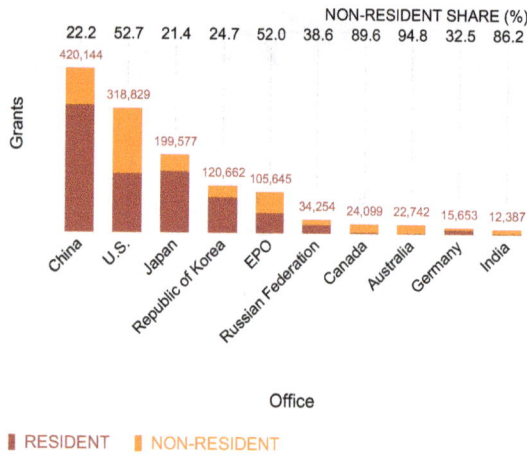

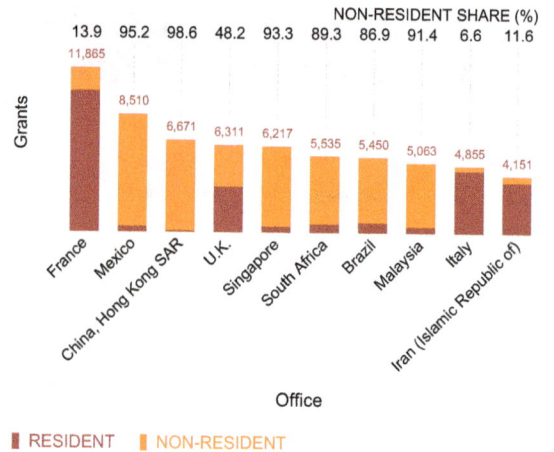

NON-RESIDENT SHARE (%)

Office	China	U.S.	Japan	Republic of Korea	EPO	Russian Federation	Canada	Australia	Germany	India
Share	22.2	52.7	21.4	24.7	52.0	38.6	89.6	94.8	32.5	86.2
Grants	420,144	318,829	199,577	120,662	105,645	34,254	24,099	22,742	15,653	12,387

NON-RESIDENT SHARE (%)

Office	France	Mexico	China, Hong Kong SAR	U.K.	Singapore	South Africa	Brazil	Malaysia	Italy	Iran (Islamic Republic of)
Share	13.9	95.2	98.6	48.2	93.3	89.3	86.9	91.4	6.6	11.6
Grants	11,865	8,510	6,671	6,311	6,217	5,535	5,450	5,063	4,855	4,151

■ RESIDENT   ■ NON-RESIDENT

Note: EPO is the European Patent Office. The procedure for issuing patents varies between offices, and differences in the numbers of patents granted among offices depend on factors such as examination capacity and procedural delays. The examination process can also be lengthy, so there is a time lag between application and grant dates. For this reason, data on applications for a given year should not be compared with data on grants for the same year.

Source: WIPO Statistics Database, September 2018.

A16. Patent grants for offices of selected low- and middle-income countries, 2017

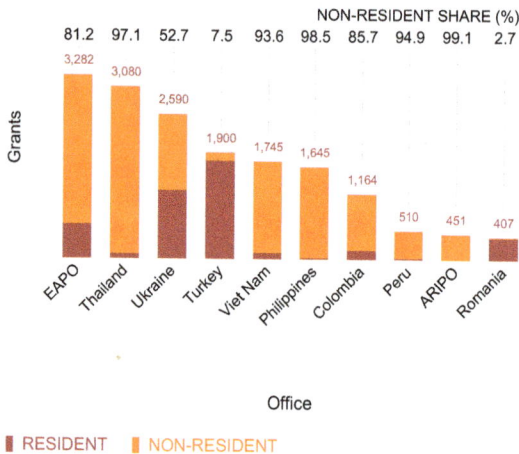

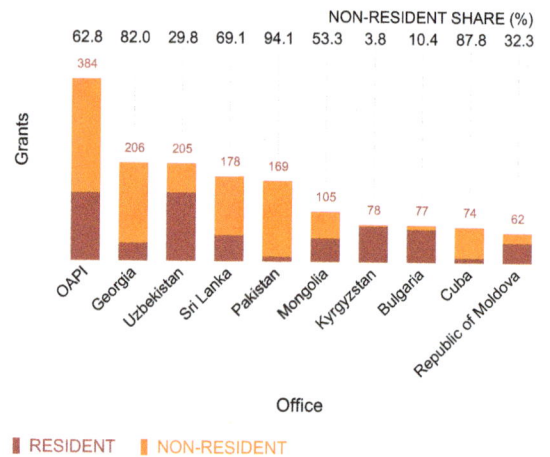

NON-RESIDENT SHARE (%)

Office	EAPO	Thailand	Ukraine	Turkey	Viet Nam	Philippines	Colombia	Peru	ARIPO	Romania
Share	81.2	97.1	52.7	7.5	93.6	98.5	85.7	94.9	99.1	2.7
Grants	3,282	3,080	2,590	1,900	1,745	1,645	1,164	510	451	407

NON-RESIDENT SHARE (%)

Office	OAPI	Georgia	Uzbekistan	Sri Lanka	Pakistan	Mongolia	Kyrgyzstan	Bulgaria	Cuba	Republic of Moldova
Share	62.8	82.0	29.8	69.1	94.1	53.3	3.8	10.4	87.8	32.3
Grants	384	206	205	178	169	105	78	77	74	62

■ RESIDENT   ■ NON-RESIDENT

Note: ARIPO is the African Regional Intellectual Property Organization, EAPO is the Eurasian Patent Organization and OAPI is the African Intellectual Property Organization. The selected offices are from different world regions and income groups (low-income, lower middle-income and upper middle-income). Where available, data for all offices are presented in table A60.

Source: WIPO Statistics Database, September 2018.

Patent applications and grants by origin

A17. Equivalent patent applications by origin, 2017

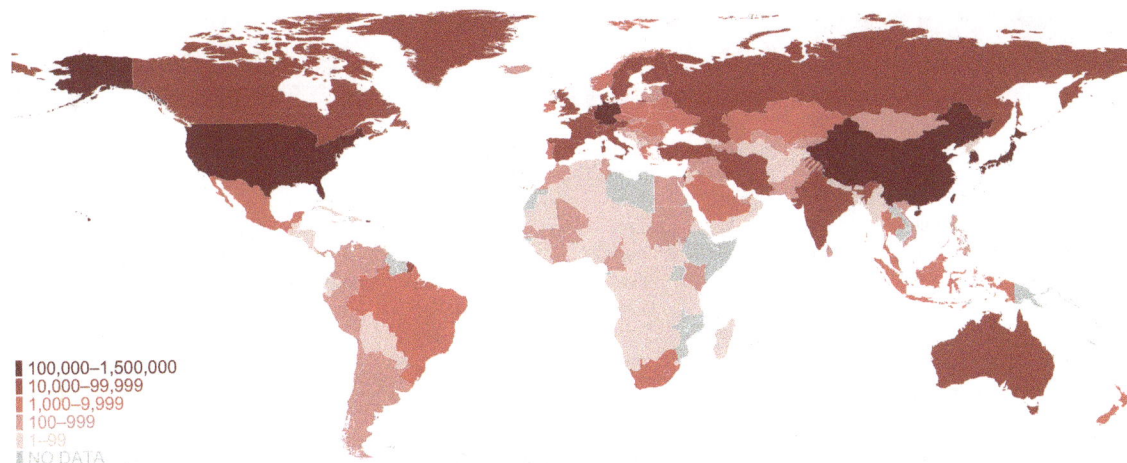

- 100,000–1,500,000
- 10,000–99,999
- 1,000–9,999
- 100–999
- 1–99
- NO DATA

Note: Patent filing activity by origin includes resident applications and applications filed abroad. The origin of a patent application is determined by the residence of the first named applicant. Applications filed at regional offices are considered equivalent to multiple applications in the relevant member states. See the glossary for the definition of equivalent application.

Source: WIPO Statistics Database, September 2018.

A18. Equivalent patent applications for the top 20 origins, 2017

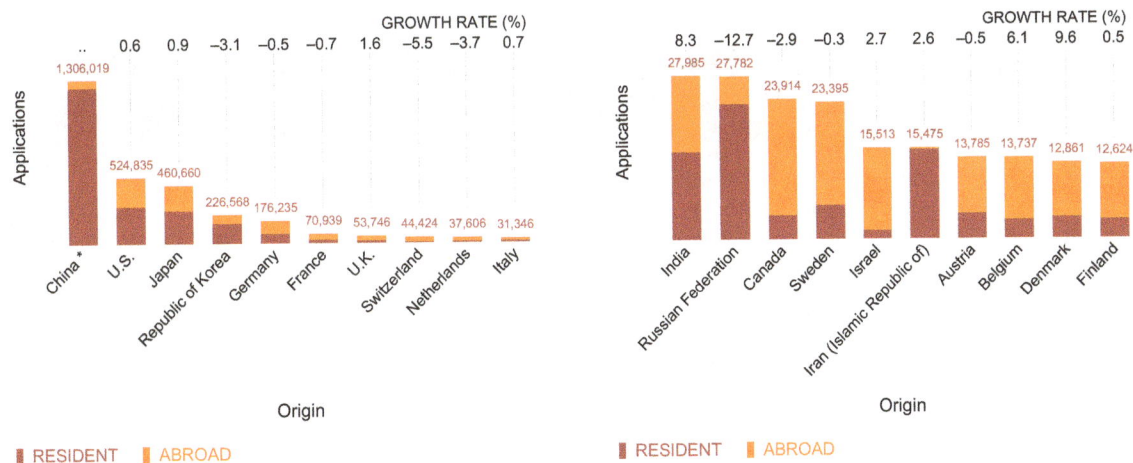

GROWTH RATE (%)

	..	0.6	0.9	−3.1	−0.5	−0.7	1.6	−5.5	−3.7	0.7
Applications	1,306,019	524,835	460,660	226,568	176,235	70,939	53,746	44,424	37,606	31,346

Origin: China *, U.S., Japan, Republic of Korea, Germany, France, U.K., Switzerland, Netherlands, Italy

GROWTH RATE (%)

	8.3	−12.7	−2.9	−0.3	2.7	2.6	−0.5	6.1	9.6	0.5
Applications	27,985	27,782	23,914	23,395	15,513	15,475	13,785	13,737	12,861	12,624

Origin: India, Russian Federation, Canada, Sweden, Israel, Iran (Islamic Republic of), Austria, Belgium, Denmark, Finland

- RESIDENT
- ABROAD

.. indicates not available.

Note: * indicates China's 2017 data are not comparable with its previous years' data due to the new way in which the IP office of China now counts its applications data. Prior to 2017, it included all applications received; however, starting in 2017, China's application count data include only those applications for which the office has received the necessary application fees (see the data description section). Due to this break in the data series, it is not possible to report an accurate 2017 growth rate. Patent activity by origin includes resident applications and applications filed abroad. The origin of a patent application is determined by the residence of the first named applicant. Applications filed at regional offices are considered equivalent to multiple applications in the relevant member states. See the glossary for the definition of equivalent application.

Source: WIPO Statistics Database, September 2018.

Patents

A19. Patent applications for the top 20 offices and origins, 2017

Origin	Office									
	Australia	Brazil	Canada	China	China, Hong Kong SAR	European Patent Office	France	Germany	India	Indonesia
Australia	2,503	156	459	675	156	842	6	22	252	83
Austria	198	200	240	828	51	2,225	6	906	232	30
Belgium	298	268	344	708	89	2,157	102	70	280	71
Canada	546	181	4,053	984	211	1,514	9	95	292	50
China	1,067	676	921	1,245,709	1,128	8,627	109	646	2,582	492
Finland	180	130	254	877	135	1,828	10	45	219	80
France	808	1,355	1,612	4,926	355	10,625	14,415	237	1,250	235
Germany	1,332	1,910	2,083	14,342	690	25,560	452	47,785	2,708	396
India	179	137	166	277	44	677	5	28	14,961	86
Iran (Islamic Republic of)	1	1	3	1		6	1	3	3	
Israel	447	170	455	884	162	1,389	2	13	317	
Italy	331	601	511	1,695	179	4,363	80	133	567	87
Japan	1,622	1,717	1,854	40,908	1,344	21,755	248	7,279	4,490	2,407
Netherlands	512	854	494	3,267	212	7,033	26	128	1,385	274
Republic of Korea	490	233	294	13,180	179	6,455	17	1,171	1,670	386
Russian Federation	33	53	70	154	12	201	3	17	80	
Sweden	427	458	402	1,842	193	3,784	29	464	1,011	
Switzerland	1,076	1,066	1,225	3,431	876	7,285	81	922	1,286	371
U.K.	1,241	657	1,139	2,296	536	5,331	42	210	1,069	
U.S.	13,388	7,949	16,363	36,980	4,740	42,542	278	6,084	10,309	1,579
Others/Unknown	2,227	6,886	2,080	7,630	2,007	12,386	326	1,454	1,619	2,676
Total	**28,906**	**25,658**	**35,022**	**1,381,594**	**13,299**	**166,585**	**16,247**	**67,712**	**46,582**	**9,303**

Origin	Office									
	Iran (Islamic Republic of)	Italy	Japan	Mexico	Republic of Korea	Russian Federation	Singapore	Turkey	U.K.	U.S.
Australia	5	6	431	110	188	69	151	1	130	3,773
Austria	23	15	378	103	262	176	59	8	44	2,584
Belgium	16	21	551	178	307	131	100		174	2,577
Canada	9	2	551	225	333	119	88	2	183	13,301
China	107	35	4,172	281	3,015	917	508	30	1,078	29,674
Finland	9	4	425	71	286	887	41		124	2,872
France	125	54	2,957	585	1,746	887	310	2	168	12,584
Germany	119	320	6,230	1,106	4,012	1,536	483	46	513	30,783
India	13	1	225	102	96	53	90	15	73	9,222
Iran (Islamic Republic of)	15,264		1	1	1	1		4	1	175
Israel		2	582	123	256	130	111	4	72	8,389
Italy	58	8,643	873	287	479	418	95	6	54	5,355
Japan	42	92	260,290	1,274	15,043	1,453	1,689	34	586	86,113
Netherlands	37	9	2,301	371	916	815	160	2	160	5,343
Republic of Korea	58	1	4,735	245	159,084	319	205	23	122	35,565
Russian Federation	19	5	107	15	69	22,777	10	2	7	1,125
Sweden	13	32	899	235	588		80	3	154	5,046
Switzerland		141	2,525	897	1,159	813	439	10	362	5,549
U.K.	37	34	1,829	379	1,026	430	392	5	13,301	14,057
U.S.	86	114	23,949	8,370	13,442	3,925	3,544	149	3,009	293,904
Others/Unknown	219	143	4,468	2,226	2,467	1,027	2,375	8,209	1,757	38,965
Total	**16,259**	**9,674**	**318,479**	**17,184**	**204,775**	**36,883**	**10,930**	**8,555**	**22,072**	**606,956**

Note: EPO is the European Patent Office. Origin data are based on absolute counts, not equivalent counts. The top 20 offices and origins are selected based on the available 2017 data, broken down by country of origin.

Source: WIPO Statistics Database, September 2018.

A20. Flows of non-resident patent applications between the top five origins and the top 10 offices, 2017

Origin   **Office**

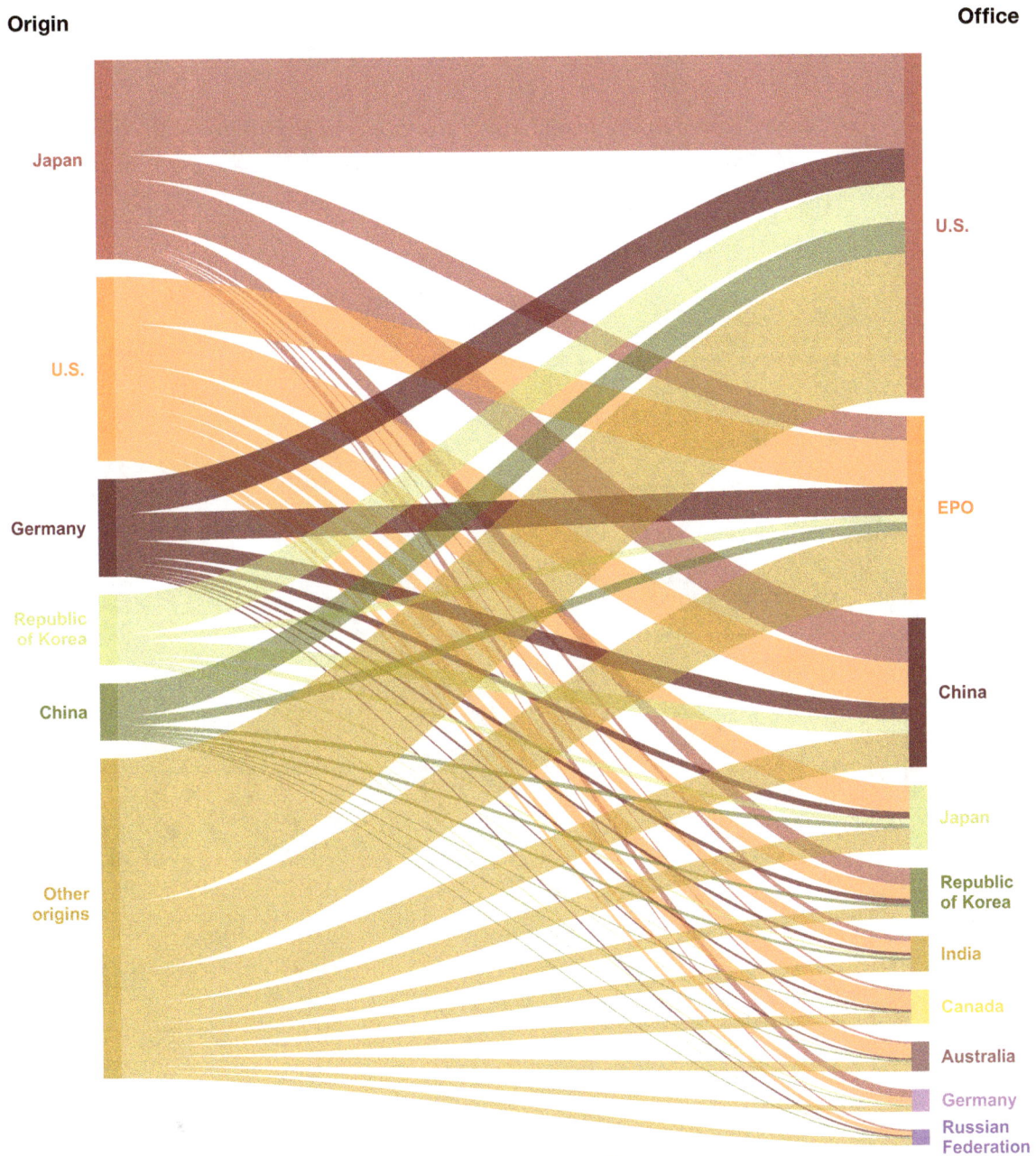

Note: EPO is the European Patent Office. Origin data are based on absolute counts, not equivalent counts.

Source: WIPO Statistics Database, September 2018.

Patents

A21. Distribution of patent applications for the top 15 offices and selected origins, 2017

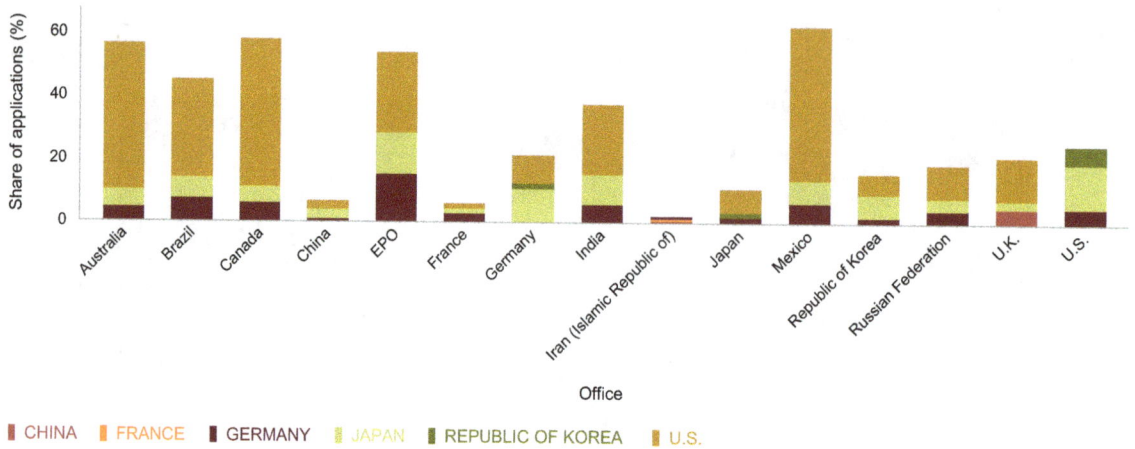

Share of applications (%) — Office

Legend: CHINA FRANCE GERMANY JAPAN REPUBLIC OF KOREA U.S.

Note: EPO is the European Patent Office. Origin data are based on absolute counts, not equivalent counts.
Source: WIPO Statistics Database, September 2018.

A22. Equivalent patent grants for the top 20 origins, 2017

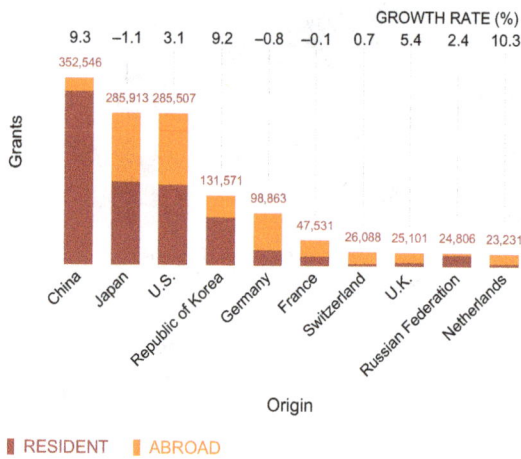

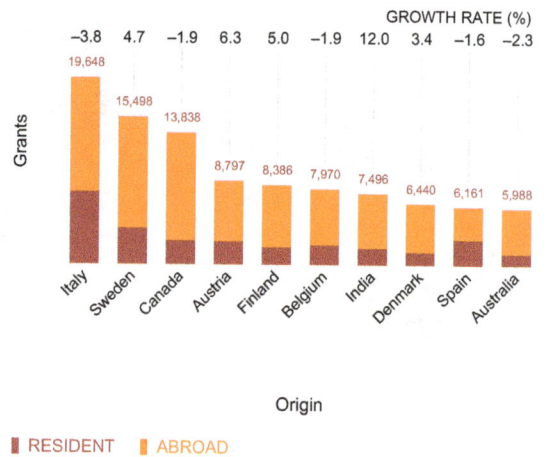

GROWTH RATE (%)
9.3 −1.1 3.1 9.2 −0.8 −0.1 0.7 5.4 2.4 10.3

Grants:
China 352,546; Japan 285,913; U.S. 285,507; Republic of Korea 131,571; Germany 98,863; France 47,531; Switzerland 26,088; U.K. 25,101; Russian Federation 24,806; Netherlands 23,231

GROWTH RATE (%)
−3.8 4.7 −1.9 6.3 5.0 −1.9 12.0 3.4 −1.6 −2.3

Grants:
Italy 19,648; Sweden 15,498; Canada 13,838; Austria 8,797; Finland 8,386; Belgium 7,970; India 7,496; Denmark 6,440; Spain 6,161; Australia 5,988

Origin — RESIDENT ABROAD

Note: See the glossary for the definition of equivalent grant.
Source: WIPO Statistics Database, September 2018.

Patent families

A23. Trend in patent families worldwide, 2001–2015

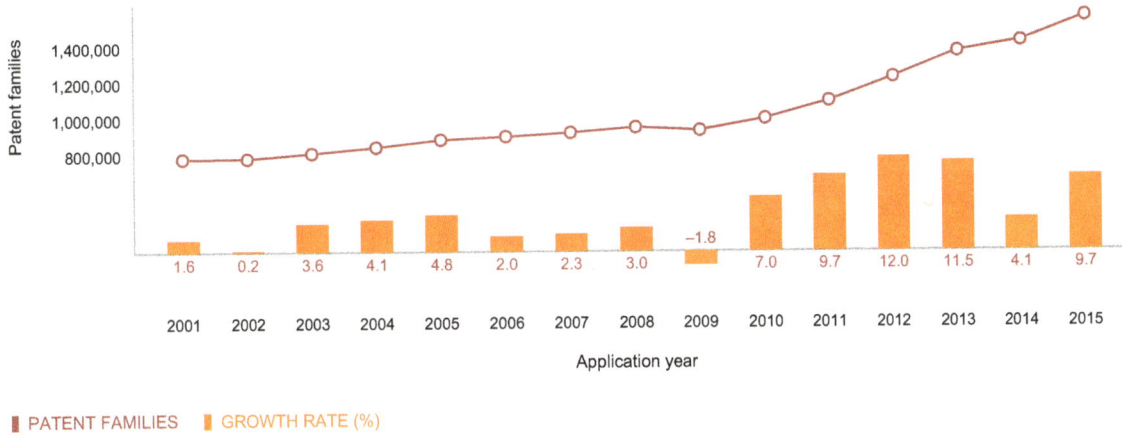

Patent families

	2001	2002	2003	2004	2005	2006	2007	2008	2009	2010	2011	2012	2013	2014	2015
	1.6	0.2	3.6	4.1	4.8	2.0	2.3	3.0	−1.8	7.0	9.7	12.0	11.5	4.1	9.7

Application year

▌ PATENT FAMILIES   ▌ GROWTH RATE (%)

Note: Applicants often file patent applications in multiple jurisdictions, so some inventions are recorded more than once. To take this into account, WIPO has indicators related to patent families, defined as patent applications interlinked by one or more of the following: priority claim, Patent Cooperation Treaty national phase entry, continuation, continuation-in-part, internal priority and addition or division. Patent families here include only those associated with patent applications for inventions and exclude patent families associated with utility model applications.

Sources: WIPO Statistics Database and EPO PATSTAT database, September 2018.

A24. Distribution of patent families by number of offices for the top 20 origins, 2013–2015

AVERAGE NUMBER OF OFFICES IN FOREIGN-ORIENTED FAMILIES

| 2.5 | 2.7 | 2.4 | 2.9 | 3.0 | 3.0 | 2.8 | 3.1 | 3.2 | 3.4 | 2.7 | 2.3 | 2.9 | 2.8 | 2.1 | 3.2 | 3.1 | 2.9 | 3.5 | 2.7 |

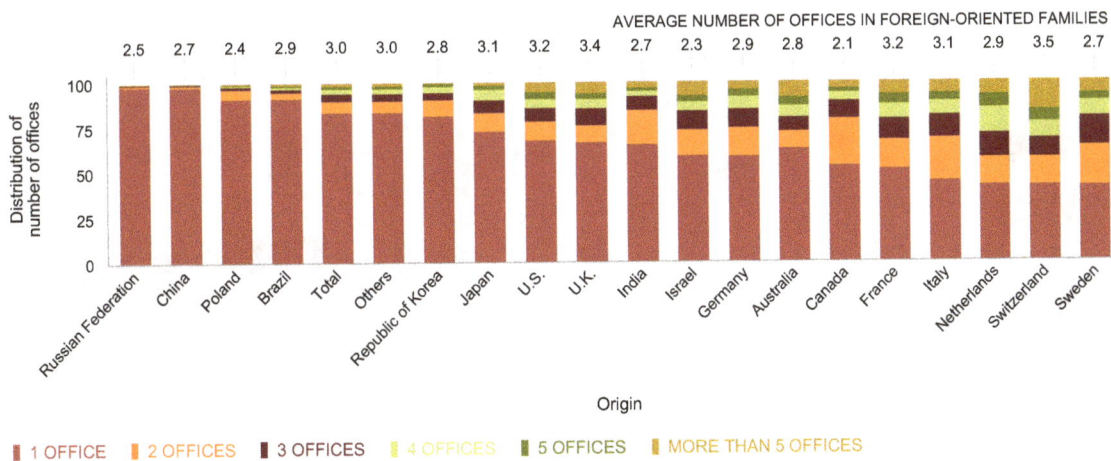

Origin

▌ 1 OFFICE   ▌ 2 OFFICES   ▌ 3 OFFICES   ▌ 4 OFFICES   ▌ 5 OFFICES   ▌ MORE THAN 5 OFFICES

Note: A patent family is defined as patent applications interlinked by one or more of the following: priority claim, Patent Cooperation Treaty national phase entry, continuation, continuation-in-part, internal priority and addition or division. Patent families here include only those associated with patent applications for inventions and exclude patent families associated with utility model applications.

Sources: WIPO Statistics Database and EPO PATSTAT database, September 2018.

Patents

A25. Trend in foreign-oriented patent families worldwide, 2000–2014

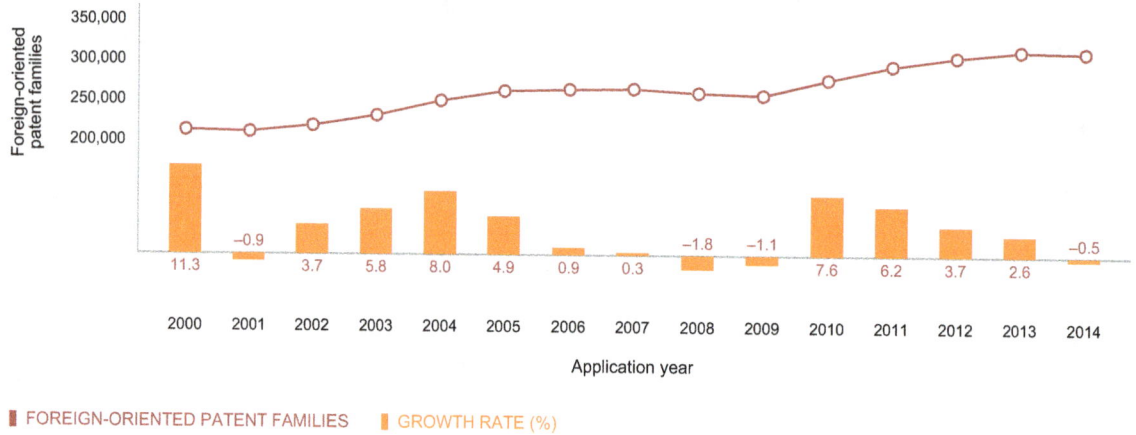

Growth rate values: 11.3 −0.9 3.7 5.8 8.0 4.9 0.9 0.3 −1.8 −1.1 7.6 6.2 3.7 2.6 −0.5

Years: 2000 2001 2002 2003 2004 2005 2006 2007 2008 2009 2010 2011 2012 2013 2014

Application year

▌ FOREIGN-ORIENTED PATENT FAMILIES   ▌ GROWTH RATE (%)

Note: A special subset of patent families comprises foreign-oriented patent families: this includes only patent families that have at least one filing office that differs from the office of the applicant's country of origin. Some foreign-oriented patent families include only one filing office, because applicants may choose to file directly with a foreign office. For example, if a Canadian applicant files a patent application directly with the United States Patent and Trademark Office (USPTO) without previously filing with the patent office of Canada, that application and applications filed subsequently with the USPTO will form a foreign-oriented patent family.

Sources: WIPO Statistics Database and EPO PATSTAT database, September 2018.

A26. Foreign-oriented patent families for the top 20 origins, 2013–2014

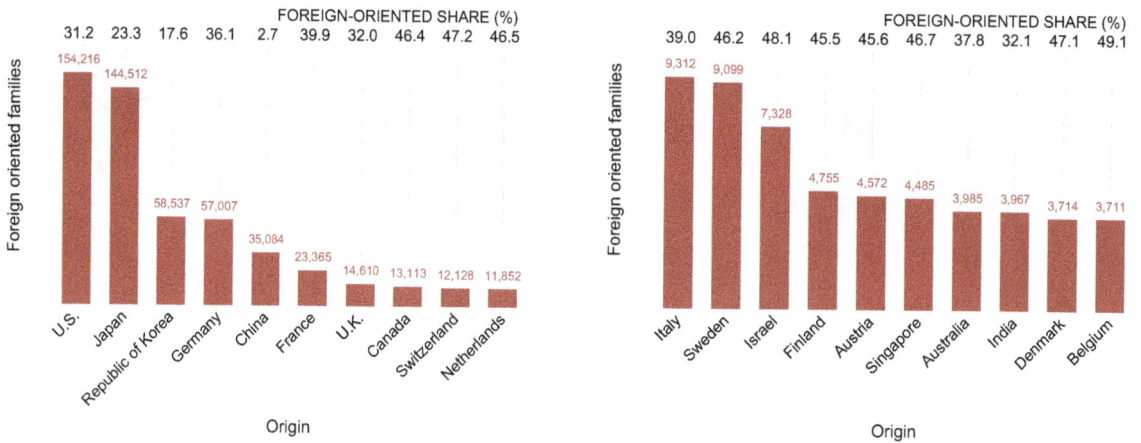

FOREIGN-ORIENTED SHARE (%)
31.2 23.3 17.6 36.1 2.7 39.9 32.0 46.4 47.2 46.5

U.S. 154,216; Japan 144,512; Republic of Korea 58,537; Germany 57,007; China 35,084; France 23,365; U.K. 14,610; Canada 13,113; Switzerland 12,128; Netherlands 11,852

FOREIGN-ORIENTED SHARE (%)
39.0 46.2 48.1 45.5 45.6 46.7 37.8 32.1 47.1 49.1

Italy 9,312; Sweden 9,099; Israel 7,328; Finland 4,755; Austria 4,572; Singapore 4,485; Australia 3,985; India 3,967; Denmark 3,714; Belgium 3,711

Origin

Sources: WIPO Statistics Database and EPO PATSTAT database, September 2018.

A27. Top 50 patent applicants worldwide, based on total number of patent families, 2013–2015

Applicant	Origin	2013	2014	2015	Total number of patent families 2013–2015
CANON INC.	Japan	7,834	8,316	7,856	24,006
SAMSUNG ELECTRONICS CO., LTD.	Republic of Korea	7,642	7,608	6,586	21,836
STATE GRID CORPORATION OF CHINA	China	6,875	9,491	5,269	21,635
MITSUBISHI ELECTRIC CORP.	Japan	5,415	5,095	4,767	15,277
INTERNATIONAL BUSINESS MACHINES CORPORATION	U.S.	4,611	4,487	5,874	14,972
TOYOTA JIDOSHA KABUSHIKI KAISHA	Japan	4,826	4,905	5,109	14,840
HUAWEI TECHNOLOGIES CO., LTD.	China	5,383	4,753	4,469	14,605
TOSHIBA KK.	Japan	5,540	4,813	4,214	14,567
LG ELECTRONICS INC.	Republic of Korea	4,329	4,988	5,244	14,561
ROBERT BOSCH GMBH	Germany	4,434	4,156	4,008	12,598
CHINA PETROLEUM & CHEMICAL CORPORATION	China	3,721	4,050	4,278	12,049
RICOH CO., LTD.	Japan	4,552	3,653	3,540	11,745
SEIKO EPSON CORP.	Japan	3,742	4,078	3,921	11,741
PANASONIC IP MAN CORP.	Japan	2,024	4,754	4,733	11,511
FUJITSU LTD.	Japan	3,520	3,283	3,373	10,176
DENSO CORP.	Japan	3,340	3,359	3,309	10,008
ZTE CORPORATION	China	2,231	3,424	3,609	9,264
HYUNDAI MOTOR CO., LTD.	Republic of Korea	2,643	3,136	3,430	9,209
SHARP CORP.	Japan	3,056	3,168	2,853	9,077
QUALCOMM INCORPORATED	U.S.	2,972	2,894	2,705	8,571
ZHEJIANG UNIVERSITY	China	2,689	2,665	2,754	8,108
SAMSUNG DISPLAY CO., LTD.	Republic of Korea	2,750	2,563	2,672	7,985
SIEMENS AG.	Germany	2,716	2,872	2,009	7,597
HONDA MOTOR CO., LTD.	Japan	2,946	2,528	2,082	7,556
HITACHI LTD.	Japan	2,590	2,487	2,391	7,468
HARBIN INSTITUTE OF TECHNOLOGY	China	2,036	2,230	3,008	7,274
SONY CORP.	Japan	2,368	2,520	2,096	6,984
LG CHEMICAL LTD.	Republic of Korea	2,029	2,320	2,583	6,932
KONICA CORP.	Japan	2,212	2,136	2,503	6,851
SCHAEFFLER TECHNOLOGIES GMBH & CO., KG.	Germany	1,852	2,488	2,282	6,622
BOE TECHNOLOGY GROUP CO., LTD.	China	1,552	2,069	2,692	6,313
NEC CORP.	Japan	2,220	2,073	2,015	6,308
DAINIPPON PRINTING CO., LTD.	Japan	2,194	2,179	1,882	6,255
LENOVO (BEIJING) CO., LTD.	China	1,799	2,316	2,029	6,144
LG DISPLAY CO., LTD.	Republic of Korea	1,870	2,022	2,190	6,082
SOUTHEAST UNIVERSITY	China	1,873	2,109	2,092	6,074
GEN ELECTRIC	U.S.	2,049	1,868	2,081	5,998
NIPPON TELEGRAPH & TELEPHONE	Japan	2,158	1,843	1,899	5,900
DAIMLER AG.	Germany	2,034	1,967	1,851	5,852
SANKYO CO.	Japan	1,874	1,822	2,086	5,782
FORD GLOBAL TECH LLC.	U.S.	1,611	2,041	2,094	5,746
FUJIFILM CORP.	Japan	1,937	1,953	1,752	5,642
INTEL CORP.	U.S.	1,794	1,740	2,093	5,627
KYOCERA DOCUMENT SOLUTIONS INC.	Japan	1,653	1,899	2,023	5,575
TSINGHUA UNIVERSITY	China	1,784	1,831	1,748	5,363
GUANGDONG OPPO MOBILE TELECOMM	China	863	915	3,454	5,232
HEWLETT PACKARD DEVELOPMENT CO.	U.S.	1,566	1,764	1,878	5,208
KOREA ELECTRONICS TELECOMM	Republic of Korea	1,640	1,738	1,802	5,180
BEIJING XIAOMI TECHNOLOGY CO.	China	637	1,386	3,137	5,160
SHANGHAI JIAO TONG UNIVERSITY	China	1,673	1,632	1,753	5,058

Note: A patent family is defined as patent applications interlinked by one or more of the following: priority claim, Patent Cooperation Treaty national phase entry, continuation, continuation-in-part, internal priority and addition or division. Patent families here include only those associated with patent applications for inventions and exclude patent families associated with utility model applications.

Sources: WIPO Statistics Database and EPO PATSTAT database, September 2018.

A28. Distribution of technology fields for each top 10 applicant based on patent families, 2013–2015

Field of technology	Canon Inc	Samsung Electronics	State Grid Corp Of China	Mitsubishi Electric Corp	IBM	Toyota Jidosha KK	Huawei Technologies	Toshiba KK	LG Electronics Inc	Robert Bosch Gmbh
Electrical machinery, apparatus, energy	3.0	4.5	31.2	20.7	1.0	24.1	2.6	12.2	4.7	17.8
Audio-visual technology	16.6	10.5	1.6	5.3	3.1	0.7	4.1	6.1	6.9	2.8
Telecommunications	6.6	7.1	2.1	4.6	1.3	0.2	10.4	3.3	16.5	0.9
Digital communication	2.8	15.9	4.1	4.0	14.9	0.5	54.8	4.2	34.4	2.1
Basic communication processes	0.4	1.7	0.2	1.7	1.3	0.2	1.7	2.1	0.5	0.5
Computer technology	14.7	26.1	7.6	6.6	51.7	1.6	20.7	15.3	10.0	3.0
IT methods for management	0.5	1.4	8.1	1.0	6.2	0.2	0.7	1.7	0.9	0.3
Semiconductors	2.9	11.9	0.3	7.5	11.3	3.4	0.6	15.4	3.0	2.3
Optics	27.5	3.4	0.5	3.2	0.9	0.1	1.6	3.0	2.1	0.9
Measurement	3.0	3.0	21.3	6.6	2.6	3.9	1.1	5.6	1.4	10.4
Analysis of biological materials	0.0	0.2	0.3	0.0	0.2	0.0	0.0	0.1	0.1	0.3
Control	0.4	0.9	5.6	4.6	2.0	2.5	0.4	3.5	0.8	4.2
Medical technology	4.5	3.3	0.1	0.6	0.4	0.6	0.1	6.5	0.5	0.3
Organic fine chemistry	0.1	0.3	0.0	0.0	0.1	0.0	0.0	0.1	0.0	0.0
Biotechnology	0.0	0.6	0.0	0.0	0.1	0.1	0.0	0.1	0.1	0.1
Pharmaceuticals	0.1	0.3	0.1	0.0	0.1	0.0	0.0	0.0	0.0	0.0
Macromolecular chemistry, polymers	0.3	0.3	0.4	0.1	0.3	0.1	0.0	0.1	0.0	0.1
Food chemistry	0.0	0.0	0.0	0.0	0.0	0.1	0.0	0.0	0.0	0.0
Basic materials chemistry	0.7	0.5	0.4	0.2	0.2	0.2	0.2	0.3	0.1	0.1
Materials, metallurgy	0.1	0.3	0.4	0.2	0.1	1.8	0.1	0.9	0.2	0.5
Surface technology, coating	0.4	0.5	0.4	0.4	0.3	1.2	0.1	1.1	0.2	0.5
Micro-structural and nanotechnology	0.1	0.1	0.0	0.0	0.2	0.0	0.0	0.2	0.0	1.5
Chemical engineering	0.2	0.5	1.0	0.5	0.2	1.1	0.0	1.3	0.7	0.7
Environmental technology	0.6	0.3	0.6	0.7	0.1	3.2	0.0	2.2	0.4	2.2
Handling	3.3	0.5	2.2	5.0	0.1	1.2	0.0	1.1	0.4	1.3
Machine tools	0.2	0.2	2.3	1.4	0.2	2.1	0.0	0.8	0.1	5.2
Engines, pumps, turbines	0.1	0.3	0.8	3.3	0.1	14.9	0.1	4.3	1.3	16.2
Textile and paper machines	9.0	0.1	0.1	0.3	0.0	0.1	0.0	1.2	0.2	0.1
Other special machines	0.9	0.4	0.8	0.5	0.2	1.1	0.0	0.5	0.3	1.0
Thermal processes and apparatus	0.0	1.4	0.8	12.0	0.2	0.4	0.2	1.4	5.0	1.4
Mechanical elements	0.5	0.3	1.1	1.1	0.1	8.7	0.1	0.6	0.4	6.8
Transport	0.0	0.1	0.9	3.8	0.3	24.9	0.0	1.2	1.4	15.2
Furniture, games	0.0	1.0	0.3	2.3	0.2	0.3	0.0	0.8	1.6	0.1
Other consumer goods	0.1	2.2	0.8	1.4	0.1	0.0	0.3	2.7	5.4	0.4
Civil engineering	0.0	0.1	3.6	0.4	0.1	0.3	0.1	0.4	0.2	0.4

Note: WIPO's International Patent Classification (IPC) technology concordance table was used to convert IPC symbols into 35 corresponding fields of technology. For an electronic version of the IPC technology concordance table, visit *www.wipo.int/ipstats*.

Sources: WIPO Statistics Database and EPO PATSTAT database, September 2018.

A29. Top five university and PRO patent applicants worldwide for selected origins, based on patent families, 2013–2015

Origin	Applicant	2013	2014	2015	Total number of patent families 2013–2015
China	ZHEJIANG UNIVERSITY	2,689	2,665	2,754	8,108
	HARBIN INSTITUTE OF TECHNOLOGY	2,036	2,230	3,008	7,274
	SOUTHEAST UNIVERSITY	1,873	2,109	2,092	6,074
	TSINGHUA UNIVERSITY	1,784	1,831	1,748	5,363
	SHANGHAI JIAO TONG UNIVERSITY	1,673	1,632	1,753	5,058
France	COMMISSARIAT À L'ÉNERGIE ATOMIQUE ET AUX ÉNERGIES ALTERNATIVES	689	682	675	2,046
	CENTRE NATIONAL DE LA RECHERCHE SCIENTIFIQUE (CNRS)	157	183	172	512
	INSTITUT NATIONAL DE LA SANTÉ ET DE LA RECHERCHE MÉDICALE (INSERM)	159	150	192	501
	IFP ÉNERGIES NOUVELLES	161	169	170	500
	INSTITUT NATIONAL DE LA RECHERCHE AGRONOMIQUE (INRA)	24	31	24	79
Germany	FRAUNHOFER-GESELLSCHAFT ZUR FÖRDERUNG DER ANGEWANDTEN FORSCHUNG E.V.	555	509	443	1,507
	DEUTSCHES ZENTRUM FÜR LUFT- UND RAUMFAHRT E.V.	235	174	158	567
	TECHNISCHE UNIVERSITÄT DRESDEN	71	91	76	238
	KARLSRUHE INSTITUT FÜR TECHNOLOGIE	50	50	46	146
	BUNDESREPUBLIK DEUTSCHLAND	42	37	28	107
Japan	NATIONAL INSTITUTE OF ADVANCED INDUSTRIAL SCIENCE AND TECHNOLOGY	465	436	373	1,274
	TOKYO UNIVERSITY	297	253	233	783
	TOHOKU UNIVERSITY	159	165	181	505
	RAILWAY TECHNICAL RESEARCH INSTITUTE	183	173	149	505
	KYOTO UNIVERSITY	141	165	146	452
Republic of Korea	KOREA ELECTRONICS TELECOMM	1,640	1,738	1,802	5,180
	KOREA ADVANCED INSTITUTE OF SCIENCE AND TECHNOLOGY	742	765	810	2,317
	KOREA ELECTRONICS TECHNOLOGY	632	636	557	1,825
	YONSEI UNIVERSITY INDUSTRY ACADEMIC COOPERATION FOUNDATION	484	714	584	1,782
	SEOUL NATIONAL UNIVERSITY INDUSTRY FOUNDATION	482	543	601	1,626
U.S.	UNIVERSITY OF CALIFORNIA	739	688	739	2,166
	MASSACHUSETTS INSTITUTE OF TECHNOLOGY	390	341	351	1,082
	THE UNIVERSITY OF TEXAS SYSTEM	260	269	258	787
	THE JOHNS HOPINS UNIVERSITY	233	287	261	781
	NORTHWESTERN UNIVERSITY	239	245	290	774

Note: PRO means public research organization. A patent family is defined as patent applications interlinked by one or more of the following: priority claim, Patent Cooperation Treaty national phase entry, continuation, continuation-in-part, internal priority and addition or division. Patent families here include only those associated with patent applications for inventions and exclude patent families associated with utility model applications.

Sources: WIPO Statistics Database and EPO PATSTAT database, September 2018.

Patents

A30. Distribution of technology fields for selected universities and PROs based on patent families, 2013–2015

Field of technology						Applicant						
	Zhejiang University	Harbin Institute of Technology	CEA	CNRS	Fraunhofer Ges Forschung	DLR	AIST	Tokyo University	Korea Electronics Telecomm	KAIST	University of California	MIT
Electrical machinery, apparatus, energy	6.7	10.1	13.0	5.1	6.4	6.7	7.8	12.4	2.5	8.6	3.8	8.4
Audio-visual technology	1.0	1.3	1.7	1.2	5.5	0.5	1.2	1.5	7.7	2.7	1.0	1.7
Telecommunications	1.1	3.5	2.5	1.4	2.7	3.8	0.6	0.9	11.7	4.8	1.0	2.5
Digital communication	2.6	4.3	1.9	0.3	2.6	4.2	0.8	1.2	31.4	7.8	0.7	1.7
Basic communication processes	0.5	0.7	1.9	1.3	2.3	4.5	0.4	0.2	2.3	2.7	1.0	1.0
Computer technology	10.5	8.4	7.3	2.5	9.5	1.5	3.0	4.8	20.9	16.1	5.0	5.2
IT methods for management	1.0	0.5	0.2	0.0	0.2	0.4	0.4	0.7	4.1	2.4	0.4	0.3
Semiconductors	1.5	0.8	17.7	4.7	5.5	1.2	12.9	2.9	3.2	6.4	4.1	5.6
Optics	2.0	3.3	3.7	4.3	5.3	1.9	3.1	2.9	3.9	3.9	2.0	3.7
Measurement	13.9	16.5	12.6	10.6	13.3	14.1	11.9	10.4	4.2	7.8	6.2	7.3
Analysis of biological materials	0.9	0.3	1.4	5.3	1.2	0.5	2.3	4.3	0.3	1.5	5.6	3.1
Control	3.7	3.8	0.7	0.8	0.9	5.6	1.0	1.4	2.3	1.4	0.5	1.4
Medical technology	2.7	1.6	2.1	3.9	3.1	2.8	3.2	5.2	1.8	3.8	11.6	8.5
Organic fine chemistry	3.8	1.0	0.8	8.1	0.8	0.2	5.2	4.9	0.0	0.9	6.6	3.5
Biotechnology	5.2	1.1	0.9	9.8	3.1	0.0	8.3	11.9	0.1	4.7	17.0	13.2
Pharmaceuticals	3.2	0.6	0.5	9.9	1.5	0.0	2.2	7.7	0.0	1.6	16.0	10.0
Macromolecular chemistry, polymers	2.4	1.8	0.6	2.8	2.2	0.1	2.6	3.4	0.0	1.2	1.7	1.3
Food chemistry	3.3	0.9	0.1	0.5	0.6	0.0	0.9	0.8	0.0	0.1	0.8	0.8
Basic materials chemistry	2.6	1.6	1.6	2.7	2.6	1.0	3.7	1.9	0.1	1.3	2.0	2.2
Materials, metallurgy	4.3	6.4	3.0	5.4	3.3	1.6	8.2	2.9	0.1	2.4	1.4	1.3
Surface technology, coating	1.5	3.2	3.7	2.2	3.5	1.2	3.1	1.1	0.2	1.6	1.5	2.0
Micro-structural and nanotechnology	1.1	0.9	2.7	1.8	1.2	0.0	1.5	0.9	0.1	1.8	1.0	1.2
Chemical engineering	3.9	3.1	3.1	5.8	2.3	0.6	5.6	2.3	0.2	3.1	3.2	4.2
Environmental technology	3.6	4.1	2.7	2.2	0.9	1.0	2.4	0.8	0.0	1.2	0.9	1.3
Handling	1.1	1.8	1.1	0.6	1.2	4.0	0.5	0.2	0.3	0.9	0.3	0.9
Machine tools	1.3	6.6	1.1	0.3	5.1	0.6	1.0	0.9	0.0	0.4	0.1	0.2
Engines, pumps, turbines	1.9	1.2	3.2	0.7	1.1	6.6	1.3	1.7	0.1	1.4	0.6	0.8
Textile and paper machines	0.5	0.8	0.2	0.3	0.8	2.6	1.0	1.2	0.0	0.4	0.4	0.6
Other special machines	3.6	1.7	1.6	1.5	3.7	8.6	2.2	3.1	0.4	1.6	1.3	3.2
Thermal processes and apparatus	1.7	1.3	3.4	0.8	1.9	5.9	0.4	1.1	0.0	0.5	0.5	0.7
Mechanical elements	2.1	1.7	1.1	0.8	1.4	5.2	0.3	0.5	0.0	0.8	0.4	0.6
Transport	1.9	3.3	1.1	0.7	1.4	11.9	0.2	1.5	1.2	2.2	0.3	0.9
Furniture, games	0.5	0.2	0.1	0.1	0.6	0.1	0.1	0.3	0.4	0.4	0.2	0.1
Other consumer goods	0.5	0.2	0.3	1.0	1.2	0.8	0.1	0.4	0.2	0.4	0.4	0.4
Civil engineering	1.9	1.6	0.4	0.3	0.9	0.2	0.4	1.5	0.1	1.1	0.3	0.4

Note: PRO means public research organization. A patent family is defined as patent applications interlinked by one or more of the following: priority claim, Patent Cooperation Treaty national phase entry, continuation, continuation-in-part, internal priority and addition or division. Patent families include only those associated with patent applications for inventions and exclude patent families associated with utility model applications. Le Centre national de la recherche scientifique (CNRS); Le Commissariat à l'énergie atomique et aux énergies alternatives (CEA); Deutsches Zentrum für Luft- und Raumfahrt E.V. (DLR); Korea Advanced Institute of Science and Technology (KAIST); Massachusetts Institute of Technology (MIT) and National Institute of Advanced Industrial Science and Technology (AIST).

Sources: WIPO Statistics Database and EPO PATSTAT database, September 2018.

Published patent applications by field of technology

A31. Published patent applications worldwide by field of technology, 2006, 2011 and 2016

Field of technology		2006	2011	2016	Share of total (%)	Average growth (%) 2006–2016
Electrical engineering	Electrical machinery, apparatus, energy	98,406	123,754	185,560	7.0	6.5
	Audio-visual technology	96,447	74,629	78,581	3.0	–2.0
	Telecommunications	67,685	50,398	53,299	2.0	–2.4
	Digital communication	59,385	81,630	133,955	5.1	8.5
	Basic communication processes	17,640	15,742	15,810	0.6	–1.1
	Computer technology	119,823	133,326	198,402	7.5	5.2
	IT methods for management	19,549	23,808	44,387	1.7	8.5
	Semiconductors	76,413	79,856	82,711	3.1	0.8
Instruments	Optics	76,064	61,824	67,958	2.6	–1.1
	Measurement	62,923	78,209	129,439	4.9	7.5
	Analysis of biological materials	10,853	11,962	15,641	0.6	3.7
	Control	26,799	28,443	56,135	2.1	7.7
	Medical technology	68,315	80,165	118,710	4.5	5.7
Chemistry	Organic fine chemistry	53,588	53,052	61,976	2.3	1.5
	Biotechnology	33,554	42,136	55,479	2.1	5.2
	Pharmaceuticals	71,236	71,804	106,704	4.0	4.1
	Macromolecular chemistry, polymers	26,935	28,990	47,138	1.8	5.8
	Food chemistry	19,765	30,720	64,389	2.4	12.5
	Basic materials chemistry	36,962	46,226	80,780	3.1	8.1
	Materials, metallurgy	28,616	39,541	66,557	2.5	8.8
	Surface technology, coating	28,960	33,711	43,933	1.7	4.3
	Micro-structural and nano-technology	2,263	3,575	4,623	0.2	7.4
	Chemical engineering	32,420	38,899	64,172	2.4	7.1
	Environmental technology	20,766	26,761	46,997	1.8	8.5
Mechanical engineering	Handling	42,300	45,081	74,271	2.8	5.8
	Machine tools	36,365	46,706	79,064	3.0	8.1
	Engines, pumps, turbines	39,689	49,025	65,442	2.5	5.1
	Textile and paper machines	37,199	30,888	40,032	1.5	0.7
	Other special machines	44,427	52,295	95,873	3.6	8.0
	Thermal processes and apparatus	24,804	30,359	43,832	1.7	5.9
	Mechanical elements	41,906	47,243	72,173	2.7	5.6
	Transport	63,652	66,623	112,496	4.2	5.9
Other fields	Furniture, games	43,727	42,788	69,174	2.6	4.7
	Other consumer goods	32,673	33,963	51,823	2.0	4.7
	Civil engineering	52,325	58,819	95,980	3.6	6.3
	Unknown	48,096	31,538	24,970	0.9	–6.3
Total		**1,662,530**	**1,794,489**	**2,648,466**	**100.0**	**4.8**

Note: Data refer to published patent applications. There is a minimum delay of 18 months between the application date and the publication date. WIPO's IPC technology concordance table was used to convert IPC symbols into 35 corresponding fields of technology. For an electronic version of the IPC technology concordance table, visit *www.wipo.int/ipstats*.

Sources: WIPO Statistics Database and EPO PATSTAT database, September 2018.

Patents

A32. Distribution of published patent applications by technology field for the top 10 origins, 2014–2016

Field of technology	China	U.S.	Japan	Republic of Korea	Germany	France	U.K.	Switzerland	Russian Federation	Netherlands
Electrical machinery, apparatus, energy	6.7	4.6	10.7	9.2	9.1	6.3	5.9	4.3	3.6	7.6
Audio-visual technology	2.1	3.0	5.0	5.6	1.5	2.4	1.7	1.0	0.6	3.0
Telecommunications	1.8	2.4	2.5	3.1	0.9	2.2	1.8	0.6	1.3	1.3
Digital communication	5.1	7.3	2.9	6.3	1.6	5.7	3.6	1.2	0.7	2.4
Basic communication processes	0.4	0.9	0.9	0.6	0.6	0.6	0.6	0.4	0.8	0.8
Computer technology	6.8	12.7	6.3	9.1	3.1	5.6	6.3	2.6	2.6	6.1
IT methods for management	1.2	3.2	1.1	3.3	0.4	1.0	1.5	0.7	0.4	0.7
Semiconductors	1.6	3.1	6.0	6.7	2.6	2.3	1.2	0.6	0.9	3.4
Optics	1.5	1.8	6.4	3.4	1.7	1.7	1.5	1.0	0.8	3.9
Measurement	6.1	3.9	4.3	3.4	5.7	5.2	5.2	8.0	7.4	5.1
Analysis of biological materials	0.4	0.9	0.3	0.4	0.6	0.9	1.4	1.4	2.1	0.7
Control	2.5	1.9	1.8	1.4	1.8	1.3	1.9	1.4	1.6	1.1
Medical technology	2.2	8.3	3.4	3.1	4.8	4.2	6.4	7.1	6.3	10.8
Organic fine chemistry	2.1	3.0	1.6	1.4	3.5	4.9	4.6	7.8	1.6	3.7
Biotechnology	1.7	3.6	0.9	1.4	1.7	2.8	4.1	5.9	1.8	3.6
Pharmaceuticals	4.5	5.6	1.2	1.9	2.5	4.2	6.6	11.5	4.2	3.5
Macromolecular chemistry, polymers	2.1	1.4	2.1	1.2	2.1	1.6	0.8	2.0	0.8	3.4
Food chemistry	4.7	1.1	0.8	1.7	0.5	0.8	1.3	3.5	15.3	3.2
Basic materials chemistry	4.4	3.0	2.1	1.6	3.4	2.1	3.3	3.2	2.9	4.9
Materials, metallurgy	3.9	1.1	2.4	2.0	2.0	2.3	1.5	1.6	4.8	0.9
Surface technology, coating	1.7	1.4	2.4	1.5	1.7	1.6	1.1	1.5	1.8	1.2
Micro-structural and nanotechnology	0.2	0.2	0.1	0.2	0.2	0.2	0.2	0.1	0.8	0.1
Chemical engineering	3.1	2.0	1.4	2.0	2.7	2.5	3.0	2.4	3.3	2.7
Environmental technology	2.5	1.0	1.3	1.6	1.5	1.5	1.9	1.2	2.1	1.8
Handling	3.1	2.0	2.9	2.0	3.3	2.3	2.6	5.8	0.9	2.9
Machine tools	4.7	1.5	2.4	2.0	3.7	1.6	1.2	1.7	2.8	1.0
Engines, pumps, turbines	1.5	2.7	3.2	1.9	6.3	4.9	3.6	2.9	4.6	1.0
Textile and paper machines	1.7	0.9	2.5	0.9	1.5	0.7	0.8	2.3	0.4	1.3
Other special machines	4.5	2.6	2.8	2.7	3.6	3.6	2.5	2.6	5.4	4.7
Thermal processes and apparatus	2.1	0.8	1.8	1.9	1.7	1.7	1.3	1.3	1.5	1.0
Mechanical elements	2.4	2.0	3.1	2.0	7.2	3.9	3.2	2.0	3.3	1.6
Transport	2.6	3.2	5.6	5.2	9.8	10.1	5.0	1.7	4.2	2.4
Furniture, games	2.1	2.3	4.1	2.5	1.6	1.6	3.3	2.8	1.0	2.4
Other consumer goods	2.1	1.7	1.5	2.7	1.9	2.3	3.9	4.2	1.2	1.8
Civil engineering	4.0	3.2	2.3	3.9	3.3	3.2	5.0	2.0	6.3	4.1

Note: Data refer to published patent applications. There is a minimum delay of 18 months between the application date and the publication date. WIPO's IPC technology concordance table was used to convert IPC symbols into 35 corresponding fields of technology. For an electronic version of the IPC technology concordance table, visit *www.wipo.int/ipstats*. The top 10 origins were selected based on their 2014–2016 total published applications.

Sources: WIPO Statistics Database and EPO PATSTAT database, September 2018.

A33. Trend in patent applications in energy-related technologies, 2002–2016

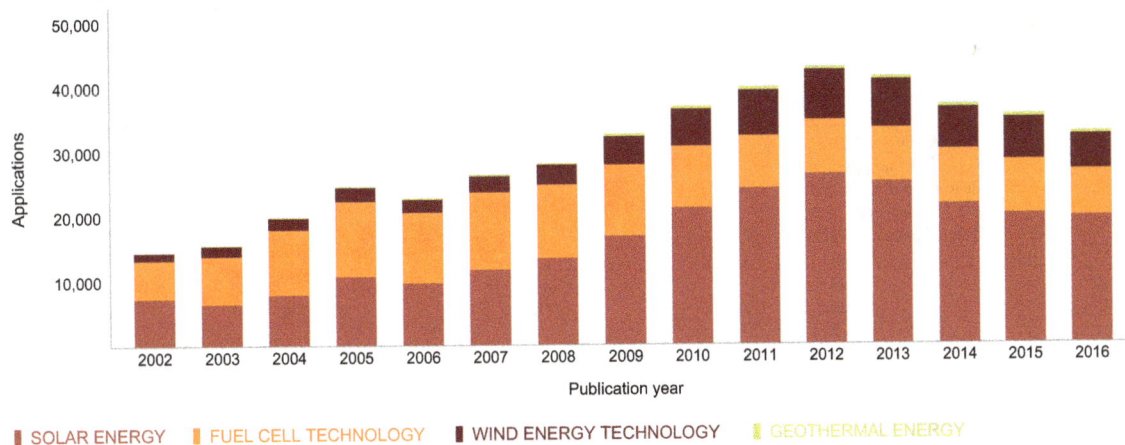

Note: For definitions of the technologies – fuel cells, geothermal, solar and wind energy – see annex A. The correspondence between IPC symbols and technology fields is not always clear (there is no one-to-one correspondence). It is therefore difficult to capture all patents in a specific technology field. Even so, the IPC-based definitions are likely to capture the vast majority of patent applications in these areas. Data refer to published patent applications.

Sources: WIPO Statistics Database and EPO PATSTAT database, September 2018.

Patents

A34. Relative specialization for patent applications in energy-related technologies for the top origins, 2014–2016

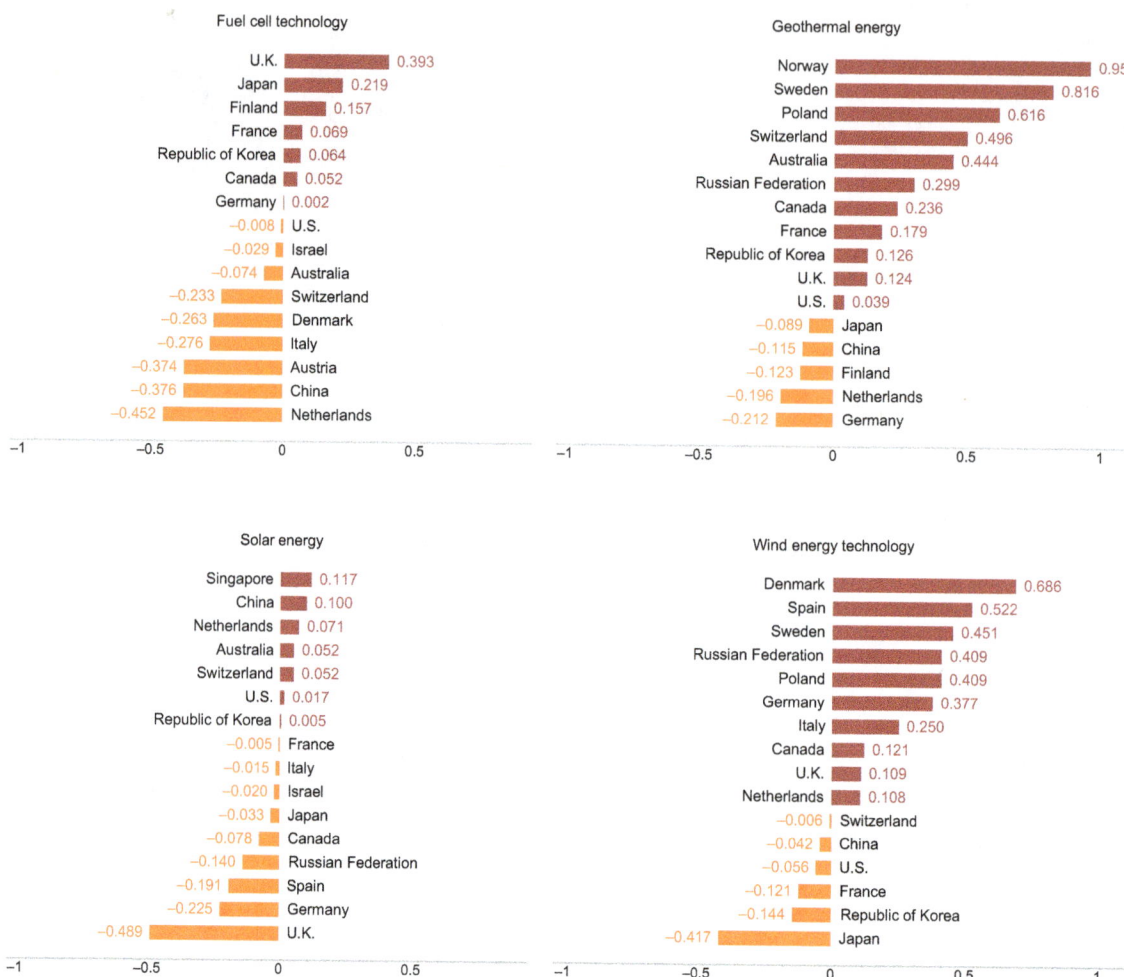

Fuel cell technology

U.K.	0.393
Japan	0.219
Finland	0.157
France	0.069
Republic of Korea	0.064
Canada	0.052
Germany	0.002
U.S.	−0.008
Israel	−0.029
Australia	−0.074
Switzerland	−0.233
Denmark	−0.263
Italy	−0.276
Austria	−0.374
China	−0.376
Netherlands	−0.452

Geothermal energy

Norway	0.954
Sweden	0.816
Poland	0.616
Switzerland	0.496
Australia	0.444
Russian Federation	0.299
Canada	0.236
France	0.179
Republic of Korea	0.126
U.K.	0.124
U.S.	0.039
Japan	−0.089
China	−0.115
Finland	−0.123
Netherlands	−0.196
Germany	−0.212

Solar energy

Singapore	0.117
China	0.100
Netherlands	0.071
Australia	0.052
Switzerland	0.052
U.S.	0.017
Republic of Korea	0.005
France	−0.005
Italy	−0.015
Israel	−0.020
Japan	−0.033
Canada	−0.078
Russian Federation	−0.140
Spain	−0.191
Germany	−0.225
U.K.	−0.489

Wind energy technology

Denmark	0.686
Spain	0.522
Sweden	0.451
Russian Federation	0.409
Poland	0.409
Germany	0.377
Italy	0.250
Canada	0.121
U.K.	0.109
Netherlands	0.108
Switzerland	−0.006
China	−0.042
U.S.	−0.056
France	−0.121
Republic of Korea	−0.144
Japan	−0.417

Note: For definitions of the technologies – fuel cells, geothermal, solar and wind energy – see annex A. The correspondence between IPC symbols and technology fields is not always clear (there is no one-to-one correspondence). It is therefore difficult to capture all patents in a specific technology field. Even so, the IPC-based definitions are likely to capture the vast majority of patent applications in these areas. Data refer to published patent applications.

Sources: WIPO Statistics Database and EPO PATSTAT database, September 2018.

Women's participation in PCT international patenting

A35. PCT applications with women inventors, 2003–2017

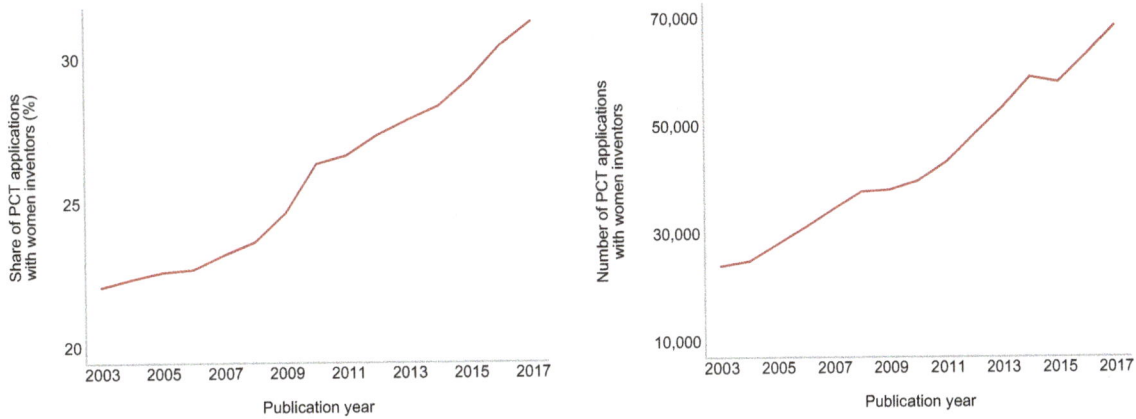

Note: In order to attribute gender to inventors' names recorded in PCT applications, WIPO produced a world gender–name dictionary based on information from 13 different public sources. Gender is attributed to a given name on a country-by-country basis because certain names can be considered male in one country but female in another.

Source: WIPO Statistics Database, September 2018.

A36. Share of PCT applications with women inventors for the top 20 origins, 2017

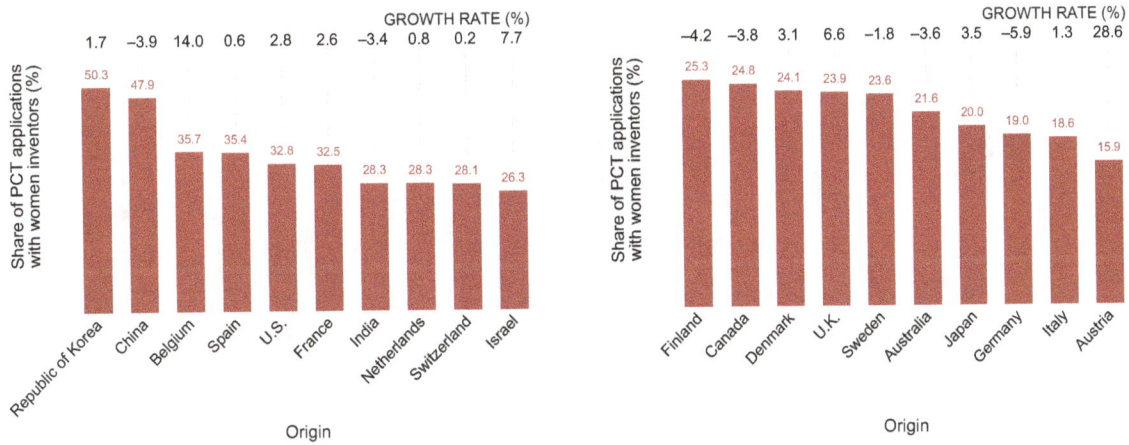

Note: In order to attribute gender to inventors' names recorded in PCT applications, WIPO produced a gender–name dictionary based on information from 13 different public sources. Gender is attributed to a given name on a country-by-country basis because certain names can be considered male in one country but female in another.

Source: WIPO Statistics Database, September 2018.

Patents

59

Patents

A37. Distribution of inventors listed in PCT applications for the top 20 origins, 2017

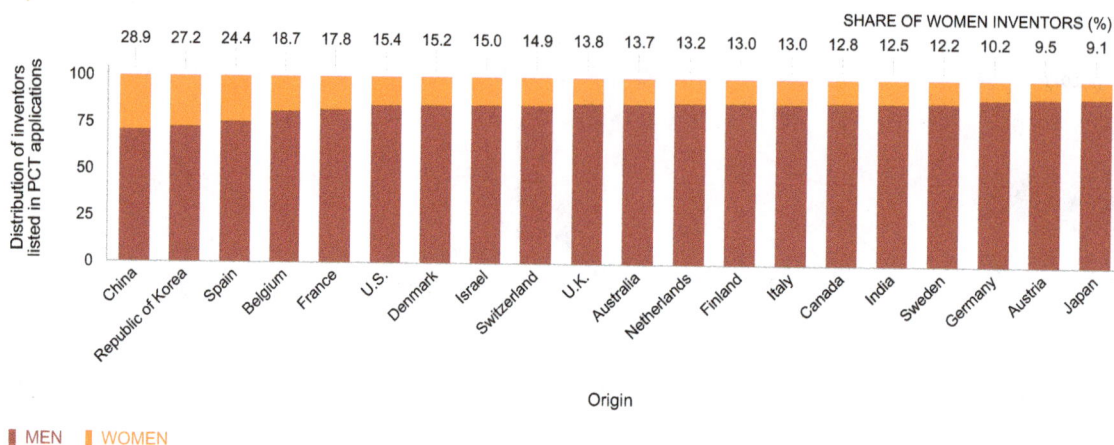

SHARE OF WOMEN INVENTORS (%)

	China	Republic of Korea	Spain	Belgium	France	U.S.	Denmark	Israel	Switzerland	U.K.	Australia	Netherlands	Finland	Italy	Canada	India	Sweden	Germany	Austria	Japan
	28.9	27.2	24.4	18.7	17.8	15.4	15.2	15.0	14.9	13.8	13.7	13.2	13.0	13.0	12.8	12.5	12.2	10.2	9.5	9.1

Distribution of inventors listed in PCT applications

Origin

■ MEN   ■ WOMEN

Note: In order to attribute gender to inventors' names recorded in PCT applications, WIPO produced a gender–name dictionary based on information from 13 different public sources. Gender is attributed to a given name on a country-by-country basis because certain names can be considered male in one country but female in another.

Source: WIPO Statistics Database, September 2018.

A38. Share of PCT patent applications with women inventors by field of technology, 2017

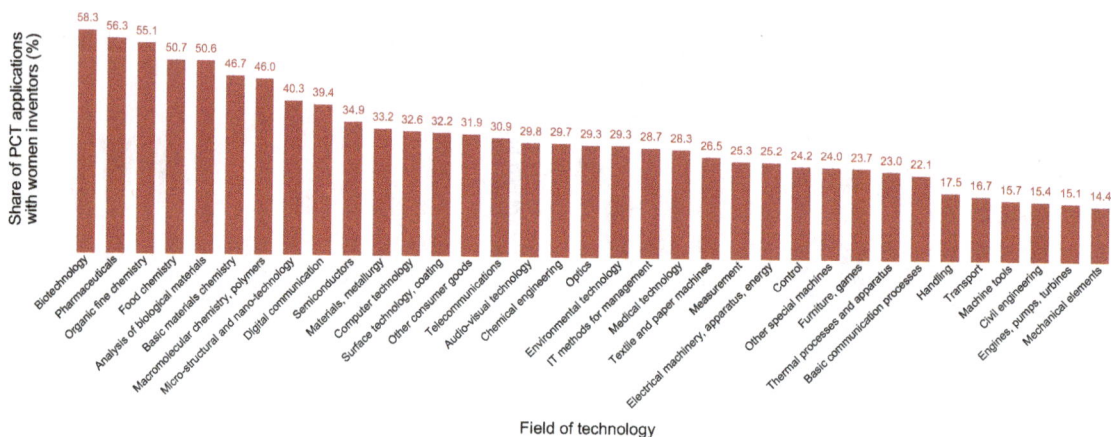

Share of PCT applications with women inventors (%)

Field of technology	%
Biotechnology	58.3
Pharmaceuticals	56.3
Organic fine chemistry	55.1
Food chemistry	50.7
Analysis of biological materials	50.6
Basic materials chemistry	46.7
Macromolecular chemistry, polymers	46.0
Micro-structural and nano-technology	40.3
Digital communication	39.4
Semiconductors	34.9
Materials, metallurgy	33.2
Computer technology	32.6
Surface technology, coating	32.2
Other consumer goods	31.9
Telecommunications	30.9
Audio-visual technology	29.8
Chemical engineering	29.7
Optics	29.3
Environmental technology	29.3
IT methods for management	28.7
Medical technology	28.3
Textile and paper machines	26.5
Measurement	25.3
Electrical machinery, apparatus, energy	25.2
Control	24.2
Other special machines	24.0
Furniture, games	23.7
Thermal processes and apparatus	23.0
Basic communication processes	22.1
Handling	17.5
Transport	16.7
Machine tools	15.7
Civil engineering	15.4
Engines, pumps, turbines	15.1
Mechanical elements	14.4

Field of technology

Note: In order to attribute gender to inventors' names recorded in PCT applications, WIPO produced a gender–name dictionary based on information from 13 different public sources. Gender is attributed to a given name on a country-by-country basis because certain names can be considered male in one country but female in another.

Source: WIPO Statistics Database, September 2018.

Patent applications in relation to GDP and population

A39. Resident patent applications per USD 100 billion GDP for the top 20 origins, 2007 and 2017

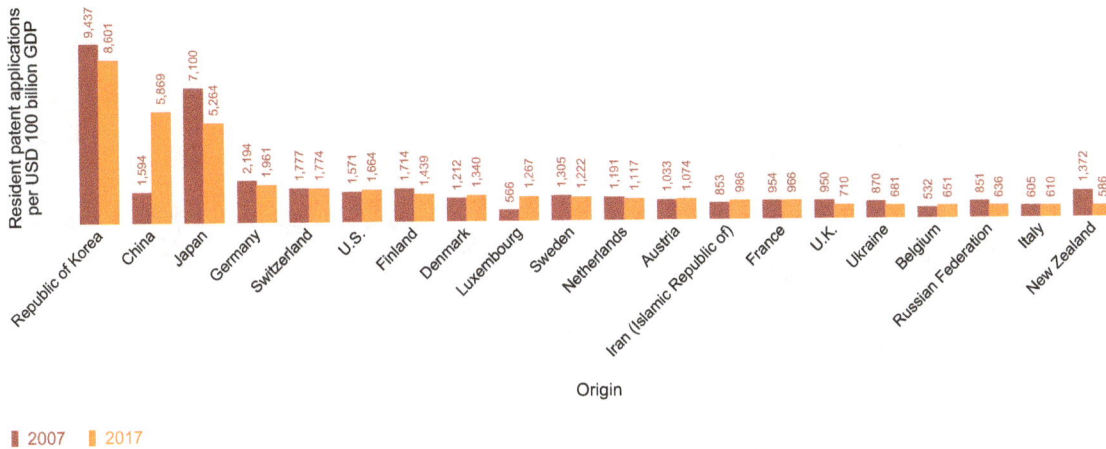

Resident patent applications per USD 100 billion GDP

Origin	2007	2017
Republic of Korea	9,437	8,601
China	1,594	5,869
Japan	7,100	5,264
Germany	2,194	1,961
Switzerland	1,777	1,774
U.S.	1,571	1,664
Finland	1,714	1,439
Denmark	1,212	1,340
Luxembourg	566	1,267
Sweden	1,305	1,222
Netherlands	1,191	1,117
Austria	1,033	1,074
Iran (Islamic Republic of)	853	986
France	954	966
U.K.	950	710
Ukraine	870	681
Belgium	532	651
Russian Federation	851	636
Italy	605	610
New Zealand	1,372	586

Origin

■ 2007 ■ 2017

Note: GDP data are in 2011 US PPP dollars. The top 20 origins were included if they had a GDP greater than USD 25 billion PPP and more than 100 resident patent applications. Due to space constraints, only the top 20 origins that fulfil these criteria are presented.

Sources: WIPO Statistics Database and World Bank, September 2018.

A40. Resident patent applications per million population for the top 20 origins, 2007 and 2017

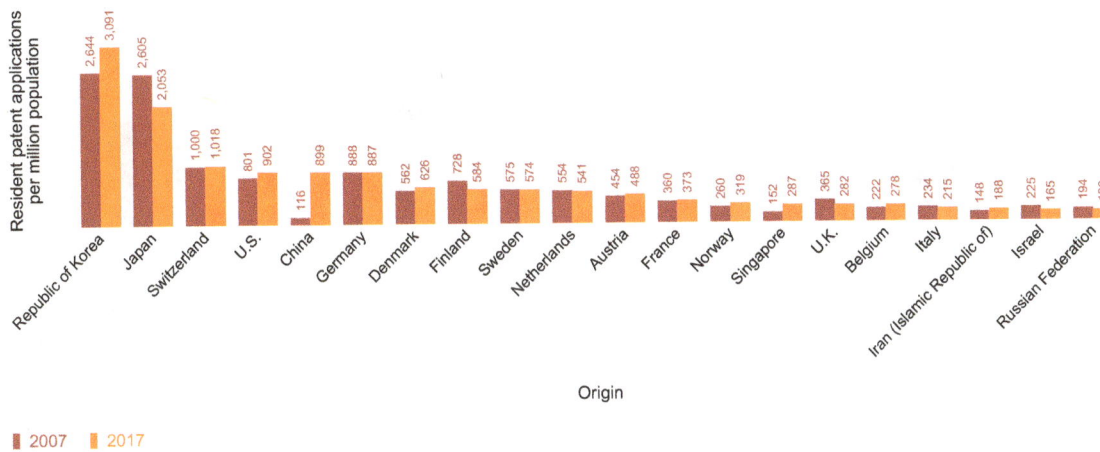

Resident patent applications per million population

Origin	2007	2017
Republic of Korea	2,644	3,091
Japan	2,605	2,053
Switzerland	1,000	1,018
U.S.	801	902
China	116	899
Germany	888	887
Denmark	562	626
Finland	728	584
Sweden	575	574
Netherlands	554	541
Austria	454	488
France	360	373
Norway	260	319
Singapore	152	287
U.K.	365	282
Belgium	222	278
Italy	234	215
Iran (Islamic Republic of)	148	188
Israel	225	165
Russian Federation	194	160

Origin

■ 2007 ■ 2017

Note: The top 20 origins were included if they had a population greater than 5 million and if they had more than 100 resident patent applications. Due to space constraints, only the top 20 origins that fulfil these criteria are presented.

Sources: WIPO Statistics Database and World Bank, September 2018.

Patents

Patents in force

A41. Trend in patents in force worldwide, 2008–2017

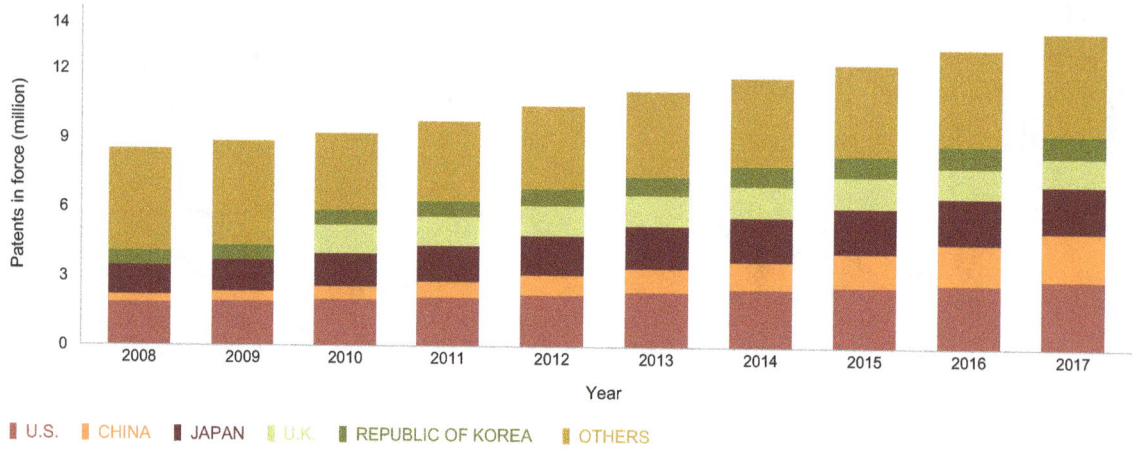

Legend: ▮ U.S. ▮ CHINA ▮ JAPAN ▮ U.K. ▮ REPUBLIC OF KOREA ▮ OTHERS

Note: World totals are WIPO estimates using data covering 122 offices.

Source: WIPO Statistics Database, September 2018.

A42. Patents in force at the top 20 offices, 2017

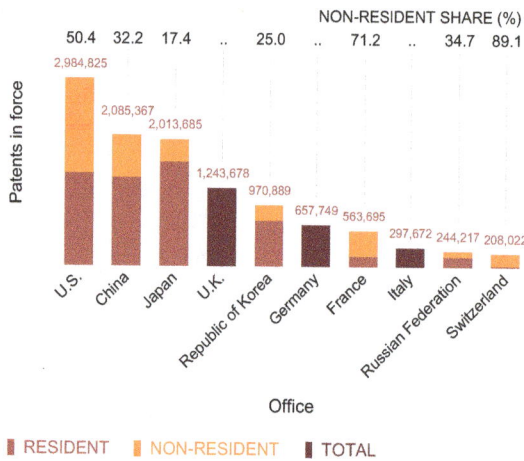

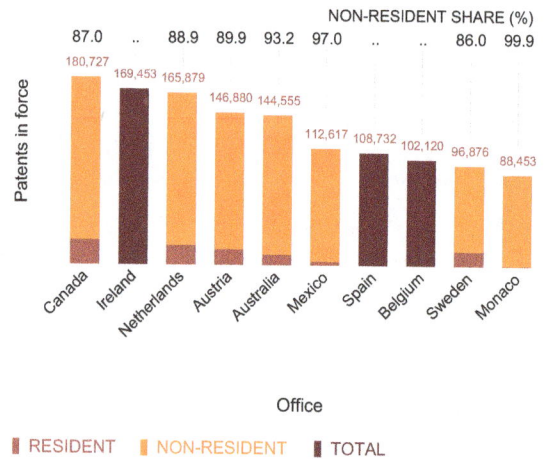

Legend: ▮ RESIDENT ▮ NON-RESIDENT ▮ TOTAL

.. indicates not available.

Source: WIPO Statistics Database, September 2018.

A43. Patents in force in 2017 as a percentage of total applications

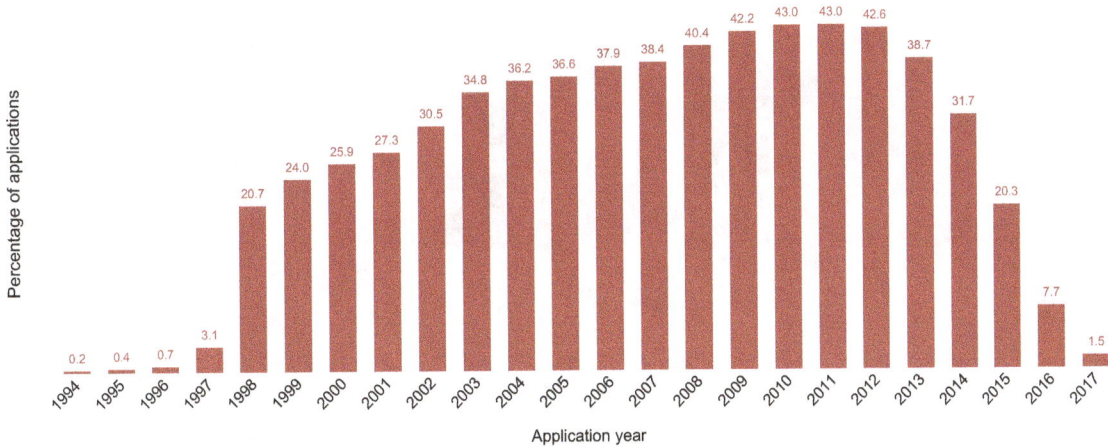

Note: Percentages are calculated as the number of patent applications filed in year *t* and in force in 2017, divided by the total number of patent applications filed in year *t*. Patent holders must pay maintenance fees to maintain the validity of their patents. Depending on technological and commercial considerations, patent holders may opt to let a patent lapse before the end of the full protection term. This figure shows the distribution of patents in force in 2017 as a percentage of total applications in the year of filing. However, not all offices provide these data. Data for 65 offices show that 40–43% of the applications for which patents were eventually granted remained in force for at least 6 to 10 years after the application date. About 21% of these patents lasted the full 20-year patent term.

Source: WIPO Statistics Database, September 2018.

A44. Average age of patents in force at selected offices, 2012 and 2017

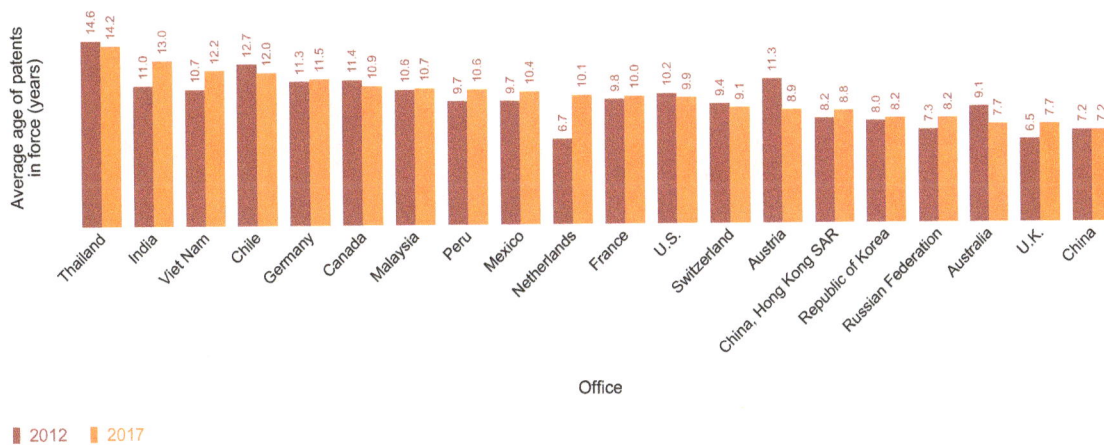

■ 2012 ■ 2017

Source: WIPO Statistics Database, September 2018.

Patent office procedural data

A45. Distribution of patent examination outcomes for selected offices, 2017

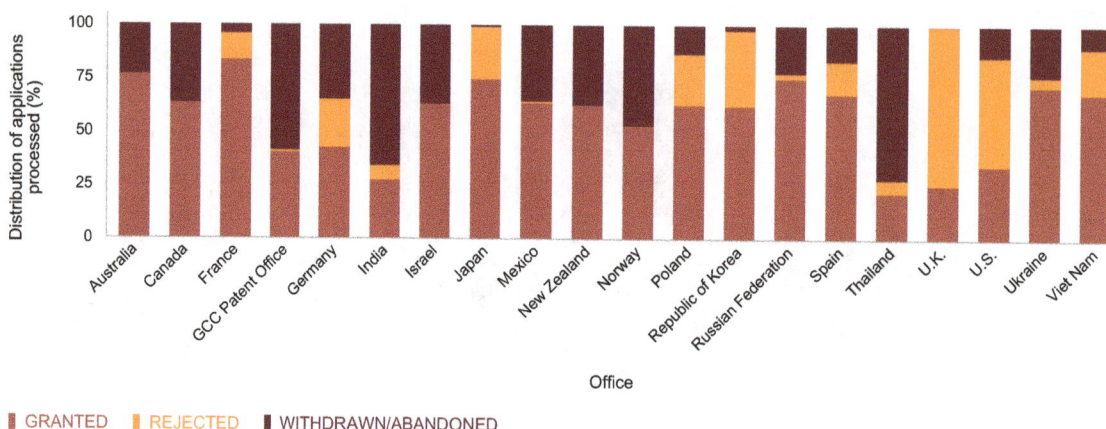

Y-axis: Distribution of applications processed (%) — 0, 25, 50, 75, 100

X-axis (Office): Australia, Canada, France, GCC Patent Office, Germany, India, Israel, Japan, Mexico, New Zealand, Norway, Poland, Republic of Korea, Russian Federation, Spain, Thailand, U.K., U.S., Ukraine, Viet Nam

Legend: ▌GRANTED ▌REJECTED ▌WITHDRAWN/ABANDONED

Note: The share of applications granted should not be interpreted as grant rates, as they are based on the examination date rather than the date when the application was filed. The number of grants in a given year relates to applications filed in previous years. WIPO collects data from IP offices using a common questionnaire and methodology. However, due to differences in patent procedures between offices, data cannot be fully harmonized. Therefore, one should exercise caution when making comparisons across offices.

Source: WIPO Statistics Database, September 2018.

A46. Potentially pending applications at the top 20 offices, 2017

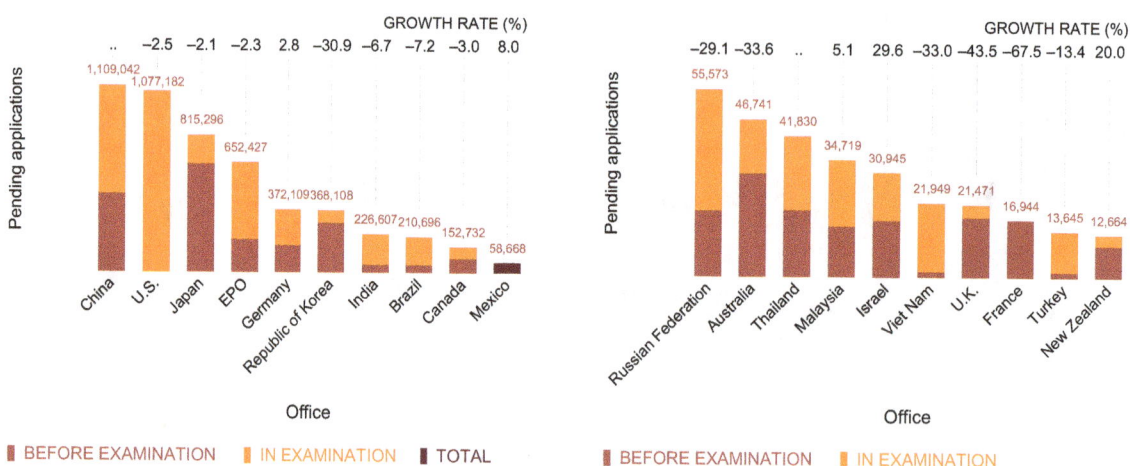

GROWTH RATE (%): .. −2.5 −2.1 −2.3 2.8 −30.9 −6.7 −7.2 −3.0 8.0

Pending applications:
- China: 1,109,042
- U.S.: 1,077,182
- Japan: 815,296
- EPO: 652,427
- Germany: 372,109
- Republic of Korea: 368,108
- India: 226,607
- Brazil: 210,696
- Canada: 152,732
- Mexico: 58,668

GROWTH RATE (%): −29.1 −33.6 .. 5.1 29.6 −33.0 −43.5 −67.5 −13.4 20.0

Pending applications:
- Russian Federation: 55,573
- Australia: 46,741
- Thailand: 41,830
- Malaysia: 34,719
- Israel: 30,945
- Viet Nam: 21,949
- U.K.: 21,471
- France: 16,944
- Turkey: 13,645
- New Zealand: 12,664

Legend (left): ▌BEFORE EXAMINATION ▌IN EXAMINATION ▌TOTAL

Legend (right): ▌BEFORE EXAMINATION ▌IN EXAMINATION

.. indicates not available.

Note: EPO is the European Patent Office. Application processing varies between offices, making it difficult to measure pending applications. In some offices, patent applications automatically proceed to the examination stage unless applicants withdraw them; in others, applications do not proceed to examination unless applicants file a separate request for examination. To take account of procedural differences, pending application data are separated between (a) all patent applications, at any stage in the process, that are awaiting a final decision by a patent office, including those for which applicants have not filed a request for examination (where applicable) and (b) patent applications undergoing examination for which the applicant has requested examination (where such separate requests are necessary). Data for Brazil include both pending patent and utility model applications, and so are not comparable with other offices.

Source: WIPO Statistics Database, September 2018.

A47. Average pendency times for first office action and final decision at selected offices, 2017

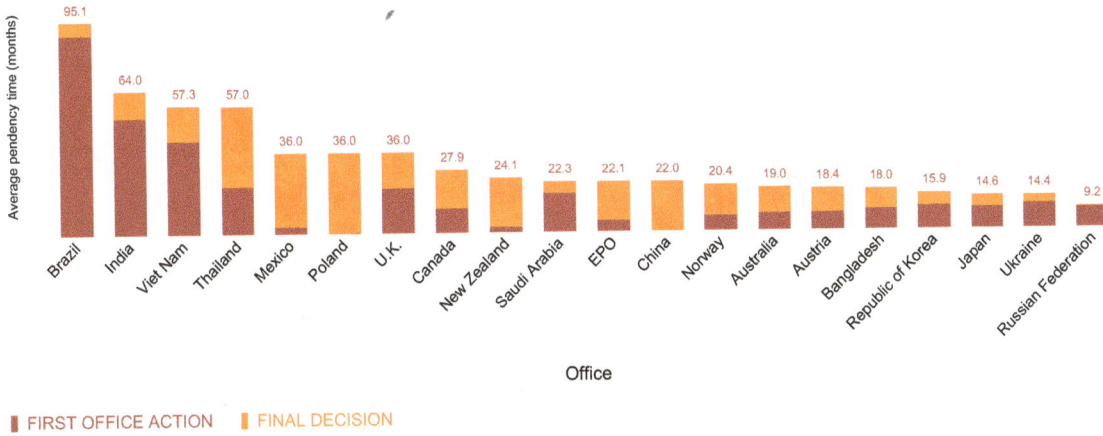

Average pendency time (months)

Office	Value
Brazil	95.1
India	64.0
Viet Nam	57.3
Thailand	57.0
Mexico	36.0
Poland	36.0
U.K.	36.0
Canada	27.9
New Zealand	24.1
Saudi Arabia	22.3
EPO	22.1
China	22.0
Norway	20.4
Australia	19.0
Austria	18.4
Bangladesh	18.0
Republic of Korea	15.9
Japan	14.6
Ukraine	14.4
Russian Federation	9.2

Office

█ FIRST OFFICE ACTION   █ FINAL DECISION

Note: EPO is the European Patent Office. WIPO collects data from IP offices using a common questionnaire and methodology. However, due to differences in patent procedures between offices, data cannot be fully harmonized. Therefore, one should exercise caution when making comparisons across offices.

Source: WIPO Statistics Database, September 2018.

A48. Average years of experience of patent examiners for selected offices, 2017

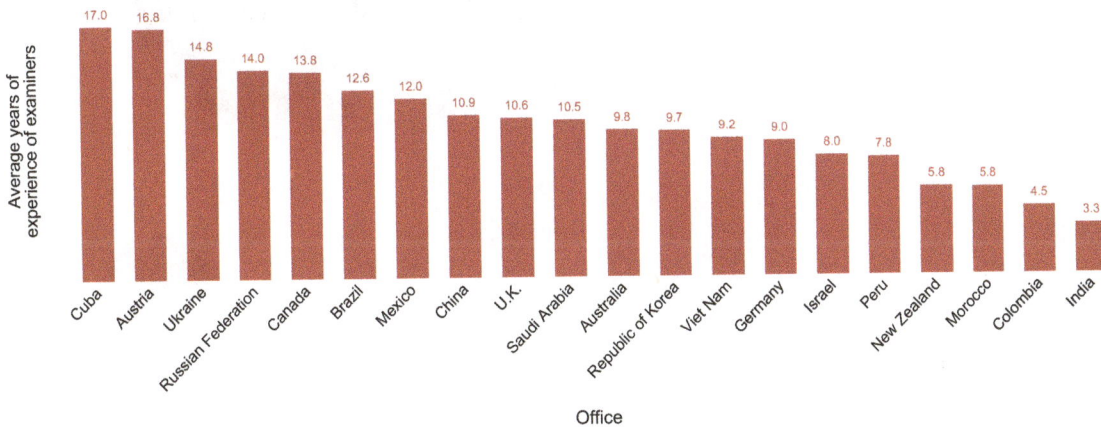

Average years of experience of examiners

Office	Value
Cuba	17.0
Austria	16.8
Ukraine	14.8
Russian Federation	14.0
Canada	13.8
Brazil	12.6
Mexico	12.0
China	10.9
U.K.	10.6
Saudi Arabia	10.5
Australia	9.8
Republic of Korea	9.7
Viet Nam	9.2
Germany	9.0
Israel	8.0
Peru	7.8
New Zealand	5.8
Morocco	5.8
Colombia	4.5
India	3.3

Office

Source: WIPO Statistics Database, September 2018.

Patent applications filed through the Patent Cooperation Treaty (PCT) System

Patents

A49. Trend in PCT applications, 2002–2017

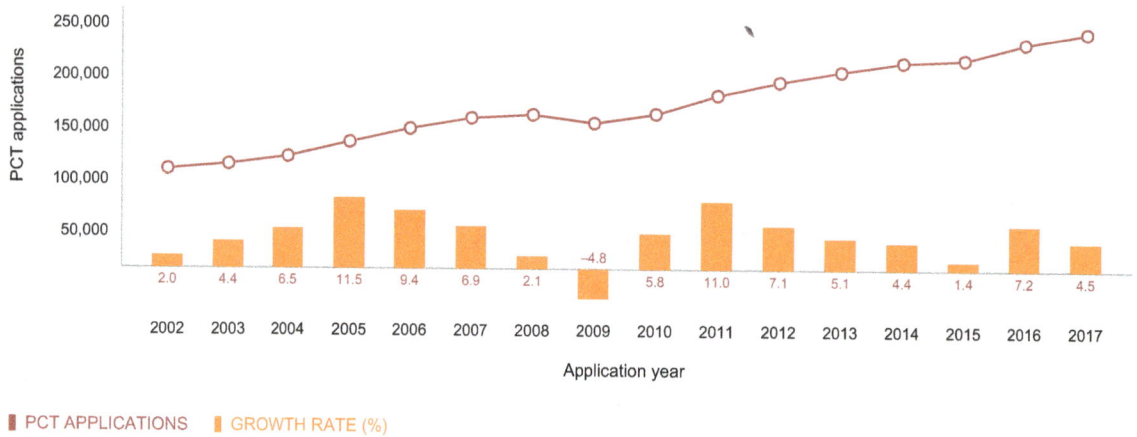

	2002	2003	2004	2005	2006	2007	2008	2009	2010	2011	2012	2013	2014	2015	2016	2017
Growth rate	2.0	4.4	6.5	11.5	9.4	6.9	2.1	–4.8	5.8	11.0	7.1	5.1	4.4	1.4	7.2	4.5

Application year

▌ PCT APPLICATIONS ▌ GROWTH RATE (%)

Note: Data refer to the international phase of the Patent Cooperation Treaty System. Counts are based on the international application date.
Source: WIPO Statistics Database, September 2018.

A50. PCT applications by origin, 2017

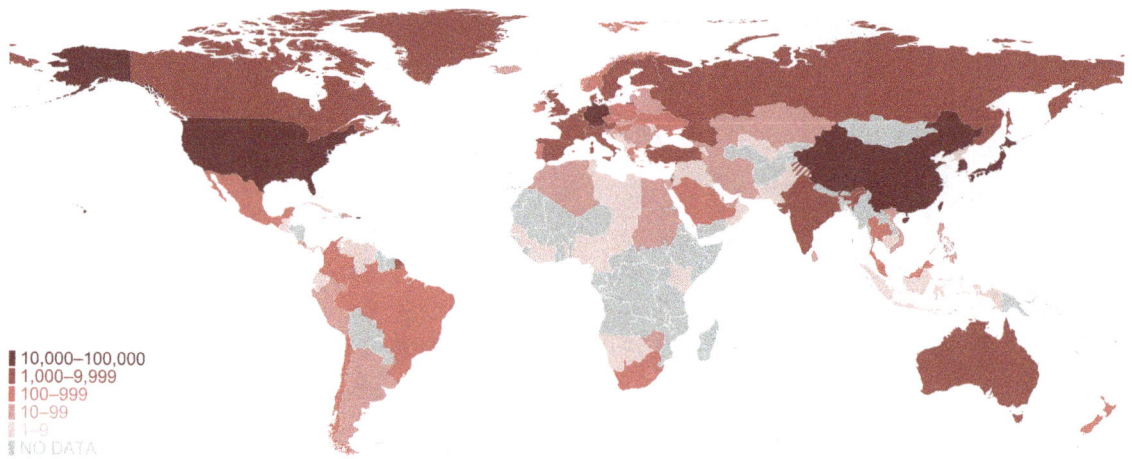

▌ 10,000–100,000
▌ 1,000–9,999
▌ 100–999
▌ 10–99
▌ 1–9
▌ NO DATA

Note: Data refer to the international phase of the Patent Cooperation Treaty System. Counts are based on the residency of the first named applicant and the international application date.
Source: WIPO Statistics Database, September 2018.

A51. PCT applications for the top 20 origins, 2017

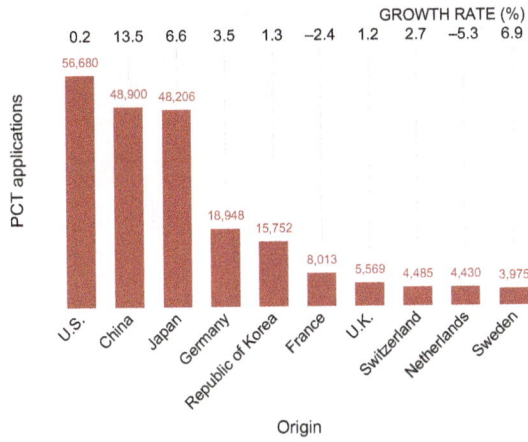

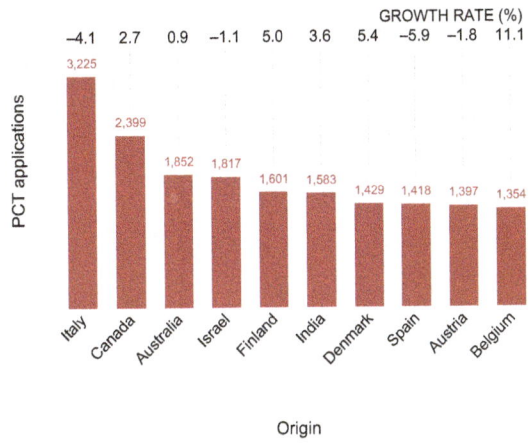

Note: Data refer to the international phase of the Patent Cooperation Treaty System. Counts are based on the residency of the first named applicant and the international application date.

Source: WIPO Statistics Database, September 2018.

Patent prosecution highway (PPH)

A52. PPH requests by offices of first filing and offices of later examination, 2017

Office of later examination	U.S.	Japan	EPO	China	Republic of Korea	Canada	Australia	U.K.	Germany	Israel	Sweden	Denmark	Russian Federation	Finland	Singapore	Others/Unknown	Total
Australia	593	120	130		41	14		10	2	5	3	16		1	2	5	942
Canada	1,640	194	203	28	56	136	71	15	6	8	4		7	9	6	6	2,389
China	1,754	1,953	818		272	12		35	56	15	33	28	12	14	5	1	5,008
Colombia	43	1	9				1						)		1	3	58
EAPO		7	3														10
EPO	578	582		138	82	46	12			25			4		4	3	1,474
Germany	205	566		10	7	3	1	29			1	4		2		2	830
Israel	281	14	135	13	9	3	9	8		32			1	1		1	507
Japan*	2,058	1,273	1,102	122	140	16	31	17	31	4	11	30	4	5	3	19	4,866
Malaysia		178															178
Mexico	236	90	102	1	12	7										15	463
New Zealand	21	7	4				18				1				1		52
Norway	13						1		1								15
Philippines	12	43			1												56
Republic of Korea	1,651	1,216	541	104	69	7	27	14	6	8	21	22	1	7	4	20	3,718
Russian Federation	316	132	97	55	72	13	9	18	12	12	7	8		11	1	8	771
Singapore	4	8	4	3	1			4	1			2			5		32
Thailand		692															692
U.K.	112	8		16	3	2			1						1		143
U.S.	589	2,296	1,827	1,133	577	219	109	90	103	83	64	21	65	33	5	66	7,280
Others/Unknown	599	514			17	3	1	2	2		1			2		17	1,158
Total	**10,705**	**9,894**	**4,975**	**1,623**	**1,359**	**482**	**289**	**243**	**220**	**193**	**145**	**131**	**94**	**85**	**38**	**166**	**30,642**

* indicates data based on office of earlier examination rather than office of first filing.

Note: EAPO is the Eurasian Patent Organization and EPO is the European Patent Office. A patent prosecution highway is a bilateral agreement between two offices that enables applicants to request a fast-track examination whereby patent examiners can use the work already undertaken by the other office.

Source: WIPO Statistics Database, September 2018.

A53. Flows of PPH requests between offices of first filing and offices of later examination, 2017

Office of first filing

Office of later examination

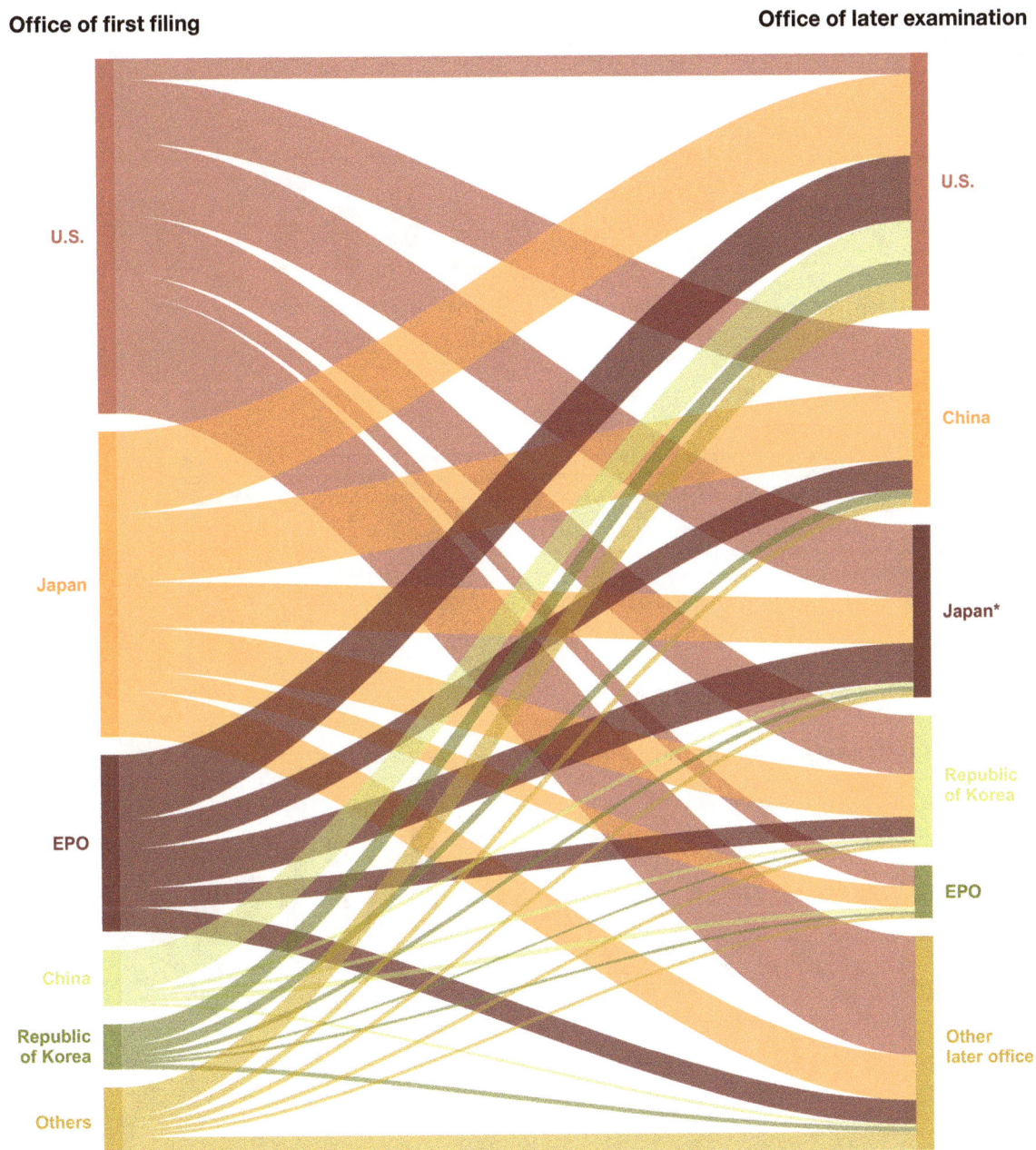

Office of first filing (left): U.S., Japan, EPO, China, Republic of Korea, Others

Office of later examination (right): U.S., China, Japan*, Republic of Korea, EPO, Other later office

* indicates data based on office of earlier examination rather than office of first filing.

Note: EPO is the European Patent Office. Japan data refers to the office of earlier examination rather than the office of first filing. A patent prosecution highway is a bilateral agreement between two offices that enables applicants to request a fast-track examination whereby patent examiners can use the work already undertaken by the other office. This graph shows the flows of PPH requests between offices of first filing and offices of later examination.

Source: WIPO Statistics Database, September 2018.

Utility model applications

Patents

A54. Trend in utility model applications worldwide, 2003–2017

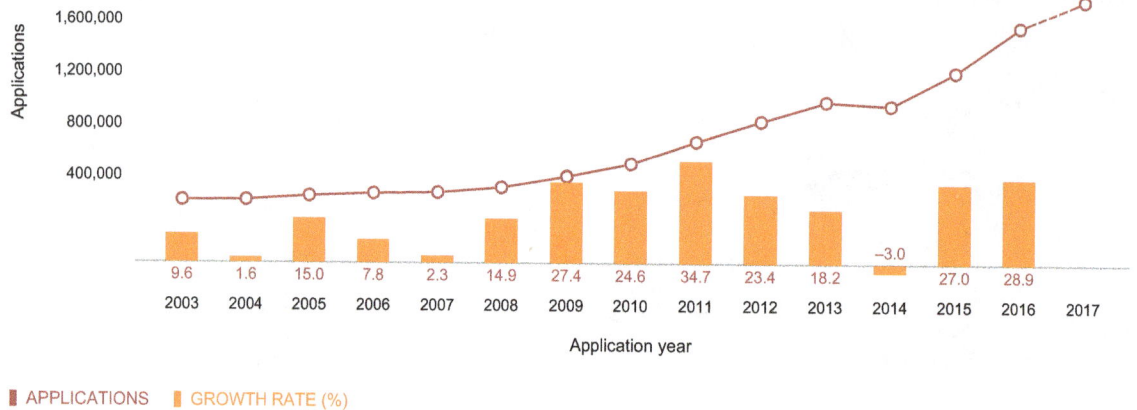

	2003	2004	2005	2006	2007	2008	2009	2010	2011	2012	2013	2014	2015	2016	2017
	9.6	1.6	15.0	7.8	2.3	14.9	27.4	24.6	34.7	23.4	18.2	−3.0	27.0	28.9	

Application year

▌ APPLICATIONS ▌ GROWTH RATE (%)

Note: China's 2017 data are not comparable with its previous years' data due to the new way in which the IP office of China now counts its applications data. Prior to 2017, it included all applications received; however, starting in 2017, China's application count data include only those applications for which the office has received the necessary application fees (see the data description section). Due to this break in the data series and to the large number of filings in China, it is not possible to report an accurate 2017 growth rate at world level. World totals are WIPO estimates using data covering 75 patent offices. These totals include applications filed directly with national and regional offices and applications entering offices through the Patent Cooperation Treaty national phase (where applicable).

Source: WIPO Statistics Database, September 2018.

A55. Utility model applications for the top 20 offices, 2017

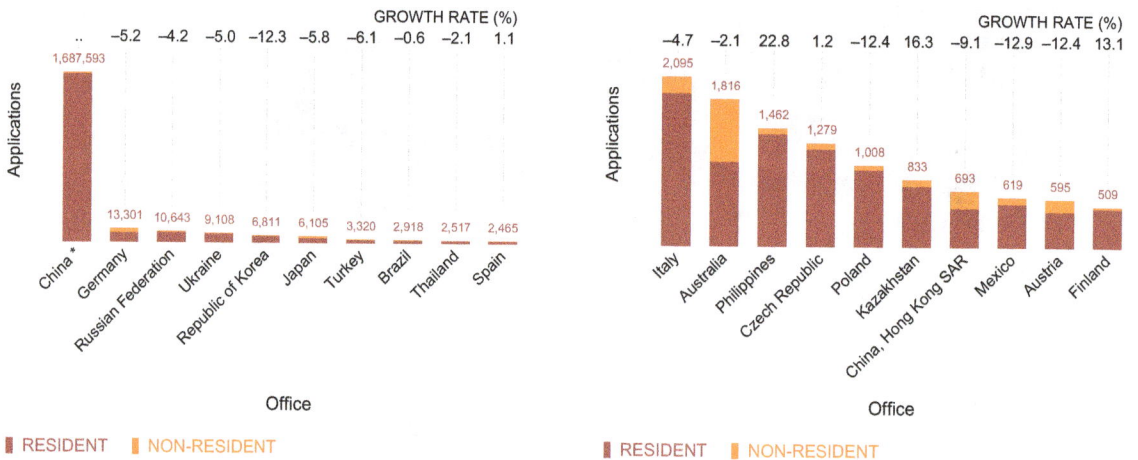

GROWTH RATE (%)

	..	−5.2	−4.2	−5.0	−12.3	−5.8	−6.1	−0.6	−2.1	1.1
	1,687,593	13,301	10,643	9,108	6,811	6,105	3,320	2,918	2,517	2,465

China * | Germany | Russian Federation | Ukraine | Republic of Korea | Japan | Turkey | Brazil | Thailand | Spain

Office

GROWTH RATE (%)

−4.7	−2.1	22.8	1.2	−12.4	16.3	−9.1	−12.9	−12.4	13.1
2,095	1,816	1,462	1,279	1,008	833	693	619	595	509

Italy | Australia | Philippines | Czech Republic | Poland | Kazakhstan | China, Hong Kong SAR | Mexico | Austria | Finland

Office

▌ RESIDENT ▌ NON-RESIDENT   ▌ RESIDENT ▌ NON-RESIDENT

.. indicates not available.

Note: * China's 2017 data are not comparable with its previous years' data due to the new way in which the IP office of China counts its applications data. Prior to 2017, the IP office of China included all applications received; however, starting in 2017, China's application count data include only those applications for which the office has received the necessary application fees (see the data description section). Due to this break in the data series, it is not possible to report an accurate growth rate for China.

Source: WIPO Statistics Database, September 2018.

A56. Utility model applications for offices of selected low- and middle-income countries, 2017

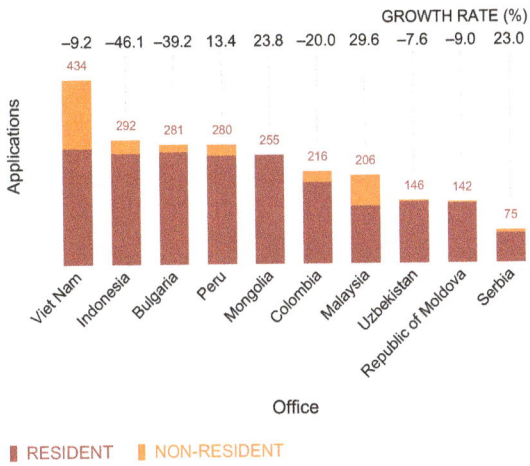

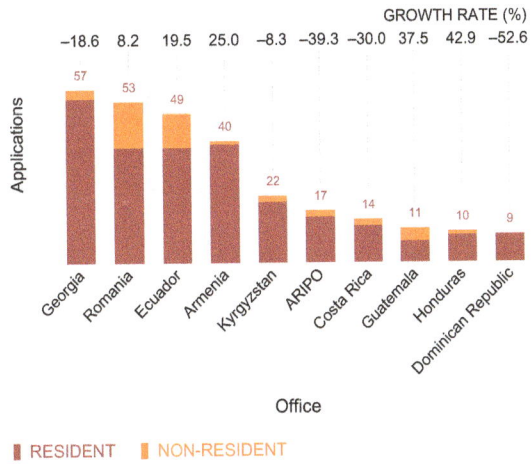

GROWTH RATE (%)

−9.2	−46.1	−39.2	13.4	23.8	−20.0	29.6	−7.6	−9.0	23.0

Applications

- Viet Nam: 434
- Indonesia: 292
- Bulgaria: 281
- Peru: 280
- Mongolia: 255
- Colombia: 216
- Malaysia: 206
- Uzbekistan: 146
- Republic of Moldova: 142
- Serbia: 75

Office

▌ RESIDENT ▌ NON-RESIDENT

GROWTH RATE (%)

−18.6	8.2	19.5	25.0	−8.3	−39.3	−30.0	37.5	42.9	−52.6

Applications

- Georgia: 57
- Romania: 53
- Ecuador: 49
- Armenia: 40
- Kyrgyzstan: 22
- ARIPO: 17
- Costa Rica: 14
- Guatemala: 11
- Honduras: 10
- Dominican Republic: 9

Office

▌ RESIDENT ▌ NON-RESIDENT

Note: ARIPO is the African Regional Intellectual Property Organization.

Source: WIPO Statistics Database, September 2018.

Patents

Microorganisms

A57. Trend in microorganism deposits worldwide, 2003–2017

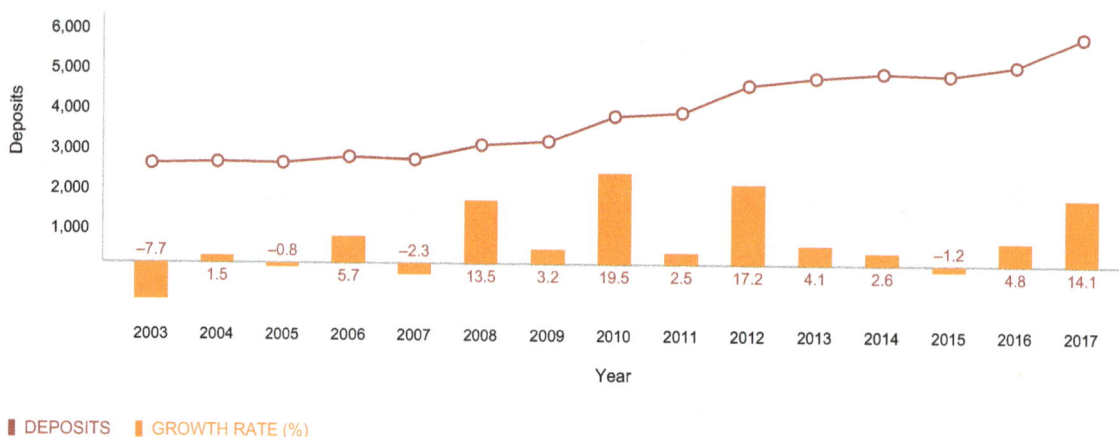

■ DEPOSITS   ■ GROWTH RATE (%)

Note: Deposits of microorganisms for patent procedures are important for biotechnological inventions. Disclosing an invention is a requirement for receiving a patent.

Source: WIPO Statistics Database, September 2018.

A58. Deposits at the top international depositary authorities, 2017

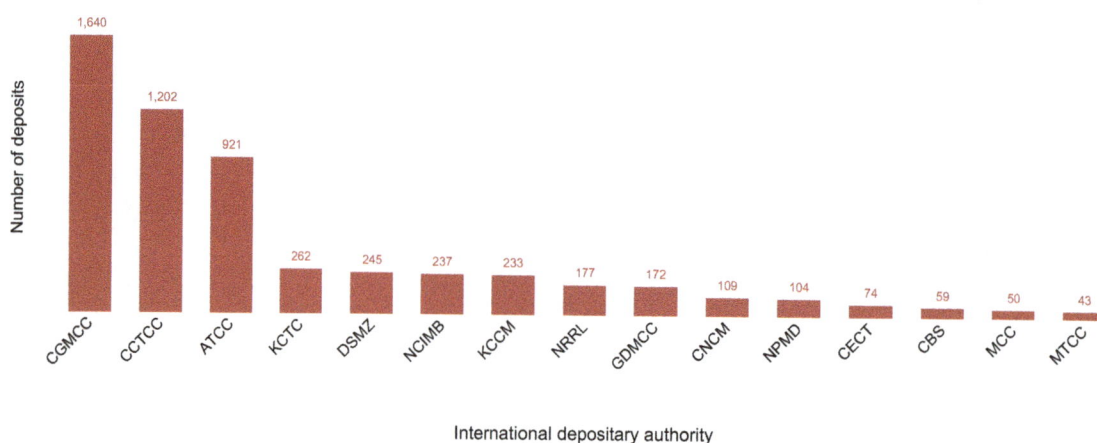

Note: ATCC is the American Type Culture Collection (U.S.), CBS is the Westerdijk Fungal Biodiversity Institute (Netherlands), CCTCC is the China Center for Type Culture Collection (China), CECT is the Colección Española de Cultivos Tipo (Spain), CGMCC is the China General Microbiological Culture Collection Center (China), CNCM is the Collection Nationale de Cultures de Micro-organismes (France), DSMZ is the Leibniz-Institut DSMZ (Deutsche Sammlung von Mikroorganismen und Zellkulturen GmbH; Germany), GDMCC is the Guangdong Microbial Culture Collection Center (China), KCCM is the Korean Culture Center of Microorganisms (Republic of Korea), KCTC is the Korean Collection for Type Cultures (Republic of Korea), MCC is the Microbial Culture Collection (India), MTCC is the Microbial Type Culture Collection and Gene Bank (India), NCIMB is the National Collection of Industrial, Food and Marine Bacteria (U.K.), NPMD is the National Institute of Technology and Evaluation, Patent Microorganisms Depositary (Japan) and NRRL is the Agriculture Research Service Culture Collection (U.S.).

Source: WIPO Statistics Database, September 2018.

Statistical tables

A59. Patent applications by office and origin, 2017

Name	Applications by office			Equivalent applications by origin	PCT international applications		PCT national phase entry	
	Total	Resident	Non-resident	Total [a]	Receiving office	Origin	Office	Origin
Afghanistan (b)	..	..	..	28	n.a.	0	..	4
African Intellectual Property Organization	519	105	414	n.a.	3	n.a.	400	n.a.
African Regional Intellectual Property Organization	747	17	730	n.a.	1	n.a.	701	n.a.
Albania	24	..	..	2	1	7	..	1
Algeria (b)	..	..	..	14	10	12	..	3
Andorra	6	0	6	42	n.a.	5	..	28
Angola (b,c)	..	..	..	5	n.a.	0	..	1
Antigua and Barbuda	8	0	8	96	0	57	8	11
Argentina	3,443	393	3,050	766	n.a.	36	..	165
Armenia	110	107	3	187	4	5	2	18
Aruba (b)	..	..	..	1	n.a.	0	..	..
Australia	28,906	2,503	26,403	11,656	1,752	1,852	19,898	7,442
Austria	2,305	2,073	232	13,785	453	1,397	565	6,720
Azerbaijan (b)	..	..	..	275	7	10	..	4
Bahamas	52	4	48	56	n.a.	5	..	24
Bahrain	245	8	237	51	0	1	229	5
Bangladesh	302	61	241	76	n.a.	0	..	3
Barbados (b,c)	..	..	..	466	n.a.	67	..	344
Belarus	524	434	90	1,525	23	28	59	27
Belgium	1,217	1,001	216	13,737	49	1,354	..	7,643
Belize (b)	..	..	..	17	0	2	..	10
Benin (b,d,g)	n.a.	n.a.	n.a.	52	n.a.	0	n.a.	..
Bermuda (b)	..	..	..	88	n.a.	0	..	40
Bhutan	3	0	3	1	n.a.	0	..	1
Bolivia (Plurinational State of)	336	59	277	61	n.a.	0	..	2
Bonaire, Sint Eustatius and Saba (b)	..	..	..	1	n.a.	0	..	1
Bosnia and Herzegovina	99	87	12	92	3	5	..	2
Botswana	7	3	4	6	0	1	..	..
Brazil	25,658	5,480	20,178	7,505	559	589	18,268	1,211
Brunei Darussalam	107	8	99	19	0	2	97	3
Bulgaria	225	202	23	425	37	50	3	113
Burkina Faso (b,d,g)	n.a.	n.a.	n.a.	102	n.a.	0	n.a.	..
Burundi (b)	..	..	..	38	n.a.	0	..	36
Cabo Verde (b)	..	..	..	1	n.a.	0	..	1
Cambodia (b)	..	..	..	..	0	1	..	..
Cameroon (b,d,g)	n.a.	n.a.	n.a.	530	n.a.	1	n.a.	..
Canada	35,022	4,053	30,969	23,914	1,875	2,399	27,350	9,147
Central African Republic (b,d,g)	n.a.	n.a.	n.a.	35	n.a.	0	n.a.	..
Chad (b,d,g)	n.a.	n.a.	n.a.	18	n.a.	1	n.a.	1
Chile	2,894	425	2,469	876	141	167	2,362	379
China	1,381,594	1,245,709	135,885	1,306,019	50,657	48,900	80,301	36,300

Name	Applications by office			Equivalent applications by origin	PCT international applications		PCT national phase entry	
	Total	Resident	Non-resident	Total (a)	Receiving office	Origin	Office	Origin
China, Hong Kong SAR	13,299	324	12,975	2,343	n.a.	0	..	408
China, Macao SAR	68	1	67	194	n.a.	0	..	14
Colombia	2,372	595	1,777	784	12	143	1,692	140
Congo (b,d,g)	n.a.	n.a.	n.a.	34	n.a.	0	n.a.	..
Costa Rica	523	19	504	82	2	10	495	21
Côte d'Ivoire (b,d,g)	n.a.	n.a.	n.a.	360	n.a.	2	n.a.	..
Croatia	159	148	11	280	19	35	5	98
Cuba	174	29	145	80	8	8	143	18
Curaçao (b)	..	..	..	15	n.a.	0	..	9
Cyprus	12	8	4	399	3	51	..	239
Czech Republic	860	794	66	2,185	144	184	25	632
Democratic People's Republic of Korea (b)	..	..	..	65	2	2	..	16
Democratic Republic of the Congo (b)	..	..	..	4	n.a.	0	..	..
Denmark	1,772	1,490	282	12,861	474	1,429	81	7,381
Dominican Republic	289	20	269	42	8	13	..	14
Ecuador	417	16	401	29	0	5	385	3
Egypt (b)	..	..	..	132	35	36	..	33
El Salvador	182	4	178	11	0	1	167	3
Eritrea (b)	..	..	..	1	n.a.	0	..	..
Estonia	41	37	4	285	8	47	4	84
Eswatini (b,f)	..	..	..	76	n.a.	0	..	2
Eurasian Patent Organization	3,302	594	2,708	n.a.	4	n.a.	2,523	n.a.
European Patent Office	166,585	78,555	88,030	n.a.	36,619	n.a.	98,431	n.a.
Fiji (b)	..	..	..	2	n.a.	0	..	..
Finland	1,529	1,390	139	12,624	980	1,601	32	6,970
France	16,247	14,415	1,832	70,939	3,803	8,013	..	37,177
Gabon (b,d,g)	n.a.	n.a.	n.a.	35	n.a.	0	n.a.	1
Gambia (f)	4	0	4	..	n.a.	0	..	..
Georgia	232	75	157	93	9	10	147	10
Germany	67,712	47,785	19,927	176,235	1,575	18,948	6,238	70,458
Ghana	26	15	11	21	0	0	..	1
Greece	589	498	91	1,225	69	110	..	437
Grenada (b)	..	..	..	1	0	0	..	..
Guatemala	278	3	275	65	0	1	268	56
Guinea (b,d,g)	n.a.	n.a.	n.a.	17	n.a.	1	n.a.	..
Guyana	23	0	23	..	n.a.	0	..	..
Honduras	193	4	189	6	0	0	184	..
Hungary	532	496	36	1,257	111	147	14	559
Iceland	44	36	8	332	14	39	1	203
India	46,582	14,961	31,621	27,985	758	1,583	26,373	4,511
Indonesia	9,303	2,271	7,032	2,320	4	8	6,186	10
International Bureau (b)	..	..	..	n.a.	10,202	n.a.	..	n.a.
Iran (Islamic Republic of)	16,259	15,264	995	15,475	2	88	..	32

Name	Applications by office			Equivalent applications by origin	PCT international applications		PCT national phase entry	
	Total	Resident	Non-resident	Total [a]	Receiving office	Origin	Office	Origin
Iraq	714	613	101	631	n.a.	2	..	..
Ireland	269	183	86	5,328	15	486	..	2,266
Israel	6,813	1,436	5,377	15,513	1,417	1,817	5,745	7,217
Italy	9,674	8,643	1,031	31,346	311	3,225	..	13,963
Jamaica	68	11	57	25	n.a.	1	..	5
Japan	318,479	260,290	58,189	460,660	47,425	48,206	62,327	129,993
Jordan	200	26	174	89	1	6	..	9
Kazakhstan	1,228	1,055	173	1,771	27	27	..	40
Kenya	178	135	43	195	3	8	38	20
Kiribati (b)	..	..	..	1	n.a.	0	..	..
Kuwait (b)	..	..	..	161	n.a.	4	..	12
Kyrgyzstan	146	137	9	170	0	0	..	..
Latvia	97	90	7	168	1	26	..	41
Lebanon (b)	..	..	..	85	n.a.	5	..	48
Liberia (b)	..	..	..	3	0	1	..	2
Libya (b)	..	..	..	..	0	3	..	..
Liechtenstein (b,e)	..	..	..	1,227	n.a.	263	..	745
Lithuania	127	81	46	214	0	30	..	94
Luxembourg	668	156	512	3,454	0	498	..	2,324
Madagascar (c)	51	9	42	11	n.a.	0	41	2
Malaysia	7,072	1,166	5,906	2,148	129	141	5,012	472
Maldives (b)	..	..	..	2	n.a.	0	..	2
Mali (b,d,g)	n.a.	n.a.	n.a.	167	n.a.	0	n.a.	7
Malta (b)	..	..	..	512	1	97	..	335
Marshall Islands (b)	..	..	..	1	n.a.	0	..	..
Mauritania (b,d,g)	n.a.	n.a.	n.a.	34	n.a.	0	n.a.	..
Mauritius	19	1	18	49	n.a.	3	..	16
Mexico	17,184	1,334	15,850	2,522	198	270	12,664	595
Monaco	35	18	17	208	0	15	..	112
Mongolia	228	124	104	128	0	0	85	1
Montenegro (b,c)	..	..	..	10	1	1	..	..
Morocco	2,224	198	2,026	265	43	47	1,668	55
Myanmar (b)	..	..	..	3	n.a.	0	..	2
Namibia (f)	25	10	15	13	n.a.	2	7	2
Nepal	63	20	43	20	n.a.	0	..	..
Netherlands	2,606	2,241	365	37,606	902	4,430	..	22,823
New Zealand	6,160	1,014	5,146	3,182	179	273	4,106	1,663
Nicaragua (b)	..	..	..	5	0	0	..	2
Niger (b,d,g)	n.a.	n.a.	n.a.	2	n.a.	0	n.a.	..
Nigeria (b,c)	..	..	..	16	n.a.	6	..	2
Norway	2,060	1,152	908	5,946	376	820	818	3,307
Oman (b,c)	..	..	..	67	1	3	..	29
Pakistan	698	193	505	245	n.a.	3	..	9
Panama	409	33	376	100	2	9	364	26

Patents

Name	Applications by office			Equivalent applications by origin	PCT international applications		PCT national phase entry	
	Total	Resident	Non-resident	Total [a]	Receiving office	Origin	Office	Origin
Paraguay (b)	..	..	..	5	n.a.	0	..	4
Patent Office of the Cooperation Council for the Arab States of the Gulf	1,846	371	1,475	n.a.	n.a.	n.a.	..	n.a.
Peru	1,219	100	1,119	167	35	33	1,061	40
Philippines	3,395	323	3,072	508	10	18	2,798	43
Poland	4,041	3,924	117	6,120	207	330	43	1,112
Portugal	680	644	36	1,508	55	201	17	555
Qatar	593	19	574	133	6	26	558	46
Republic of Korea	204,775	159,084	45,691	226,568	15,790	15,752	37,248	26,161
Republic of Moldova	110	73	37	103	8	8	34	19
Romania	1,178	1,098	80	1,451	21	31	17	116
Russian Federation	36,883	22,777	14,106	27,782	1,133	1,061	10,838	2,137
Rwanda	456	3	453	4	0	0	451	..
Saint Kitts and Nevis	9	0	9	13	n.a.	1	9	9
Saint Lucia (b,c)	..	..	..	1	n.a.	0	..	..
Saint Vincent and the Grenadines (c)	3	0	3	2	n.a.	0	3	..
Samoa (b)	..	..	..	84	n.a.	1	..	35
San Marino (b)	..	..	..	41	1	5	..	4
Sao Tome and Principe (b,c)	..	..	..	1	n.a.	0	..	..
Saudi Arabia	3,191	909	2,282	4,405	26	378	2,325	688
Senegal (b,d,g)	n.a.	n.a.	n.a.	397	n.a.	4	n.a.	1
Serbia	184	171	13	296	18	19	1	67
Seychelles (b)	..	..	..	64	0	4	..	19
Sierra Leone (b,f)	..	..	..	1	n.a.	0	..	1
Singapore	10,930	1,609	9,321	6,950	664	867	7,263	2,970
Slovakia	206	183	23	440	24	52	7	122
Slovenia (b)	..	..	..	373	45	99	..	164
South Africa	7,544	728	6,816	2,178	97	295	6,216	1,309
South Sudan (b)	..	..	..	1	n.a.	0	..	..
Spain	2,343	2,167	176	10,788	1,008	1,418	57	4,982
Sri Lanka (c)	543	277	266	331	n.a.	19	227	23
Sudan	293	281	12	288	5	11	..	6
Sweden	2,297	1,992	305	23,395	1,414	3,975	86	15,408
Switzerland	1,628	1,337	291	44,424	109	4,485	72	24,753
Syrian Arab Republic	136	120	16	130	0	1	16	3
Tajikistan (b)	..	..	..	33	0	0	..	..
Thailand	7,865	979	6,886	1,611	91	156	6,082	436
The former Yugoslav Republic of Macedonia (b)	..	..	..	2	0	2	..	..
Togo (b,d,g)	n.a.	n.a.	n.a.	34	n.a.	1	n.a.	..
Trinidad and Tobago	171	0	171	9	0	3	171	1
Tunisia	555	172	383	188	8	9	555	173
Turkey	8,555	8,175	380	11,144	846	1,203	359	1,750
Turkmenistan (b)	..	..	..	9	0	0	..	..

Name	Applications by office			Equivalent applications by origin	PCT international applications		PCT national phase entry	
	Total	Resident	Non-resident	Total [a]	Receiving office	Origin	Office	Origin
Ukraine	4,047	2,283	1,764	2,791	131	141	1,555	247
United Arab Emirates (c)	1,800	52	1,748	717	n.a.	95	1,744	247
United Kingdom	22,072	13,301	8,771	53,746	3,933	5,569	2,873	26,749
United Republic of Tanzania (b,f)	..	..	..	20	n.a.	0	..	17
United States of America	606,956	293,904	313,052	524,835	56,296	56,680	154,403	190,896
Uruguay	523	23	500	103	n.a.	14	..	11
Uzbekistan	553	357	196	366	2	4	185	5
Vanuatu (b)	..	..	..	5	n.a.	1	..	3
Venezuela (Bolivarian Republic of)	434	96	338	112	n.a.	2	..	3
Viet Nam	5,382	592	4,790	663	9	23	4,104	26
Yemen	28	15	13	21	n.a.	0	..	1
Zambia	22	12	10	14	0	0	10	2
Zimbabwe (b)	..	..	..	6	0	21	..	5
Others/Unknown	..	..	..	32,930	n.a.	249	..	3,609
Total (2017 estimates)	**3,168,900**	**2,251,500**	**917,400**	**n.a.**	**243,464**	**243,464**	**630,000**	**n.a.**

(a) Equivalent applications by origin data are incomplete because some offices do not report by origin.

(b) The office did not report resident applications. Therefore, the equivalent applications by origin data may be incomplete.

(c) The International Bureau acts as the receiving office for PCT applications.

(d) The African Intellectual Property Organization (OAPI) acts as the receiving office for PCT applications.

(e) The Swiss Federal Institute of Intellectual Property (IFPI) acts as the receiving office for PCT applications.

(f) The African Regional Intellectual Property Organization (ARIPO) acts as the receiving office for PCT applications.

(g) The African Intellectual Property Organization (OAPI) acts as the national office for patent applications.

.. indicates not available.

n.a. indicates not applicable.

Source: WIPO Statistics Database, September 2018.

A60. Patent grants by office and origin, and patents in force, 2017

Name	Total	Resident	Grants by office Non-resident	Equivalent grants by origin Total [a]	In force by office Total
Afghanistan	..	..	..	4	..
African Intellectual Property Organization	384	143	241	n.a.	..
African Regional Intellectual Property Organization	451	4	447	n.a.	..
Albania	10	..	..	1	4,946
Algeria	..	..	..	5	..
Andorra	4	0	4	9	4
Argentina	2,302	176	2,126	354	13,115
Armenia	74	74	0	115	209
Australia	22,742	1,188	21,554	5,988	144,555
Austria	1,102	980	122	8,797	146,880
Azerbaijan	..	..	..	283	..
Bahamas	20	0	20	97	1,082
Bahrain	..	..	..	18	245
Bangladesh	144	..	..	11	..
Barbados	..	..	..	365	..
Belarus	861	771	90	2,295	2,250
Belgium	1,016	859	157	7,970	102,120
Belize	..	..	..	9	..
Benin (b)	n.a.	n.a.	n.a.	136	..
Bermuda	..	..	..	116	..
Bhutan	..	..	..	1	1
Bolivia (Plurinational State of)	63	3	60	4	..
Bosnia and Herzegovina	4	0	4	3	367
Botswana	4	0	4	2	2,035
Brazil	5,450	714	4,736	1,622	25,664
Brunei Darussalam	41	6	35	11	1,213
Bulgaria	77	69	8	192	12,039
Burkina Faso (b)	n.a.	n.a.	n.a.	120	..
Cameroon (b)	n.a.	n.a.	n.a.	530	..
Canada	24,099	2,500	21,599	13,838	180,727
Central African Republic (b)	n.a.	n.a.	n.a.	51	..
Chad (b)	n.a.	n.a.	n.a.	52	..
Chile	1,574	161	1,413	477	12,389
China	420,144	326,970	93,174	352,546	2,085,367
China, Hong Kong SAR	6,671	96	6,575	1,150	45,059
China, Macao SAR	21	0	21	40	416
Colombia	1,164	166	998	234	7,024
Congo (b)	n.a.	n.a.	n.a.	102	..
Costa Rica	190	2	188	18	834
Côte d'Ivoire (b)	n.a.	n.a.	n.a.	443	..
Croatia	20	5	15	63	7,845
Cuba	74	9	65	105	816
Curaçao	..	..	..	12	..

Name	Total	Grants by office Resident	Grants by office Non-resident	Equivalent grants by origin Total [a]	In force by office Total
Cyprus	..	..	..	227	37
Czech Republic	669	567	102	1,437	41,606
Democratic People's Republic of Korea	..	..	..	8	..
Denmark	419	243	176	6,440	58,494
Djibouti	..	..	..	1	..
Dominican Republic	42	..	..	4	282
Ecuador	17	4	13	9	63
Egypt	..	..	..	52	..
El Salvador	24	0	24	1	..
Eritrea	..	..	..	1	..
Estonia	15	13	2	142	9,710
Eswatini	..	..	..	7	..
Eurasian Patent Organization	3,282	616	2,666	n.a.	n.a.
European Patent Office	105,645	50,662	54,983	n.a.	n.a.
Finland	704	593	111	8,386	50,764
France	11,865	10,216	1,649	47,531	563,695
Gabon (b)	n.a.	n.a.	n.a.	68	..
Gambia	4	0	4	..	8
Georgia	206	37	169	39	1,172
Germany	15,653	10,564	5,089	98,863	657,749
Ghana	5	1	4	1	30
Greece	261	252	9	514	26,936
Guatemala	50	1	49	2	908
Guinea (b)	n.a.	n.a.	n.a.	17	..
Guyana	23	0	23	..	..
Honduras	54	0	54	..	1,654
Hungary	155	88	67	632	26,225
Iceland	36	6	30	154	6,613
India	12,387	1,712	10,675	7,496	60,777
Indonesia	2,309	..	..	43	..
Iran (Islamic Republic of)	4,151	3,668	483	3,726	42,447
Iraq	388	323	65	330	..
Ireland	87	41	46	2,968	169,453
Israel	..	..	..	6,720	32,764
Italy	4,855	4,536	319	19,648	297,672
Jamaica	2	0	2	12	265
Japan	199,577	156,844	42,733	285,913	2,013,685
Jordan	119	4	115	45	407
Kazakhstan	869	650	219	1,091	2,625
Kenya	43	11	32	19	..
Kuwait	..	..	..	65	..
Kyrgyzstan	78	75	3	110	256
Latvia	87	75	12	173	8,808

Name	Total	Grants by office Resident	Grants by office Non-resident	Equivalent grants by origin Total [a]	In force by office Total
Lebanon	..	..	..	27	..
Liberia	..	..	..	1	..
Liechtenstein	..	..	..	694	..
Lithuania	143	93	50	173	..
Luxembourg	487	123	364	2,120	..
Madagascar	23	1	22	3	206
Malaysia	5,063	437	4,626	945	25,313
Mali (b)	n.a.	n.a.	n.a.	170	..
Malta	..	..	..	244	..
Marshall Islands	..	..	..	13	..
Mauritania (b)	n.a.	n.a.	n.a.	17	..
Mauritius	4	0	4	35	46
Mexico	8,510	407	8,103	1,094	112,617
Monaco	10	6	4	55	88,453
Mongolia	105	49	56	51	..
Montenegro	..	..	..	1	..
Morocco	413	74	339	92	4,145
Namibia	16	7	9	14	451
Netherlands	2,307	1,937	370	23,231	165,879
New Zealand	2,430	177	2,253	1,167	36,157
Nicaragua	..	..	..	1	..
Niger (b)	n.a.	n.a.	n.a.	155	..
Nigeria	..	..	..	11	..
Norway	2,147	513	1,634	3,579	33,150
Oman	..	..	..	15	..
Pakistan	169	10	159	43	1,745
Panama	4	0	4	28	..
Paraguay	..	..	..	2	..
Patent Office of the Cooperation Council for the Arab States of the Gulf	2,240	298	1,942	n.a.	6,095
Peru	510	26	484	42	2,791
Philippines	1,645	25	1,620	138	21,254
Poland	2,904	2,795	109	3,808	75,982
Portugal	55	52	3	448	36,821
Qatar	37	2	35	47	..
Republic of Korea	120,662	90,847	29,815	131,571	970,889
Republic of Moldova	62	42	20	57	333
Romania	407	396	11	553	20,711
Russian Federation	34,254	21,037	13,217	24,806	244,217
Rwanda	176	2	174	2	456
Saint Kitts and Nevis	..	..	..	1	..
Saint Vincent and the Grenadines	10	0	10	18	10
Samoa	..	..	..	16	51
San Marino	..	..	..	21	..
Saudi Arabia	501	90	411	2,905	3,277

Name	Total	Grants by office Resident	Grants by office Non-resident	Equivalent grants by origin Total [a]	In force by office Total
Senegal (b)	n.a.	n.a.	n.a.	544	..
Serbia	47	35	12	64	4,644
Seychelles	..	..	..	65	..
Sierra Leone	..	..	..	1	..
Singapore	6,217	414	5,803	3,111	49,514
Slovakia	82	59	23	183	17,815
Slovenia	..	..	..	358	..
South Africa	5,535	595	4,940	1,419	63,151
South Sudan	..	..	..	1	..
Spain	2,011	1,873	138	6,161	108,732
Sri Lanka	178	55	123	68	826
Sudan	177	165	12	165	177
Sweden	1,031	904	127	15,498	96,876
Switzerland	771	541	230	26,088	208,022
Syrian Arab Republic	3	0	3	2	13
Tajikistan	..	..	..	32	..
Thailand	3,080	88	2,992	249	16,591
The former Yugoslav Republic of Macedonia	..	..	..	5	..
Togo (b)	n.a.	n.a.	n.a.	34	..
Trinidad and Tobago	66	0	66	4	..
Tunisia	555	..	..	19	..
Turkey	1,900	1,757	143	2,888	68,886
Turkmenistan	..	..	..	16	..
Uganda	2	..	..	1	..
Ukraine	2,590	1,224	1,366	1,523	23,705
United Arab Emirates	..	..	..	271	874
United Kingdom	6,311	3,267	3,044	25,101	1,243,678
United Republic of Tanzania	..	..	..	1	..
United States of America	318,829	150,949	167,880	285,507	2,984,825
Uruguay	27	2	25	179	410
Uzbekistan	205	144	61	158	952
Vanuatu	..	..	..	4	..
Venezuela (Bolivarian Republic of)	..	..	..	19	..
Viet Nam	1,745	111	1,634	159	15,226
Yemen	28	1	27	24	..
Zambia	18	5	13	12	7,705
Others/Unknown	..	..	..	17,967	..
Total (2017 estimates)	**1,404,600**	**866,700**	**537,900**	**n.a.**	**13,718,050**

(a) Equivalent grants by origin data are incomplete because some offices do not report by origin.

(b) The African Intellectual Property Organization (OAPI) acts as the national office for patent grants.

.. indicates not available.

n.a. indicates not applicable.

Source: WIPO Statistics Database, September 2018.

A61. Patent office procedural data, 2017

Office	Total applications processed	Granted	Rejected	Withdrawn or abandoned	Number of examiners (FTE)	First office action (months)	Final office decision (months)
Albania	..	769	..	..	2.0	12.0	3.0
Armenia	107	93	4	10	8.0	3.3	1.5
Australia	29,773	22,742	21	7,010	379.6	19.0	7.5
Austria	1,892	1,161	615	116	98.0	18.4	7.7
Bangladesh	277	144	33	100	9.0	18.0	9.0
Belarus	..	917	281	..	19.0	..	..
Bhutan	..	..	..	..	3.0	..	..
Bolivia (Plurinational State of)	445	63	178	204	4.0	6.0	6.0
Bosnia and Herzegovina	..	..	..	..	7.0	27.0	2.0
Brazil	9,847	5,450	3,874	523	183.0	95.1	89.0
Brunei Darussalam	..	6	..	..	..	8.0	3.0
Bulgaria	226	72	48	106	13.0	60.0	48.0
Canada	..	24,099	..	13,952	322.9	27.9	10.7
China	..	420,144	..	..	2,302.0	22.0	..
China, Macao SAR	..	21	32	..	..	11.7	5.3
Colombia	2,416	1,164	862	390	43.0	15.5	7.6
Costa Rica	903	190	340	373	19.0	60.0	54.0
Croatia	82	20	37	25	6.0	58.0	40.0
Cuba	150	74	6	70	11.0	32.0	4.0
Czech Republic	1,266	669	390	207	32.0	..	..
Denmark	1,871	419	3	1,449	64.0	24.9	5.6
Dominican Republic	187	42	101	44	10.0	..	..
Ecuador	875	17	843	15	6.0	60.0	24.0
El Salvador	..	..	..	..	2.0	36.0	24.0
Estonia	26	6	1	19	7.8	24.5	4.5
European Patent Office	..	105,645	..	..	4,378.0	22.1	4.8
Finland	2,372	704	15	1,653	107.0	30.0	6.5
France	14,646	12,205	1,841	600	92.0	..	..
Georgia	328	206	33	89	18.0	21.0	15.0
Germany	36,833	15,653	8,356	12,824	721.0	..	..
Honduras	..	102	82	..	4.0	36.0	1.0
Hungary	860	155	40	665	47.0	23.4	6.0
India	45,379	12,387	3,203	29,789	571.0	64.0	52.0
Iraq	668	388	165	115	..	..	..
Israel	7,659	4,815	12	2,832	114.0	21.0	28.5
Japan	246,500	183,919	60,613	1,968	1,696.0	14.6	9.4
Jordan	..	125	259	..	5.0	20.0	12.0
Kyrgyzstan	..	102	..	20	9.0	12.0	12.0
Latvia	98	87	6	5	6.0	..	..
Lithuania	162	139	13	10	5.0	5.0	1.0
Madagascar	..	23	..	1	2.0	12.0	7.0
Mexico	13,921	8,843	120	4,958	129.0	36.0	3.0
Monaco	..	10	14	..	1.5	9.0	4.0
Morocco	745	403	264	78	18.0	20.2	10.5
Namibia	..	..	..	..	1.0	..	..
New Zealand	..	2,430	..	1,439	43.0	24.1	2.3
Norway	4,073	2,148	14	1,911	75.0	20.4	6.5
Panama	..	..	..	..	4.0	..	..
Patent Office of the Cooperation Council for the Arab States of the Gulf	5,548	2,240	56	3,252	40.0	46.0	14.0
Peru	..	1,029	338	..	27.0	35.9	31.8
Philippines	..	..	..	..	106.0	..	..
Poland	4,937	3,097	1,185	655	78.0	36.0	0.1

Patents

Office	Total applications processed	Granted	Rejected	Withdrawn or abandoned	Number of examiners (FTE)	First office action (months)	Final office decision (months)
Portugal	352	116	223	13	20.0	27.6	..
Qatar	..	37	..	..	7.0	24.0	12.0
Republic of Korea	177,118	110,408	62,869	3,841	866.0	15.9	10.3
Republic of Moldova	153	86	42	25	15.0	12.0	4.0
Romania	1,239	407	337	495	35.0	52.0	36.0
Russian Federation	45,217	33,988	1,147	10,082	587.0	9.2	9.0
Saint Vincent and the Grenadines	..	..	..	..	2.0	6.0	6.0
Saudi Arabia	1,512	501	713	298	55.0	22.3	17.1
Serbia	158	43	45	70	12.0	18.0	12.0
Slovakia	233	82	62	89	25.0	49.6	47.7
Spain	2,965	2,011	462	492	176.0	11.8	3.8
Sri Lanka	..	178	898	..	8.0	24.0	0.5
Sudan	293	186	12	95	16.0	..	..
Sweden	2,313	1,031	25	1,257	111.0	29.9	7.6
Thailand	14,204	3,080	906	10,218	73.0	57.0	21.0
Trinidad and Tobago	..	..	..	..	6.0	..	..
Turkey	2,422	2,100	257	65	112.0	17.4	3.6
Ukraine	3,818	2,734	178	906	115.0	14.4	11.0
United Kingdom	..	6,311	18,644	..	318.0	36.0	20.0
United States of America	922,859	318,828	469,976	134,055	..	..	..
Uruguay	784	27	30	727	10.0	144.0	120.0
Uzbekistan	455	216	13	226	9.0	..	..
Viet Nam	3,386	2,309	727	350	62.0	57.3	41.6
Zambia	..	..	..	..	2.0	..	..

Note: FTE is full time equivalent. Grant data differ slightly from grant data reported elsewhere in this report due to different dates of extraction. Every effort has been made to compile procedural data based on common definitions and concepts, but procedural differences make it extremely difficult to fully harmonize such data. For instance, "rejection" is not recorded as a final decision in Canada. Applicants are informed of the action that they must take or questions that they must answer in order for their application to be considered, and if an applicant cannot provide the required information, they are regarded as having abandoned the application. A similar situation exists in Australia.

.. indicates not available.

Source: WIPO Statistics Database, September 2018.

A62. Utility model applications and grants by office and origin, 2017

Name	Applications by office			Equivalent applications by origin	Grants by office		
	Total	Resident	Non-resident	Total [a]	Total	Resident	Non-resident
African Regional Intellectual Property Organization	17	15	2	n.a.	8	2	6
Albania	1	1	0	1	3	1	2
Andorra	..	..	..	5	..	..	..
Argentina	225	195	30	216	39	33	6
Armenia	40	39	1	44	27	26	1
Australia	1,816	1,047	769	1,134	1,855	1,015	840
Austria	595	449	146	792	348	267	81
Azerbaijan	..	..	..	1	..	..	..
Barbados	..	..	..	3	..	..	..
Belarus	453	400	53	491	306	266	40
Belgium	..	..	..	91	..	..	..
Belize	..	..	..	8	..	..	..
Bolivia (Plurinational State of)	18	11	7	11	2	0	2
Bosnia and Herzegovina	..	..	..	1	..	..	..
Botswana	5	5	0	5	..	..	..
Brazil	2,918	2,843	75	2,901	788	763	25
Brunei Darussalam	..	..	..	6	..	..	..
Bulgaria	281	264	17	295	464	443	21
Canada	..	..	..	117	..	..	..
Chile	142	102	40	108	51	44	7
China	1,687,593	1,679,807	7,786	1,681,657	973,294	967,416	5,878
China, Hong Kong SAR	693	483	210	601	582	369	213
China, Macao SAR	18	2	16	41	7	2	5
Colombia	216	191	25	202	134	115	19
Cook Islands	..	..	..	4	..	..	..
Costa Rica	14	12	2	13	14	5	9
Croatia	53	51	2	55	66	60	6
Cuba	2	0	2	..	..	..	..
Cyprus	..	..	..	221	..	..	..
Czech Republic	1,279	1,205	74	1,392	1,107	1,036	71
Democratic Republic of the Congo	..	..	..	1	..	..	..
Denmark	132	100	32	158	120	92	28
Dominican Republic	9	9	0	10	4	4	0
Ecuador	49	38	11	45	7	6	1
Egypt	..	..	..	3	..	..	..
El Salvador	104	4	100	4	3	2	1
Estonia	55	53	2	63	37	35	2
Fiji	..	..	..	2	..	..	..
Finland	509	486	23	723	417	395	22
France	428	174	254	632	..	..	..
Gambia	1	1	0	1	1	1	0
Georgia	57	54	3	56	37	34	3

Name	Applications by office			Equivalent applications by origin	Grants by office		
	Total	Resident	Non-resident	Total [a]	Total	Resident	Non-resident
Germany	13,301	9,479	3,822	10,613	11,882	7,895	3,987
Ghana	7	7	0	7	..	..	..
Greece	16	12	4	20	33	30	3
Guatemala	11	7	4	7	4	3	1
Honduras	10	9	1	9	10	9	1
Hungary	235	207	28	226	157	132	25
India	..	..	..	34	..	..	..
Indonesia	292	261	31	265	103	79	24
Iran (Islamic Republic of)	..	..	..	8	..	..	..
Iraq	..	..	..	1	..	..	..
Ireland	..	..	..	12	..	..	..
Israel	..	..	..	89	..	..	..
Italy	2,095	1,888	207	2,315	1,402	1,357	45
Japan	6,105	4,577	1,528	6,881	6,024	4,526	1,498
Kazakhstan	833	754	79	762	591	532	59
Kenya	153	152	1	152	79	79	0
Kyrgyzstan	22	20	2	24	11	10	1
Latvia	..	..	..	9	..	..	..
Lebanon	..	..	..	1	..	..	..
Liechtenstein	..	..	..	15	..	..	..
Lithuania	..	..	..	3	..	..	..
Luxembourg	..	..	..	56	..	..	..
Malaysia	206	134	72	179	64	37	27
Mali	..	..	..	4	..	..	..
Malta	..	..	..	6	..	..	..
Mauritius	..	..	..	1	..	..	..
Mexico	619	541	78	558	164	134	30
Monaco	..	..	..	1	..	..	..
Mongolia	255	255	0	256	164	164	0
Morocco	..	..	..	1	..	..	..
Netherlands	..	..	..	212	..	..	..
New Zealand	..	..	..	37	..	..	..
Norway	..	..	..	18	..	..	..
Panama	4	2	2	3	2	1	1
Peru	280	255	25	268	128	117	11
Philippines	1,462	1,392	70	1,406	572	542	30
Poland	1,008	953	55	1,009	810	776	34
Portugal	97	72	25	89	61	38	23
Republic of Korea	6,811	6,451	360	7,408	2,993	2,810	183
Republic of Moldova	142	140	2	144	110	108	2
Romania	53	38	15	46	26	14	12
Russian Federation	10,643	10,152	491	10,347	8,774	8,376	398

Patents

Name	Applications by office			Equivalent applications by origin	Grants by office		
	Total	Resident	Non-resident	Total [a]	Total	Resident	Non-resident
Rwanda	9	9	0	9	..	..	..
Saint Kitts and Nevis	..	..	..	1	..	..	..
Samoa	..	..	..	19	..	..	..
San Marino	..	..	..	6	..	..	..
Saudi Arabia	..	..	..	3	..	..	..
Serbia	75	69	6	70	43	37	6
Seychelles	..	..	..	8	..	..	..
Singapore	..	..	..	550	..	..	..
Slovakia	412	343	69	402	307	246	61
Slovenia	..	..	..	9	..	..	..
South Africa	..	..	..	12	..	..	..
Spain	2,465	2,313	152	2,533	2,171	2,040	131
Sweden	..	..	..	135	..	..	..
Switzerland	..	..	..	479	..	..	..
Syrian Arab Republic	..	..	..	1	..	..	..
Thailand	2,517	2,335	182	2,383	1,155	1,038	117
Turkey	3,320	3,256	64	3,327	2,088	2,014	74
Ukraine	9,108	8,973	135	9,099	9,442	9,365	77
United Arab Emirates	17	0	17	7	..	..	..
United Kingdom	..	..	..	246	..	..	..
United Republic of Tanzania	..	..	..	1	..	..	..
United States of America	..	..	..	3,367	..	..	..
Uruguay	36	25	11	32	17	13	4
Uzbekistan	146	144	2	146	107	105	2
Venezuela (Bolivarian Republic of)	..	..	..	3	..	..	..
Viet Nam	434	273	161	273	146	118	28
Yemen	..	..	..	..	2	2	0
Others/Unknown	..	..	..	2,185	..	..	..
Total (2017 estimates)	**1,761,200**	**1,743,790**	**17,410**	**n.a.**	..	..	..

(a) Equivalent applications by origin data are incomplete because some offices do not report by origin.

.. indicates not available.

n.a. indicates not applicable.

Source: WIPO Statistics Database, September 2018.

Trademarks

Highlights

Applications grew by an extraordinary 30% in 2017

An estimated 9.11 million trademark applications were filed worldwide in 2017, 30% more than in 2016 (see figure 2.1). This marks the eighth consecutive year of growth and the highest level of growth recorded in recent decades. There are currently almost three times as many trademark applications being filed around the world than in 2007 – applications have increased every year except for two during this 11-year period, and five years saw annual growth exceed 10%.

After slowing in 2007 and showing slight declines in 2008 and 2009, trademark applications rebounded in 2010 and have continued to increase year on year. In 2010, the large number of applications filed in China accounted for 53% of the increase in overall growth. Since then, China's share has climbed to 90%. About 60% of all applications in 2017 were filed in China alone.

An estimated 9.11 million trademark applications were filed worldwide

2.1. Trademark applications worldwide, 2007–2017

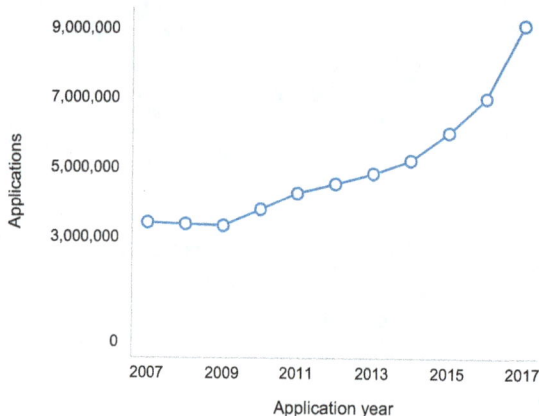

Source: Figure B1.

When differences in filing systems across national and regional offices are harmonized using the application class count, trademark filing activity in 2017 also saw a double-digit increase, up 26.8% on the previous year. The total number of classes specified in applications – known as the application class count – reached an estimated 12.39 million (see figure 2.2). Excluding the 2017 application class count for China, trademark filing activity grew by a more moderate 9.5% in the rest of the world.

The total number of classes specified in trademark applications grew by 26.8%

2.2. Trademark application class counts worldwide, 2007–2017

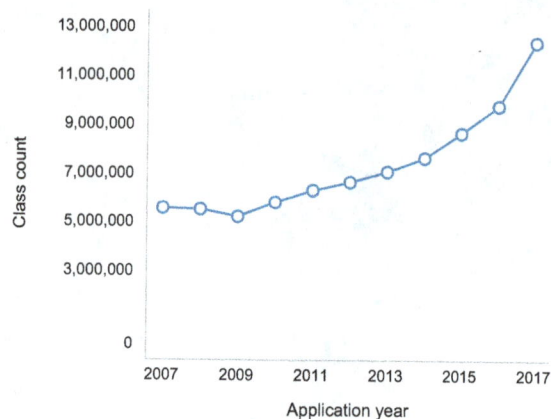

Source: Figure B2.

Class count

A trademark application may refer to different classes of goods or services. Many offices use the Nice Classification, an international classification of goods and services for registering trademarks and service marks. Applications received by these offices are classified in one or more of the 45 Nice classes (see *www.wipo.int/classifications/nice*). Some offices allow single-class filing only, meaning that applicants have to file a separate application for each class. Others permit multi-class filings, enabling applicants to file a single application in which a number of classes can be specified. To improve international comparisons of the numbers of applications received, it helps to compare class counts across offices. Class counts are also used to make trademark registration activity internationally comparable. This method for comparing offices began in 2004, the first year for which complete class count data are available.

Offices with the most filing activity

As with other forms of intellectual property (IP), the increase in trademark filing activity (measured in application class counts) largely reflects the strong growth in the number of trademark applications filed in China. In 2017, the trademark office of China accounted for 78% of the annual increase in global trademark filing activity using this measure. It was followed by the offices of the Islamic Republic of Iran (6%) and Japan (4%), which accounted for considerably smaller portions of total growth.

The office of China's class count of over 5.7 million was followed by a count of 613,921 at the office of the United States of America (U.S.) (see figure 2.3). These have been the top two offices since the early 2000s

Non-resident applicants accounted for 30.2% of total trademark filing activity in the U.S.

2.3. Trademark application class counts for the top 10 offices, 2017

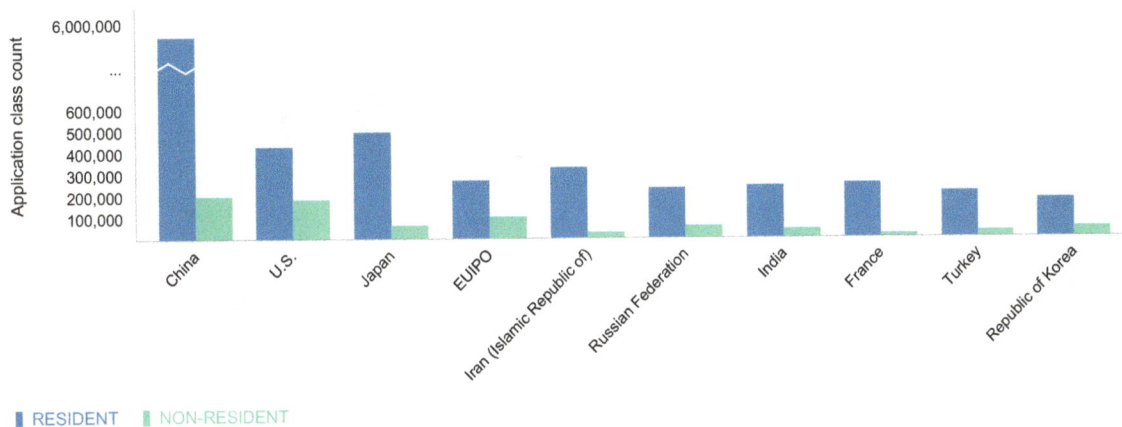

■ RESIDENT ■ NON-RESIDENT

Source: Figure B10.

Trademarks

but, since 2007, China's class count has grown from close to twice that of the U.S. to over nine times as much. These two offices were followed by that of Japan (560,269), the European Union Intellectual Property Office (EUIPO) (371,508) and that of the Islamic Republic of Iran (358,353). The top five offices in 2017 accounted for 62% of all trademark filing activity, up from the 33% shared by the top five offices a decade earlier, in 2007.

Among the top 20 offices, 16 had higher levels of trademark filing activity in 2017 than in 2016, of which eight recorded growth exceeding 10%. The largest increases were in the Islamic Republic of Iran (+87.9%) and China (+55.2), followed by Japan (+24.2%), the United Kingdom (U.K.) (+24.1%) and Canada (+19.5%). In contrast, the office of India (−9.5%) saw the largest annual drop, while the offices of France (−1.4%), Italy (−1%) and the Republic of Korea (−0.6%) recorded small declines (see figure B11).

For offices located in low- and middle-income countries, annual growth was particularly high in Namibia (+47.1%), Gambia (+21.6%) and Georgia (+14.1%) (see figure B13). The office of South Africa, however, witnessed a large decrease of 30.9% in trademark filing activity from 2016 to 2017.

At most offices, trademark applications are filed mainly by residents seeking protection within their domestic jurisdiction. In 2017, residents accounted for 83.1% of global filing activity. In fact, domestic filing is becoming increasingly pronounced as a share of total filing activity, with the world resident application class count having increased by 32% on the previous year's total; in contrast, the application class count for non-residents increased by only 6%.

Due largely to the high number of resident trademark applications in China, the global non-resident share of filing activity declined by about 16 percentage points, from a peak of 33.1% in 2004 to 16.9% in 2017. However, when the figures for China are excluded, the non-resident share fell by only around 8 percentage points over the same period.

Of the top 20 offices, half had non-resident filing shares of 20% or greater, with Australia (41.9%), Canada (43.5%), Switzerland (55.6%), the U.S. (30.2%) and Viet Nam (34.7%) recording the highest shares. The lowest non-resident shares were recorded at the offices of China (3.5%), France (6.5%) and the Islamic Republic of Iran (8.2%) (see figure B10). The low non-resident shares for France and other European Union (EU) member state offices can be explained by the fact that many non-resident applicants file for protection in these countries via the EUIPO.

Resident filing activity overwhelmingly drove the double-digit growth in Brazil, Canada, China, the Islamic Republic of Iran, Japan and the Russian Federation, whereas non-resident filing activity accounted for most or all of the total growth in Australia, the EUIPO and Viet Nam (see figure B11). For the U.K. and the U.S., the annual increases in filing activity by residents and non-residents were more balanced. In France, India, Italy and the Republic of Korea, declines in total filing activity can be attributed entirely or mainly to a drop in resident applications.

The list of top 20 offices in 2017 is largely similar to the 2016 list, but ranked somewhat differently. For example, the Islamic Republic of Iran was the largest mover, shifting up six places to become the fifth largest

Trademarks

The share for offices of high-income countries declined from 56.3% in 2007 to 31.6% in 2017

2.4. Trademark application class counts by income group, 2007 and 2017

Offices located in Asia accounted for 66.6% of all trademark filing activity in 2017

2.5. Trademark application class counts by region, 2007 and 2017

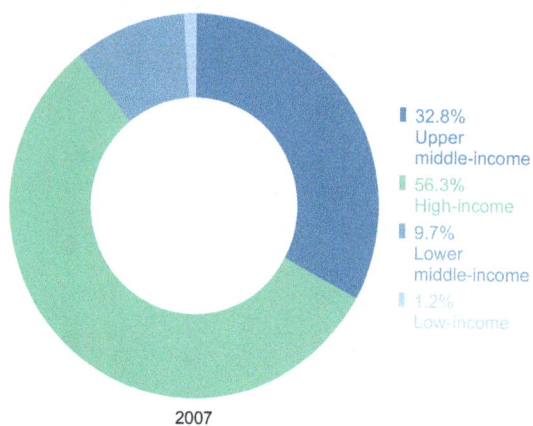

- 32.8% Upper middle-income
- 56.3% High-income
- 9.7% Lower middle-income
- 1.2% Low-income

2007

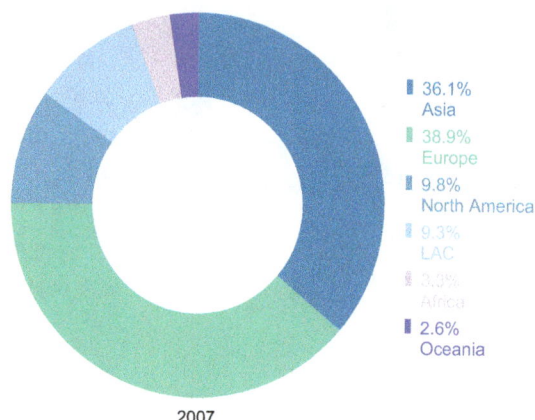

- 36.1% Asia
- 38.9% Europe
- 9.8% North America
- 9.3% LAC
- 3.3% Africa
- 2.6% Oceania

2007

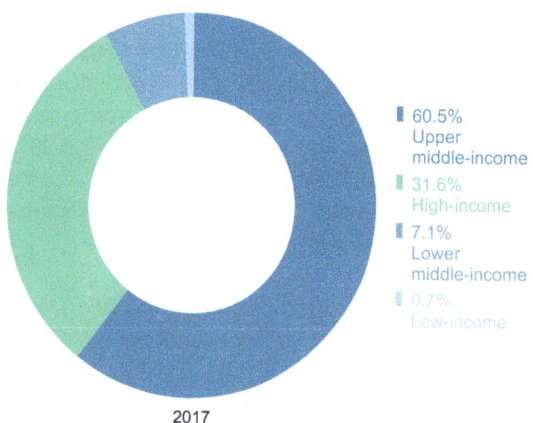

- 60.5% Upper middle-income
- 31.6% High-income
- 7.1% Lower middle-income
- 0.7% Low-income

2017

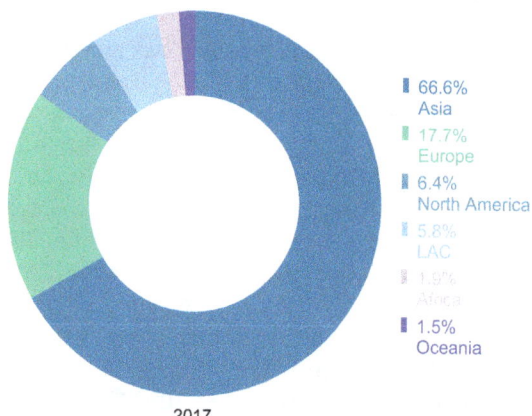

- 66.6% Asia
- 17.7% Europe
- 6.4% North America
- 5.8% LAC
- 1.9% Africa
- 1.5% Oceania

2017

Source: Table B7.

Source: Table B8.

office in terms of trademark filing activity. In addition, the Russian Federation and Switzerland moved up one spot each, to rank sixth and 17th, respectively. In contrast, France, India and the Republic of Korea each moved down two places from their previous year's rankings.

Total application class counts at offices of high-income economies grew only slightly (+2.3%) between 2007 and 2017. This is lower than the average annual growth rates for all other income groups. The highest growth (+15.2%) over this 11-year period was recorded for offices of upper middle-income countries. Offices of lower middle-income (+5%) and low-income (+3.1%) countries also saw growth over the same period.

Twelve of the top 20 offices are in high-income economies, six are in upper middle-income countries (Brazil, China, the Islamic Republic of Iran, Mexico, the Russian

Federation and Turkey) and two are in lower middle-income countries (India and Viet Nam). In 2017, the offices of high-income countries together received 31.6% of total global filing activity, down from 56.3% in 2007. In contrast, the share for offices of upper middle-income countries rose from 32.8% in 2007 to 60.5% in 2017, due to their combined high average annual growth (see figure 2.4). When China's statistics are removed from the upper middle-income group, the application class count for the other countries in this group still grew between 2007 and 2017, but at a lower rate of 4.6%. However, the combined share of the world total claimed by this group of upper middle-income countries actually decreased from 20.1% to 14.2%. The shares of total filing activity for lower middle-income (7.1% in 2017) and low-income countries (0.7%) also fell over the same period, although to a lesser extent.

Trademark filings since 1883

Trademark filings were fairly low and stable until the mid-1980s. Filings at China's office took off in the 1990s, and in 2001 they exceeded those received by that of the U.S., making China's office the largest in terms of the number of applications received. Even so, filings in the U.S. have doubled since the mid-1990s, despite declines at the end of the dot-com era in 2001 and 2002 and again during the financial crisis in 2008 and 2009. Having remained below 100,000 until 2006, India's trademark annual filings now exceed 260,000. Similar numbers of trademark applications are now filed in both Brazil and Japan, where the volumes are approaching 190,000.

Trend in trademark applications for the top five offices, 1883–2017

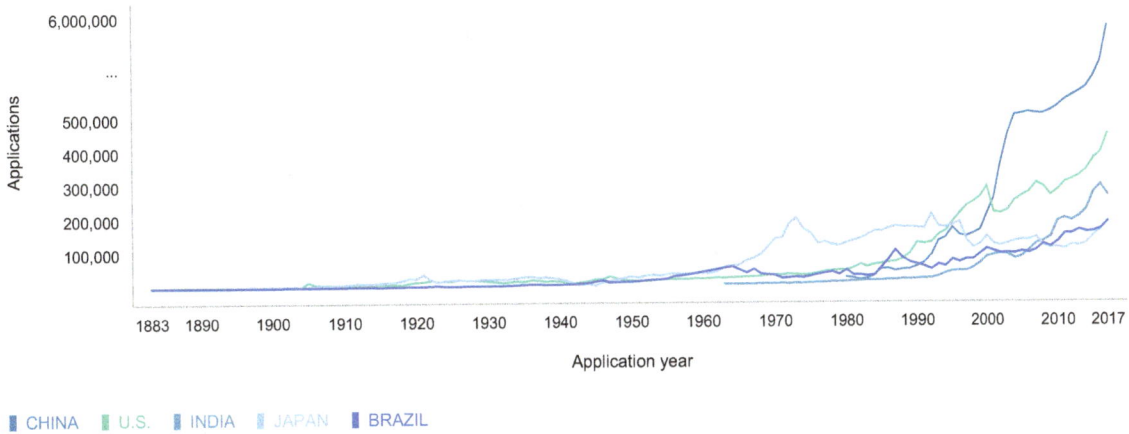

CHINA   U.S.   INDIA   JAPAN   BRAZIL

Source: Figure B9.

Trademark filing activity was concentrated in a few origins

2.6. Equivalent trademark application class counts by origin, 2017

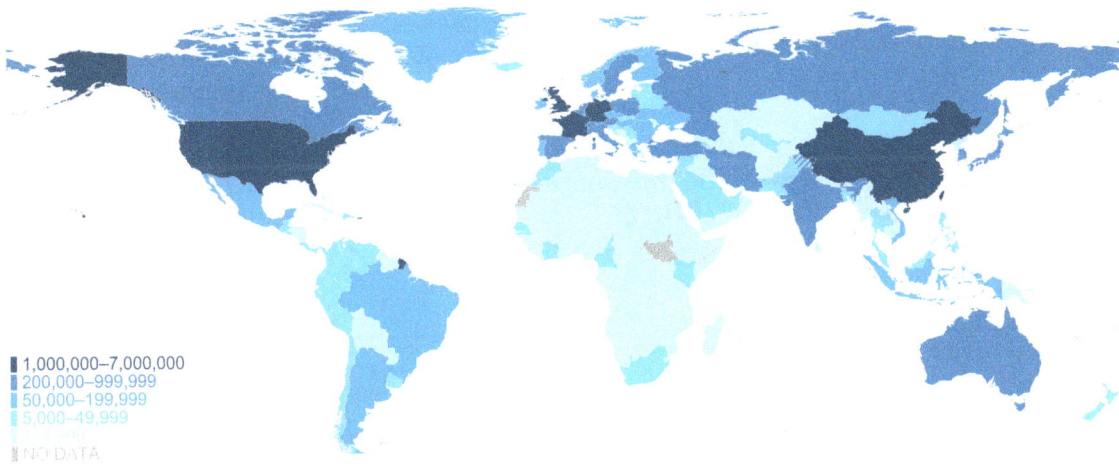

1,000,000–7,000,000
200,000–999,999
50,000–199,999
5,000–49,999
NO DATA

Source: Map B19.

Eight of the top 20 offices in 2017 were located in Europe, seven in Asia, two each in Latin America and the Caribbean (LAC) and North America, and one in Oceania. Offices in Asia accounted for 66.6% of all trademark filing activity, up from 36.1% in 2007. This partly explains the decline in overall shares for the other five geographical regions over the same period (see figure 2.5). Offices in Europe accounted for 17.7% of the world total in 2017, followed by North America (6.4%), LAC (5.8%), Africa (1.9%) and Oceania (1.5%).

Equivalent application class count

Applications at some regional IP offices are equivalent to multiple applications in the countries that are members of the organizations establishing those offices. For example, to calculate the number of equivalent applications for the EUIPO, each application is multiplied by the corresponding number of EU member states. So an application filed with the EUIPO by an applicant residing outside the EU is counted as 28 applications abroad – equivalent to the 28 member countries of the EU in 2016. An application filed by an applicant residing in an EU country is counted as one resident application and 27 applications abroad. The same multiplier is applied to the classes specified in these applications. The equivalent application class count concept is used for reporting data by origin.

German applicants continue to file the greatest number of applications abroad

Trademark applications received by offices from resident and non-resident applicants are referred to as office data, whereas applications filed by applicants at a national/regional office (resident applications) or at foreign offices (applications abroad) are referred to as origin data. Here, trademark statistics based on the origin of the residence of the applicant are reported in order to complement the picture of trademark filing activity worldwide.

In terms of filing activity abroad based on equivalent class count, a greater number of applicants from Germany than from any other origin seek protection for their trademarks outside their country, a position Germany has held since 2006. In 2017, German filing activity abroad reached an equivalent application class count of 2.11 million, followed by applicants from the U.S. (1.22 million), the U.K. (982,367) and France (868,198) (see figure B22).[1] The high equivalent class counts for applications abroad from these origins can be explained, not only by their high application class counts at numerous offices abroad, but also by their frequent use of the EUIPO – with its multiplier effect – to seek protection within the EU as a whole.

Looking at absolute counts, and so removing the EUIPO's multiplier effect, 96% of all filing activity (application class counts) by China-based applicants was in China alone, with only 4% attributed to those seeking protection abroad. The shares for resident filing and filing abroad were similar for applicants

Applicants from the U.S. were the most active foreign filers in China, Mexico and at the EUIPO.

2.7. Share of total non-resident filing activity by origin at selected offices, 2017

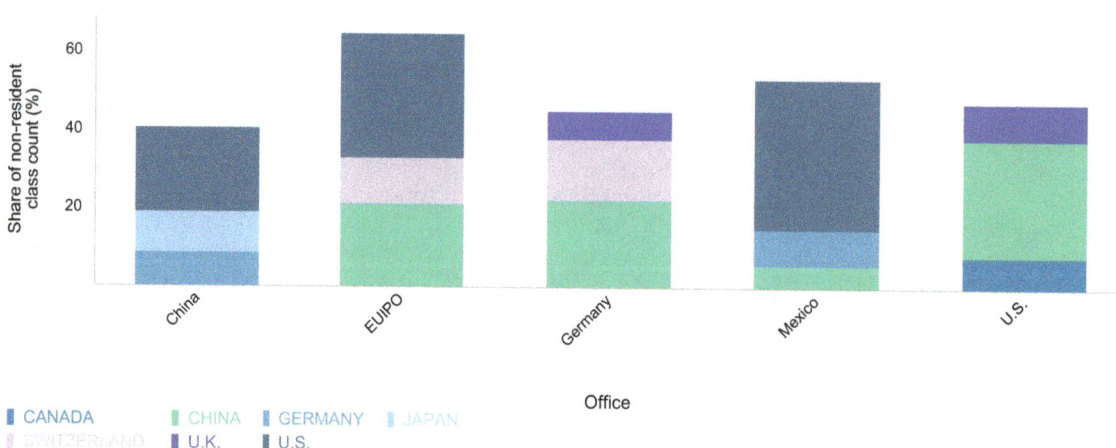

CANADA   CHINA   GERMANY   JAPAN
SWITZERLAND   U.K.   U.S.

Office

Source: Figure B25.

from Argentina, Brazil and India. Applicants residing in many other low- and middle-income countries also dedicated less than 10% of their trademark filing activity to seeking protection abroad.

Among the top 20 origins, about 72% of filing activity by Switzerland-based applicants occurred outside the country. This highest ranking share of applications abroad as a proportion of total filing activity was followed by that of applicants from the U.S. (44%), the Netherlands (43%) and Germany (42%).

Applicants from the upper middle-income countries Armenia (32%), Bulgaria (27%) and Mauritius (63%) sought protection abroad for more than one-quarter of their trademark filing activity. For the upper middle-income countries Colombia, Kyrgyzstan, the Russian Federation, South Africa and Thailand, the share was 12–17%.

When deciding where to seek trademark protection, applicants consider such factors as the appeal of various foreign markets in which to sell their goods and services, geographical proximity to these markets or well-established historical ties between the trademark holder's country of residence and the destination country. For example, 38% of all non-resident filing activity in Mexico in 2017 came from U.S. applicants, 9% from Germany and 6% from China (see figure 2.7). Applicants from China (30%) and the U.K. (9%) accounted for the largest shares of non-resident trademark filing activity in the U.S, followed by applicants from Canada (8%). In China, the three origins accounting for the largest shares of non-resident filing activity were the U.S. (21%), Japan (10%) and Germany (9%). For non-resident filing activity

at the EUIPO, applicants from the U.S. (32%), China (21%) and Switzerland (12%) constituted the largest shares.

For the second year in a row, applicants from China remained the most active foreign filers at the German IP office, accounting for 22% of application class counts in filings that the office received from abroad.

Adjusting for GDP and population

Differences in trademark filing activity across countries may reflect both the size of their economies and their level of economic development. To compare trademark filing intensity across countries, it helps to measure resident application class counts relative to GDP or population level.

When resident trademark applications are viewed as class counts and adjusted by GDP, countries with a lower number of classes specified in resident applications, such as Chile, New Zealand and Switzerland, may rank higher than some countries that otherwise show higher class counts (for example, India and the U.S.). Of selected origins, China (26,098), New Zealand (9,884), the Republic of Korea (9,798), Switzerland (8,643) and Chile (7,717) exhibited among the highest ratios of resident application class count to GDP in 2017 (see figure 2.8). China (+19,797), the U.K. (+2,020) and Brazil (+2,081) saw particularly large increases in resident application class count per unit of GDP between 2007 and 2017. In contrast, New Zealand (–1,740), Chile (–1,697) and the Republic of Korea (–1,016) saw decreases in their class count to GDP ratio over the same period.

Brazil, China and the U.K. saw large increases in resident application class count per unit of GDP between 2007 and 2017

2.8. Resident trademark application class count per USD 100 billion GDP for selected origins, 2007 and 2017

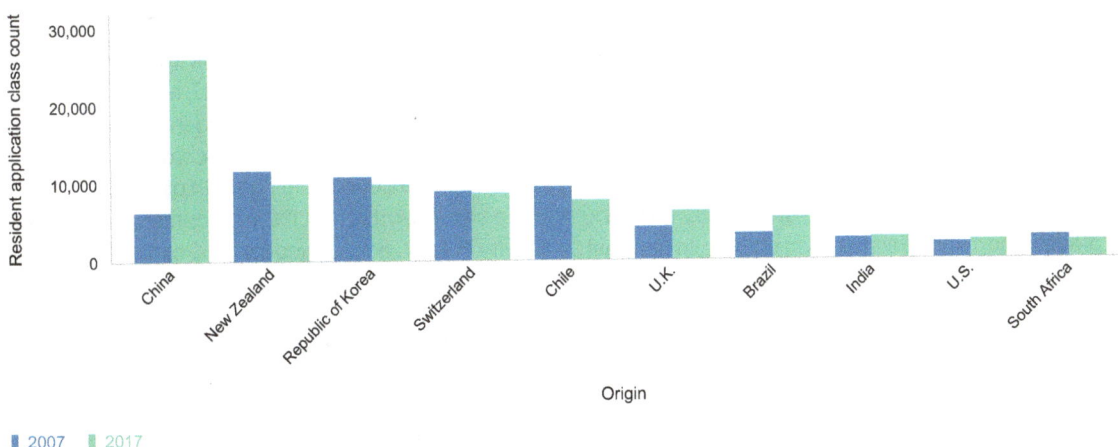

■ 2007 ■ 2017

Source: Figure B33.

Trademarks

The data reflecting application class count per million population present a somewhat different picture. Switzerland, with a population of about 8.5 million, reported a resident application class count of 4,962 per million – one of the most intensive among all countries of origin in 2017. Among other selected origins, the resident application class count per million population exceeded 3,000 for Australia (3,262), China (3,995), Germany (3,310) and the Republic of Korea (3,521). Argentina, the Russian Federation and the U.S. each had ratios of about 1,300–1,600, while the ratios for Ecuador, Serbia and Thailand were all between 400 and 500 (see figure B34).

Which classes and industries saw the most filing activity?

Trademarks are registered in relation to particular classes of goods or services. The Nice Classification of goods and services is used in the international trademark system and at certain national and regional offices. Nice Classification statistics offer insights into the relative importance of different goods and services. Service class 35 (advertising, business management, business administration and office functions) has been number one since 2004 – when complete class counts first became available – and, in 2017, was represented in 11% of all reported trademark filing activity by class. Nice class 35 is followed by goods class 25 (7%), which includes articles of clothing; goods class 9 (6.6%), which includes scientific, photographic, measuring instruments, recording equipment, computers and software; and service class 41 (5.5%), which relates to education, entertainment and sports activities (see figure B26).

The 11 service-related classes accounted for about 37% of all Nice classes specified in applications filed in 2017, up from 30% in 2004. Services classes accounted for between 31% and 35% of all filing activity in Canada, China, India and the Russian Federation, and over 50% in the offices of Brazil, France, Japan and Spain.

It is useful to group the 45 Nice classes into 10 industry sectors. Agriculture, research and technology, business services and clothing were the top four sectors in 2017, each accounting for between 13% and 18% of global reported trademark filing activity. In contrast, industries relating to chemicals (2.4%) and transportation (5.4%) accounted for the smallest shares (see figure B28). The distribution of total trademark applications across industries has remained stable for more than a decade.

Concordant with being the global top industry in terms of trademark filing activity, agriculture was the top sector at the offices of China (22%), the Islamic Republic of Iran (22%), the Republic of Korea (19%) and the Russian Federation (16%) (see figure B29). Agriculture was the second top sector in India and Turkey, accounting for between 15 and 17% of all trademark filing activity in these countries in 2017. Research and technology was the top industry sector at the EUIPO (21%) and the offices of France (20%), Japan (27%) and the U.S. (20%), but ranked third in Turkey (11%), the Republic of Korea (13%) and the Russian Federation (12%). In Turkey, business services topped the list of industry sectors, accounting for 21% of all trademark filing activity. Among the top 10, only the offices of India (20%) and the Republic of Korea (17%) listed health among their top three industry sectors for trademark filing, and only the office of the Islamic Republic of Iran (19%) included the transportation sector among its top three.

A total of 5.45 million trademark registrations were recorded worldwide in 2017

After concluding the examination process, an office may decide to register a trademark. The number of registrations issued can fluctuate greatly from year to year, due in part to the resources dedicated by offices to examining trademark applications. For this reason, it is not possible to accurately compare the number of applications filed at an office in a given year with the number of registrations issued by that office in the same year.

The estimated 5.45 million trademark registrations recorded worldwide in 2017 represent an increase of 18.2%, or 836,500 additional registrations, on the previous year's total.

Just as class counts make application activity internationally comparable, they also permit a more meaningful comparison of registrations. In 2017, an estimated 7.62 million classes were specified in trademark registrations. After the modest growth of 2.7% recorded in 2016, 2017 saw a return to double-digit growth of 16.3%. China's office saw growth of 24.1% in trademark registration activity in 2017, accounting for 51% of the total global annual increase.

China's office registered trademarks in which about 2.82 million classes were specified, followed by the offices of the U.S. (361,759), India (339,692) and the EUIPO (335,435) (see figure B17).

Along with the high annual growth in China, several other offices among the top 20 experienced large increases in registration activity, including Brazil (+23.4%), India (+68.2%), Italy (+102.2%) and the U.K. (+32.2%). In contrast, the offices of Canada (–18.6%) and Turkey (–5.4%) saw the most significant declines among the top 20.

Active trademarks increased by 9.7%

Unlike most forms of IP, trademarks can be maintained indefinitely by payment of renewal fees at defined time intervals. In 2017, there were an estimated 43.2 million active trademark registrations at 138 offices worldwide, representing an increase of 9.7% on 2016 figures.

Once again, the office of China accounted for the greatest number of trademark registrations in force in 2017, with about 14.92 million – a 20.6% increase on its 2016 total. It was followed by the offices of the U.S. (2.19 million), Japan (1.87 million) and India (1.61 million). With between 1 million and 1.25 million trademark registrations in force each, the EUIPO and the offices of Brazil, Mexico and the Republic of Korea also recorded high numbers of active trademarks. Germany (940,991) had almost the same number of trademark registrations in force as Turkey (945,154), while Argentina (830,640) and France (840,000) also had similar figures (see figure B38).

About 15.2 million trademark registrations in force at 66 offices in 2017 can be distributed according to the year in which they were initially registered. This represents 57% of the total of approximately 26.5 million trademark registrations recorded at these offices between 1991 and 2017.

About one-fifth of these trademarks registered in 1991 remained in force in 2017, reflecting the enduring value of marks. For those registered in 2007 and later, the percentage rises above 50%. Almost half of these 15.2 million registrations in force have a recent registration date, dating back only to 2012.

Demand for Madrid international trademark registrations continues to grow

To obtain trademark protection in multiple countries or jurisdictions, applicants can either file their applications directly at each individual office – known as the "Paris route" – or file an application for international registration through the Madrid System – the "Madrid route" (see the glossary). In 2017, the Madrid System offered trademark holders the ability to obtain protection for their branded products and services in an area covering a total of 116 countries.

Madrid international applications[2] totaled 57,139 in 2017, up 6.7% on 2016, marking the eighth consecutive year of growth. In fact, since 2004 the number of applications has increased in all but one year, which coincided with the economic downturn in 2009. This prevailing growth is due partly to the expanding membership of the Madrid System and partly to a general upward trend in trademark application volumes worldwide.

For the fourth year in a row, the U.S. remained the largest user of the Madrid System. International applications filed by applicants located in the U.S. reached 7,889 (see figure B49). These were followed by applications from Germany (7,319), China (6,066) and France (4,260). Applicants domiciled in China filed about 2,200 more Madrid applications in 2017 than in 2016, which translated to a high growth rate of 57.8% and allowed China to surpass France to become the third largest origin of Madrid applications.

The EU (22,914) attracted the highest number of designations in international Madrid applications in 2017, edging slightly ahead of China (22,565), which was last year's top destination for international trademark registrations. The U.S. (21,990) ranked third. Madrid applicants sought to extend protection for their marks to the 28 EU member countries as a whole more than to any other Madrid member jurisdiction. Middle-income countries, including the Russian Federation (15,322), India (12,124) and Mexico (9,388) were also among the top 10 destinations for international trademark registration via the Madrid System. For further information and statistics, see the *Madrid Yearly Review 2018*.

1. Equivalent application class counts differ from absolute class counts, which are presented in figure B20 and do not take into the account the multiplying effect of regional offices.
2. Due to continual updating of statistics, figures for Madrid applications and designations published in this report have been revised from their values presented in the *Madrid Yearly Review 2018*.

Trademark applications and registrations worldwide

B1. Trend in trademark applications worldwide, 2004–2017

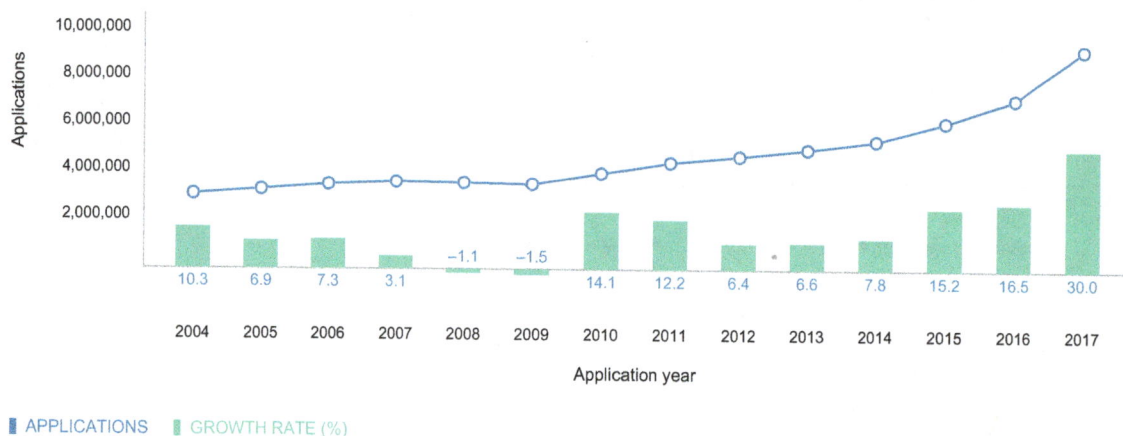

	2004	2005	2006	2007	2008	2009	2010	2011	2012	2013	2014	2015	2016	2017
Growth rate	10.3	6.9	7.3	3.1	−1.1	−1.5	14.1	12.2	6.4	6.6	7.8	15.2	16.5	30.0

Application year

▌ APPLICATIONS ▌ GROWTH RATE (%)

Note: World totals are WIPO estimates using data covering 164 IP offices. Each total includes the number of applications filed directly with national and regional offices (the "Paris route") as well as the number of designations received by offices via the Madrid System (where applicable).

Source: WIPO Statistics Database, September 2018.

B2. Trend in trademark application class counts worldwide, 2004–2017

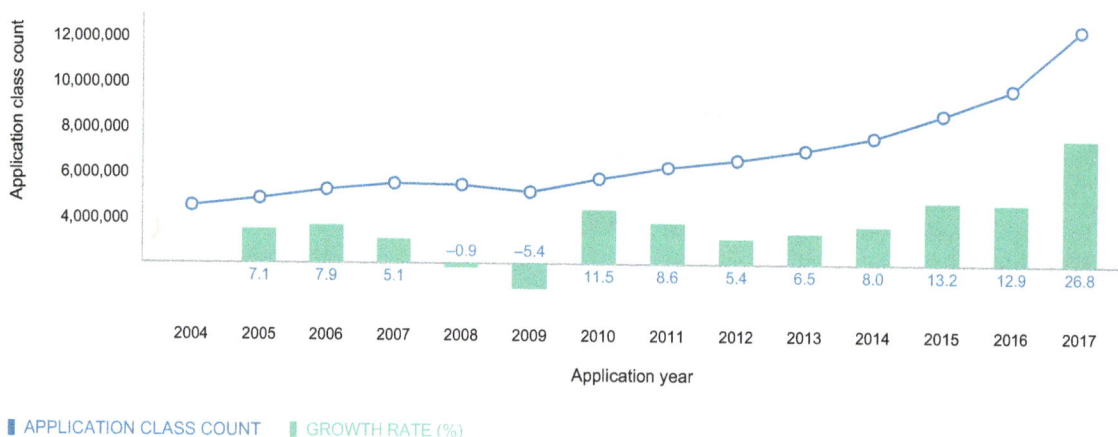

	2004	2005	2006	2007	2008	2009	2010	2011	2012	2013	2014	2015	2016	2017
Growth rate		7.1	7.9	5.1	−0.9	−5.4	11.5	8.6	5.4	6.5	8.0	13.2	12.9	26.8

Application year

▌ APPLICATION CLASS COUNT ▌ GROWTH RATE (%)

Note: World totals are WIPO estimates using data covering 164 IP offices. These totals include class counts in applications filed directly with national and regional offices (the "Paris route") as well as class counts in designations received by offices via the Madrid System (where applicable). See the glossary for the definition of class count.

Source: WIPO Statistics Database, September 2018.

Trademarks

B3. Resident and non-resident trademark application class counts worldwide, 2004–2017

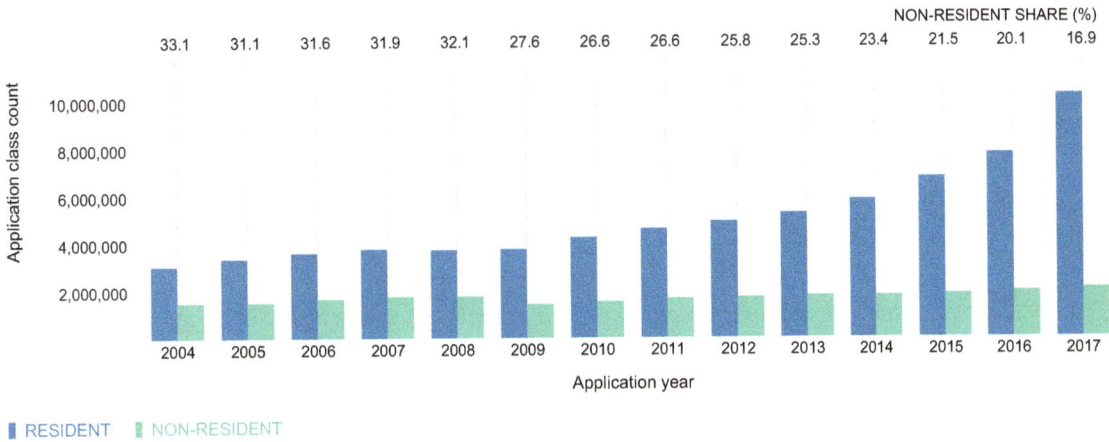

NON-RESIDENT SHARE (%)

| 33.1 | 31.1 | 31.6 | 31.9 | 32.1 | 27.6 | 26.6 | 26.6 | 25.8 | 25.3 | 23.4 | 21.5 | 20.1 | 16.9 |

Application class count

| 10,000,000 |
| 8,000,000 |
| 6,000,000 |
| 4,000,000 |
| 2,000,000 |

2004 2005 2006 2007 2008 2009 2010 2011 2012 2013 2014 2015 2016 2017

Application year

■ RESIDENT ■ NON-RESIDENT

Note: World totals are WIPO estimates using data covering 164 IP offices. These totals include class counts in applications filed directly with national and regional offices (the "Paris route") as well as class counts in designations received by offices via the Madrid System (where applicable). See the glossary for definitions of class count, resident and non-resident.

Source: WIPO Statistics Database, September 2018.

B4. Trend in trademark registrations worldwide, 2004–2017

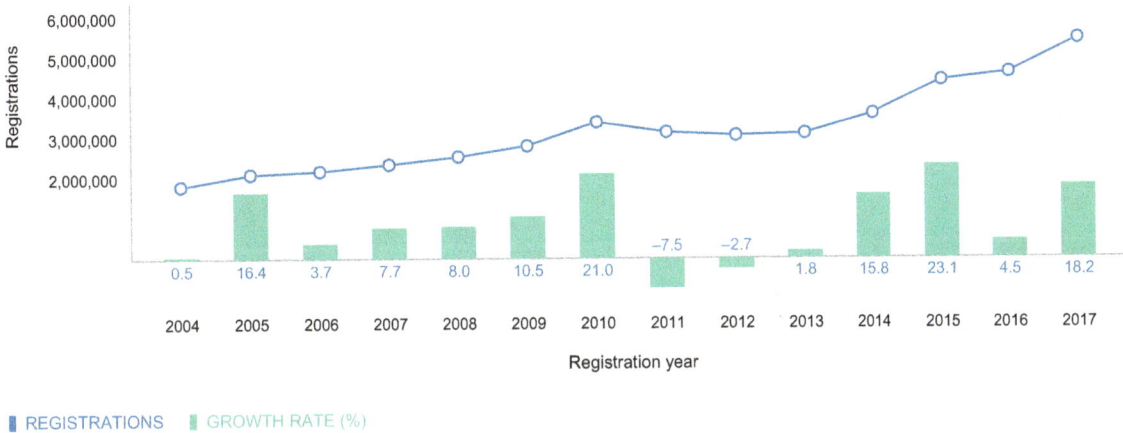

Registrations

| 6,000,000 |
| 5,000,000 |
| 4,000,000 |
| 3,000,000 |
| 2,000,000 |

| 0.5 | 16.4 | 3.7 | 7.7 | 8.0 | 10.5 | 21.0 | −7.5 | −2.7 | 1.8 | 15.8 | 23.1 | 4.5 | 18.2 |

2004 2005 2006 2007 2008 2009 2010 2011 2012 2013 2014 2015 2016 2017

Registration year

■ REGISTRATIONS ■ GROWTH RATE (%)

Note: World totals are WIPO estimates using data covering 163 IP offices. Each total includes the number of registrations issued by national and regional offices for applications filed directly with offices (the "Paris route") as well as the number of designations received by offices via the Madrid System (where applicable).

Source: WIPO Statistics Database, September 2018.

Trademarks

Trademarks

B5. Trend in trademark registration class counts worldwide, 2004–2017

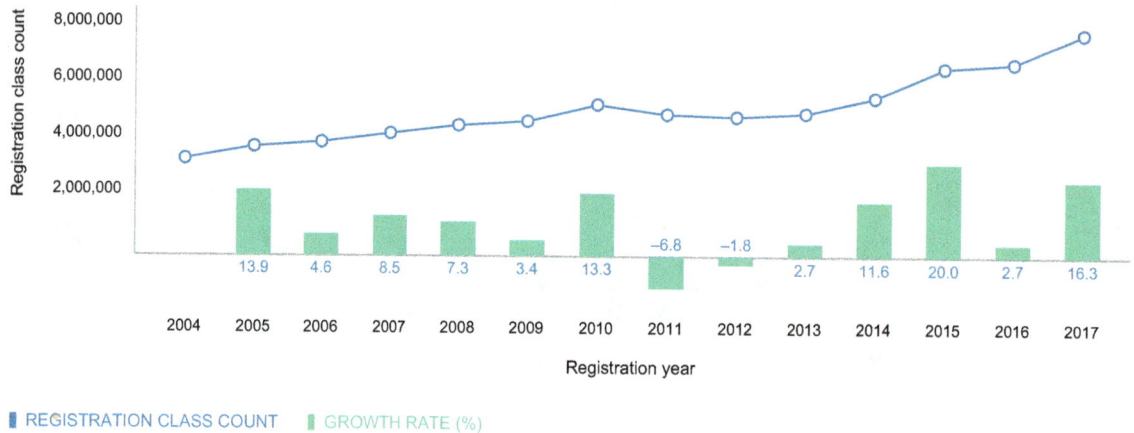

Registration class count

	2004	2005	2006	2007	2008	2009	2010	2011	2012	2013	2014	2015	2016	2017
Growth rate		13.9	4.6	8.5	7.3	3.4	13.3	−6.8	−1.8	2.7	11.6	20.0	2.7	16.3

Registration year

▌ REGISTRATION CLASS COUNT   ▌ GROWTH RATE (%)

Note: World totals are WIPO estimates using data covering 163 IP offices. These totals include class counts in registrations issued by national and regional offices for applications filed directly with offices (the "Paris route") as well as designations received by offices via the Madrid System (where applicable). See the glossary for the definition of class count.

Source: WIPO Statistics Database, September 2018.

B6. Resident and non-resident trademark registration class counts worldwide, 2004–2017

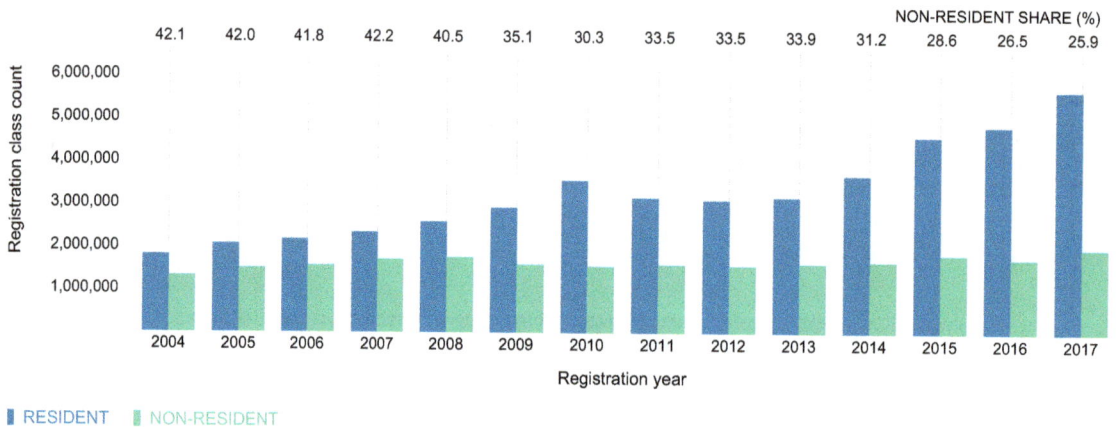

NON-RESIDENT SHARE (%)

	2004	2005	2006	2007	2008	2009	2010	2011	2012	2013	2014	2015	2016	2017
Non-resident share	42.1	42.0	41.8	42.2	40.5	35.1	30.3	33.5	33.5	33.9	31.2	28.6	26.5	25.9

Registration class count

Registration year

▌ RESIDENT   ▌ NON-RESIDENT

Note: World totals are WIPO estimates using data covering 163 IP offices. These totals include class counts in registrations issued by national and regional offices for applications filed directly with offices (the "Paris route") as well as for designations received by offices via the Madrid System (where applicable). See the glossary for definitions of class count, resident and non-resident.

Source: WIPO Statistics Database, September 2018.

Trademark applications and registrations by office

B7. Trademark application class counts by income group, 2007 and 2017

Income group	Application class count		Resident share (%)		Share of world total (%)		Average growth (%)
	2007	2017	2007	2017	2007	2017	2007–2017
High-income	3,126,400	3,916,400	68.7	71.1	56.3	31.6	2.3
Upper middle-income	1,822,400	7,499,800	70.7	91.3	32.8	60.5	15.2
Upper middle-income without China	*1,117,500*	*1,760,000*	*61.2*	*74.4*	*20.1*	*14.2*	*4.6*
Lower middle-income	539,800	879,100	59.6	66.2	9.7	7.1	5.0
Low-income	67,900	92,300	40.1	44.2	1.2	0.7	3.1
World	**5,556,500**	**12,387,600**	**68.1**	**83.1**	**100.0**	**100.0**	**8.3**

Note: Totals by income group are WIPO estimates using data covering 164 IP offices. Each category includes the following number of offices: high-income (62), upper middle-income (46), lower middle-income (35) and low-income (21). Data for the European Union Intellectual Property Office are allocated to the high-income group because most EU member states are high-income countries. For similar reasons, data for the African Regional Intellectual Property Organization and the African Intellectual Property Organization are allocated to the low-income group. For information on income group classification, see the data description section.

Source: WIPO Statistics Database, September 2018.

B8. Trademark application class counts by region, 2007 and 2017

Region	Application class count		Resident share (%)		Share of world total (%)		Average growth (%)
	2007	2017	2007	2017	2007	2017	2007–2017
Africa	185,000	240,300	41.9	48.2	3.3	1.9	2.6
Asia	2,005,300	8,252,600	72.6	89.5	36.1	66.6	15.2
Europe	2,158,900	2,194,600	66.9	74.4	38.9	17.7	0.2
Latin America and the Caribbean	518,200	715,900	62.9	69.0	9.3	5.8	3.3
North America	543,400	797,700	73.1	66.7	9.8	6.4	3.9
Oceania	145,700	186,500	57.2	52.3	2.6	1.5	2.5
World	**5,556,500**	**12,387,600**	**68.1**	**83.1**	**100.0**	**100.0**	**8.3**

Note: Totals by geographical region are WIPO estimates using data covering 164 IP offices. Each region includes the following number of offices: Africa (34), Asia (45), Europe (42), Latin America and the Caribbean (36), North America (2) and Oceania (5).

Source: WIPO Statistics Database, September 2018.

B9. Trend in trademark applications for the top five offices, 1883–2017

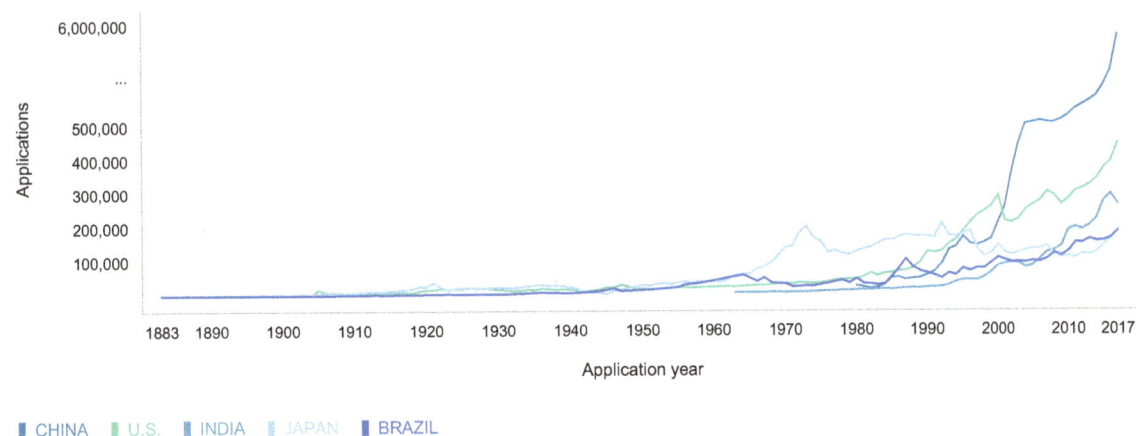

CHINA   U.S.   INDIA   JAPAN   BRAZIL

Note: Data are based on the numbers of applications filed; that is, differences between single-class and multi-class filing systems across IP offices are not taken into account. The top five offices were selected based on their 2017 totals.

Source: WIPO Statistics Database, September 2018.

Trademarks

B10. Trademark application class counts for the top 20 offices, 2017

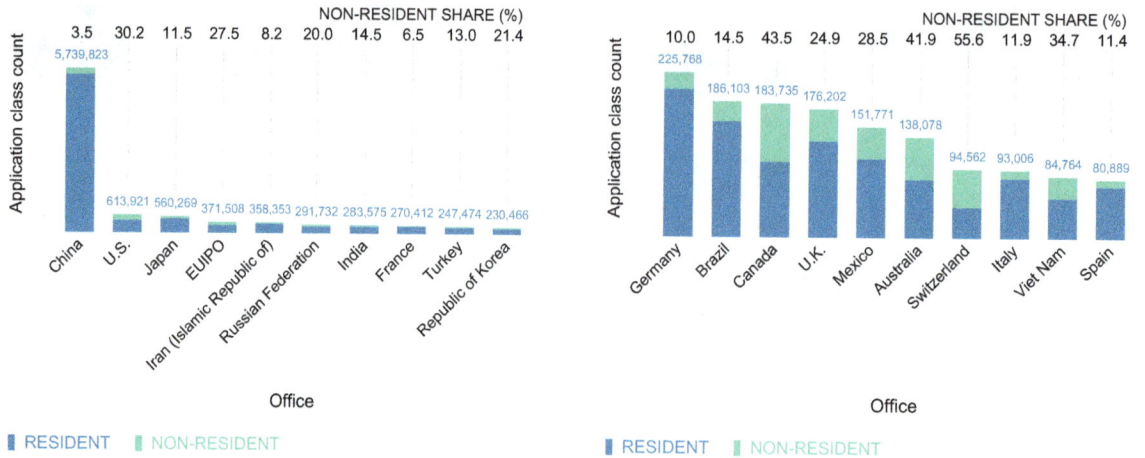

NON-RESIDENT SHARE (%)

3.5	30.2	11.5	27.5	8.2	20.0	14.5	6.5	13.0	21.4

Application class count

5,739,823 (China)

613,921 (U.S.) 560,269 (Japan) 371,508 (EUIPO) 358,353 (Iran (Islamic Republic of)) 291,732 (Russian Federation) 283,575 (India) 270,412 (France) 247,474 (Turkey) 230,466 (Republic of Korea)

Office

■ RESIDENT ■ NON-RESIDENT

NON-RESIDENT SHARE (%)

10.0	14.5	43.5	24.9	28.5	41.9	55.6	11.9	34.7	11.4

Application class count

225,768 (Germany) 186,103 (Brazil) 183,735 (Canada) 176,202 (U.K.) 151,771 (Mexico) 138,078 (Australia) 94,562 (Switzerland) 93,006 (Italy) 84,764 (Viet Nam) 80,889 (Spain)

Office

■ RESIDENT ■ NON-RESIDENT

Note: EUIPO is the European Union Intellectual Property Office.

Source: WIPO Statistics Database, September 2018.

B11. Contribution of resident and non-resident application class counts to total growth for the top 20 offices, 2016–2017

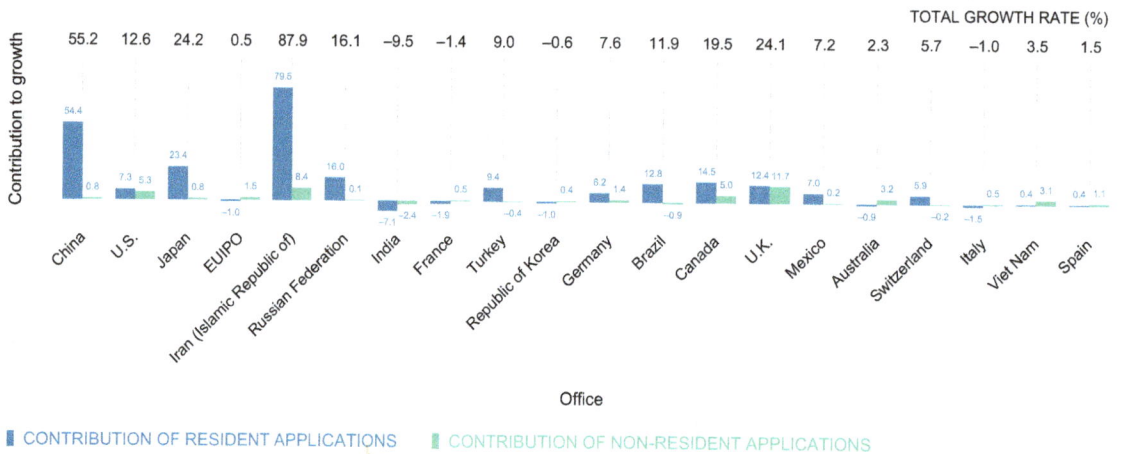

TOTAL GROWTH RATE (%)

55.2	12.6	24.2	0.5	87.9	16.1	−9.5	−1.4	9.0	−0.6	7.6	11.9	19.5	24.1	7.2	2.3	5.7	−1.0	3.5	1.5

Contribution to growth

China 54.4 / 0.8; U.S. 7.3 / 5.3; Japan 23.4 / 0.8; EUIPO −1.0 / 1.5; Iran (Islamic Republic of) 79.5 / 8.4; Russian Federation 16.0 / 0.1; India −7.1 / −2.4; France −1.9 / 0.5; Turkey 9.4 / −0.4; Republic of Korea −1.0 / 0.4; Germany 8.2 / 1.4; Brazil 12.8 / −0.9; Canada 14.5 / 5.0; U.K. 12.4 / 11.7; Mexico 7.0 / 0.2; Australia −0.9 / 3.2; Switzerland 5.9 / −0.2; Italy −1.5 / 0.5; Viet Nam 0.4 / 3.1; Spain 0.4 / 1.1

Office

■ CONTRIBUTION OF RESIDENT APPLICATIONS ■ CONTRIBUTION OF NON-RESIDENT APPLICATIONS

Note: EUIPO is the European Union Intellectual Property Office. This figure shows, for each office, the total growth or decrease in application class counts, broken down by the respective contributions of resident and non-resident filing activity. For example, the total number of classes specified in trademark applications in the U.S. grew by 12.6%. Growth in resident filing activity accounted for 7.3 percentage points of this increase, whereas the remaining 5.3 percentage points came from non-resident filing activity.

Source: WIPO Statistics Database, September 2018.

B12. Trademark application class counts for offices of selected low- and middle-income countries, 2017

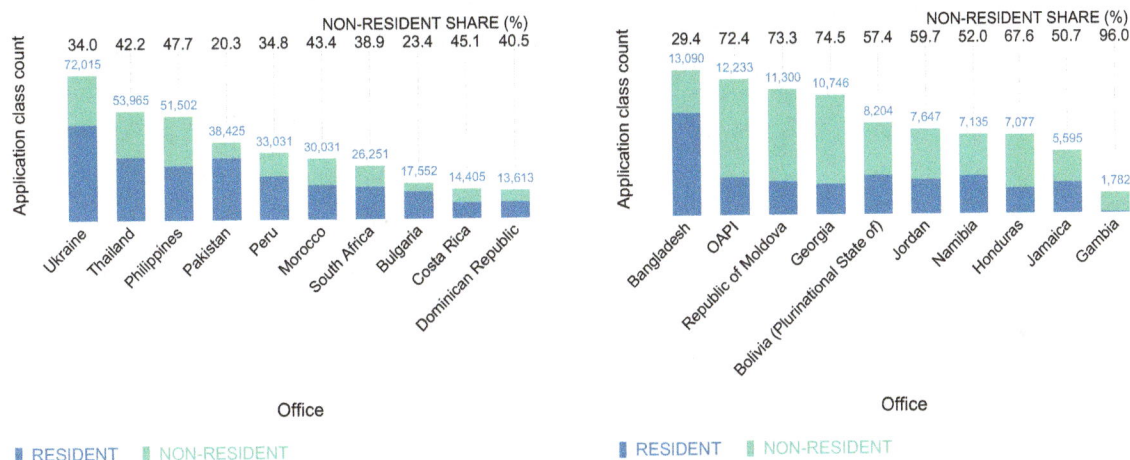

NON-RESIDENT SHARE (%)

| | 34.0 | 42.2 | 47.7 | 20.3 | 34.8 | 43.4 | 38.9 | 23.4 | 45.1 | 40.5 |

Ukraine 72,015
Thailand 53,965
Philippines 51,502
Pakistan 38,425
Peru 33,031
Morocco 30,031
South Africa 26,251
Bulgaria 17,552
Costa Rica 14,405
Dominican Republic 13,613

NON-RESIDENT SHARE (%)

| | 29.4 | 72.4 | 73.3 | 74.5 | 57.4 | 59.7 | 52.0 | 67.6 | 50.7 | 96.0 |

Bangladesh 13,090
OAPI 12,233
Republic of Moldova 11,300
Georgia 10,746
Bolivia (Plurinational State of) 8,204
Jordan 7,647
Namibia 7,135
Honduras 7,077
Jamaica 5,595
Gambia 1,782

Office

■ RESIDENT ■ NON-RESIDENT

■ RESIDENT ■ NON-RESIDENT

Note: The selected offices are from different world regions and income groups (low-income, lower middle-income and upper middle-income). OAPI is the African Intellectual Property Organization, which receives applications on behalf of its 17 member states. Where available, data for all offices are presented in statistical table B51 at the end of this section.

Source: WIPO Statistics Database, September 2018.

B13. Contribution of resident and non-resident application class counts to total growth for offices of selected low- and middle-income countries, 2016–2017

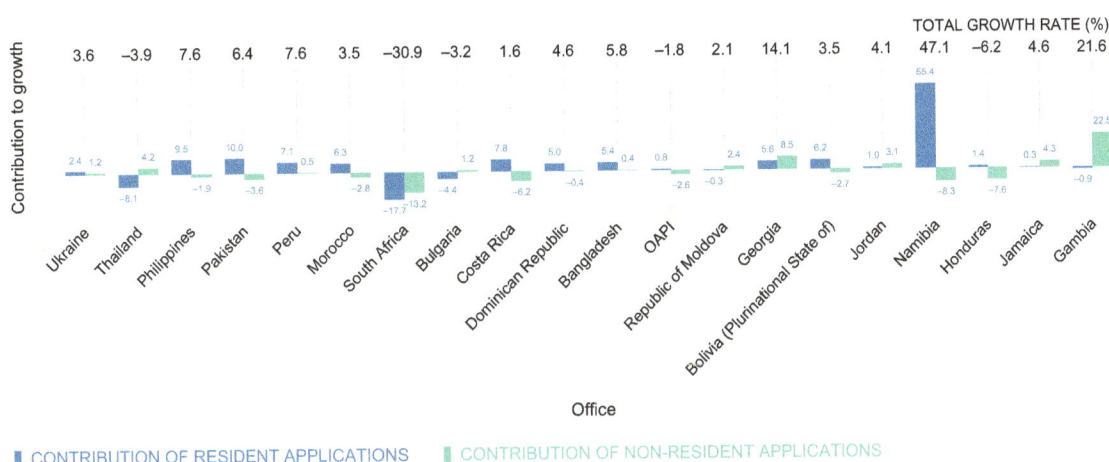

TOTAL GROWTH RATE (%)

| 3.6 | −3.9 | 7.6 | 6.4 | 7.6 | 3.5 | −30.9 | −3.2 | 1.6 | 4.6 | 5.8 | −1.8 | 2.1 | 14.1 | 3.5 | 4.1 | 47.1 | −6.2 | 4.6 | 21.6 |

Ukraine, Thailand, Philippines, Pakistan, Peru, Morocco, South Africa, Bulgaria, Costa Rica, Dominican Republic, Bangladesh, OAPI, Republic of Moldova, Georgia, Bolivia (Plurinational State of), Jordan, Namibia, Honduras, Jamaica, Gambia

Office

■ CONTRIBUTION OF RESIDENT APPLICATIONS   ■ CONTRIBUTION OF NON-RESIDENT APPLICATIONS

Note: The selected offices are from different world regions and income groups (low-income, lower middle-income and upper middle-income). OAPI is the African Intellectual Property Organization, which receives applications on behalf of its 17 member states. Where available, data for all offices are presented in statistical table B51 at the end of this section. This figure shows, for each office, the total growth or decrease in application class counts, broken down by the respective contributions of resident and non-resident applications. For example, the total number of classes specified in trademark applications at the IP office of Ukraine grew by 3.6%. Growth in resident filing activity accounted for 2.4 percentage points of this increase, whereas the remaining 1.2 percentage points came from non-resident filing activity.

Source: WIPO Statistics Database, September 2018.

Trademarks

B14. Trademark registration class counts by income group, 2007 and 2017

Income group	Registration class count		Resident share (%)		Share of world total (%)		Average growth (%)
	2007	2017	2007	2017	2007	2017	2007–2017
High-income	2,394,500	2,782,300	60.9	64.1	59.4	36.5	1.5
Upper middle-income	1,155,400	4,019,900	57.4	84.4	28.7	52.8	13.3
Upper middle-income without China	*877,500*	*1,202,400*	*51.1*	*61.3*	*21.8*	*15.8*	*3.2*
Lower middle-income	423,800	740,700	46.0	60.7	10.5	9.7	5.7
Low-income	55,600	76,000	22.1	22.1	1.4	1.0	3.2
World	**4,029,300**	**7,618,900**	**57.8**	**74.1**	**100.0**	**100.0**	**6.6**

Note: Totals by income group are WIPO estimates using data covering 163 IP offices. Each category includes the following number of offices: high-income (62), upper middle-income (46), lower middle-income (34) and low-income (21). Data for the European Union Intellectual Property Office are allocated to the high-income group because most EU member states are high-income countries. For similar reasons, data for the African Regional Intellectual Property Organization and the African Intellectual Property Organization are allocated to the low-income group. For information on income group classification, see the data description section.

Source: WIPO Statistics Database, September 2018.

B15. Trademark registration class counts by region, 2007 and 2017

Region	Registration class count		Resident share (%)		Share of world total (%)		Average growth (%)
	2007	2017	2007	2017	2007	2017	2007–2017
Africa	136,100	194,100	29.5	29.9	3.4	2.5	3.6
Asia	1,232,900	4,486,000	58.0	82.5	30.6	58.9	13.8
Europe	1,789,400	1,789,300	58.1	68.1	44.4	23.5	0.0
Latin America and the Caribbean	460,000	546,000	62.2	58.8	11.4	7.2	1.7
North America	319,500	439,700	63.0	61.3	7.9	5.8	3.2
Oceania	91,400	163,800	51.0	45.2	2.3	2.1	6.0
World	**4,029,300**	**7,618,900**	**57.8**	**74.1**	**100.0**	**100.0**	**6.6**

Note: Totals by geographical region are WIPO estimates based on data covering 163 offices. Each region includes the following number of offices: Africa (33), Asia (45), Europe (42), Latin America and the Caribbean (36), North America (2) and Oceania (5).

Source: WIPO Statistics Database, September 2018.

B16. Trend in trademark registrations for the top five offices, 1883–2017

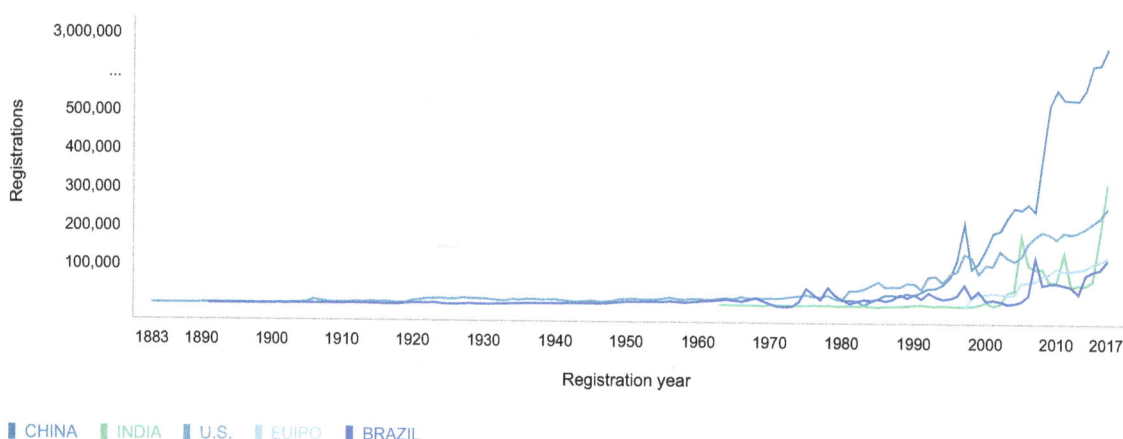

CHINA   INDIA   U.S.   EUIPO   BRAZIL

Note: EUIPO is the European Union Intellectual Property Office. Data are based on the numbers of registrations recorded; that is, differences between single-class and multi-class registration systems across IP offices are not taken into account. The top five offices were selected based on their 2017 totals.

Source: WIPO Statistics Database, September 2018.

B17. Trademark registration class counts for the top 20 offices, 2017

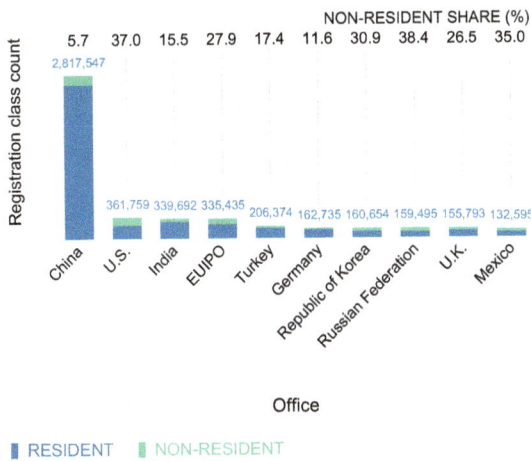

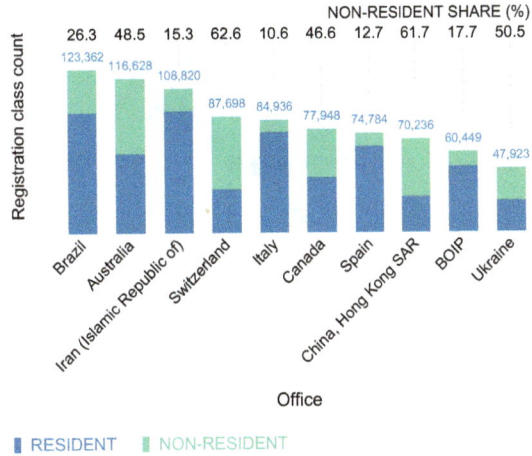

Note: EUIPO is the European Union Intellectual Property Office and BOIP is the Benelux Office for Intellectual Property. Figures for the office of France are not presented here because the data are not available. On the basis of an examination, a registration may be issued for a trademark application. The number of registrations issued may fluctuate greatly from one year to the next, in part reflecting the resources that IP offices dedicate to examining trademark applications.

Source: WIPO Statistics Database, September 2018.

B18. Trademark registration class counts for offices of selected low- and middle-income countries, 2017

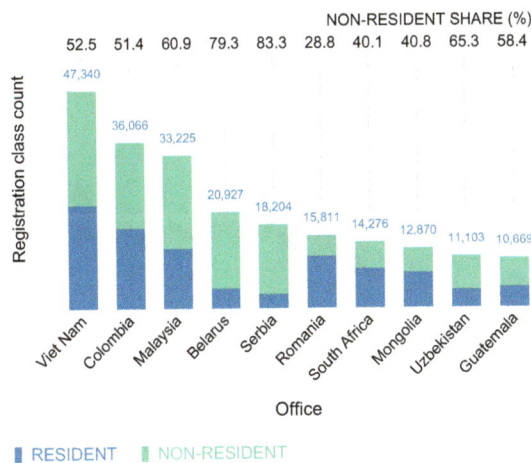

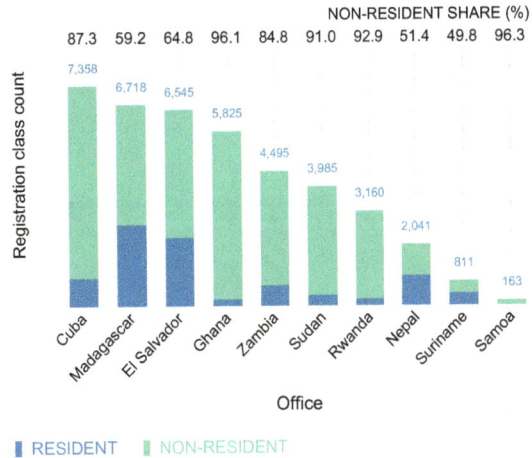

Note: The selected offices are from different world regions and income groups (low-income, lower middle-income and upper middle-income). Where available, data for all offices are presented in statistical table B52 at the end of this section.

Source: WIPO Statistics Database, September 2018.

Trademark applications by origin

B19. Equivalent trademark application class counts by origin, 2017

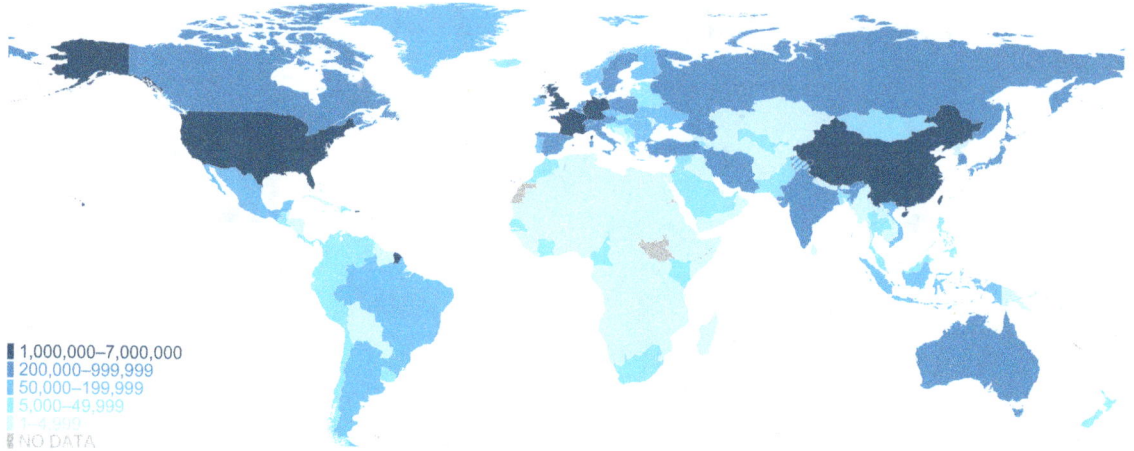

- 1,000,000–7,000,000
- 200,000–999,999
- 50,000–199,999
- 5,000–49,999
- NO DATA

Note: Trademark filing activity by origin includes the number of classes specified in resident applications and in applications filed abroad. The origin of a trademark application is determined by the residence of the applicant. Applications filed at regional offices are considered equivalent to multiple applications in the relevant member states and the classes specified in these applications are multiplied accordingly. See the glossary for the definition of equivalent application.

Source: WIPO Statistics Database, September 2018.

B20. Trademark application class counts for the top 20 origins, 2017

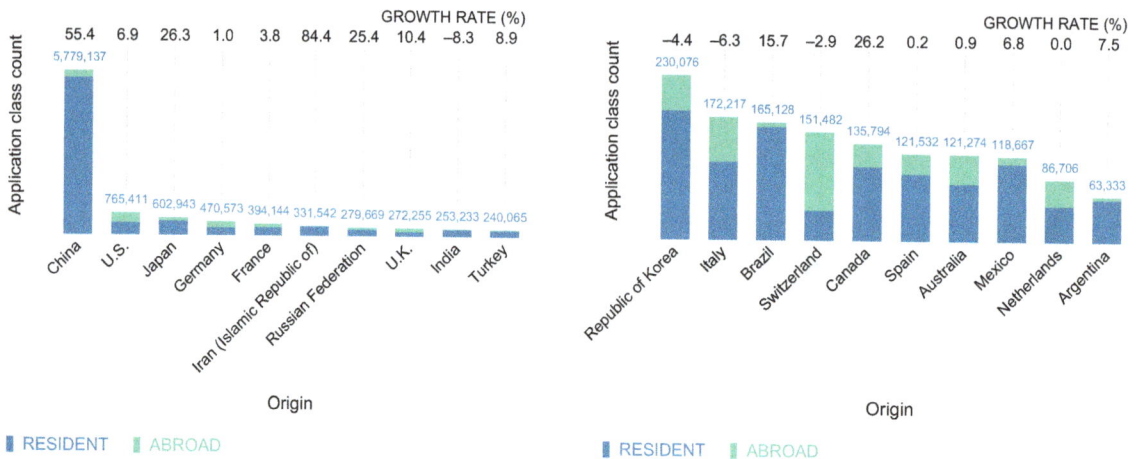

GROWTH RATE (%)
55.4 6.9 26.3 1.0 3.8 84.4 25.4 10.4 −8.3 8.9

China	U.S.	Japan	Germany	France	Iran (Islamic Republic of)	Russian Federation	U.K.	India	Turkey
5,779,137	765,411	602,943	470,573	394,144	331,542	279,669	272,255	253,233	240,065

GROWTH RATE (%)
−4.4 −6.3 15.7 −2.9 26.2 0.2 0.9 6.8 0.0 7.5

Republic of Korea	Italy	Brazil	Switzerland	Canada	Spain	Australia	Mexico	Netherlands	Argentina
230,076	172,217	165,128	151,482	135,794	121,532	121,274	118,667	86,706	63,333

Origin

RESIDENT   ABROAD

Note: In this figure, trademark application filing activity by origin includes the number of classes specified in resident applications and in applications filed abroad and is based on absolute count, not equivalent count. The origin of a trademark application is determined by the residence of the applicant. An application filed at a regional office is considered a resident filing if the applicant is a resident of one of the relevant member states.

Source: WIPO Statistics Database, September 2018.

B21. Trademark application class counts for selected low- and middle-income origins, 2017

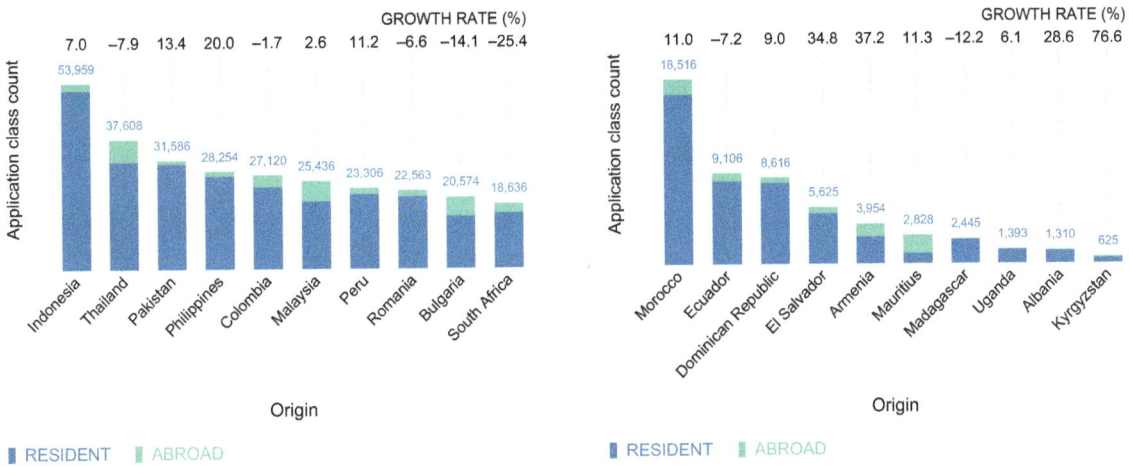

GROWTH RATE (%)

| 7.0 | −7.9 | 13.4 | 20.0 | −1.7 | 2.6 | 11.2 | −6.6 | −14.1 | −25.4 |

Application class count

- Indonesia: 53,959
- Thailand: 37,608
- Pakistan: 31,586
- Philippines: 28,254
- Colombia: 27,120
- Malaysia: 25,436
- Peru: 23,306
- Romania: 22,563
- Bulgaria: 20,574
- South Africa: 18,636

Origin

■ RESIDENT ■ ABROAD

GROWTH RATE (%)

| 11.0 | −7.2 | 9.0 | 34.8 | 37.2 | 11.3 | −12.2 | 6.1 | 28.6 | 76.6 |

Application class count

- Morocco: 18,516
- Ecuador: 9,106
- Dominican Republic: 8,616
- El Salvador: 5,625
- Armenia: 3,954
- Mauritius: 2,828
- Madagascar: 2,445
- Uganda: 1,393
- Albania: 1,310
- Kyrgyzstan: 625

Origin

■ RESIDENT ■ ABROAD

Note: In this figure, trademark application filing activity by origin includes the number of classes specified in resident applications and in applications filed abroad and is based on absolute count, not equivalent count. The origin of a trademark application is determined by the residence of the applicant. The selected origins are from different world regions and income groups (low-income, lower middle-income and upper middle-income). Where available, data for all origins are presented in statistical table B51 at the end of this section.

Source: WIPO Statistics Database, September 2018.

B22. Trademark application class counts abroad for the top 20 origins, 2017

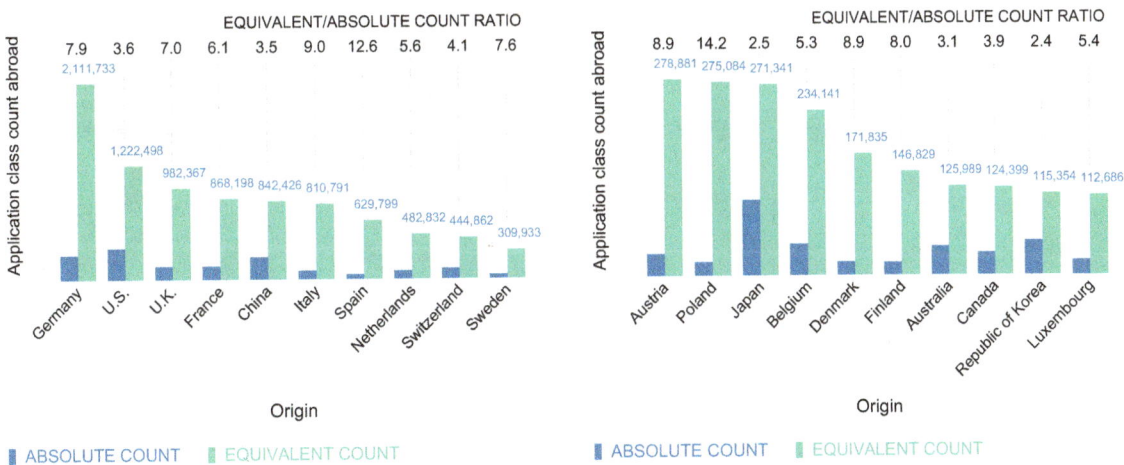

EQUIVALENT/ABSOLUTE COUNT RATIO

| 7.9 | 3.6 | 7.0 | 6.1 | 3.5 | 9.0 | 12.6 | 5.6 | 4.1 | 7.6 |

Application class count abroad

- Germany: 2,111,733
- U.S.: 1,222,498
- U.K.: 982,367
- France: 868,198
- China: 842,426
- Italy: 810,791
- Spain: 629,799
- Netherlands: 482,832
- Switzerland: 444,862
- Sweden: 309,933

Origin

■ ABSOLUTE COUNT ■ EQUIVALENT COUNT

EQUIVALENT/ABSOLUTE COUNT RATIO

| 8.9 | 14.2 | 2.5 | 5.3 | 8.9 | 8.0 | 3.1 | 3.9 | 2.4 | 5.4 |

Application class count abroad

- Austria: 278,881
- Poland: 275,084
- Japan: 271,341
- Belgium: 234,141
- Denmark: 171,835
- Finland: 146,829
- Australia: 125,989
- Canada: 124,399
- Republic of Korea: 115,354
- Luxembourg: 112,686

Origin

■ ABSOLUTE COUNT ■ EQUIVALENT COUNT

Note: This figure distinguishes between absolute counts and equivalent counts for filing activity abroad – that is, resident applications are excluded. Based on equivalent application class counts, applicants from Germany had the highest level of trademark filing activity abroad. This was due not only to their high application class counts at numerous foreign offices, but also to their frequent use of the European Union Intellectual Property Office (EUIPO) – with its multiplier effect – to seek trademark protection within the entire EU. See the glossary for the definition of equivalent application. The origin of a trademark application is determined by the residence of the applicant.

Source: WIPO Statistics Database, September 2018.

Trademarks

Trademarks

B23. Trademark application class counts for the top 25 offices and origins, 2017

Origin	Office												
	China	U.S.	Japan	EUIPO	Iran (Islamic Republic of)	Russian Federation	India	France	Turkey	Republic of Korea	Germany	Brazil	Canada
Argentina	147	292	11	126	7	16	6	6	3	9	3	406	22
Australia	7,553	6,372	1,332	3,115	174	451	949	170	181	909	198	194	1,873
Brazil	369	875	71	487	33	41	30	11	14	34	8	159,192	124
Canada	3,396	15,126	541	3,399	117	373	239	130	168	645	231	358	103,776
China	5,539,086	55,370	11,786	21,537	3,912	5,084	4,873	3,335	2,136	6,803	4,993	1,561	4,841
France	9,253	7,694	3,922	26,672	2,641	4,046	2,290	252,960	2,223	2,803	1,217	1,843	3,992
Germany	17,267	14,093	6,177	70,497	4,563	8,270	5,372	1,380	6,264	4,345	203,252	2,483	5,010
India	470	1,148	140	575	167	387	242,483	31	123	89	40	110	280
Indonesia	676	87	30	30	9	12	24	3	3	56	15	4	11
Iran (Islamic Republic of)	336	41	20	121	329,107	95	77	18	139	23	49	3	25
Italy	6,870	5,140	2,438	27,589	2,224	3,428	1,410	437	1,794	1,808	357	1,009	1,798
Japan	20,651	7,857	496,092	5,920	872	1,964	2,124	586	1,076	7,105	478	1,144	2,692
Mexico	634	2,003	72	499	18	91	98	29	32	87	55	362	297
Netherlands	3,875	3,358	1,083	13,720	447	1,235	994	558	1,010	774	834	582	1,610
Poland	844	704	146	9,825	200	668	171	62	187	148	262	29	126
Republic of Korea	15,931	4,393	3,280	2,376	469	916	508	146	491	181,218	168	462	978
Russian Federation	3,135	1,318	339	1,246	894	233,430	845	547	861	560	814	64	199
Spain	2,235	2,436	753	22,191	701	987	484	438	485	437	310	547	644
Sweden	2,423	2,671	1,182	10,325	502	980	732	40	572	887	109	395	1,172
Switzerland	7,291	6,454	3,479	12,051	1,403	3,410	2,044	2,247	2,009	2,480	3,479	1,463	2,683
Turkey	834	1,115	201	1,960	2,265	1,003	364	422	215,220	145	728	36	147
U.K.	15,314	17,083	3,706	32,103	986	3,008	2,720	936	1,705	2,570	1,599	1,206	8,727
U.S.	43,034	428,225	15,221	32,132	1,657	7,058	7,936	1,502	4,841	10,627	1,450	8,528	34,209
Ukraine	260	422	25	426	35	888	41	119	146	17	276	16	83
Viet Nam	281	209	108	50	53	64	68	35	31	145	44	7	30
Others	37,658	29,435	8,114	72,536	4,897	13,827	6,693	4,264	5,760	5,742	4,799	4,099	8,386
Total	**5,739,823**	**613,921**	**560,269**	**371,508**	**358,353**	**291,732**	**283,575**	**270,412**	**247,474**	**230,466**	**225,768**	**186,103**	**183,735**

Origin	Office											
	U.K.	Mexico	Australia	Switzerland	Italy	Viet Nam	Spain	China, Hong Kong SAR	Argentina	Ukraine	Indonesia	BOIP
Argentina	14	227	13		10	5	33	7	59,669	1	2	5
Australia	2,385	357	80,230	224	87	612	64	1,127	106	116	321	92
Brazil	65	386	77	33	9	12	14	28	573	17	26	5
Canada	770	719	1,164	214	27	132	21	436	151	67	96	128
China	6,243	2,494	6,502	1,896	1,943	3,824	1,420	12,134	771	1,722	2,559	1,030
France	2,159	2,148	2,381	5,941	1,341	1,540	1,420	1,684	941	1,681	596	2,419
Germany	3,665	3,931	4,822	19,441	1,199	2,184	936	2,209	1,103	3,240	745	1,425
India	390	111	333	60	45	184	40	100	78	237	177	39
Indonesia	19	16	30		4	96	3	65	5	2	51,918	5
Iran (Islamic Republic of)	24	8	27	63	21	20	12	12		48	2	2
Italy	645	1,250	1,393	2,706	81,926	698	292	989	431	1,069	274	185
Japan	1,932	1,376	2,471	1,153	388	3,956	296	5,319	520	518	2,122	197
Mexico	74	108,590	92	61	32	17	104	128	485	31	16	16
Netherlands	795	752	1,059	1,414	215	494	240	513	256	520	342	36,078
Poland	111	86	159	188	44	101	57	44	38	762	20	50
Republic of Korea	389	766	998	232	138	2,232	69	1,619	158	247	885	36
Russian Federation	630	282	232	465	576	736	426	85	28	2,122	40	358
Spain	251	2,000	595	558	201	217	71,649	291	697	302	113	99
Sweden	372	489	1,046	1,320	15	291	20	399	200	244	124	60
Switzerland	2,277	2,272	2,443	42,009	1,279	948	815	1,368	924	1,614	539	910
Turkey	519	156	242	279	404	128	309	96	10	582	68	464
U.K.	132,300	1,657	5,780	2,331	334	875	407	2,295	645	900	617	1,099
U.S.	10,598	16,448	15,620	5,309	694	3,958	851	7,564	4,100	2,054	2,655	642
Ukraine	106	25	41	104	124	20	102	9	1	47,531	1	57
Viet Nam	42	37	73	14	20	55,313	22	51	6	21	50	19
Others	9,427	5,188	10,255	8,547	1,930	6,171	1,267	37,949	2,826	6,367	3,800	21,785
Total	**176,202**	**151,771**	**138,078**	**94,562**	**93,006**	**84,764**	**80,889**	**76,521**	**74,722**	**72,015**	**68,108**	**67,205**

Note: EUIPO is the European Union Intellectual Property Office and BOIP is the Benelux Office for Intellectual Property. The office and origin data shown here consist of absolute application class counts rather than equivalent application class counts.

Source: WIPO Statistics Database, September 2018.

Trademarks

B24. Flows of non-resident trademark application class counts between selected top origins and offices, 2017

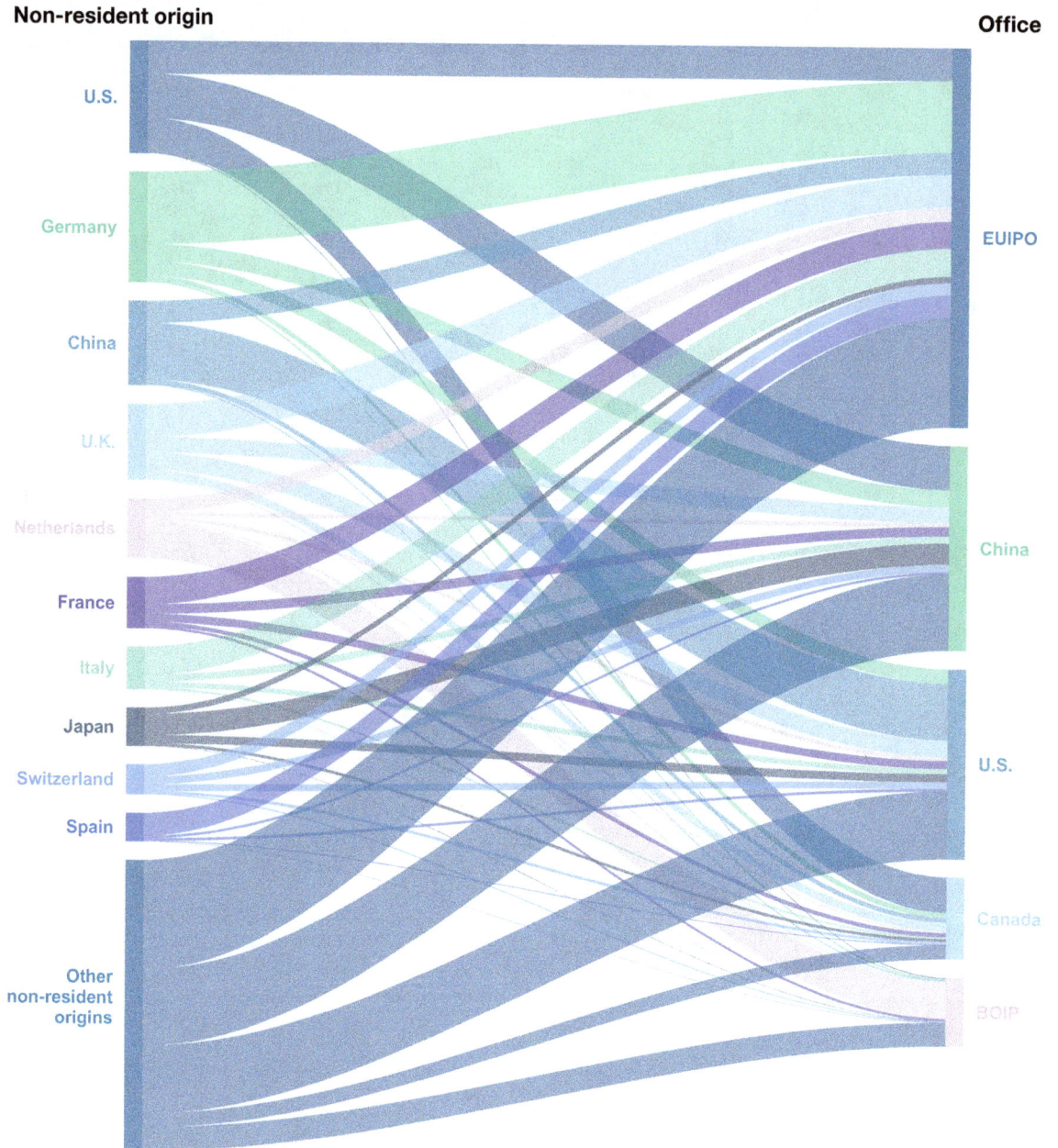

Non-resident origin

Trademarks

Office

U.S.

Germany

China

U.K.

Netherlands

France

Italy

Japan

Switzerland

Spain

Other
non-resident
origins

EUIPO

China

U.S.

Canada

BOIP

Note: EUIPO is the European Union Intellectual Property Office and BOIP is the Benelux Office for Intellectual Property. The office and non-resident origin data shown here consist of absolute application class counts rather than equivalent application class counts.

Source: WIPO Statistics Database, September 2018.

B25. Distribution of trademark application class counts for the top 15 offices and selected non-resident origins, 2017

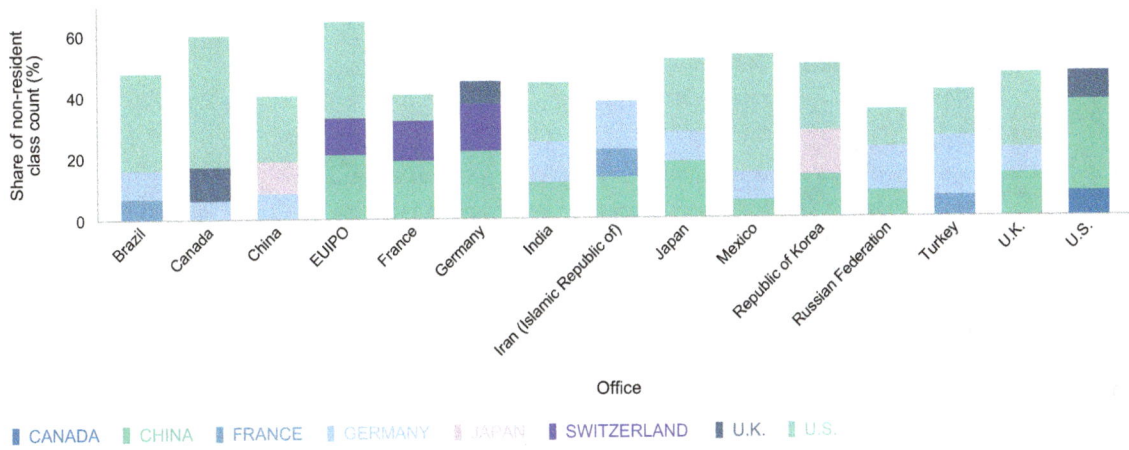

Note: EUIPO is the European Union Intellectual Property Office. The office and origin data shown here consist of absolute application class counts rather than equivalent application class counts.

Source: WIPO Statistics Database, September 2018.

Trademark applications by Nice class and industry sector

B26. Distribution of trademark applications by top Nice classes, 2017

Rank		Class	Class share (%)
1	35	Advertising, business management, business administration and office functions	11.0
2	25	Clothing, footwear, headgear	7.0
3	9	Scientific, photographic, measuring instruments; recording equipment; computers and software	6.6
4	41	Education, entertainment, and sporting activities	5.5
5	30	Coffee, tea, cocoa, rice, flour, bread, pastry and confectionery, sugar, honey, yeast, salt, mustard, vinegar, sauces (condiments) and spices	4.8
6	42	Scientific and technological services, design and development of computer hardware and software	4.3
7	5	Pharmaceutical preparations, baby food, dietary supplements for humans and animals, disinfectants, fungicides and herbicides	4.0
8	43	Services for providing food and drink; temporary accommodation	3.9
9	3	Bleaching preparations and other substances for laundry use; cleaning and abrasive preparations; soaps, perfumery and cosmetics	3.5
10	29	Foodstuffs of animal origin and vegetables	3.4
		Remaining classes	**46.0**

Note: These figures are based on filing data from 131 IP offices. Some classes listed are abbreviated. See *www.wipo.int/classifications/nice* for a complete list of all classes.

Source: WIPO Statistics Database, September 2018.

B27. Trademark applications by goods and services classes, 2017

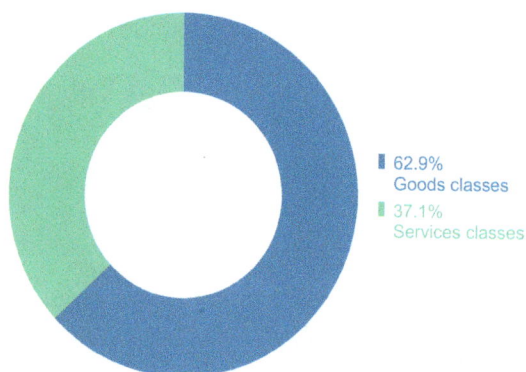

62.9%
Goods classes

37.1%
Services classes

Note: In the 45-class Nice Classification, the first 34 classes indicate goods and the remaining 11 refer to services. See *www.wipo.int/classifications/nice* for a complete list of all classes. These figures are based on filing data from 131 IP offices.

Source: WIPO Statistics Database, September 2018.

B28. Trademark applications by industry sector, 2017

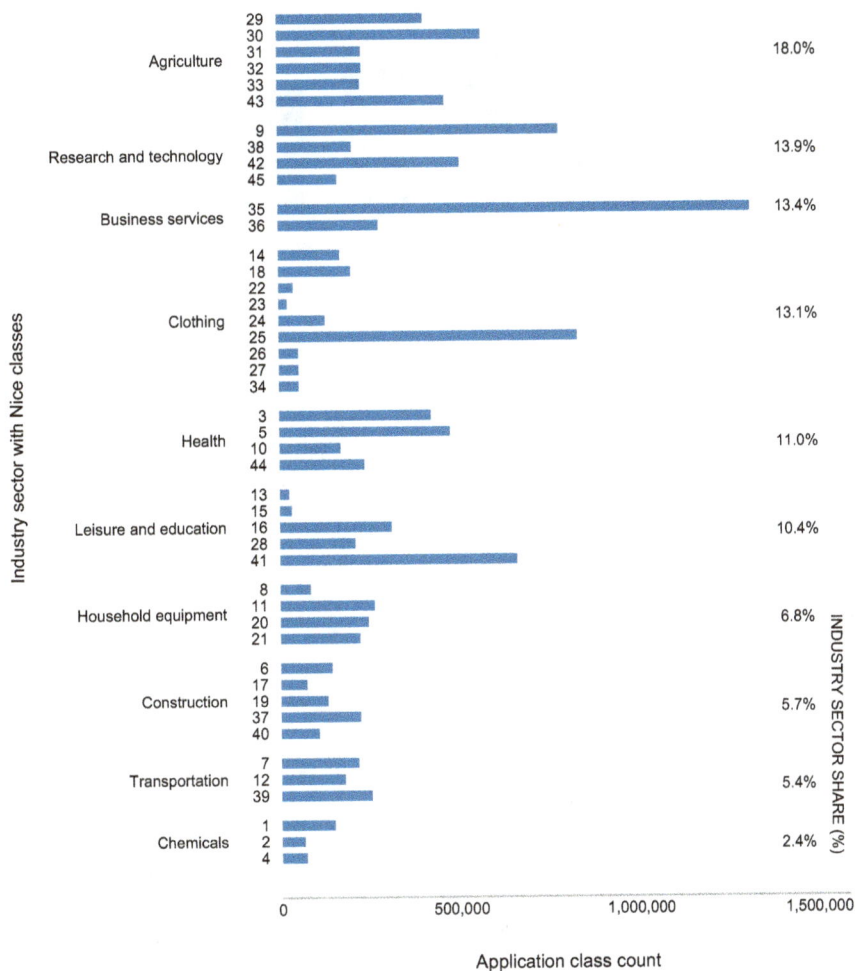

Industry sector with Nice classes

Sector	Nice classes	Industry sector share (%)
Agriculture	29, 30, 31, 32, 33, 43	18.0%
Research and technology	9, 38, 42, 45	13.9%
Business services	35, 36	13.4%
Clothing	14, 18, 22, 23, 24, 25, 26, 27, 34	13.1%
Health	3, 5, 10, 44	11.0%
Leisure and education	13, 15, 16, 28, 41	10.4%
Household equipment	8, 11, 20, 21	6.8%
Construction	6, 17, 19, 37, 40	5.7%
Transportation	7, 12, 39	5.4%
Chemicals	1, 2, 4	2.4%

Application class count

INDUSTRY SECTOR SHARE (%)

Note: Industry sectors based on class groups are those defined by Edital. Some industry sectors are abbreviated. See annex B for full definitions and composition of Nice goods and services classes. These figures are based on filing data from 131 IP offices.

Source: WIPO Statistics Database, September 2018.

Trademarks

Trademarks

B29. Trademark applications by top three sectors at the top offices, 2017

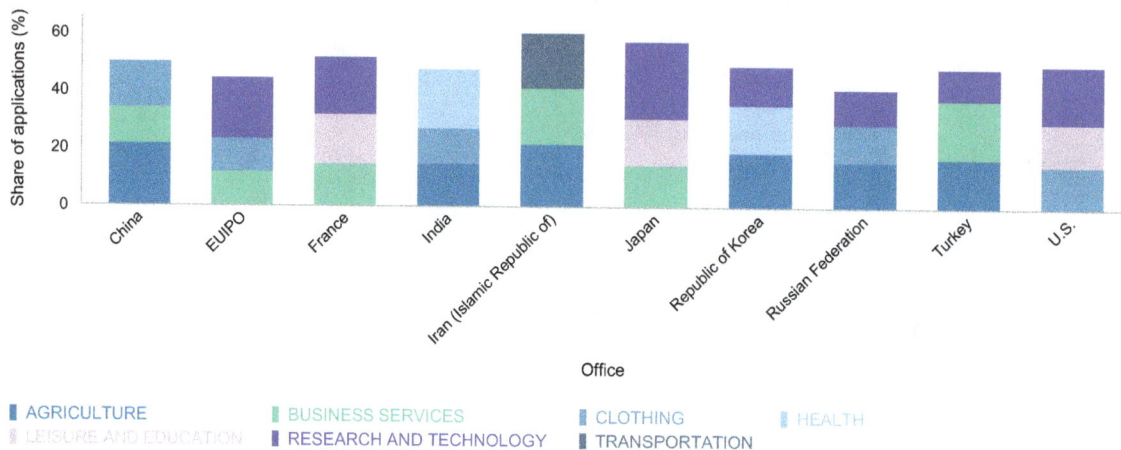

Share of applications (%) — vertical axis: 0, 20, 40, 60

Offices (horizontal axis): China, EUIPO, France, India, Iran (Islamic Republic of), Japan, Republic of Korea, Russian Federation, Turkey, U.S.

Office

■ AGRICULTURE ■ BUSINESS SERVICES ■ CLOTHING ■ HEALTH
■ LEISURE AND EDUCATION ■ RESEARCH AND TECHNOLOGY ■ TRANSPORTATION

Note: EUIPO is the European Union Intellectual Property Office. Industry sectors based on class groups are those defined by Edital. Some industry sectors are abbreviated. See *www.wipo.int/classifications/nice* for a complete list of all classes. The top three sectors and top offices were selected based on their 2017 totals.

Source: WIPO Statistics Database, September 2018.

B30. Distribution of trademark applications by goods and services at the top offices, 2017

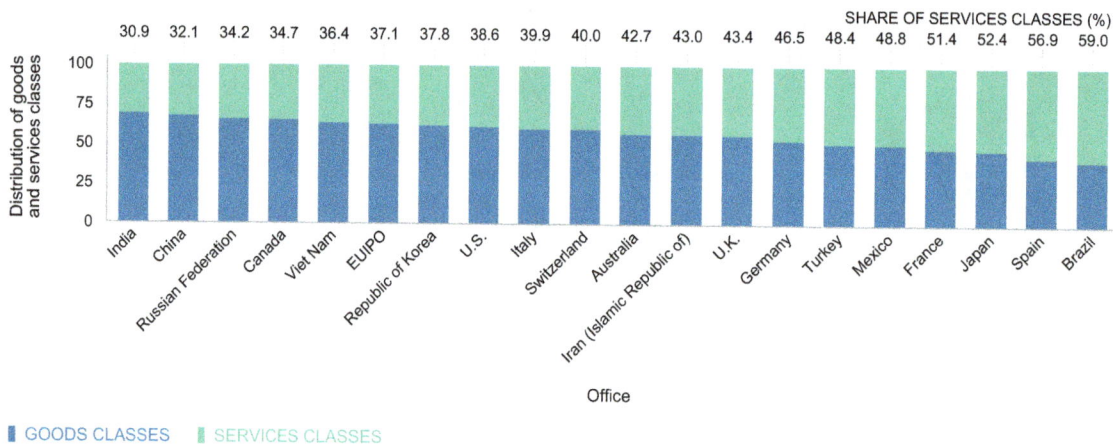

SHARE OF SERVICES CLASSES (%)

30.9 32.1 34.2 34.7 36.4 37.1 37.8 38.6 39.9 40.0 42.7 43.0 43.4 46.5 48.4 48.8 51.4 52.4 56.9 59.0

Distribution of goods and services classes — vertical axis: 0, 25, 50, 75, 100

Offices (horizontal axis): India, China, Russian Federation, Canada, Viet Nam, EUIPO, Republic of Korea, U.S., Italy, Switzerland, Australia, Iran (Islamic Republic of), U.K., Germany, Turkey, Mexico, France, Japan, Spain, Brazil

Office

■ GOODS CLASSES ■ SERVICES CLASSES

Note: EUIPO is the European Union Intellectual Property Office.
Source: WIPO Statistics Database, September 2018.

B31. Trademark applications by top three sectors for the top origins, 2017

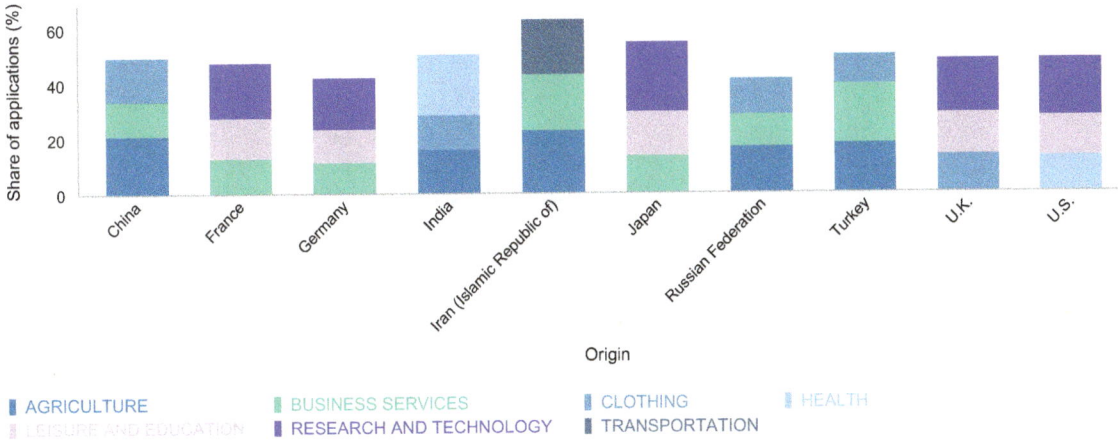

Note: Industry sectors based on class groups are those defined by Edital. Some industry sectors are abbreviated. See annex B for full definitions. The top three sectors and top origins were selected based on their 2017 totals.

Source: WIPO Statistics Database, September 2018.

B32. Distribution of trademark applications by goods and services for the top origins, 2017

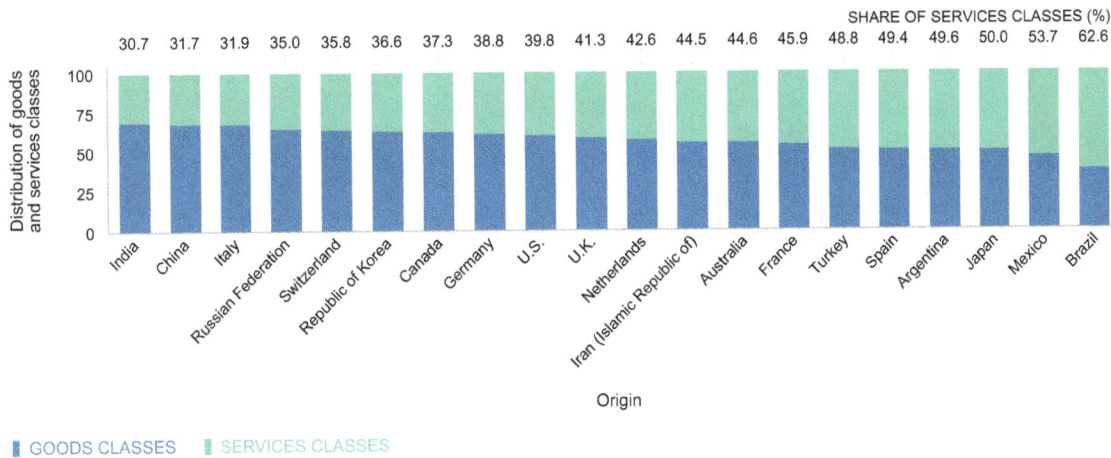

Source: WIPO Statistics Database, September 2018.

Trademarks

Trademark application class count in relation to GDP and population

B33. Resident trademark application class count per USD 100 billion GDP for selected origins, 2007 and 2017

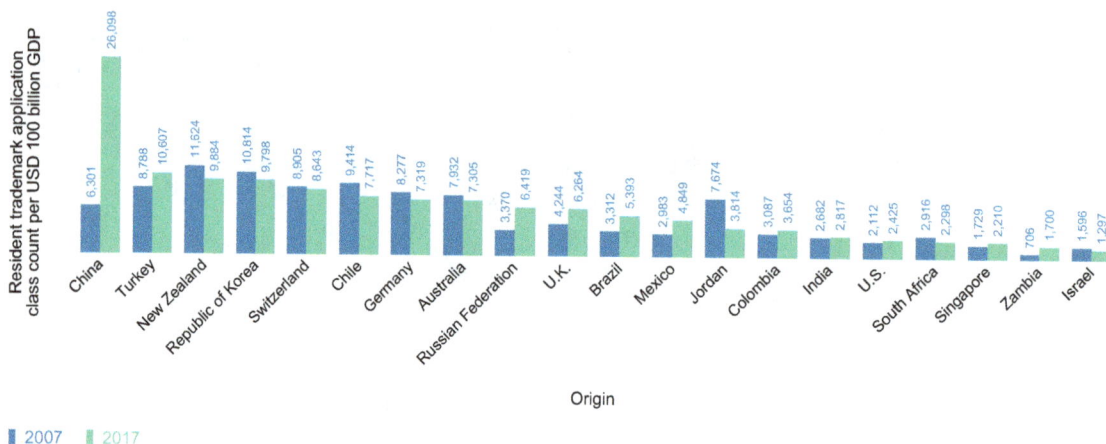

Resident trademark application class count per USD 100 billion GDP

Origin	2007	2017
China	6,301	26,098
Turkey	8,788	10,607
New Zealand	11,624	9,884
Republic of Korea	10,814	9,798
Switzerland	8,905	8,643
Chile	9,414	7,717
Germany	8,277	7,319
Australia	7,932	7,305
Russian Federation	3,370	6,419
U.K.	4,244	6,264
Brazil	3,312	5,393
Mexico	2,983	4,849
Jordan	7,674	3,814
Colombia	3,087	3,654
India	2,682	2,817
U.S.	2,112	2,425
South Africa	2,916	2,298
Singapore	1,729	2,210
Zambia	706	1,700
Israel	1,596	1,297

■ 2007 ■ 2017

Note: GDP data are in constant 2011 U.S. PPP dollars. This figure does not provide an overall ranking of all origins; rather, it shows a selection across geographical regions and income groups.

Sources: WIPO Statistics Database and World Bank, September 2018.

B34. Resident trademark application class count per million population for selected origins, 2007 and 2017

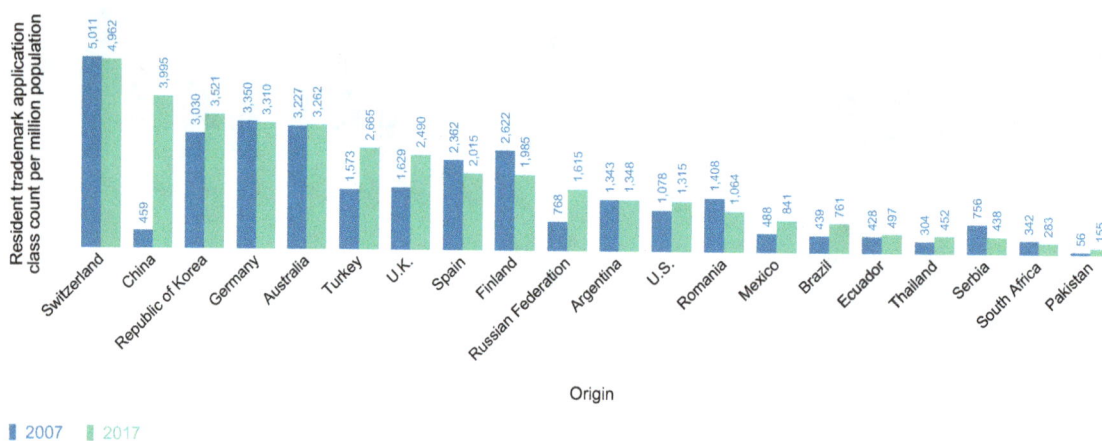

Resident trademark application class count per million population

Origin	2007	2017
Switzerland	5,011	4,962
China	459	3,995
Republic of Korea	3,030	3,521
Germany	3,350	3,310
Australia	3,227	3,262
Turkey	1,573	2,665
U.K.	1,629	2,490
Spain	2,362	2,015
Finland	2,622	1,985
Russian Federation	768	1,615
Argentina	1,343	1,348
U.S.	1,078	1,315
Romania	1,408	1,064
Mexico	488	841
Brazil	439	761
Ecuador	428	497
Thailand	304	452
Serbia	756	438
South Africa	342	283
Pakistan	56	155

■ 2007 ■ 2017

Note: This figure does not provide an overall ranking of all origins; rather, it shows a selection across geographical regions and income groups.
Sources: WIPO Statistics Database and World Bank, September 2018.

Collective and certification trademark applications by office

B35. Collective trademark applications for the top 20 offices, 2017

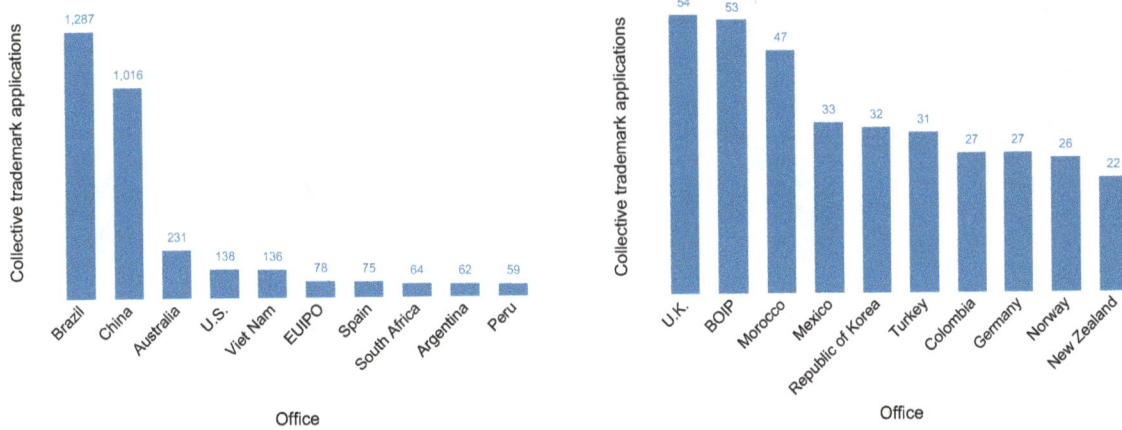

Collective trademark applications / Office

Brazil 1,287; China 1,016; Australia 231; U.S. 138; Viet Nam 136; EUIPO 78; Spain 75; South Africa 64; Argentina 62; Peru 59

U.K. 54; BOIP 53; Morocco 47; Mexico 33; Republic of Korea 32; Turkey 31; Colombia 27; Germany 27; Norway 26; New Zealand 22

Note: EUIPO is the European Union Intellectual Property Office. BOIP is the Benelux Office for Intellectual Property.
Source: WIPO Statistics Database, September 2018.

B36. Certification trademark applications for the top 20 offices, 2017

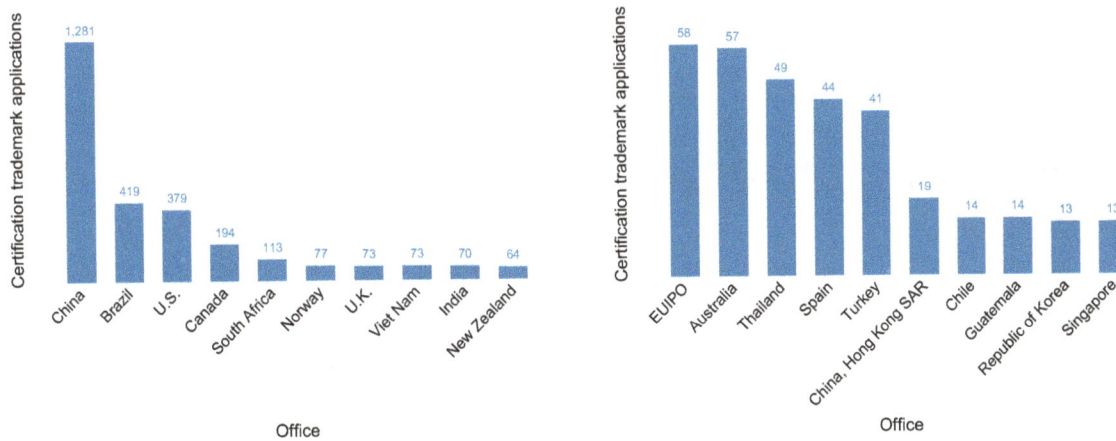

Certification trademark applications / Office

China 1,281; Brazil 419; U.S. 379; Canada 194; South Africa 113; Norway 77; U.K. 73; Viet Nam 73; India 70; New Zealand 64

EUIPO 58; Australia 57; Thailand 49; Spain 44; Turkey 41; China, Hong Kong SAR 19; Chile 14; Guatemala 14; Republic of Korea 13; Singapore 13

Note: EUIPO is the European Union Intellectual Property Office.
Source: WIPO Statistics Database, September 2018.

Trademarks

117

Trademark registrations in force

Trademarks

B37. Trend in trademark registrations in force worldwide, 2010–2017

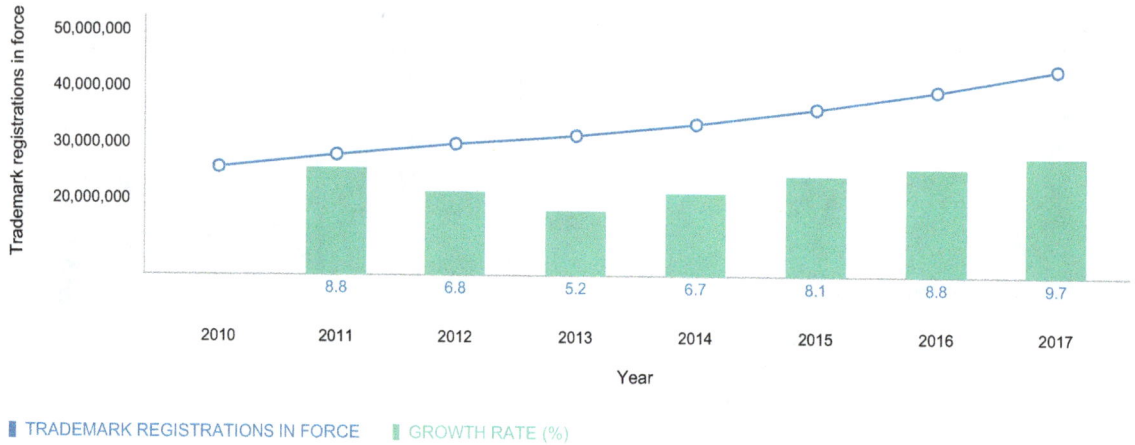

	2011	2012	2013	2014	2015	2016	2017
Growth rate (%)	8.8	6.8	5.2	6.7	8.1	8.8	9.7

▮ TRADEMARK REGISTRATIONS IN FORCE   ▮ GROWTH RATE (%)

Note: World totals are WIPO estimates using data covering 138 IP offices. Data refer to the number of trademark registrations in force, not the number of classes specified in those registrations. Trademark rights can be maintained indefinitely by paying renewal fees at defined time intervals. Trademarks in force provide information on the volume of trademark registrations currently active as well as the historical trademark life cycle.

Source: WIPO Statistics Database, September 2018.

B38. Trademark registrations in force for the top 20 offices, 2017

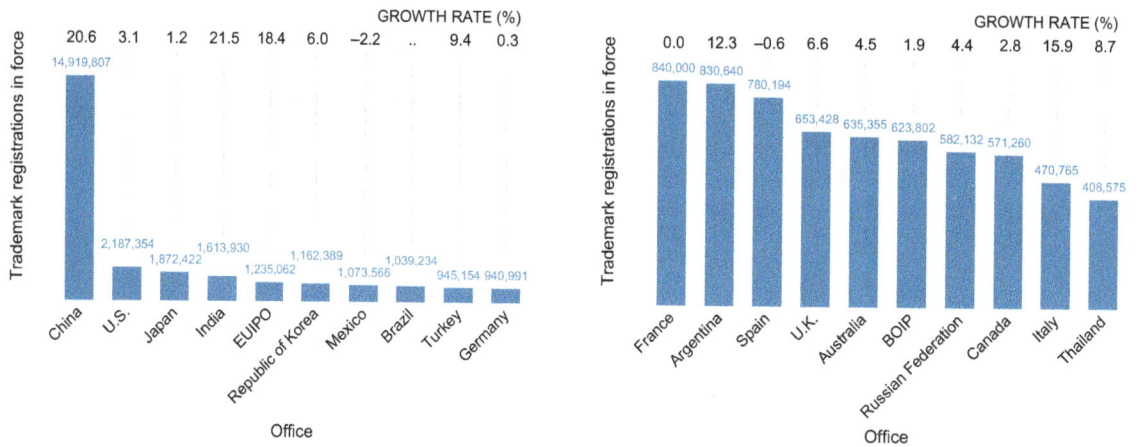

.. indicates unavailable.

Note: EUIPO is the European Union Intellectual Property Office and BOIP is the Benelux Office for Intellectual Property. Data refer to the number of trademark registrations in force, not the number of classes specified in those registrations.

Source: WIPO Statistics Database, September 2018.

B39. Trademark registrations in force in 2017 as a percentage of total registrations recorded between 1991 and 2017

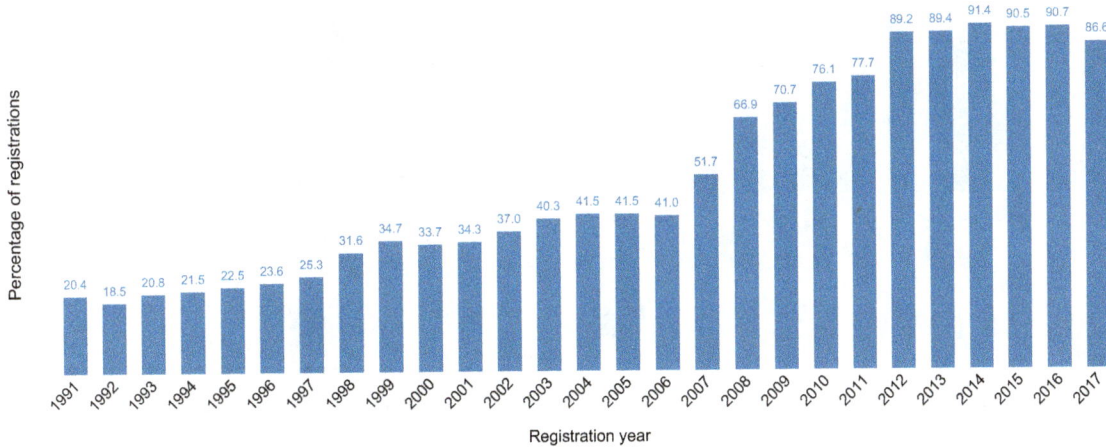

Note: Percentages are calculated as follows: the number of trademark registrations issued in year t and in force in 2017 divided by the total number of trademark registrations issued in year t. Trademark holders must pay renewal fees to maintain the validity of their marks, which in most cases can be maintained indefinitely. This figure is based on about 15.2 million active trademark registrations reported by 66 offices that provided a breakdown by year of registration. Detailed data for several larger offices, such as those of China, France, Italy and Japan, are not available.

Source: WIPO Statistics Database, September 2018.

B40. Average age of trademarks in force at selected offices, 2012 and 2017

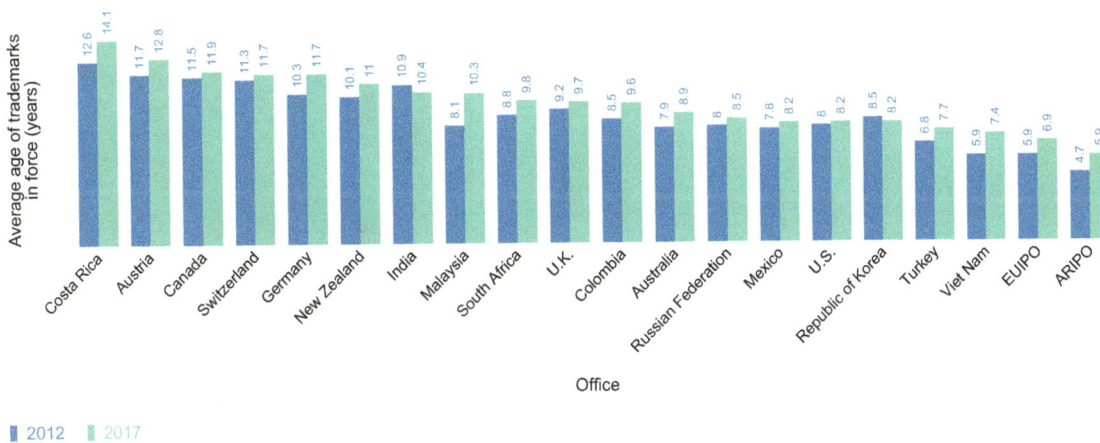

■ 2012   ■ 2017

Note: EUIPO is the European Union Intellectual Property Office and ARIPO is the African Regional Intellectual Property Organization.

Source: WIPO Statistics Database, September 2018.

Trademarks

Trademark office procedural data

B41. Trademark examination decisions for selected offices, 2017

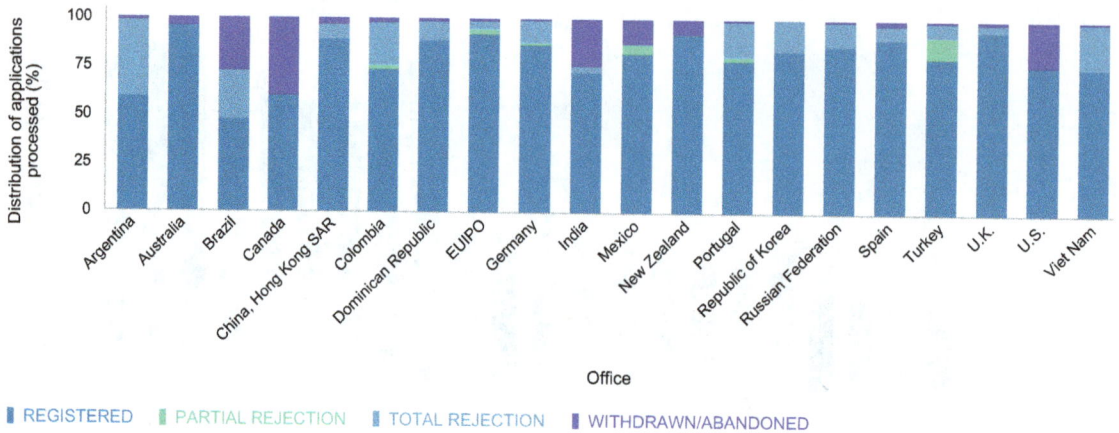

Note: EUIPO is the European Union Intellectual Property Office. WIPO collects data from IP offices using a common questionnaire and methodology. However, due to differences in application processing procedures between offices, data cannot be fully harmonized. Therefore, one should exercise caution when making comparisons across offices.

Source: WIPO Statistics Database, September 2018.

B42. Trademark applications pending for selected offices, 2017

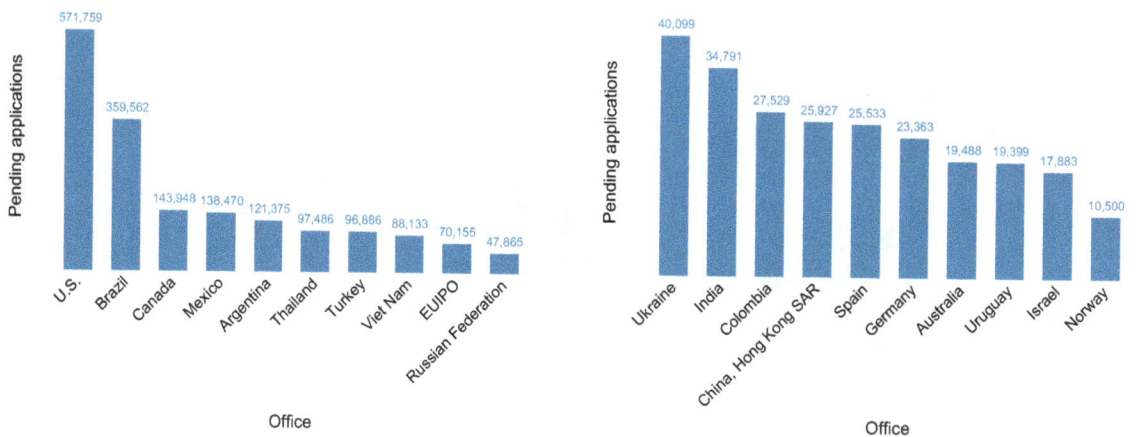

Note: EUIPO is the European Union Intellectual Property Office. WIPO collects data from IP offices using a common questionnaire and methodology. However, due to differences in application processing procedures between offices, data cannot be fully harmonized. Therefore, one should exercise caution when making comparisons across offices.

Source: WIPO Statistics Database, September 2018.

B43. Trademark examiners for selected offices, 2017

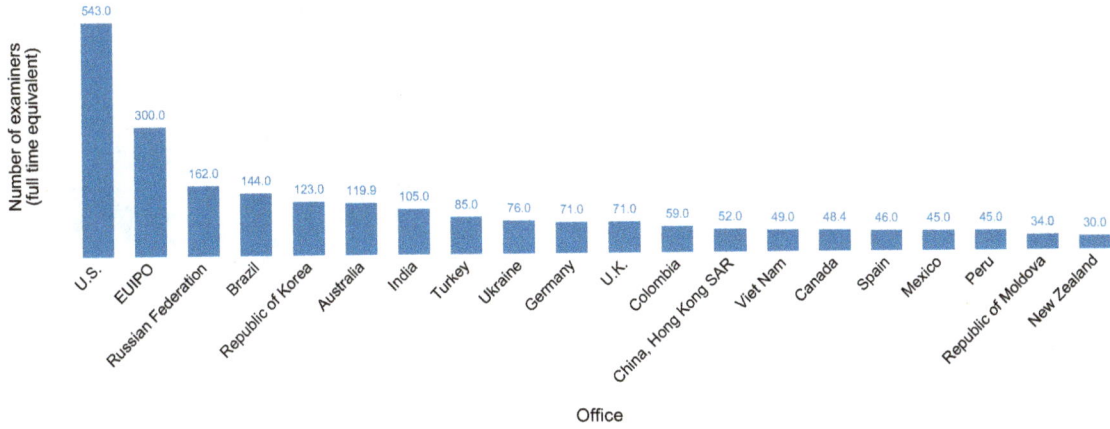

Number of examiners (full time equivalent)

- U.S. 543.0
- EUIPO 300.0
- Russian Federation 162.0
- Brazil 144.0
- Republic of Korea 123.0
- Australia 119.9
- India 105.0
- Turkey 85.0
- Ukraine 76.0
- Germany 71.0
- U.K. 71.0
- Colombia 59.0
- China, Hong Kong SAR 52.0
- Viet Nam 49.0
- Canada 48.4
- Spain 46.0
- Mexico 45.0
- Peru 45.0
- Republic of Moldova 34.0
- New Zealand 30.0

Office

Note: EUIPO is the European Union Intellectual Property Office.

Source: WIPO Statistics Database, September 2018.

B44. Duration of trademark examination for selected offices, 2017

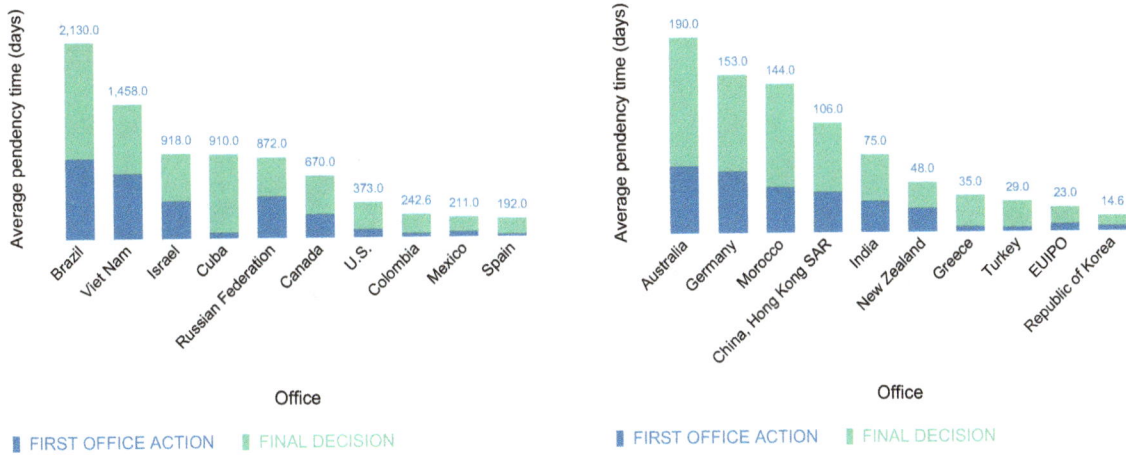

Average pendency time (days)

- Brazil 2,130.0
- Viet Nam 1,458.0
- Israel 918.0
- Cuba 910.0
- Russian Federation 872.0
- Canada 670.0
- U.S. 373.0
- Colombia 242.6
- Mexico 211.0
- Spain 192.0

Office

Average pendency time (days)

- Australia 190.0
- Germany 153.0
- Morocco 144.0
- China, Hong Kong SAR 106.0
- India 75.0
- New Zealand 48.0
- Greece 35.0
- Turkey 29.0
- EUIPO 23.0
- Republic of Korea 14.6

Office

■ FIRST OFFICE ACTION   ■ FINAL DECISION

■ FIRST OFFICE ACTION   ■ FINAL DECISION

Note: EUIPO is the European Union Intellectual Property Office. WIPO collects data from IP offices using a common questionnaire and methodology. However, due to differences in application processing procedures between offices, data cannot be fully harmonized. Therefore, one should exercise caution when making comparisons across offices.

Source: WIPO Statistics Database, September 2018.

Trademarks

Trademarks

B45. Third party oppositions for selected offices, 2017

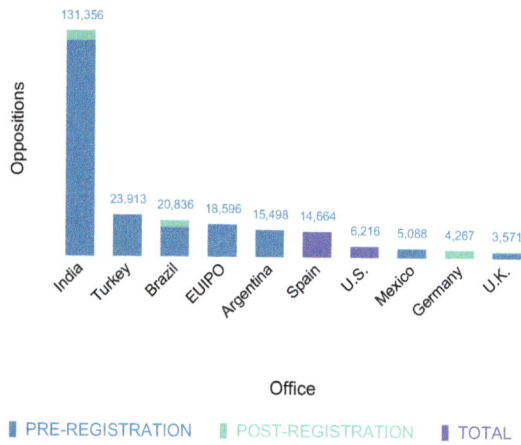

Oppositions

India 131,356
Turkey 23,913
Brazil 20,836
EUIPO 18,596
Argentina 15,498
Spain 14,664
U.S. 6,216
Mexico 5,088
Germany 4,267
U.K. 3,571

Office

■ PRE-REGISTRATION   ■ POST-REGISTRATION   ■ TOTAL

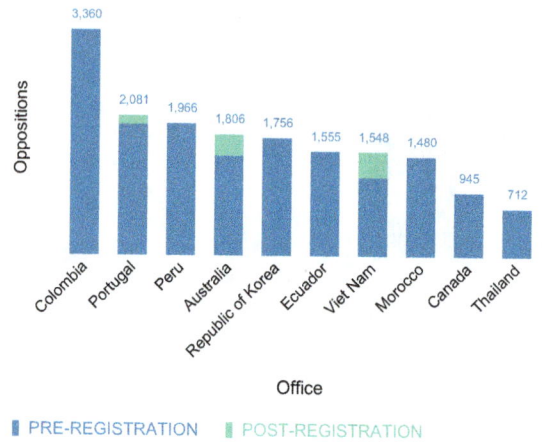

Oppositions

Colombia 3,360
Portugal 2,081
Peru 1,966
Australia 1,806
Republic of Korea 1,756
Ecuador 1,555
Viet Nam 1,548
Morocco 1,480
Canada 945
Thailand 712

Office

■ PRE-REGISTRATION   ■ POST-REGISTRATION

Note: EUIPO is the European Union Intellectual Property Office.
Source: WIPO Statistics Database, September 2018.

B46. Appeals to decisions by selected offices, 2017

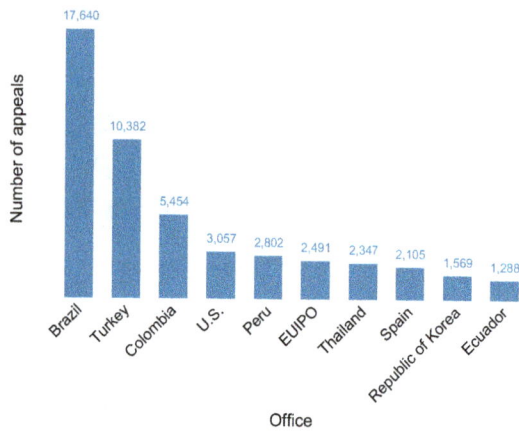

Number of appeals

Brazil 17,640
Turkey 10,382
Colombia 5,454
U.S. 3,057
Peru 2,802
EUIPO 2,491
Thailand 2,347
Spain 2,105
Republic of Korea 1,569
Ecuador 1,288

Office

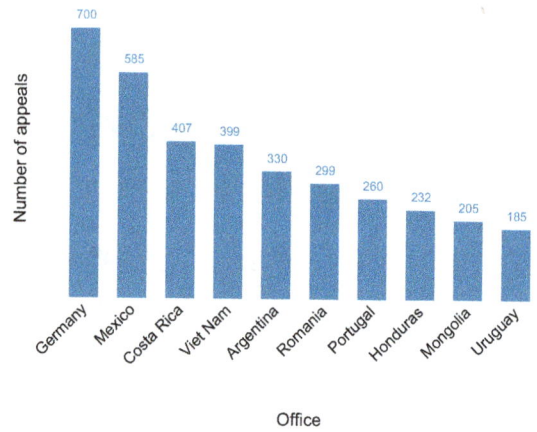

Number of appeals

Germany 700
Mexico 585
Costa Rica 407
Viet Nam 399
Argentina 330
Romania 299
Portugal 260
Honduras 232
Mongolia 205
Uruguay 185

Office

Note: EUIPO is the European Union Intellectual Property Office.
Source: WIPO Statistics Database, September 2018.

Trademark applications through the Madrid System

B47. Trend in Madrid international applications, 2004–2017

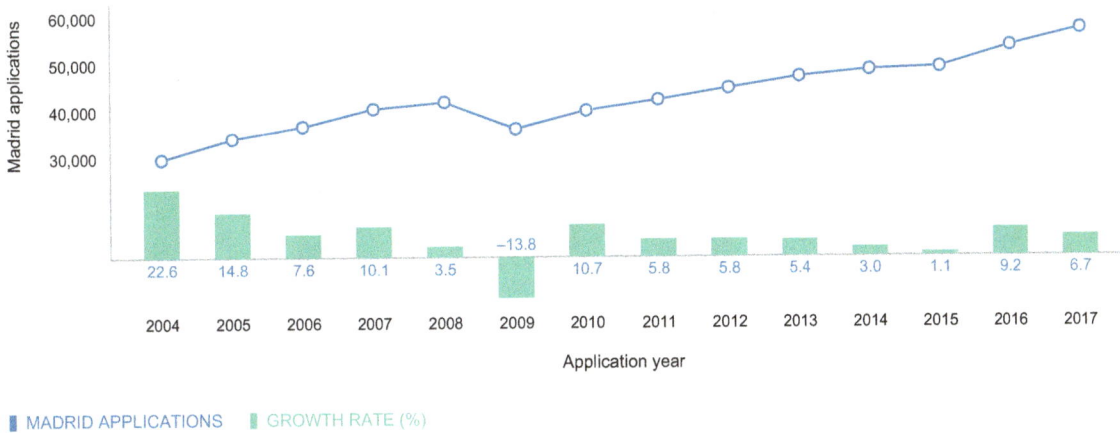

Legend: ▌ MADRID APPLICATIONS ▌ GROWTH RATE (%)

Growth rate values by year: 2004: 22.6, 2005: 14.8, 2006: 7.6, 2007: 10.1, 2008: 3.5, 2009: −13.8, 2010: 10.7, 2011: 5.8, 2012: 5.8, 2013: 5.4, 2014: 3.0, 2015: 1.1, 2016: 9.2, 2017: 6.7

Source: WIPO Statistics Database, September 2018.

B48. Madrid international applications by origin, 2017

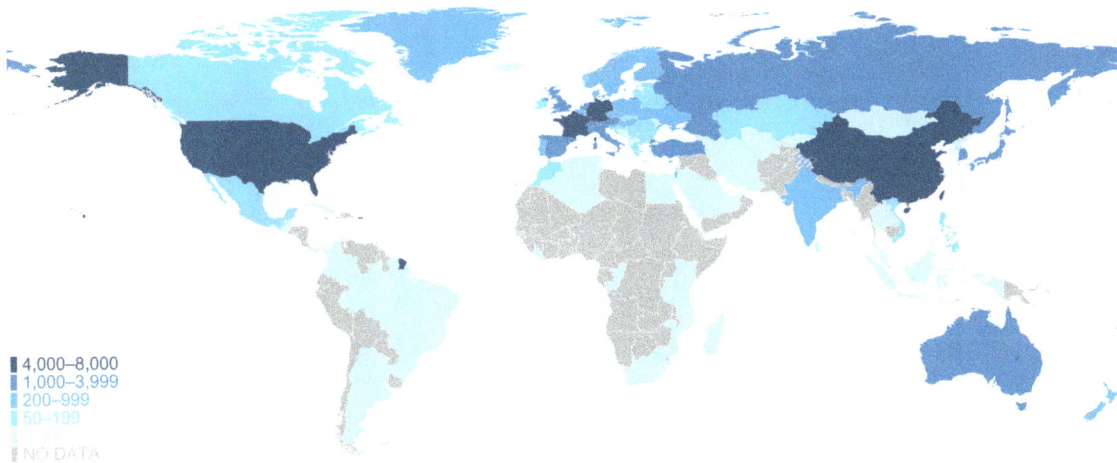

Legend:
▌ 4,000–8,000
▌ 1,000–3,999
▌ 200–999
▌ 50–199
▌ NO DATA

Note: Counts are based on the country of the applicant's address, not the office of origin.
Source: WIPO Statistics Database, September 2018.

Trademarks

B49. Madrid applications for the top 20 origins, 2017

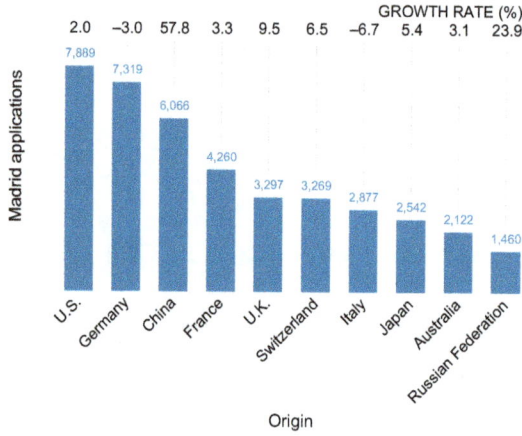

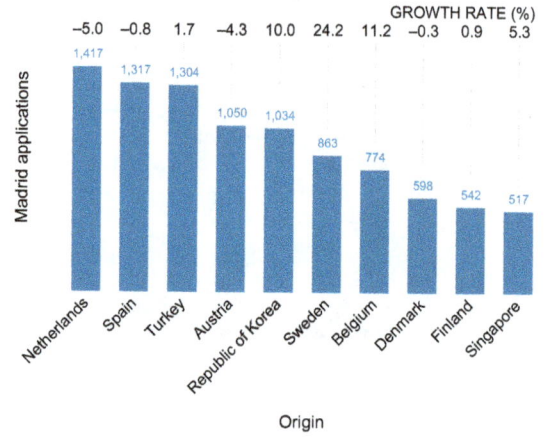

GROWTH RATE (%)

2.0	−3.0	57.8	3.3	9.5	6.5	−6.7	5.4	3.1	23.9

Madrid applications

- U.S. — 7,889
- Germany — 7,319
- China — 6,066
- France — 4,260
- U.K. — 3,297
- Switzerland — 3,269
- Italy — 2,877
- Japan — 2,542
- Australia — 2,122
- Russian Federation — 1,460

Origin

GROWTH RATE (%)

−5.0	−0.8	1.7	−4.3	10.0	24.2	11.2	−0.3	0.9	5.3

Madrid applications

- Netherlands — 1,417
- Spain — 1,317
- Turkey — 1,304
- Austria — 1,050
- Republic of Korea — 1,034
- Sweden — 863
- Belgium — 774
- Denmark — 598
- Finland — 542
- Singapore — 517

Origin

Note: Origin data are based on the country of the applicant's address.
Source: WIPO Statistics Database, September 2018.

B50. Designations in Madrid international applications for the top 20 designated Madrid members, 2017

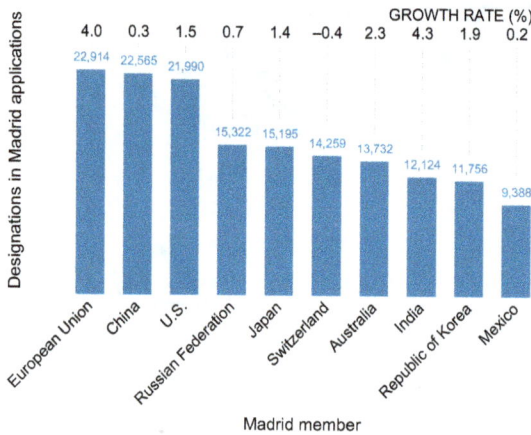

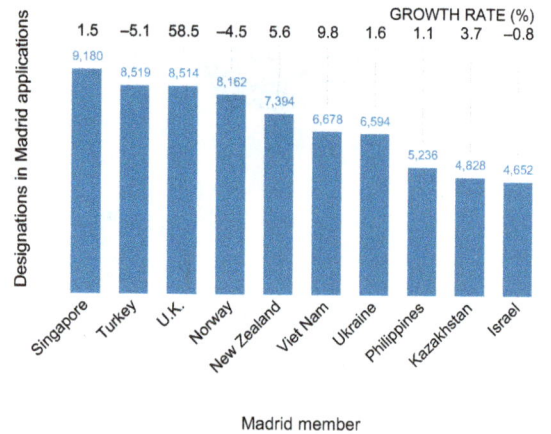

GROWTH RATE (%)

4.0	0.3	1.5	0.7	1.4	−0.4	2.3	4.3	1.9	0.2

Designations in Madrid applications

- European Union — 22,914
- China — 22,565
- U.S. — 21,990
- Russian Federation — 15,322
- Japan — 15,195
- Switzerland — 14,259
- Australia — 13,732
- India — 12,124
- Republic of Korea — 11,756
- Mexico — 9,388

Madrid member

GROWTH RATE (%)

1.5	−5.1	58.5	−4.5	5.6	9.8	1.6	1.1	3.7	−0.8

Designations in Madrid applications

- Singapore — 9,180
- Turkey — 8,519
- U.K. — 8,514
- Norway — 8,162
- New Zealand — 7,394
- Viet Nam — 6,678
- Ukraine — 6,594
- Philippines — 5,236
- Kazakhstan — 4,828
- Israel — 4,652

Madrid member

Note: The numbers of designations in applications for all Madrid members are reported in statistical table B51.
Source: WIPO Statistics Database, September 2018.

Statistical tables

B51. Trademark applications by office and origin, 2017

Name	Application class count by office			Application class count by origin	Equivalent application class count by origin	Madrid international applications	
	Total	Resident	Non-resident	Total [a]	Total [a]	Origin [f]	Designated Madrid member
Afghanistan (b)	..	..	..	295	322	..	n.a.
African Intellectual Property Organization	12,233	3,379	8,854	n.a.	n.a.	n.a.	1,960
African Regional Intellectual Property Organization	782	386	396	n.a.	n.a.	n.a.	n.a.
Albania	8,391	1,232	7,159	1,310	2,012	12	2,319
Algeria (b)	..	..	..	249	549	9	2,623
Andorra	3,086	691	2,395	1,315	10,225	..	n.a.
Angola (b)	..	..	..	28	71	..	n.a.
Antigua and Barbuda (b)	..	..	..	26	188	..	621
Argentina	74,722	59,669	15,053	63,333	66,793	3	n.a.
Armenia	10,043	2,685	7,358	3,954	5,062	37	2,631
Aruba (b)	..	..	..	2	2	..	n.a.
Australia	138,078	80,230	57,848	121,274	206,219	2,122	13,732
Austria	22,748	14,039	8,709	45,306	302,402	1,050	2,632
Azerbaijan (b)	..	..	..	292	589	12	3,017
Bahamas	1,002	199	803	2,136	8,724	12	n.a.
Bahrain	9,418	253	9,165	505	899	..	1,787
Bangladesh	13,090	9,247	3,843	9,388	9,490	..	n.a.
Barbados	861	21	840	791	2,838	4	n.a.
Belarus	18,961	4,453	14,508	7,261	9,784	142	4,559
Belgium (c)	n.a.	n.a.	n.a.	44,482	258,377	774	n.a.
Belize (b)	..	..	..	1,224	2,126	37	n.a.
Benelux Office for Intellectual Property (d)	67,205	56,762	10,443	n.a.	n.a.	n.a.	2,592
Benin (b,h)	n.a.	n.a.	n.a.	197	3,045	..	n.a.
Bermuda (b)	..	..	..	687	3,473	8	n.a.
Bhutan	1,921	16	1,905	18	18	..	717
Bolivia (Plurinational State of)	8,204	3,491	4,713	3,609	3,663	..	n.a.
Bonaire, Sint Eustatius and Saba (b)	..	..	..	6	6	1	500
Bosnia and Herzegovina	10,031	742	9,289	1,208	2,510	33	2,922
Botswana	3,134	464	2,670	707	707	..	807
Brazil	186,103	159,192	26,911	165,128	178,367	3	n.a.
Brunei Darussalam	2,834	176	2,658	262	262	2	701
Bulgaria	17,552	13,438	4,114	20,574	66,903	190	1,436
Burkina Faso (b,h)	n.a.	n.a.	n.a.	210	3,506	..	n.a.
Burundi	534	53	481	53	53	..	n.a.
Cabo Verde (b)	..	..	..	15	231	..	n.a.
Cambodia (b)	..	..	..	66	66	..	2,025
Cameroon (b,h)	n.a.	n.a.	n.a.	537	8,980	..	n.a.
Canada	183,735	103,776	79,959	135,794	228,175	60	n.a.
Central African Republic (b,h)	n.a.	n.a.	n.a.	5	37	..	n.a.
Chad (b,h)	n.a.	n.a.	n.a.	9	121	..	n.a.
Chile	45,360	31,720	13,640	36,169	40,259	..	n.a.
China	5,739,823	5,539,086	200,737	5,779,137	6,381,512	6,066	22,565
China, Hong Kong SAR	76,521	29,536	46,985	49,060	122,529	..	n.a.
China, Macao SAR	13,135	2,030	11,105	2,520	2,839	..	n.a.
Colombia	41,076	23,762	17,314	27,120	29,636	32	3,727

Trademarks

Trademarks

Name	Application class count by office			Application class count by origin	Equivalent application class count by origin	Madrid international applications	
	Total	Resident	Non-resident	Total [a]	Total [a]	Origin [f]	Designated Madrid member
Comoros (b)	..	..	..	17	257	..	n.a.
Congo (b,h)	n.a.	n.a.	n.a.	52	641	1	n.a.
Cook Islands (b)	..	..	..	33	87	..	n.a.
Costa Rica	14,405	7,902	6,503	8,726	9,158	..	n.a.
Côte d'Ivoire (b,h)	n.a.	n.a.	n.a.	957	15,865	..	n.a.
Croatia	8,272	4,348	3,924	7,210	18,762	110	1,366
Cuba	7,308	2,099	5,209	2,692	3,354	9	1,563
Curaçao	1,996	0	1,996	452	4,001	11	626
Cyprus (b)	..	..	..	10,723	58,615	204	814
Czech Republic	25,339	20,031	5,308	30,303	117,910	298	1,740
Democratic People's Republic of Korea (b)	..	..	..	175	229	6	1,066
Democratic Republic of the Congo (b)	..	..	..	29	29	..	n.a.
Denmark	11,135	7,036	4,099	26,271	184,715	598	1,314
Djibouti (b)	..	..	..	3	3	..	n.a.
Dominica (b)	..	..	..	25	25	..	n.a.
Dominican Republic	13,613	8,094	5,519	8,616	9,053	..	n.a.
Ecuador	14,551	8,262	6,289	9,106	9,677	..	n.a.
Egypt (b)	..	..	..	710	2,587	20	4,164
El Salvador	9,082	5,026	4,056	5,625	5,679	..	n.a.
Equatorial Guinea (b,h)	n.a.	n.a.	n.a.	12	204	..	n.a.
Eritrea (b)	..	..	..	3	3	..	n.a.
Estonia	5,493	2,197	3,296	5,106	37,036	73	1,095
Eswatini (b)	..	..	..	47	47	..	713
Ethiopia (b)	..	..	..	9	90	..	n.a.
European Union Intellectual Property Office (e)	371,508	269,422	102,086	n.a.	n.a.	n.a.	22,914
Fiji (b)	..	..	..	57	57	..	n.a.
Finland	9,376	6,019	3,357	24,396	157,771	542	1,087
France	270,412	252,960	17,452	394,144	1,147,830	4,260	3,584
Gabon (b,h)	n.a.	n.a.	n.a.	158	2,254	..	n.a.
Gambia	1,782	72	1,710	85	229	..	735
Georgia	10,746	2,742	8,004	3,227	3,828	30	2,662
Germany	225,768	203,252	22,516	470,573	2,385,482	7,319	4,564
Ghana	5,041	928	4,113	944	1,120	..	1,177
Greece (b)	..	..	..	5,160	65,907	141	1,171
Grenada	41	41	0	68	68	..	n.a.
Guatemala	12,012	6,215	5,797	7,236	7,484	1	n.a.
Guinea (b,h)	n.a.	n.a.	n.a.	241	4,001	..	n.a.
Guinea-Bissau (b,h)	n.a.	n.a.	n.a.	11	171	..	n.a.
Guyana (b)	..	..	..	5	5	..	n.a.
Haiti (b)	..	..	..	13	67	..	n.a.
Holy See (b)	..	..	..	8	224	..	n.a.
Honduras	7,077	2,292	4,785	2,559	2,559	..	n.a.
Hungary	14,324	9,978	4,346	17,236	64,770	239	1,491
Iceland	9,179	1,706	7,473	3,128	8,312	43	2,305
India	283,575	242,483	41,092	253,233	271,972	233	12,124
Indonesia	68,108	51,918	16,190	53,959	54,827	1	n.a.

Name	Application class count by office			Application class count by origin	Equivalent application class count by origin	Madrid international applications	
	Total	Resident	Non-resident	Total [a]	Total [a]	Origin [l]	Designated Madrid member
Iran (Islamic Republic of)	358,353	329,107	29,246	331,542	335,021	37	3,931
Iraq (b)	..	..	..	977	1,220	..	n.a.
Ireland (g)	7,648	..	..	10,524	92,540	164	990
Israel	19,491	3,745	15,746	10,904	35,587	323	4,652
Italy	93,006	81,926	11,080	172,217	920,306	2,877	3,434
Jamaica	5,595	2,759	2,836	3,011	3,231	..	n.a.
Japan	560,269	496,092	64,177	602,943	767,433	2,542	15,195
Jordan	7,647	3,085	4,562	3,754	6,469	1	n.a.
Kazakhstan (b)	..	..	..	1,790	2,141	111	4,828
Kenya	12,043	5,321	6,722	5,513	6,103	2	1,793
Kiribati (b)	..	..	..	26	26	..	n.a.
Kuwait (b)	..	..	..	814	3,912	..	n.a.
Kyrgyzstan	7,503	519	6,984	625	652	5	2,493
Lao People's Democratic Republic (b)	..	..	..	21	48	2	1,166
Latvia	7,099	3,434	3,665	5,804	18,630	109	1,246
Lebanon (b)	..	..	..	961	4,043	1	n.a.
Lesotho (b)	..	..	..	12	12	..	646
Liberia (b)	..	..	..	48	955	1	734
Libya (b)	..	..	..	10	26	..	n.a.
Liechtenstein	8,877	388	8,489	7,412	19,045	87	2,369
Lithuania	7,858	3,993	3,865	6,954	31,773	120	1,282
Luxembourg (c)	n.a.	n.a.	n.a.	20,811	119,075	386	n.a.
Madagascar	5,396	2,405	2,991	2,445	2,685	2	876
Malawi (b)	..	..	..	1	1	..	n.a.
Malaysia	41,093	19,481	21,612	25,436	29,030	13	n.a.
Maldives (b)	..	..	..	8	8	..	n.a.
Mali (b,h)	n.a.	n.a.	n.a.	243	3,731	..	n.a.
Malta	1,167	771	396	6,292	48,687	72	n.a.
Marshall Islands (b)	..	..	..	220	630	..	n.a.
Mauritania (g,h)	n.a.	n.a.	n.a.	75	811	..	n.a.
Mauritius	2,092	1,035	1,057	2,828	7,319	13	n.a.
Mexico	151,771	108,590	43,181	118,667	132,188	107	9,388
Monaco	9,208	1,659	7,549	4,831	15,039	52	2,352
Mongolia	13,845	9,101	4,744	9,200	9,200	1	1,852
Montenegro (b)	..	..	..	1,297	2,953	15	2,458
Morocco	30,031	17,001	13,030	18,516	26,203	110	3,788
Mozambique (b)	..	..	..	64	214	4	1,033
Myanmar (b)	..	..	..	78	84	..	n.a.
Namibia	7,135	3,423	3,712	3,850	4,066	..	897
Nauru (b)	..	..	..	10	10	..	n.a.
Nepal	5,682	4,005	1,677	4,056	4,110	..	n.a.
Netherlands (c)	n.a.	n.a.	n.a.	86,706	532,630	1,417	n.a.
New Zealand	47,173	17,099	30,074	26,317	41,242	419	7,394
Nicaragua (b)	..	..	..	141	141	..	n.a.
Niger (b,h)	n.a.	n.a.	n.a.	156	1,148	..	n.a.
Nigeria (b)	..	..	..	131	883	..	n.a.

Trademarks

Name	Application class count by office			Application class count by origin	Equivalent application class count by origin	Madrid international applications	
	Total	Resident	Non-resident	Total [a]	Total [a]	Origin [f]	Designated Madrid member
Norway	42,897	12,934	29,963	23,754	75,645	376	8,162
Oman (b)	..	..	..	264	642	..	1,972
Pakistan	38,425	30,632	7,793	31,586	32,163	..	n.a.
Palau (b)	..	..	..	2	2	..	n.a.
Panama	10,582	4,306	6,276	7,545	12,265	3	n.a.
Papua New Guinea (b)	..	..	..	99	99	..	n.a.
Paraguay (b)	..	..	..	765	1,008	..	n.a.
Peru	33,031	21,535	11,496	23,306	23,819	..	n.a.
Philippines	51,502	26,922	24,580	28,254	29,349	54	5,236
Poland	40,434	33,128	7,306	52,566	318,037	416	2,318
Portugal	33,287	27,340	5,947	34,721	131,755	265	1,612
Qatar	8,124	1,117	7,007	2,294	4,300	1	n.a.
Republic of Korea	230,466	181,218	49,248	230,076	296,572	1,034	11,756
Republic of Moldova	11,300	3,015	8,285	3,667	3,982	49	2,621
Romania	22,987	18,583	4,404	22,563	83,547	106	1,636
Russian Federation	291,732	233,430	58,302	279,669	314,811	1,460	15,322
Rwanda	2,536	255	2,281	256	283	..	765
Saint Kitts and Nevis	339	28	311	195	405	3	n.a.
Saint Lucia (b)	..	..	..	97	178	..	n.a.
Saint Vincent and the Grenadines	365	5	360	59	194	..	n.a.
Samoa	246	28	218	443	875	..	n.a.
San Marino (b)	..	..	..	457	2,470	10	1,116
Sao Tome and Principe	1,267	11	1,256	12	12	..	510
Saudi Arabia (b)	..	..	..	2,091	6,617	3	n.a.
Senegal (b,h)	n.a.	n.a.	n.a.	659	10,627	..	n.a.
Serbia	16,090	3,079	13,011	6,136	11,128	178	4,067
Seychelles	50	50	0	1,482	3,387	10	n.a.
Sierra Leone (b)	..	..	..	19	19	..	737
Singapore	48,548	10,608	37,940	33,324	53,993	517	9,180
Sint Maarten (Dutch Part) (b)	..	..	..	12	174	1	555
Slovakia	14,080	8,804	5,276	12,278	44,712	123	1,363
Slovenia (b)	..	..	..	5,245	33,934	208	1,265
Solomon Islands (b)	..	..	..	4	4	..	n.a.
Somalia (b)	..	..	..	2	29	..	n.a.
South Africa	26,251	16,027	10,224	18,636	30,094	3	n.a.
Spain	80,889	71,649	9,240	121,532	723,639	1,317	2,980
Sri Lanka (b)	..	..	..	508	1,496	2	n.a.
Sudan	5,004	1,558	3,446	1,607	1,623	..	1,153
Suriname	1,162	530	632	565	597	1	n.a.
Sweden	22,815	18,462	4,353	59,009	338,720	863	1,414
Switzerland	94,562	42,009	52,553	151,482	486,871	3,269	14,259
Syrian Arab Republic	17,461	8,211	9,250	8,670	9,740	..	1,101
Tajikistan (b)	..	..	..	12	12	..	2,125
Thailand	53,965	31,183	22,782	37,608	43,109	25	584
The former Yugoslav Republic of Macedonia (b)	..	..	..	800	2,401	39	2,586
Timor-Leste (b)	..	..	..	2	2	..	n.a.

Name	Application class count by office			Application class count by origin	Equivalent application class count by origin	Madrid international applications	
	Total	Resident	Non-resident	Total [a]	Total [a]	Origin [f]	Designated Madrid member
Togo (b,h)	n.a.	n.a.	n.a.	157	2,525	..	n.a.
Trinidad and Tobago	2,558	594	1,964	698	729	..	n.a.
Tunisia (g)	13,281	..	..	793	3,385	24	2,306
Turkey	247,474	215,220	32,254	240,065	296,665	1,304	8,519
Turkmenistan (b)	..	..	..	136	136	7	1,909
Uganda	1,474	1,359	115	1,393	1,393	..	n.a.
Ukraine	72,015	47,531	24,484	54,719	66,335	388	6,594
United Arab Emirates	19,042	6,075	12,967	15,205	36,987	20	n.a.
United Kingdom	176,202	132,300	43,902	272,255	1,146,770	3,297	8,514
United Republic of Tanzania (b)	..	..	..	95	446	1	n.a.
United States of America	613,921	428,225	185,696	765,411	1,650,723	7,889	21,990
Uruguay	9,311	3,705	5,606	4,747	5,395	..	n.a.
Uzbekistan	13,242	6,750	6,492	7,201	7,368	16	2,052
Vanuatu (b)	..	..	..	31	85	..	n.a.
Venezuela (Bolivarian Republic of)	22,439	18,414	4,025	18,840	19,272	..	n.a.
Viet Nam	84,764	55,313	29,451	58,076	59,752	91	6,678
Yemen	4,713	2,941	1,772	3,135	3,210	..	n.a.
Zambia	4,474	1,072	3,402	1,132	1,132	..	947
Zimbabwe (b)	..	..	..	15	31	..	1,013
Others/Unknown	..	..	..	70,146	167,807	25	2
Total (2017 estimates)	**12,387,600**	**10,300,000**	**2,087,600**	**12,387,600**	**n.a.**	**57,139**	**373,864**

(a) Data on application class count by origin are incomplete because some offices do not report detailed statistics containing the origin of application class counts.

(b) Only Madrid designation data are available, so application class count by office and origin data may be incomplete.

(c) This country does not have a national trademark office. All applications for trademark protection are filed at the Benelux Office for Intellectual Property or the European Union Intellectual Property Office.

(d) Resident applications include those filed by residents of Belgium, Luxembourg and the Netherlands.

(e) Resident applications include those filed by residents of EU member states.

(f) Origin is defined as the country/territory of the stated residence of the applicant in an international application.

(g) Total includes an aggregate direct application class count that cannot be broken down into direct and non-resident components.

(h) The African Intellectual Property Office (OAPI) is the competent office for processing applications.

n.a. indicates not applicable.

.. indicates not available.

Source: WIPO Statistics Database, September 2018.

Trademarks

B52. Trademark registrations by office and origin, and trademarks in force, 2017

Name	Registration class count by office			Registration class count by origin	Equivalent registration class count by origin	Madrid international registration	In force by office
	Total	Resident	Non-resident	Total [a]	Total [a]	Origin [f]	Total
Afghanistan (b)	..	..	..	139	166	..	..
African Intellectual Property Organization	12,868	2,835	10,033	n.a.	n.a.	n.a.	..
African Regional Intellectual Property Organization	362	68	294	n.a.	n.a.	n.a.	1,786
Albania	8,720	639	8,081	686	983	4	10,000
Algeria (b)	..	..	..	164	449	7	..
Andorra	3,090	691	2,399	942	4,992	1	20,113
Angola (b)	..	..	..	52	484	..	..
Antigua and Barbuda (b)	..	..	..	6	60	..	8,536
Argentina	36,494	27,066	9,428	29,848	33,334	1	830,640
Armenia	10,488	2,011	8,477	2,827	4,079	32	..
Australia	116,628	60,070	56,558	97,177	185,759	2,348	635,355
Austria	21,018	11,813	9,205	45,855	284,807	1,085	100,917
Azerbaijan (b)	..	..	..	205	321	4	..
Bahamas	1,104	47	1,057	1,274	6,674	5	..
Bahrain	13,228	461	12,767	724	1,118	..	..
Bangladesh	4,464	919	3,545	1,021	1,382	..	33,790
Barbados	321	21	300	867	3,211	6	..
Belarus	20,927	4,323	16,604	7,379	9,559	159	126,018
Belgium (c)	n.a.	n.a.	n.a.	37,562	236,213	823	n.a.
Belize (b)	..	..	..	787	1,809	22	..
Benelux Office for Intellectual Property (d)	60,449	49,747	10,702	n.a.	n.a.	n.a.	623,802
Benin (b,h)	n.a.	n.a.	n.a.	156	2,556	..	..
Bermuda (b)	..	..	..	696	3,660	7	..
Bhutan	2,098	15	2,083	17	17	..	..
Bolivia (Plurinational State of)	6,445	2,395	4,050	2,484	2,565	..	52,379
Bonaire, Sint Eustatius and Saba (b)	..	..	..	9	90	1	..
Bosnia and Herzegovina	11,794	433	11,361	691	1,449	14	16,383
Botswana	3,563	249	3,314	253	253	..	17,522
Brazil	123,362	90,859	32,503	94,974	107,052	3	1,039,234
Brunei Darussalam	2,643	135	2,508	346	508	2	..
Bulgaria	17,982	13,301	4,681	22,951	68,335	248	52,511
Burkina Faso (b,h)	n.a.	n.a.	n.a.	148	2,516	..	..
Burundi	534	53	481	53	53	..	..
Cabo Verde (b)	..	..	..	5	5	..	..
Cambodia (b)	..	..	..	21	21	1	..
Cameroon (b,h)	n.a.	n.a.	n.a.	516	8,181	2	..
Canada	77,948	41,627	36,321	61,313	130,216	70	571,260
Central African Republic (b,h)	n.a.	n.a.	n.a.	3	35	..	..
Chad (b,h)	n.a.	n.a.	n.a.	28	396	..	..
Chile	34,735	20,996	13,739	24,664	27,626	1	366,033
China	2,817,547	2,656,147	161,400	2,833,631	3,329,750	3,622	14,919,807
China, Hong Kong SAR	70,236	26,900	43,336	40,037	104,315	..	402,099
China, Macao SAR	11,484	1,645	9,839	2,048	2,356	..	105,031
Colombia	36,066	17,517	18,549	20,354	22,193	21	309,926
Comoros (b)	..	..	..	2	2	..	..

Trademarks

Name	Registration class count by office			Registration class count by origin	Equivalent registration class count by origin	Madrid international registration	In force by office
	Total	Resident	Non-resident	Total [a]	Total [a]	Origin [f]	Total
Congo (b,h)	n.a.	n.a.	n.a.	51	848	1	..
Cook Islands (b)	..	..	..	24	186	..	..
Costa Rica	10,535	4,841	5,694	5,496	5,901	..	196,215
Côte d'Ivoire (b,h)	n.a.	n.a.	n.a.	777	13,015	..	..
Croatia	7,608	3,182	4,426	6,131	14,867	117	28,165
Cuba	7,358	938	6,420	1,227	2,055	8	14,535
Curaçao	2,436	0	2,436	757	4,191	14	23,276
Cyprus (b)	..	..	..	9,922	50,626	222	..
Czech Republic	29,814	23,608	6,206	35,130	113,272	289	123,876
Democratic People's Republic of Korea (b)	..	..	..	200	335	12	..
Democratic Republic of the Congo (b)	..	..	..	3	3	..	..
Denmark	10,478	6,132	4,346	26,889	154,818	684	83,697
Dominica (b)	..	..	..	29	29	..	..
Dominican Republic	11,268	5,940	5,328	6,216	6,907	..	130,649
Ecuador	8,349	4,691	3,658	5,243	6,011	..	..
Egypt (b)	..	..	..	1,172	2,945	23	..
El Salvador	6,545	2,302	4,243	2,836	2,879	..	87,743
Equatorial Guinea (b,h)	n.a.	n.a.	n.a.	3	84	..	..
Estonia	4,697	1,537	3,160	3,759	28,332	57	54,947
Eswatini (b)	..	..	..	30	111	..	..
Ethiopia (b)	..	..	..	15	123	..	..
European Union Intellectual Property Office (e)	335,435	241,820	93,615	n.a.	n.a.	n.a.	1,235,062
Fiji (b)	..	..	..	71	183	3	..
Finland	8,789	5,421	3,368	24,903	164,388	571	100,136
France (b)	..	..	..	143,347	849,399	4,525	840,000
Gabon (b,h)	n.a.	n.a.	n.a.	42	698	..	..
Gambia	1,686	7	1,679	14	126	..	..
Georgia	10,368	1,164	9,204	1,559	2,304	33	60,088
Germany	162,735	143,893	18,842	419,637	2,093,590	7,606	940,991
Ghana	5,825	225	5,600	254	506	..	47,535
Greece (b)	..	..	..	4,124	56,031	137	..
Grenada	41	41	0	43	43	..	201
Guatemala	10,669	4,433	6,236	5,805	5,940	1	159,741
Guinea (b,h)	n.a.	n.a.	n.a.	204	3,378	..	..
Guinea-Bissau (b,h)	n.a.	n.a.	n.a.	18	306	..	..
Guyana (g)	400	..	..	10	10	..	1,179
Haiti (b)	..	..	..	16	70	..	..
Holy See (b)	..	..	..	8	224	..	..
Honduras	6,286	1,407	4,879	1,660	1,714	..	..
Hungary	10,966	6,431	4,535	10,882	49,184	150	55,056
Iceland	10,105	1,367	8,738	2,647	7,183	40	60,681
India	339,692	287,139	52,553	296,026	313,206	207	1,613,930
Indonesia (b)	..	..	..	1,291	2,397	..	..
Iran (Islamic Republic of)	108,820	92,165	16,655	93,973	96,715	34	172,123
Iraq (b)	..	..	..	325	460	..	..
Ireland (g)	6,480	..	..	9,890	82,325	165	78,807

Name	Registration class count by office			Registration class count by origin	Equivalent registration class count by origin	Madrid international registration	In force by office
	Total	Resident	Non-resident	Total [a]	Total [a]	Origin [f]	Total
Israel	20,913	2,619	18,294	8,214	31,326	330	130,276
Italy	84,936	75,911	9,025	177,961	867,886	3,094	470,765
Jamaica	4,648	2,101	2,547	2,214	2,434	..	66,231
Japan (b)	..	..	..	89,320	244,732	2,553	1,872,422
Jordan	4,351	1,724	2,627	2,366	4,633	1	..
Kazakhstan (b)	..	..	..	1,295	1,916	99	41,499
Kenya (b)	..	..	..	288	1,205	9	..
Kiribati (b)	..	..	..	11	11	..	..
Kuwait (b)	..	..	..	638	2,074	..	..
Kyrgyzstan	7,930	262	7,668	462	525	7	10,238
Lao People's Democratic Republic (b)	..	..	..	13	40	1	..
Latvia	6,002	2,291	3,711	4,619	15,630	97	25,198
Lebanon (b)	..	..	..	895	4,649	1	..
Lesotho (b)	..	..	..	15	15	..	..
Liberia (b)	..	..	..	15	420	..	..
Libya (b)	..	..	..	22	22	..	..
Liechtenstein (b)	..	..	..	6,916	17,783	98	..
Lithuania	7,533	3,798	3,735	6,357	25,251	118	36,889
Luxembourg (c)	n.a.	n.a.	n.a.	26,593	128,900	438	n.a.
Madagascar	6,718	2,738	3,980	2,749	2,749	1	21,021
Malawi (b)	..	..	..	2	2	..	..
Malaysia	33,225	12,977	20,248	17,721	20,754	12	333,325
Maldives (b)	..	..	..	10	10	..	..
Mali (b,h)	n.a.	n.a.	n.a.	259	4,067	..	..
Malta	900	589	311	5,756	38,569	74	22,390
Marshall Islands (b)	..	..	..	206	616	2	..
Mauritania (b,h)	n.a.	n.a.	n.a.	44	684	..	..
Mauritius	2,004	1,048	956	2,178	5,637	11	21,000
Mexico	132,595	86,201	46,394	95,941	107,864	79	1,073,566
Monaco	9,628	1,341	8,287	3,673	16,242	68	10,313
Mongolia	12,870	7,625	5,245	7,678	7,759	1	13,298
Montenegro (b)	..	..	..	1,212	3,786	17	..
Morocco	30,238	15,185	15,053	16,627	25,402	110	112,586
Mozambique (b)	..	..	..	113	320	1	..
Myanmar (b)	..	..	..	48	48	..	..
Namibia	4,556	298	4,258	315	396	..	2,768
Nauru (b)	..	..	..	9	25	..	..
Nepal	2,041	991	1,050	1,031	1,058	..	..
Netherlands (c)	n.a.	n.a.	n.a.	78,860	463,384	1,521	n.a.
New Zealand	46,117	13,819	32,298	21,557	37,799	414	233,036
Nicaragua (b)	..	..	..	200	308	..	..
Niger (b,h)	n.a.	n.a.	n.a.	44	748	..	..
Nigeria (b)	..	..	..	91	541	..	..
Norway	40,365	8,495	31,870	18,341	63,633	386	219,492
Oman (b)	..	..	..	218	785	..	..
Pakistan	12,112	7,420	4,692	7,917	8,970	..	137,585
Palau (b)	..	..	..	1	1	..	..

| Name | Registration class count by office | | | Registration class count by origin | Equivalent registration class count by origin | Madrid international registration | In force by office |
	Total	Resident	Non-resident	Total [a]	Total [a]	Origin [f]	Total
Panama	14,023	4,831	9,192	7,621	12,056	4	136,906
Papua New Guinea (b)	..	..	..	8	8	..	..
Paraguay (b)	..	..	..	290	452	..	..
Peru	33,565	20,757	12,808	22,268	23,104	..	320,843
Philippines	40,478	16,282	24,196	17,329	18,002	44	..
Poland	46,728	38,687	8,041	57,357	282,084	432	234,792
Portugal	29,388	23,354	6,034	30,359	111,887	271	210,366
Qatar	8,418	692	7,726	2,092	3,899	..	29,185
Republic of Korea	160,654	111,059	49,595	155,945	231,351	1,037	1,162,389
Republic of Moldova	11,396	2,033	9,363	2,760	3,117	52	20,057
Romania	15,811	11,255	4,556	14,394	59,364	91	..
Russian Federation	159,495	98,190	61,305	138,037	169,447	1,361	582,132
Rwanda	3,160	223	2,937	225	225	..	..
Saint Kitts and Nevis (b)	..	..	..	113	329	3	5,527
Saint Lucia (b)	..	..	..	108	648	..	..
Saint Vincent and the Grenadines	104	1	103	26	107	..	..
Samoa	163	6	157	402	807	..	..
San Marino (b)	..	..	..	560	3,011	11	..
Sao Tome and Principe (b)	..	..	..	..	..	..	..
Saudi Arabia (b)	..	..	..	2,080	5,528	2	..
Senegal (b,h)	n.a.	n.a.	n.a.	513	8,673	..	..
Serbia	18,204	3,041	15,163	7,407	13,216	207	29,086
Seychelles	22	22	0	1,223	3,092	11	..
Sierra Leone (b)	..	..	..	3	3	..	..
Singapore	47,362	8,605	38,757	29,488	51,032	542	307,566
Sint Maarten (Dutch Part) (b)	..	..	..	13	202	1	..
Slovakia	11,032	6,206	4,826	9,433	34,011	101	47,678
Slovenia (b)	..	..	..	5,194	28,563	215	..
Solomon Islands (b)	..	..	..	16	16	..	..
Somalia (b)	..	..	..	1	28	..	..
South Africa	14,276	8,549	5,727	10,468	21,707	6	348,627
Spain	74,784	65,253	9,531	113,425	646,923	1,396	780,194
Sri Lanka (b)	..	..	..	351	1,538	1	..
Sudan	3,985	359	3,626	374	390	..	..
Suriname	811	407	404	447	475	1	10,611
Sweden	15,522	11,020	4,502	47,116	300,106	839	127,813
Switzerland	87,698	32,772	54,926	148,701	469,805	3,163	236,014
Syrian Arab Republic	5,706	1,621	4,085	1,946	3,426	8	..
Tajikistan (b)	..	..	..	1	1	..	..
Thailand	37,989	19,245	18,744	23,218	28,849	16	408,575
The former Yugoslav Republic of Macedonia (b)	..	..	..	846	2,071	47	..
Togo (b,h)	n.a.	n.a.	n.a.	165	2,937	..	..
Trinidad and Tobago	2,626	445	2,181	516	520	..	22,126
Tunisia (g)	15,241	..	..	810	3,002	23	..
Turkey	206,374	170,393	35,981	198,630	253,047	1,339	945,154
Turkmenistan (b)	..	..	..	68	68	3	..
Uganda (g)	2,611	..	..	8	8	..	..

Trademarks

Trademarks

Name	Registration class count by office			Registration class count by origin	Equivalent registration class count by origin	Madrid international registration	In force by office
	Total	Resident	Non-resident	Total [a]	Total [a]	Origin [f]	Total
Ukraine	47,923	23,742	24,181	30,575	40,050	355	177,353
United Arab Emirates	26,149	4,601	21,548	11,120	30,411	21	223,813
United Kingdom	155,793	114,536	41,257	237,993	1,084,328	3,323	653,428
United Republic of Tanzania (b)	..	..	..	69	150	1	..
United States of America	361,759	227,913	133,846	529,592	1,381,631	8,277	2,187,354
Uruguay	5,962	2,169	3,793	3,098	3,864	..	89,959
Uzbekistan	11,103	3,852	7,251	4,086	4,167	11	21,190
Vanuatu (b)	..	..	..	38	92	..	..
Venezuela (Bolivarian Republic of)	14,142	8,903	5,239	9,311	9,689	..	..
Viet Nam	47,340	22,504	24,836	25,285	27,555	104	226,044
Yemen	2,791	1,658	1,133	1,779	1,854	..	..
Zambia	4,495	683	3,812	713	713	..	33,066
Zimbabwe (b)	..	..	..	6	22	..	..
Others/Unknown	..	..	..	60,727	144,129	17	..
Total (2017 estimates)	**7,618,900**	**5,642,100**	**1,976,800**	**7,618,900**	**n.a.**	**56,267**	**43,235,000**

(a) Data on registration class count by origin are incomplete because some offices do not report detailed statistics containing the origin of registration class counts.

(b) Only Madrid designation data are available, so registration class count by office and origin data may be incomplete.

(c) This country does not have a national trademark office. All trademark registrations for this country are issued by the Benelux Office for Intellectual Property or the European Union Intellectual Property Office.

(d) Resident registrations include those issued to residents of Belgium, Luxembourg and the Netherlands.

(e) Resident registrations include those issued to residents of EU member states.

(f) Origin is defined as the country/territory of the stated residence of the holder of an international registration.

(g) Total includes an aggregate direct registration class count that cannot be broken down into direct and non-resident components.

(h) The African Intellectual Property Office (OAPI) is the competent office for issuing registrations.

n.a. indicates not applicable.

.. indicates not available.

Source: WIPO Statistics Database, September 2018.

B53. Trademark office procedural data, 2017

Office	Total examination decisions	Number registered	Partial rejections	Total rejections	Applications withdrawn or abandoned	Applications pending	Number of examiners (FTE)	First office action (average number of days)	Final office decision (average number of days)	Total third party oppositions	Pre-registration oppositions	Post-registration oppositions	Appeals to decisions
African Intellectual Property Organization	3,791	3,591	..	200	..	300	4.0	30	180	127	..	127	23
Albania	540	451	6	83	..	621	4.0	45	120	94	94	..	..
Argentina	62,456	36,970	..	24,608	878	121,375	15.0	..	405	15,498	15,498	..	330
Armenia	2,974	1,435	1,435	94	10	773	12.0	10	120	100	100	..	50
Australia	54,443	52,147	..	25	2,271	19,488	119.9	65	125	1,806	1,490	316	25
Bangladesh	..	..	..	..	..	..	14.0	45	60	101	101	..	6
Belarus	3,100	2,848	..	..	252	2,819	16.0	90	365	..	..	..	39
Benelux Office for Intellectual Property	..	..	..	..	..	..	..	..	..	..	..	..	..
Bhutan	..	..	..	..	..	..	4.0	..	..	..	..	..	..
Bolivia (Plurinational State of)	6,496	6,445	..	..	51	381	5.0	21	150	279	..	..	..
Bosnia and Herzegovina	716	631	12	30	43	956	3.0	8	350	7	7	..	1
Botswana	..	..	..	..	..	1,070	3.0	..	..	..	..	..	..
Brazil	258,823	123,362	..	65,503	69,958	359,562	144.0	870	1,260	20,836	16,968	3,868	17,640
Brunei Darussalam	230	180	..	..	50	697	1.0	14	60	5	5	..	..
Canada	47,796	28,621	13	61	19,101	143,948	48.4	254	416	945	945	..	15
China	..	..	..	..	..	..	..	..	..	..	..	..	..
China, Hong Kong SAR	39,559	35,234	..	3,091	1,234	25,927	52.0	39	67	564	423	141	2
China, Macao SAR	11,660	11,076	20	518	46	5,138	5.0	201	201	147	147	..	..
Colombia	32,959	24,314	797	7,201	647	27,529	59.0	40	203	3,360	3,360	..	5,454
Costa Rica	10,763	9,092	..	67	1,604	..	17.0	8	8	211	185	26	407
Croatia	1,051	865	37	86	63	445	2.0	51	51	57	57	..	23
Cuba	1,054	862	40	122	30	4,646	8.0	60	850	47	47	..	91
Denmark	2,590	2,293	114	110	73	474	..	49	49	115	..	..	..
Dominican Republic	10,696	9,488	6	1,055	147	3,005	11.0	14	14	196	196	..	14
Ecuador	11,878	11,468	277	133	..	3,298	13.0	120	100	1,555	1,555	..	1,288
El Salvador	13,514	6,491	1,761	1,669	3,593	1,893	18.0	4	7	164	164	..	101
Estonia	1,333	1,122	89	5	117	1,343	12.0	3	269	43	43	..	1
European Union Intellectual Property Office	114,573	105,552	3,232	4,547	1,242	70,155	300.0	7	16	18,596	18,596	..	2,491
Finland	3,729	2,860	44	196	629	1,270	8.0	99	137	73	..	73	19
Gambia	..	..	..	..	..	..	3.0	..	..	..	..	..	..
Georgia	1,253	960	93	187	13	1,261	12.0	60	240	17	17	..	115
Germany	58,774	50,947	775	6,682	370	23,363	71.0	60	93	4,267	..	4,267	700
Ghana	..	..	..	..	..	2,151	..	..	..	..	..	..	..
Greece	..	..	..	..	..	..	5.0	5	30	..	..	..	..
Honduras	6,838	6,285	..	397	156	100	4.0	5	15	150	..	..	232
Hungary	3,868	2,869	20	116	863	2,804	14.0	15	195	174	144	30	90
Iceland	5,378	4,517	517	122	222	1,598	6.0	56	63	40	..	..	..
India	423,447	307,811	..	13,875	101,761	34,791	105.0	30	45	131,356	125,785	5,571	128
Indonesia	..	..	..	..	..	..	..	..	..	..	..	..	..
Israel	..	..	..	..	..	17,883	16.0	405	513	70	70	..	..
Jamaica	..	..	..	..	..	..	2.0	..	..	..	..	..	7
Kyrgyzstan	655	588	5	22	40	15	5.0	30	365	..	..	..	7
Latvia	1,519	1,260	15	140	104	1,031	6.0	1	145	79	..	79	7
Lithuania	3,219	2,678	3	245	293	..	5.0	105	107	123	..	123	6
Madagascar	134	..	45	84	5	137	1.0	210	240	..	..	..	25
Malta	1,045	920	..	44	81	110	2.8	1	80	..	..	..	..
Mauritius	..	..	..	..	..	..	2.0	..	..	..	..	..	..
Mexico	128,142	105,686	6,493	..	15,963	138,470	45.0	53	158	5,088	5,088	..	585

Trademarks

Office	Total examination decisions	Number registered	Partial rejections	Total rejections	Applications withdrawn or abandoned	Applications pending	Number of examiners (FTE)	First office action (average number of days)	Final office decision (average number of days)	Total third party oppositions	Pre-registration oppositions	Post-registration oppositions	Appeals to decisions
Monaco	37	..	..	4	33	3	2.0	5	33	..	..	..	..
Mongolia	2,276	1,482	205	136	453	876	3.0	180	270	7	1	6	205
Morocco	1,048	111	339	427	171	1,363	12.0	44	100	1,480	1,480	..	58
Namibia	..	..	..	..	..	..	3.0	..	..	..	..	..	..
New Zealand	8,841	8,165	14	..	662	3,039	30.0	23	25	181	..	..	3
Norway	14,635	12,228	..	91	2,316	10,500	26.5	150	200	114	..	114	114
Panama	..	..	..	..	..	24	6.0	..	..	..	..	..	..
Peru	34,619	26,785	..	5,180	2,654	6,103	45.0	5	74	1,966	1,966	..	2,802
Portugal	23,739	18,754	524	4,278	183	1,190	18.0	100	100	2,081	1,959	122	260
Qatar	501	167	200	80	54	128	6.0	30	180	130	130	..	69
Republic of Korea	245,791	206,377	..	39,414	..	..	123.0	5	10	1,756	1,756	..	1,569
Republic of Moldova	1,841	1,297	219	277	48	2,549	34.0	20	391	72	58	14	96
Romania	7,177	6,073	..	665	439	3,893	25.0	7	150	630	..	..	299
Russian Federation	48,657	42,149	..	6,128	380	47,865	162.0	446	426	..	..	..	27
Saint Kitts and Nevis	..	..	..	..	..	214	..	..	..	..	..	..	..
Saint Vincent and the Grenadines	87	86	..	1	..	155	3.0	7	21	..	..	..	..
Serbia	2,743	2,201	40	260	242	902	6.0	150	210	..	..	..	51
Slovakia	2,431	2,107	12	232	80	1,282	15.0	29	160	108	108	..	86
Spain	26,508	23,998	..	1,876	634	25,533	46.0	25	167	14,664	..	..	2,105
Sudan	2,332	1,759	..	262	311	311	20.0	3	10	80	50	30	3
Suriname	..	..	..	..	..	643	2.0	..	..	..	..	..	..
Sweden	8,571	6,329	163	390	1,689	3,707	25.0	70	149	154	..	154	143
Thailand	106,797	37,260	..	51,463	18,074	97,486	22.0	162	426	712	712	..	2,347
Trinidad and Tobago	..	..	..	..	..	..	8.0	..	..	..	..	..	..
Turkey	106,036	85,573	11,779	7,573	1,111	96,886	85.0	4	25	23,913	23,913	..	10,382
Ukraine	23,571	16,453	..	1,851	5,267	40,099	76.0	205	428	..	..	..	91
United Arab Emirates	..	..	..	..	..	..	..	..	..	..	..	..	..
United Kingdom	66,403	62,809	..	2,530	1,064	3,914	71.0	..	9	3,571	3,172	399	64
United States of America	326,750	250,833	..	..	75,917	571,759	543.0	85	288	6,216	..	..	3,057
Uruguay	3,917	3,440	68	233	176	19,399	5.0	737	751	422	..	..	185
Uzbekistan	3,522	2,580	..	213	729	393	8.0	210	210	..	..	..	25
Viet Nam	27,227	20,661	..	6,347	219	88,133	49.0	708	750	1,548	1,173	375	399
Zambia	..	..	..	..	..	515	4.0	..	..	..	..	..	..

Note: WIPO collects data from IP offices using a common questionnaire and methodology. However, due to differences in application processing procedures between offices, data cannot be fully harmonized. Therefore, one should exercise caution when making comparisons across offices.

Source: WIPO Statistics Database, September 2018.

Industrial designs

Highlights

Designs contained in applications totaled 1.24 million in the world

An estimated 945,100 applications were filed worldwide in 2017 (see figure 3.1). The number of designs contained in these applications (design count) totaled 1.24 million (see figure 3.2). Unfortunately, it is not possible to calculate a meaningful growth rate for global design applications in 2017. The intellectual property (IP) office of China changed its methodology in 2017 and now counts only those industrial design application filings for which the filing fees have been paid. As filings in China account for more than half of all industrial design applications filed around the world, comparison of 2016 and 2017 estimated world totals would not reflect the actual trend in global filing activity.

An estimated 945,100 industrial design applications were filed worldwide
3.1. Industrial design applications worldwide, 2007–2017

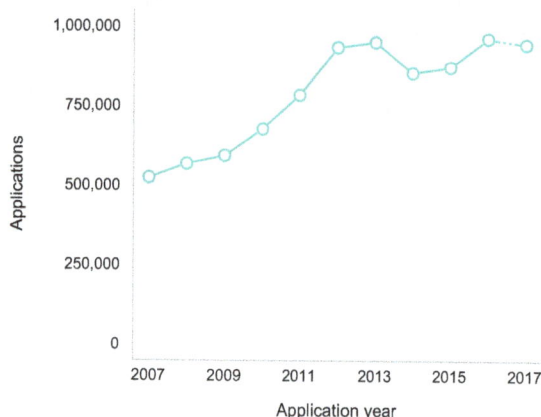

Source: Figure C1.

The number of designs contained in applications totaled 1.24 million
3.2. Number of designs in industrial design applications worldwide, 2007–2017

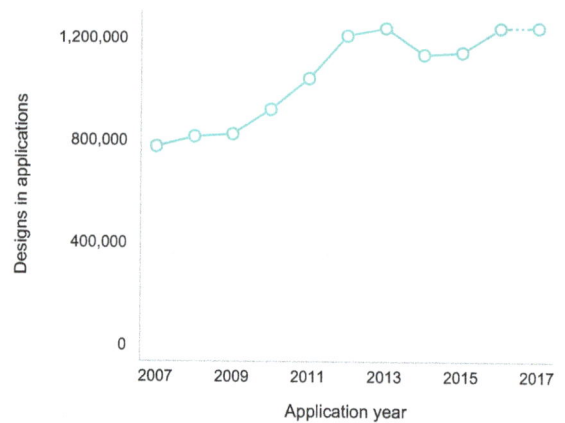

Source: Figure C2.

Designs contained in applications filed at the U.K. IP office almost doubled

The office of China received applications containing 50.6% of all designs in applications filed worldwide in 2017, representing 628,658 designs. The office of China was followed by the European Union Intellectual Property Office (EUIPO) (111,021), the offices of the Republic of Korea (67,357), of Turkey (46,875) and of the United States of America (U.S.) (45,881) (see figure 3.3).

The top 20 offices combined accounted for 92.3% of designs in all applications. The 2017 annual growth rate for the office of China is not available due to its change in methodology, mentioned earlier. Of the 19 remaining offices, 13 saw increases in their application design count, among which six experienced double-digit growth (see figure C11). The offices of the United Kingdom (U.K.) (+92.1%), Spain (+23.5%) and Switzerland (+17.9%) saw the sharpest increases. The EUIPO (+6.2%) and the office of Japan (+4.7%) also had higher design counts in 2017 than in the previous year. In contrast, the offices of Germany (–18.5%), France (–17.8%) and Morocco (–12.5%) all saw significant decreases.

Among offices located in low- and middle-income countries, annual growth in 2017 was particularly high for Georgia (+82.1%), Ghana (+69.2%), Mongolia (+52%) and Malaysia (+27.1%). The offices of Bangladesh, Egypt, the African Intellectual Property Organization (OAPI) and the Republic of Moldova saw double-digit growth of between 12% and 18% (see figure C13).

Designs contained in resident applications accounted for 83.7% of the world total design count in 2017. The proportion was boosted by the high resident design share in China (97.2%). Resident design counts accounted for the majority of filing activity in all of the top 20 offices except for Canada (12.5%), Switzerland (32.9%) and Australia (37%).

An increase in the number of designs contained in resident applications had a positive impact on the overall annual growth rates for 10 of the top 20 offices, and for seven of them, it was the primary driver of growth, with particularly high contributions to total growth in both Spain and the U.K. The increases in resident design counts explain the overall growth seen at the offices of Brazil, India, the Islamic Republic of Iran and the Russian Federation (see figure C11). An increase in the non-resident design count was the main or sole driver of growth at nine offices, which included the offices of Canada, the EUIPO, Switzerland and the U.S.

Design count

Some offices allow industrial design applications to contain more than one design for the same good or in the same class; others allow only one design per application. To capture the differences in application filing systems across offices, one needs to compare their respective application and registration design counts.

Equivalent design count

Designs in applications filed at regional offices are equivalent to multiple designs in applications filed in the respective member states of those offices. To calculate the number of equivalent designs for the African Intellectual Property Organization (OAPI) which has 17 member states, the Benelux Office for Intellectual Property (BOIP) which has three, and the EUIPO (28), each design is multiplied by the corresponding number of member states. However, the African Regional Intellectual Property Organization (ARIPO) does not register industrial designs with automatic region-wide applicability. Therefore, for this office, each application is counted as one application abroad if the applicant does not reside in a member state or as one resident application and one application abroad if the applicant resides in a member state.

The offices of all upper middle-income countries combined received 59.1% of all designs contained in applications filed in 2017 (see table C7). China accounted for the vast majority of this share, with the other upper middle-income countries receiving only 8.5% of the world total. The combined share of the high-income countries stood at 36.8%. Offices of lower middle-income countries received 3.9% of the total, and those of low-income countries only 0.3%.

Between 2007 and 2017, average annual growth in design counts was 8% for upper middle-income countries.[1] Over the same period, offices in high-income (+1.6%), lower middle-income (+1.8%) and low-income (+1.3%) economies had much lower growth rates in comparison.

Asia accounted for more than two-thirds (67.9%) of all designs in applications filed worldwide in 2017 (see figure 3.4). It was followed by Europe (24.4%) and North America (4.2%). All geographical regions experienced positive average annual growth between 2007 and 2017, with Asia (+6.9%) and North America (+4.8%) experiencing the largest increases.

Industrial designs

China received 50.6% of all designs contained in applications filed worldwide

3.3. Application design counts for the top 10 offices, 2017

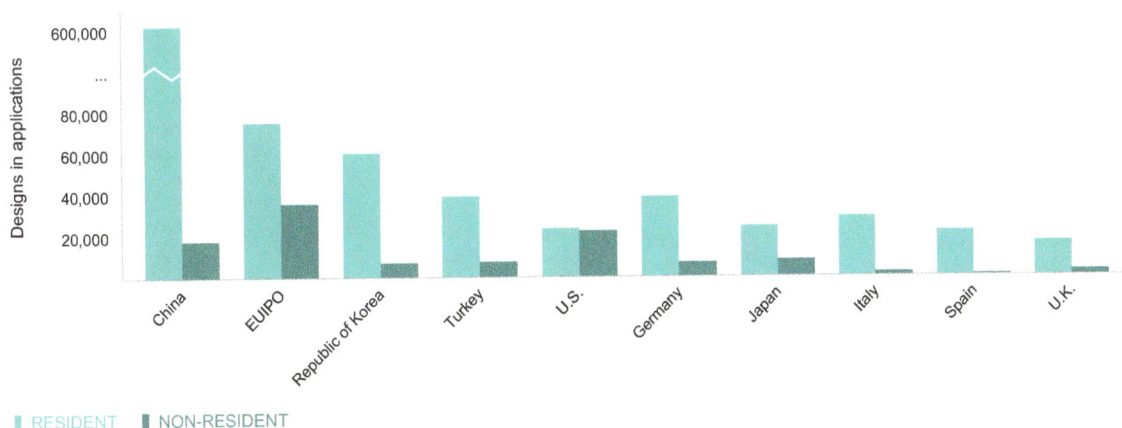

RESIDENT   NON-RESIDENT

Source: Figure C10.

Offices located in Asia accounted for more than two-thirds of total filing activity
3.4. Application design counts by region, 2007 and 2017

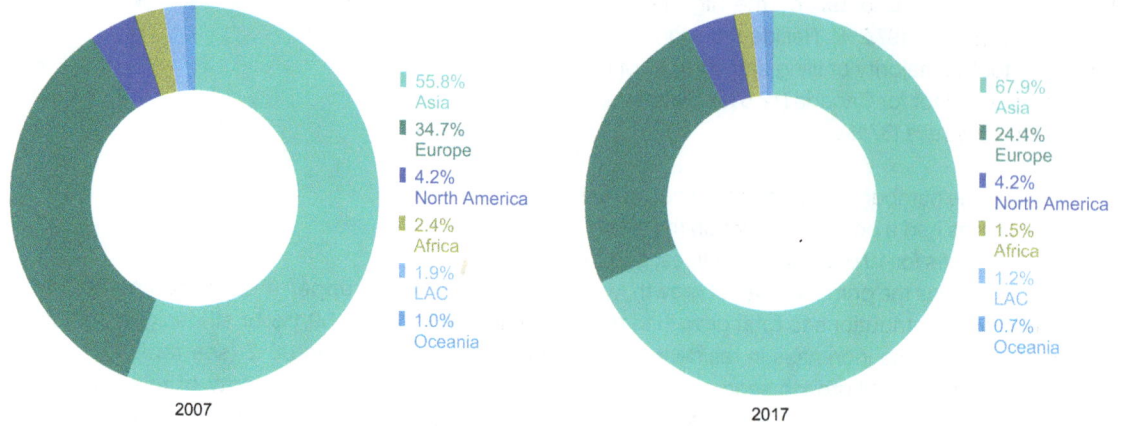

2007

- 55.8% Asia
- 34.7% Europe
- 4.2% North America
- 2.4% Africa
- 1.9% LAC
- 1.0% Oceania

2017

- 67.9% Asia
- 24.4% Europe
- 4.2% North America
- 1.5% Africa
- 1.2% LAC
- 0.7% Oceania

Source: Table C8.

Industrial designs

Industrial design applications filed since 1883

Between 1883 and the early 1950s, the offices of Japan and the U.S. averaged similar numbers of applications, rarely exceeding 10,000. The office of Japan received the largest number of applications per year from the 1950s to the late 1990s, reaching approximately 50,000 annual filings at its peak. The office of China began receiving applications in 1985 and saw unprecedented growth: from 640 in 1985 to 660,000 in 2013. The office of the Republic of Korea surpassed the office of Japan in 2004 and has remained in second position since then. In 2012, the office of the U.S. moved ahead of the office of Japan to become the third largest. Ranked fifth is the EUIPO, which began receiving applications in 2003. Unlike the other four offices, the EUIPO has a multiple design system. Applications filed at the EUIPO contained 111,021 designs in 2017.

Trend in industrial design applications for the top five offices, 1883–2017

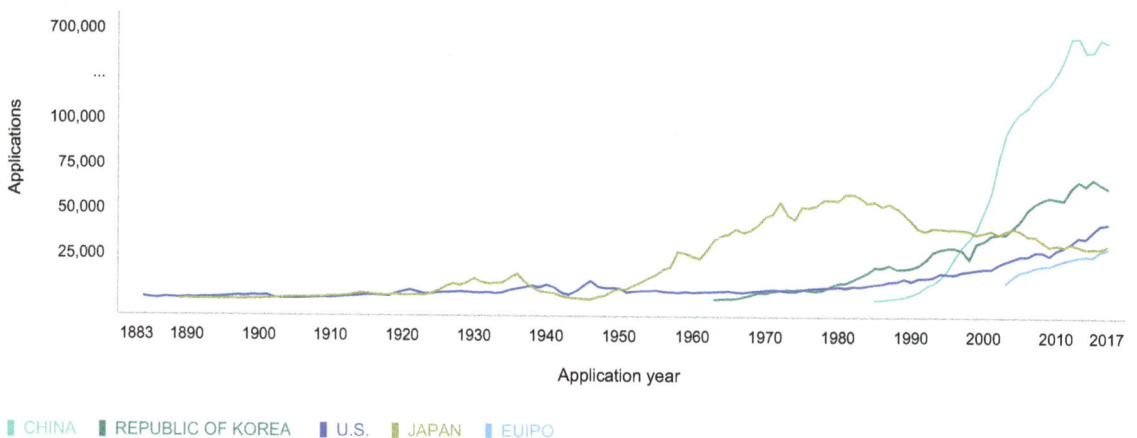

CHINA   REPUBLIC OF KOREA   U.S.   JAPAN   EUIPO

Source: Table C8

Equivalent design counts from applicants in Japan increased by 16.2%

Applications received by offices from resident and non-resident applicants are referred to as office data, whereas applications filed by applicants at their home office (resident applications) or at foreign offices (applications abroad) are referred to as origin data. Here, industrial design statistics based on the origin of residence of the first named applicant are reported in order to complement the picture of industrial design activity worldwide. As with the office data, the 2017 annual growth rate for applicants residing in China is not available due to the change in how the office of China counts the applications it receives.

Applicants from China had the highest equivalent design count in 2017, numbering almost 858,000 (see map 3.5). They were followed by applicants residing in Germany (676,139), the U.S. (353,707) and Italy (304,664). Equivalent designs in applications filed abroad accounted for between 79% and 98% of the total for applicants from all of the top 20 origins, except for those from China (28.8%), Turkey (30.7%) and the Republic of Korea (48.9%).

Among the top 10 origins, the largest increases in equivalent design counts were experienced in Japan (+16.2%), Switzerland (+11.3%) and in the U.S. (+10.4%). In contrast, applicants from Italy (–16.5%), Spain (–12.4%) and the Republic of Korea (–11.5%) saw the sharpest decreases in equivalent design count compared to 2016 (see figure C17).

European countries dominate the top 20 origins with a total of 13, followed by five origins located in Asia and one each in Oceania and North America. In terms of income categories, 18 of the top 20 origins belong to the high-income group, while two upper middle-income countries – China and Turkey – also feature.

Applicants from Germany (615,045), the U.S. (330,139) and Italy (266,177) had the highest number of equivalent designs in applications filed abroad in 2017. Among the top 10 origins of equivalent designs in applications filed abroad, applicants from China (+54.9%), Japan (+20.5%), the U.S. (+11.5%) and Switzerland (+11.3%) saw the most pronounced increases.

The Republic of Korea tops the ranking when adjusting for GDP and population

The Republic of Korea (3,265) had the highest resident design count per 100 billion US dollars (USD) of gross domestic product (GDP) in 2017 (see figure 3.6). It was followed by China (2,878) and Turkey (1,938). Germany, Italy and Spain each had ratios between 1,500 and 2,000. Among other European countries, Switzerland (887), France (689) and the Russian Federation (104) had much lower ratios.

The Republic of Korea (1,174) was also the country with by far the highest resident design count per million population in 2017 (see figure C26). It was followed by Germany (739) and Italy (636). Compared to the 2007 ratios, those for 2017 sharply increased for China (441) and Spain (543). Even though residents of Japan

Applicants from China had the highest equivalent design count
3.5. Equivalent design counts by origin, 2017

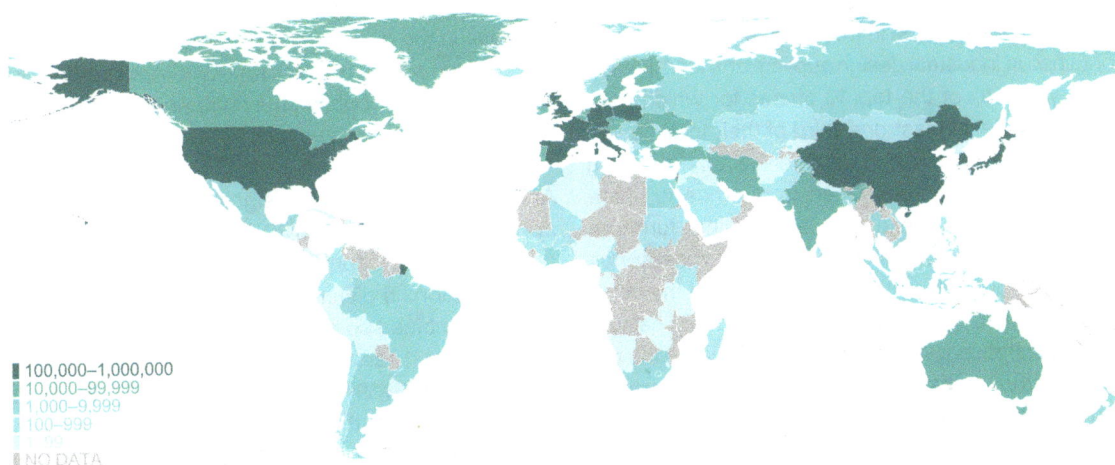

100,000–1,000,000
10,000–99,999
1,000–9,999
100–999

NO DATA

Source: Map C16.

The Republic of Korea had the highest number of designs per unit of GDP both in 2007 and 2017

3.6. Resident application design count per USD 100 billion GDP for the top 10 origins, 2007 and 2017

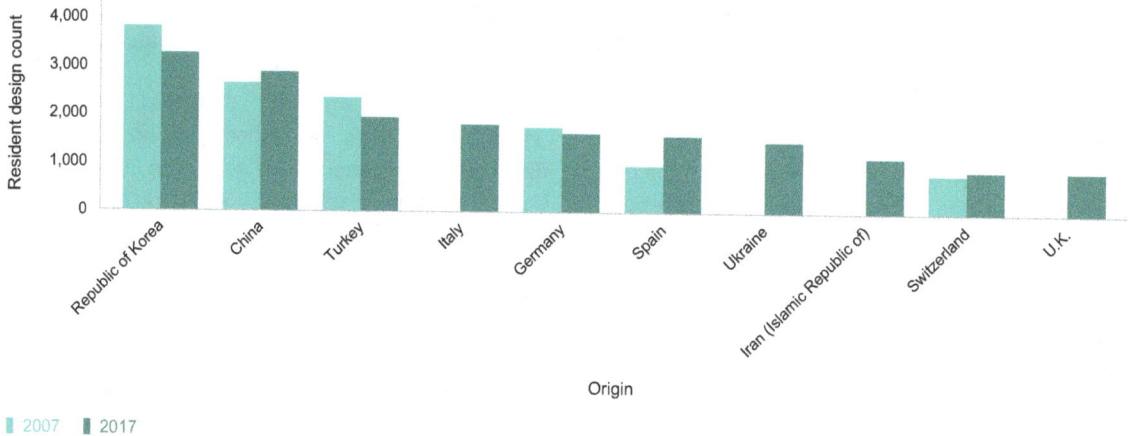

■ 2007   ■ 2017

Source: Figure C25.

Industrial designs

and the U.S. ranked among the top five in terms of industrial design application filings, their 2017 ratios of resident design count per million population were relatively low, with ratios of 193 and 72, respectively.

Furnishing and clothing remained the most recorded classes

The Locarno classification includes 32 classes of industrial designs. In 2017, the classes that accounted for the largest shares of the world total remained furnishings (10%), clothing (8.5%) and packages and containers (7.2%). These three classes combined accounted for one-quarter of all designs in applications (see figure C22).

Grouping the Locarno classes into 12 industry sectors highlights the most important sectors for designs contained in industrial design applications filed in each country. For all of the top 10 offices for which data were available, at least one-third of their total design count was concentrated in just three sectors, although these top three sectors varied from office to office (see figure 3.7). For example, advertising, furniture and household goods and textiles and accessories accounted for 71.4% of total design count at the office of France and 64.8% at the office of Germany. Leisure and education, packaging and transport were the top three sectors at the office of the Russian Federation and represented 35.4% of total design count.

In half of the top 10 countries of origin, the majority of designs in applications were filed among their top three sectors, with applicants residing in Switzerland (70.1%) and Italy (67.7%) recording the highest level of concentration among their top three sectors (see figure C24). The textiles and accessories sector was among the top three sectors for nine of the top 10 origins, whereas furniture and household goods featured in the top three sectors for six of them.

Industrial design registrations worldwide rose to 711,400

An estimated 711,400 industrial designs were registered worldwide in 2017. This represents an annual increase of 0.8%, following a drop of 3.5% in 2016 (see figure C4). This growth was mainly due to a considerable increase in the number of registrations issued by the U.K. office, which registered 17,195 applications in 2017, more than doubling the number of registrations it recorded the previous year.

An estimated 985,900 designs were contained in applications registered in 2017, up 1.5% on 2016. The office of China accounted for nearly 45% of all designs in applications registered worldwide, and the top 20 offices combined comprised 91% of the total. Among these offices, 12 saw annual growth, including the U.K. (+102.7%), India (+39%), Spain (+27.6%) and Switzerland (+19%). In contrast, the offices of the Republic of Korea (–11.6%), Brazil (–10.8%) and Canada (–9.1%) all saw sharp decreases in the number of designs registered (see figure C14).

Designs related to textiles and accessories accounted for a fifth of total design in India and the Republic of Korea

3.7. Distribution of application design counts by the top three sectors and for the top 10 offices, 2017

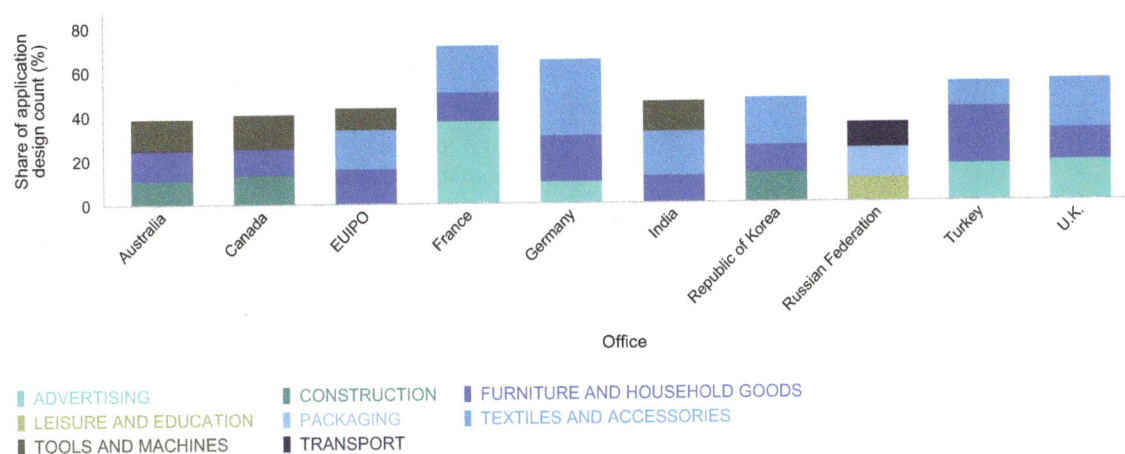

Legend:
- ADVERTISING
- LEISURE AND EDUCATION
- TOOLS AND MACHINES
- CONSTRUCTION
- PACKAGING
- TRANSPORT
- FURNITURE AND HOUSEHOLD GOODS
- TEXTILES AND ACCESSORIES

Source: Figure C23.

Around 1.46 million industrial design registrations were in force in China

A record 3.75 million industrial design registrations were in force worldwide in 2017, up 5% on 2016 (see figure C27). The number of registrations in force in China increased by 105,504 to reach 1.46 million, representing 38.9% of the world total. China was followed by the Republic of Korea (339,350), the U.S. (321,314), Japan (254,060) and the EUIPO (210,605). The top five offices saw growth of between 0.3% (Republic of Korea) and 8.1% (EUIPO).

German applicants remained the largest users of the Hague System

The Hague System offers applicants an advantageous way to seek industrial design protection internationally as an alternative to using the Paris Convention for the Protection of Industrial Property. For further information and statistics on the System, see the *Hague Yearly Review 2018*.

In 2017, the Hague System received 5,213 international applications, down 6.3% on 2016. These applications contained 19,429 designs, representing an annual growth of 3.8% (see figure C31). It was the 11th consecutive year of growth in application design counts.

Applicants residing in Germany remained the largest users of the Hague System, with 4,261 designs in applications. They were followed by those residing in Switzerland (2,935), the Republic of Korea (1,742), the U.S. (1,661) and France (1,396). These five origins

combined accounted for 61.7% of the total. While the U.S. (+17.8%), France (+15.2%), Switzerland (+14.9%) and Germany (+8.8%) all experienced sharp increases in design count, the Republic of Korea (–7.4%) saw its first drop since joining the System in 2014.

The European Union (EU) was the most designated Hague member with 15,124 designs in designations in 2017. It was followed by Switzerland (9,604), Turkey (6,615), the U.S. (4,534) and Norway (3,546). Of these top five designated Hague members, all saw annual growth ranging from 1.2% for the EU to 9% for Switzerland, except for the U.S., which saw its design count decrease by 4% compared to 2016.

1   The recent methodological change of the office of China affects this growth rate but, given the long-term nature of the comparisons, the resulting bias is relatively small.

Industrial design statistics

Industrial designs

Industrial design applications and registrations worldwide

C1. Trend in industrial design applications worldwide, 2004–2017

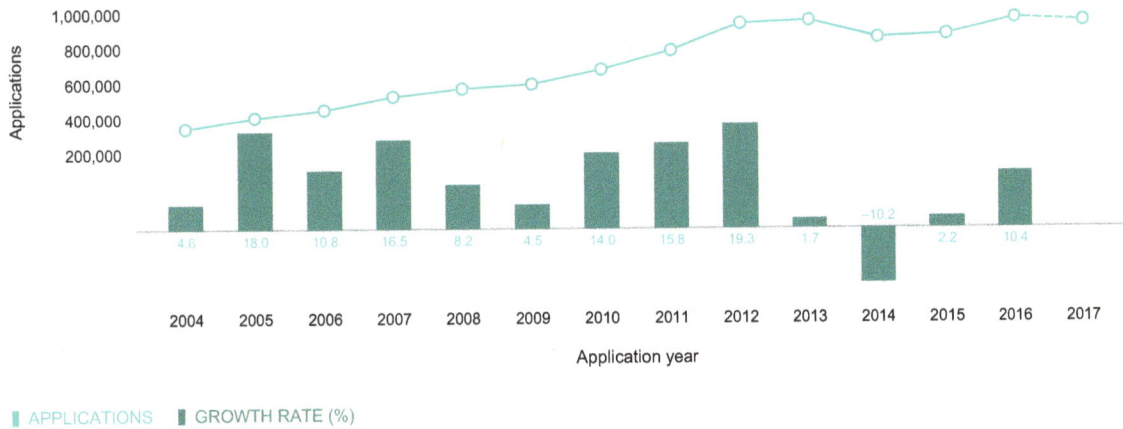

APPLICATIONS   GROWTH RATE (%)

Note: China's 2017 data are not comparable with its previous year's data due to the new way in which the IP office of China counts its applications data. Prior to 2017, it included all applications received; however, starting in 2017, China's application count data include only those applications for which the office has received the necessary application fees. As China accounts for the bulk of the global total, it is not possible to report the 2017 worldwide application growth rate. World totals are WIPO estimates using data covering 151 IP offices. These totals include the numbers of applications filed directly with national and regional offices (known as the "Paris route") as well as the numbers of designations received via the Hague System (where applicable).

Source: WIPO Statistics Database, September 2018.

C2. Trend in application design counts worldwide, 2004–2017

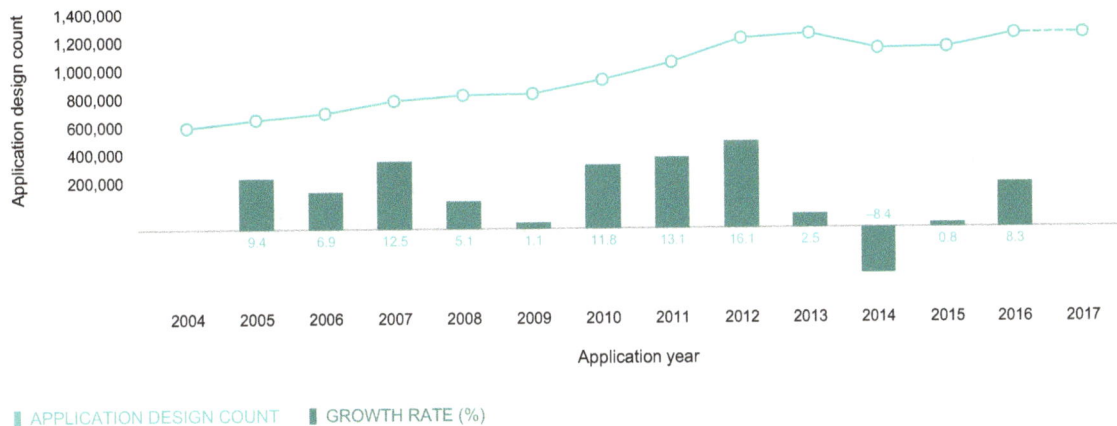

APPLICATION DESIGN COUNT   GROWTH RATE (%)

Note: China's 2017 data are not comparable with its previous year's data due to the new way in which the IP office of China counts its applications data. Prior to 2017, it included all applications received; however, starting in 2017, China's application count data include only those applications for which the office has received the necessary application fees. As China accounts for the bulk of the global total, it is not possible to report the 2017 worldwide application growth rate. World totals are WIPO estimates using data covering 151 IP offices. These totals include design counts in applications filed directly with national and regional offices (known as the "Paris route") as well as design counts in designations received via the Hague System (where applicable). See the glossary for the definition of design count.

Source: WIPO Statistics Database, September 2018.

C3. Resident and non-resident application design counts worldwide, 2004–2017

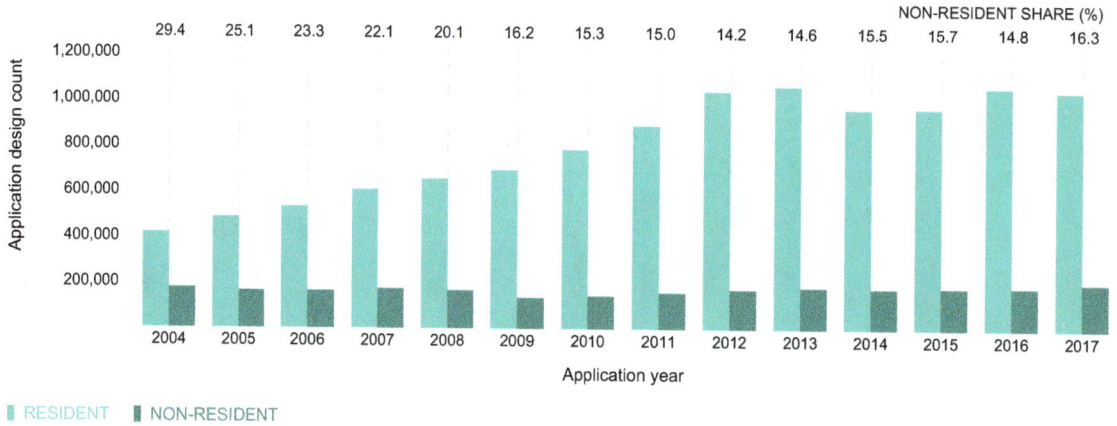

NON-RESIDENT SHARE (%)

| | 29.4 | 25.1 | 23.3 | 22.1 | 20.1 | 16.2 | 15.3 | 15.0 | 14.2 | 14.6 | 15.5 | 15.7 | 14.8 | 16.3 |

Application design count

1,200,000

1,000,000

800,000

600,000

400,000

200,000

2004 2005 2006 2007 2008 2009 2010 2011 2012 2013 2014 2015 2016 2017

Application year

■ RESIDENT   ■ NON-RESIDENT

Note: World totals are WIPO estimates using data covering 151 IP offices. These totals include design counts in applications filed directly with national and regional offices (known as the "Paris route") as well as design counts in designations received via the Hague System (where applicable). See the glossary for the definition of design count.

Source: WIPO Statistics Database, September 2018.

Industrial designs

C4. Trend in industrial design registrations worldwide, 2004–2017

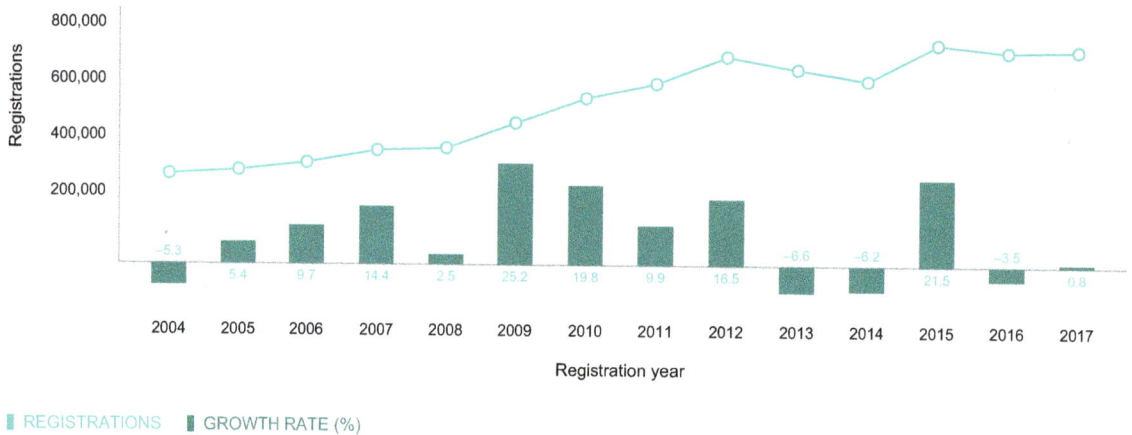

Registrations

800,000

600,000

400,000

200,000

| -5.3 | 5.4 | 9.7 | 14.4 | 2.5 | 25.2 | 19.8 | 9.9 | 16.5 | -6.6 | -6.2 | 21.5 | -3.5 | 0.8 |

2004 2005 2006 2007 2008 2009 2010 2011 2012 2013 2014 2015 2016 2017

Registration year

■ REGISTRATIONS   ■ GROWTH RATE (%)

Note: World totals are WIPO estimates using data covering 147 IP offices. These totals include the numbers of registrations issued by national and regional offices for applications filed directly with offices (known as the "Paris route") as well as for designations received via the Hague System (where applicable).

Source: WIPO Statistics Database, September 2018.

C5. Trend in registration design counts worldwide, 2004–2017

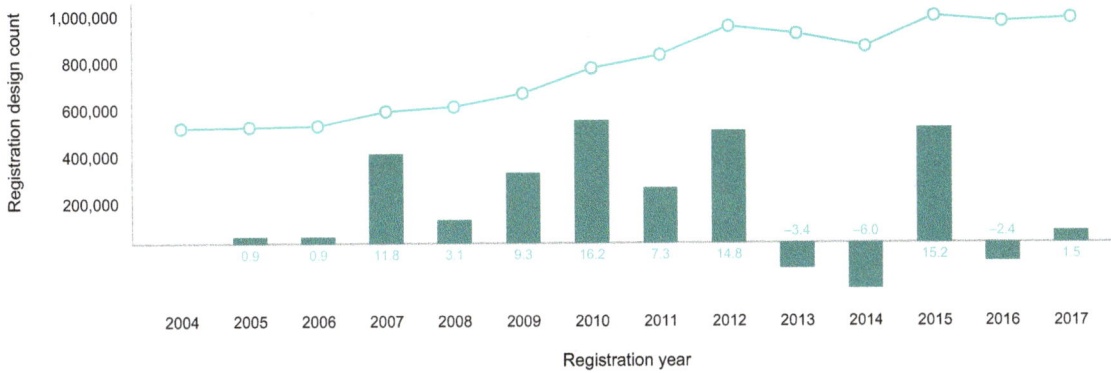

Registration design count (y-axis)

Year	Growth rate (%)
2004	
2005	0.9
2006	0.9
2007	11.8
2008	3.1
2009	9.3
2010	16.2
2011	7.3
2012	14.8
2013	-3.4
2014	-6.0
2015	15.2
2016	-2.4
2017	1.5

Registration year (x-axis)

REGISTRATION DESIGN COUNT   GROWTH RATE (%)

Note: World totals are WIPO estimates using data covering 147 IP offices. These totals include design counts in registrations issued by national and regional offices for applications filed directly with offices (known as the "Paris route") as well as for designations received via the Hague System (where applicable). See the glossary for the definition of design count.

Source: WIPO Statistics Database, September 2018.

Industrial designs

C6. Resident and non-resident registration design counts worldwide, 2004–2017

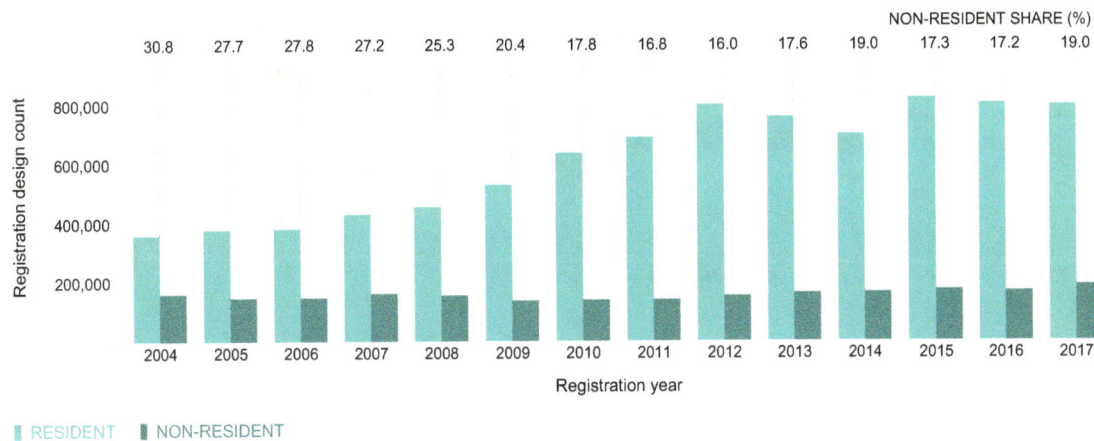

NON-RESIDENT SHARE (%)

2004	2005	2006	2007	2008	2009	2010	2011	2012	2013	2014	2015	2016	2017
30.8	27.7	27.8	27.2	25.3	20.4	17.8	16.8	16.0	17.6	19.0	17.3	17.2	19.0

Registration design count (y-axis)

Registration year (x-axis)

RESIDENT   NON-RESIDENT

Note: World totals are WIPO estimates using data covering 147 IP offices. These totals include design counts in registrations issued by national and regional offices for applications filed directly with offices (known as the "Paris route") as well as for designations received via the Hague System (where applicable). See the glossary for the definition of design count.

Source: WIPO Statistics Database, September 2018.

Industrial design applications and registrations by office

C7. Application design counts by income group, 2007 and 2017

Income group	Number of designs in applications		Resident share (%)		Share of world total (%)		Average growth (%)
	2007	2017	2007	2017	2007	2017	2007–2017
High-income	390,800	456,500	71.1	70.8	50.4	36.8	1.6
Upper middle-income	341,200	734,100	88.6	93.4	44.0	59.1	8.0
Upper middle-income without China	*73,800*	*105,400*	*66.2*	*71.3*	*9.5*	*8.5*	*3.6*
Lower middle-income	40,400	48,100	48.4	61.5	5.2	3.9	1.8
Low-income	3,000	3,400	33.4	29.9	0.4	0.3	1.3
World	**775,400**	**1,242,100**	**77.5**	**83.7**	**100.0**	**100.0**	**4.8**

Note: Average growth rate is provided for 2007–2017, as the change in the method of reporting application data at the IP office of China has limited impact on long-term average growth rates. Totals by income group are WIPO estimates using data covering 151 IP offices. Each category includes the following number of offices: high-income countries/economies (57), upper middle-income (43), lower middle-income (37) and low-income (14). Data for the European Union Intellectual Property Office are allocated to the high-income group because most EU member states are high-income countries. For similar reasons, data for the African Regional Intellectual Property Organization and the African Intellectual Property Organization are allocated to the low-income group. For information on income group classification, see the data description section.

Source: WIPO Statistics Database, September 2018.

C8. Application design counts by region, 2007 and 2017

Region	Number of designs in applications		Resident share (%)		Share of world total (%)		Average growth (%)
	2007	2017	2007	2017	2007	2017	2007–2017
Africa	18,400	18,900	47.4	55.7	2.4	1.5	0.3
Asia	432,900	843,700	89.6	92.1	55.8	67.9	6.9
Europe	268,800	302,600	66.5	71.7	34.7	24.4	1.2
Latin America and the Caribbean	14,600	15,500	41.3	47.9	1.9	1.2	0.6
North America	32,800	52,400	48.9	46.5	4.2	4.2	4.8
Oceania	7,900	9,000	42.2	35.6	1.0	0.7	1.3
Total	**775,400**	**1,242,100**	**77.5**	**83.7**	**100.0**	**100.0**	**4.8**

Note: Average growth rate is provided for 2007–2017, as the change in the method of reporting application data at the IP office of China has limited impact on long-term average growth rates. Totals by geographical region are WIPO estimates using data covering 151 IP offices. Each region includes the following number of offices: Africa (29), Asia (41), Europe (46), Latin America and the Caribbean (28), North America (2) and Oceania (5). For information on geographical region classification, see the data description section.

Source: WIPO Statistics Database, September 2018.

Industrial designs

C9. Trend in industrial design applications for the top five offices, 1883–2017

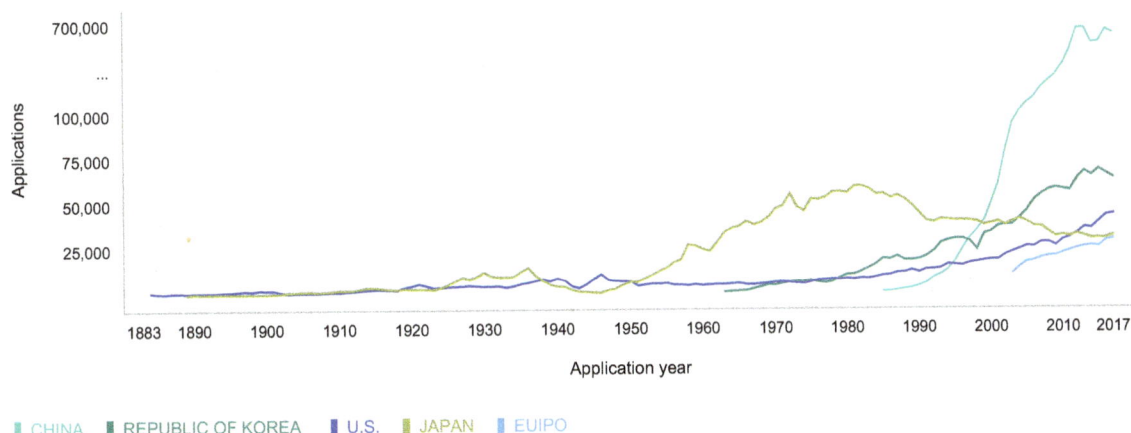

CHINA   REPUBLIC OF KOREA   U.S.   JAPAN   EUIPO

Note: The decrease in applications at the IP office of China in 2017 is mostly explained by the new way in which the office counts its applications data. Prior to 2017, it included all applications received; however, starting in 2017, China's application count data include only those applications for which the office has received the necessary application fees. EUIPO is the European Union Intellectual Property Office. Data are based on the numbers of applications filed; that is, differences between single-design and multiple-design filing systems across IP offices are not taken into account. The top five offices were selected based on their 2017 totals.

Source: WIPO Statistics Database, September 2018.

C10. Application design counts for the top 20 offices, 2017

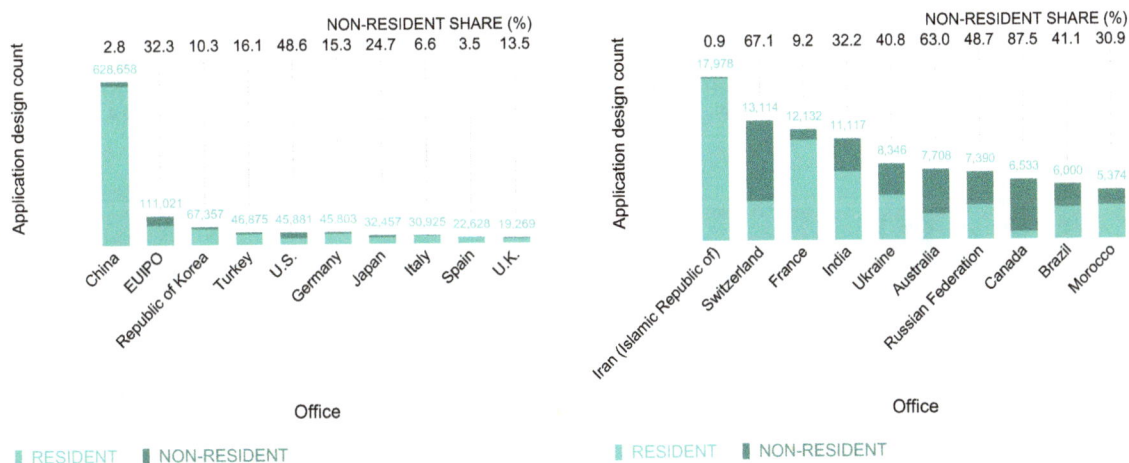

RESIDENT   NON-RESIDENT

RESIDENT   NON-RESIDENT

Note: EUIPO is the European Union Intellectual Property Office.
Source: WIPO Statistics Database, September 2018.

Industrial designs

C11. Contribution of resident and non-resident application design counts to total growth for the top 20 offices, 2016–2017

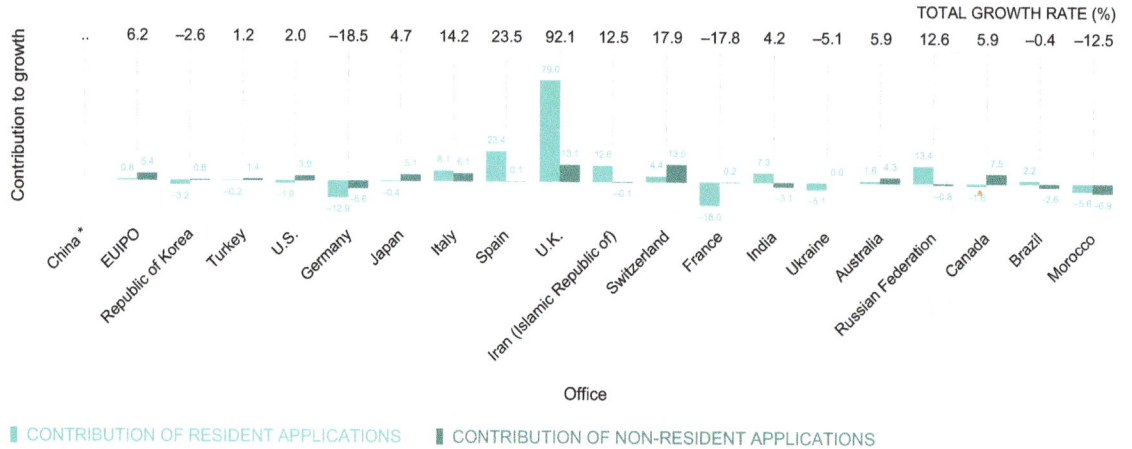

TOTAL GROWTH RATE (%)

China*	EUIPO	Republic of Korea	Turkey	U.S.	Germany	Japan	Italy	Spain	U.K.	Iran (Islamic Republic of)	Switzerland	France	India	Ukraine	Australia	Russian Federation	Canada	Brazil	Morocco
..	6.2	−2.6	1.2	2.0	−18.5	4.7	14.2	23.5	92.1	12.5	17.9	−17.8	4.2	−5.1	5.9	12.6	5.9	−0.4	−12.5

■ CONTRIBUTION OF RESIDENT APPLICATIONS   ■ CONTRIBUTION OF NON-RESIDENT APPLICATIONS

.. indicates not available.

Note: * China's 2017 data are not comparable with its previous year's data due to the new way in which the IP office of China counts its applications data. Prior to 2017, it included all applications received; however, starting in 2017, China's application count data include only those applications for which the office has received the necessary application fees. For this reason, it is not possible to report China's 2017 growth rate. EUIPO is the European Union Intellectual Property Office. This figure shows total growth in application design counts, broken down by the respective contributions of resident and non-resident filings. For example, total design counts in Italy grew by 14.2%, with resident applicants contributing 8.1 percentage points to this overall growth.

Source: WIPO Statistics Database, September 2018.

C12. Application design counts for offices of selected low- and middle-income countries, 2017

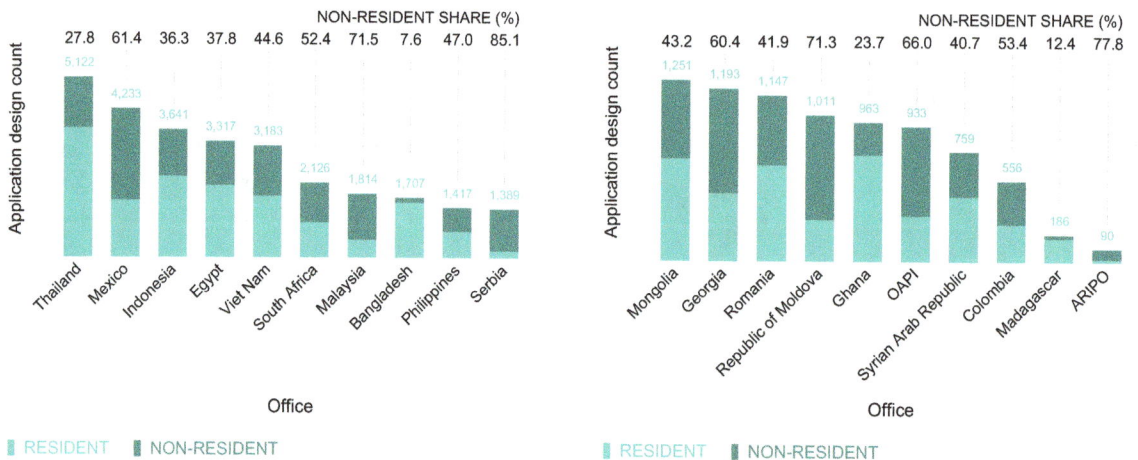

NON-RESIDENT SHARE (%)

Thailand	Mexico	Indonesia	Egypt	Viet Nam	South Africa	Malaysia	Bangladesh	Philippines	Serbia
27.8	61.4	36.3	37.8	44.6	52.4	71.5	7.6	47.0	85.1
5,122	4,233	3,641	3,317	3,163	2,126	1,814	1,707	1,417	1,389

NON-RESIDENT SHARE (%)

Mongolia	Georgia	Romania	Republic of Moldova	Ghana	OAPI	Syrian Arab Republic	Colombia	Madagascar	ARIPO
43.2	60.4	41.9	71.3	23.7	66.0	40.7	53.4	12.4	77.8
1,251	1,193	1,147	1,011	963	933	759	556	186	90

■ RESIDENT   ■ NON-RESIDENT

Note: ARIPO is the African Regional Intellectual Property Organization. OAPI is the African Intellectual Property Organization. The selected offices are from different world regions and income groups (low-income, lower middle-income and upper middle-income). Where available, data for all offices are presented in the statistical table at the end of this section.

Source: WIPO Statistics Database, September 2018.

C13. Contribution of resident and non-resident application design counts to total growth for offices of selected low- and middle-income countries, 2016–2017

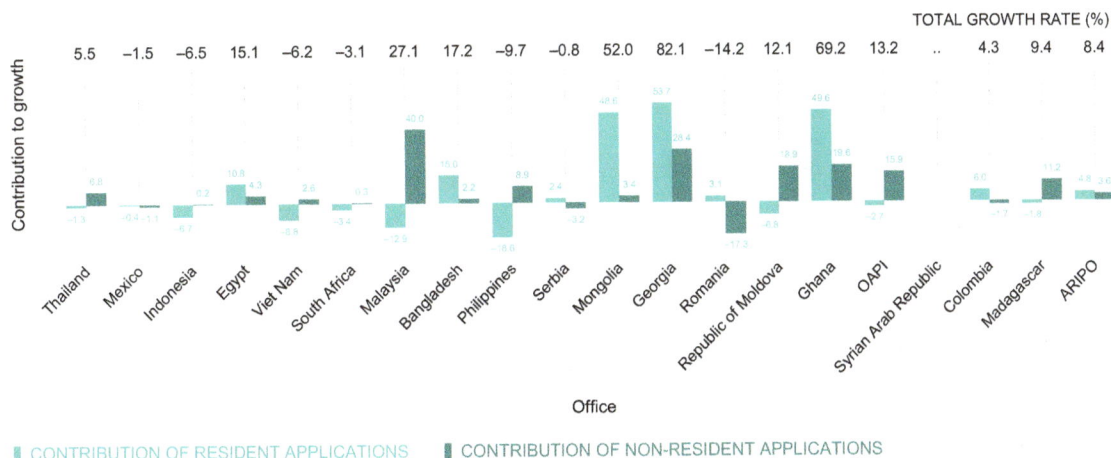

TOTAL GROWTH RATE (%)

Thailand	Mexico	Indonesia	Egypt	Viet Nam	South Africa	Malaysia	Bangladesh	Philippines	Serbia	Mongolia	Georgia	Romania	Republic of Moldova	Ghana	OAPI	Syrian Arab Republic	Colombia	Madagascar	ARIPO
5.5	−1.5	−6.5	15.1	−6.2	−3.1	27.1	17.2	−9.7	−0.8	52.0	82.1	−14.2	12.1	69.2	13.2	..	4.3	9.4	8.4

Contribution to growth / Office

▊ CONTRIBUTION OF RESIDENT APPLICATIONS   ▊ CONTRIBUTION OF NON-RESIDENT APPLICATIONS

.. indicates not available.

Note: ARIPO is the African Regional Intellectual Property Organization. OAPI is the African Intellectual Property Organization. The selected offices are from different world regions and income groups (low-income, lower middle-income and upper middle-income). Where available, data for all offices are in the statistical table at the end of this section. This figure shows total growth in design counts, broken down by the respective contributions of resident and non-resident filings. For example, the total design count in Ghana grew by 69.2%, with resident applicants contributing 49.6 percentage points to this overall growth.

Source: WIPO Statistics Database, September 2018.

C14. Registration design counts for the top 20 offices, 2017

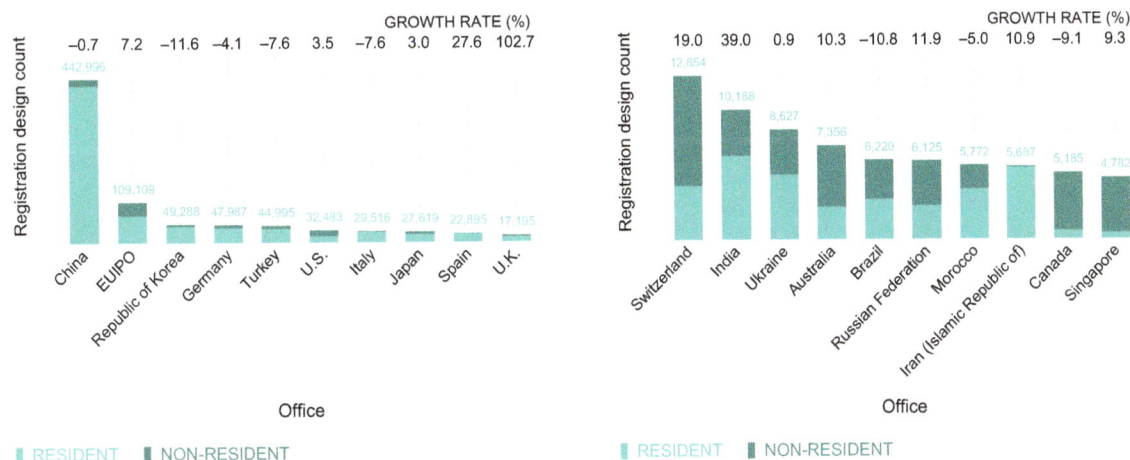

GROWTH RATE (%)

China	EUIPO	Republic of Korea	Germany	Turkey	U.S.	Italy	Japan	Spain	U.K.
−0.7	7.2	−11.6	−4.1	−7.6	3.5	−7.6	3.0	27.6	102.7
442,996	109,109	49,288	47,987	44,995	32,483	29,516	27,619	22,895	17,195

Registration design count / Office

▊ RESIDENT   ▊ NON-RESIDENT

GROWTH RATE (%)

Switzerland	India	Ukraine	Australia	Brazil	Russian Federation	Morocco	Iran (Islamic Republic of)	Canada	Singapore
19.0	39.0	0.9	10.3	−10.8	11.9	−5.0	10.9	−9.1	9.3
12,654	10,188	8,627	7,356	6,220	6,125	5,772	5,687	5,185	4,782

Registration design count / Office

▊ RESIDENT   ▊ NON-RESIDENT

Note: EUIPO is the European Union Intellectual Property Office. Registration design count data for France are not available.

Source: WIPO Statistics Database, September 2018.

C15. Registration design counts for offices of selected low- and middle-income countries, 2017

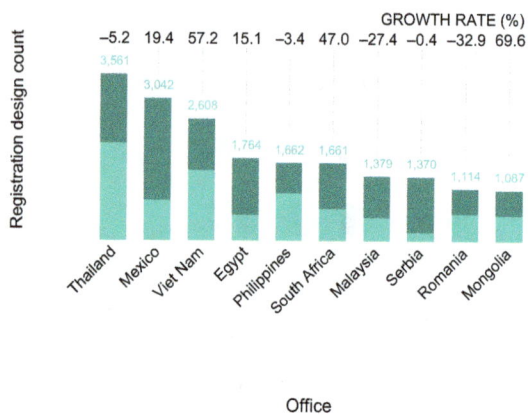

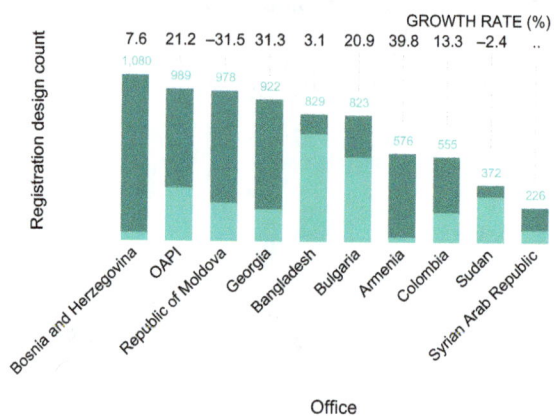

GROWTH RATE (%)

−5.2 19.4 57.2 15.1 −3.4 47.0 −27.4 −0.4 −32.9 69.6

Registration design count

- Thailand: 3,561
- Mexico: 3,042
- Viet Nam: 2,608
- Egypt: 1,764
- Philippines: 1,662
- South Africa: 1,661
- Malaysia: 1,379
- Serbia: 1,370
- Romania: 1,114
- Mongolia: 1,087

Office

■ RESIDENT ■ NON-RESIDENT

GROWTH RATE (%)

7.6 21.2 −31.5 31.3 3.1 20.9 39.8 13.3 −2.4 ..

Registration design count

- Bosnia and Herzegovina: 1,080
- OAPI: 989
- Republic of Moldova: 978
- Georgia: 922
- Bangladesh: 829
- Bulgaria: 823
- Armenia: 576
- Colombia: 555
- Sudan: 372
- Syrian Arab Republic: 226

Office

■ RESIDENT ■ NON-RESIDENT

.. indicates not available.

Note: OAPI is the African Intellectual Property Organization. The selected offices are from different world regions and income groups (low-income, lower middle-income and upper middle-income). Where available, data for all offices are presented in the statistical table at the end of this section.

Source: WIPO Statistics Database, September 2018.

Industrial designs

Application design counts by origin

C16. Equivalent application design counts by origin, 2017

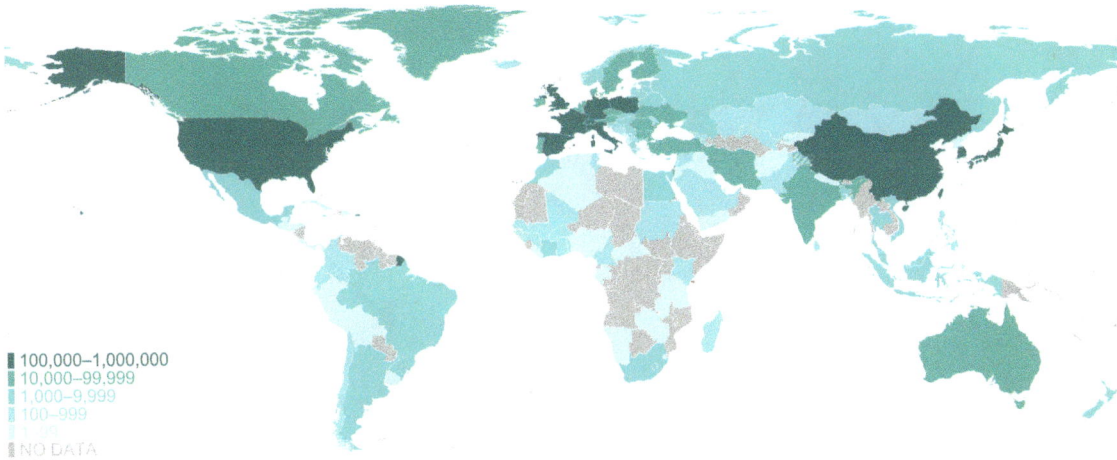

- 100,000–1,000,000
- 10,000–99,999
- 1,000–9,999
- 100–999
- 1–99
- NO DATA

Note: Equivalent application design count includes resident applications and applications filed abroad. The origin of an industrial design application is determined by the residence of the first named applicant. Applications filed at some regional offices are considered equivalent to multiple applications in the member states of those offices. See the glossary for the full definition of equivalent application and design count.

Source: WIPO Statistics Database, September 2018.

C17. Equivalent application design counts for the top 20 origins, 2017

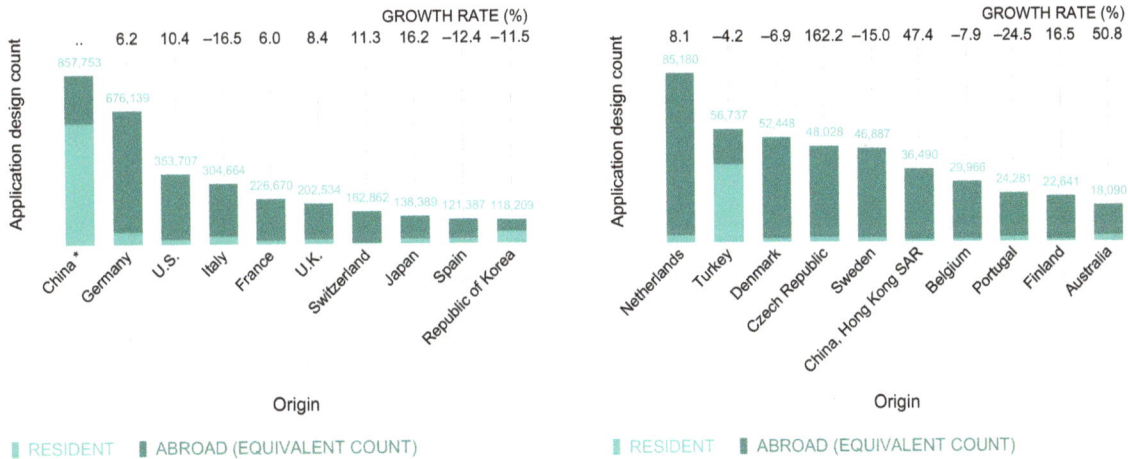

GROWTH RATE (%)

.. 6.2 10.4 −16.5 6.0 8.4 11.3 16.2 −12.4 −11.5

Origin	Count
China *	857,753
Germany	676,139
U.S.	353,707
Italy	304,664
France	226,670
U.K.	202,534
Switzerland	162,862
Japan	138,389
Spain	121,387
Republic of Korea	118,209

GROWTH RATE (%)

8.1 −4.2 −6.9 162.2 −15.0 47.4 −7.9 −24.5 16.5 50.8

Origin	Count
Netherlands	85,180
Turkey	56,737
Denmark	52,448
Czech Republic	48,028
Sweden	46,887
China, Hong Kong SAR	36,490
Belgium	29,966
Portugal	24,281
Finland	22,641
Australia	18,090

RESIDENT   ABROAD (EQUIVALENT COUNT)

.. indicates not available.

Note: * China's 2017 data are not comparable with its previous year's data due to the new way in which the IP office of China counts its applications data. Prior to 2017, it included all applications received; however, starting in 2017, China's application count data include only those applications for which the office has received the necessary application fees. For this reason, it is not possible to report China's 2017 growth rate (see the data description section for further details). The origin of an industrial design application is determined by the residence of the first named applicant. An application filed at a regional office is considered to be a resident filing if the applicant is a resident of one of that office's member states. See the glossary for the definition of equivalent application and design count.

Source: WIPO Statistics Database, September 2018.

C18. Application design counts for the top 20 origins, 2017

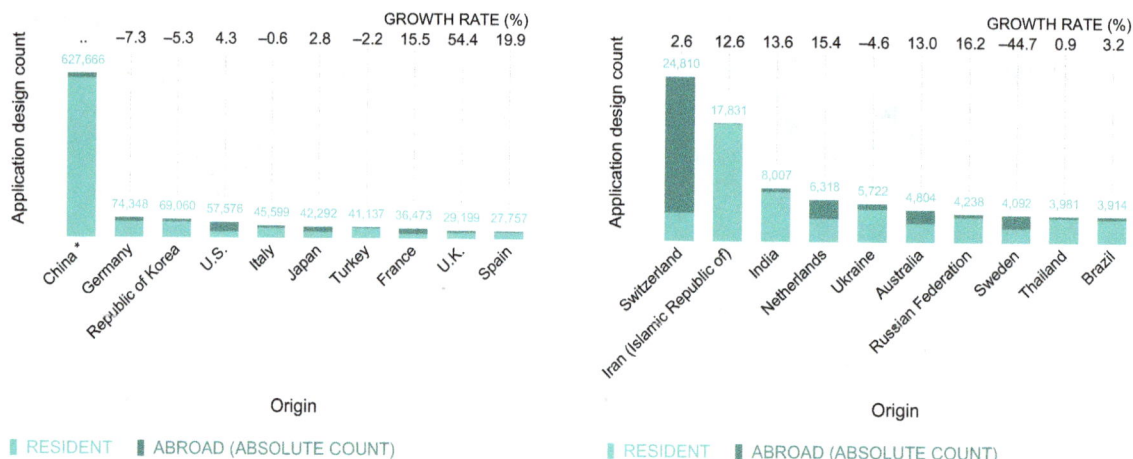

GROWTH RATE (%)

	..	−7.3	−5.3	4.3	−0.6	2.8	−2.2	15.5	54.4	19.9

Application design count

China * — 627,666
Germany — 74,348
Republic of Korea — 69,060
U.S. — 57,576
Italy — 45,599
Japan — 42,292
Turkey — 41,137
France — 36,473
U.K. — 29,199
Spain — 27,757

Origin

■ RESIDENT   ■ ABROAD (ABSOLUTE COUNT)

GROWTH RATE (%)

2.6	12.6	13.6	15.4	−4.6	13.0	16.2	−44.7	0.9	3.2

Application design count

Switzerland — 24,810
Iran (Islamic Republic of) — 17,831
India — 8,007
Netherlands — 6,318
Ukraine — 5,722
Australia — 4,804
Russian Federation — 4,238
Sweden — 4,092
Thailand — 3,981
Brazil — 3,914

Origin

■ RESIDENT   ■ ABROAD (ABSOLUTE COUNT)

.. indicates not available.

Note: China's 2017 data are not comparable with its previous year's data due to the new way in which the IP office of China counts its applications data. Prior to 2017, it included all applications received; however, starting in 2017, China's application count data include only those applications for which the office has received the necessary application fees. For this reason, it is not possible to report China's 2017 growth rate (see the data description section for further details). Data are based on absolute count, not equivalent count. The origin of an industrial design application is determined by the residence of the first named applicant. An application filed at a regional office is considered to be a resident filing if the applicant is a resident of one of that office's member states.

Source: WIPO Statistics Database, September 2018.

C19. Application design counts for selected low- and middle-income origins, 2017

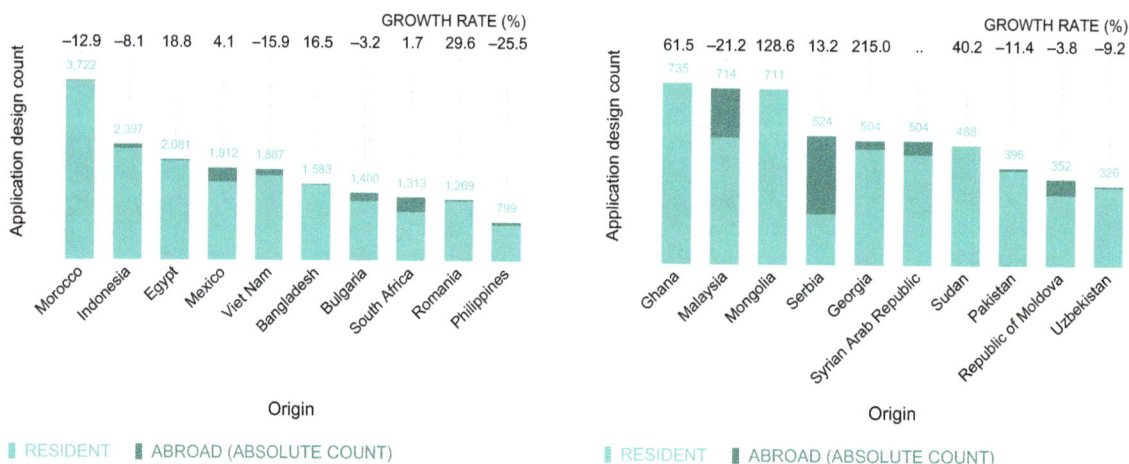

GROWTH RATE (%)

−12.9	−8.1	18.8	4.1	−15.9	16.5	−3.2	1.7	29.6	−25.5

Application design count

Morocco — 3,722
Indonesia — 2,397
Egypt — 2,081
Mexico — 1,912
Viet Nam — 1,887
Bangladesh — 1,583
Bulgaria — 1,400
South Africa — 1,313
Romania — 1,269
Philippines — 799

Origin

■ RESIDENT   ■ ABROAD (ABSOLUTE COUNT)

GROWTH RATE (%)

61.5	−21.2	128.6	13.2	215.0	..	40.2	−11.4	−3.8	−9.2

Application design count

Ghana — 735
Malaysia — 714
Mongolia — 711
Serbia — 524
Georgia — 504
Syrian Arab Republic — 504
Sudan — 488
Pakistan — 396
Republic of Moldova — 352
Uzbekistan — 326

Origin

■ RESIDENT   ■ ABROAD (ABSOLUTE COUNT)

.. indicates not available.

Note: Data are based on absolute count, not equivalent count. The selected origins are from different world regions and income groups (low-income, lower middle-income and upper middle-income). Where available, data for all origins are presented in the statistical table at the end of this section. The origin of an industrial design application is determined by the residence of the first named applicant.

Source: WIPO Statistics Database, September 2018.

Industrial designs

C20. Flows of non-resident design counts for the top five origins and the top 10 offices of high-income economies, 2017

Origin   **Office**

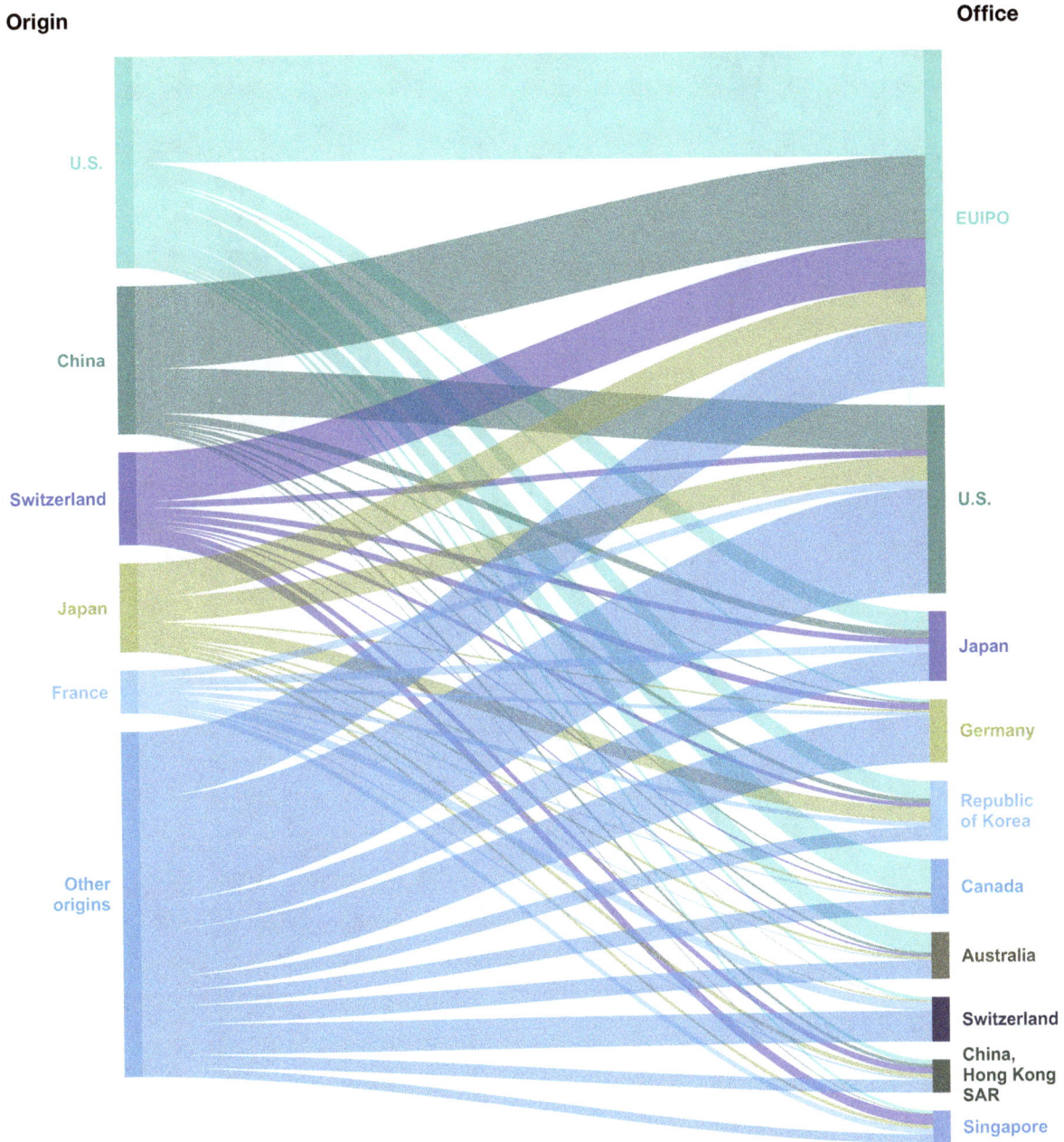

Note: EUIPO is the European Union Intellectual Property Office. Data are based on absolute count, not equivalent count.

Source: WIPO Statistics Database, September 2018.

C21. Flows of non-resident design counts for the top five origins and the top 10 offices of low- and middle-income economies, 2017

Industrial designs

Origin　　　　　　　　　　　　　　　　　　　　　　　　　**Office**

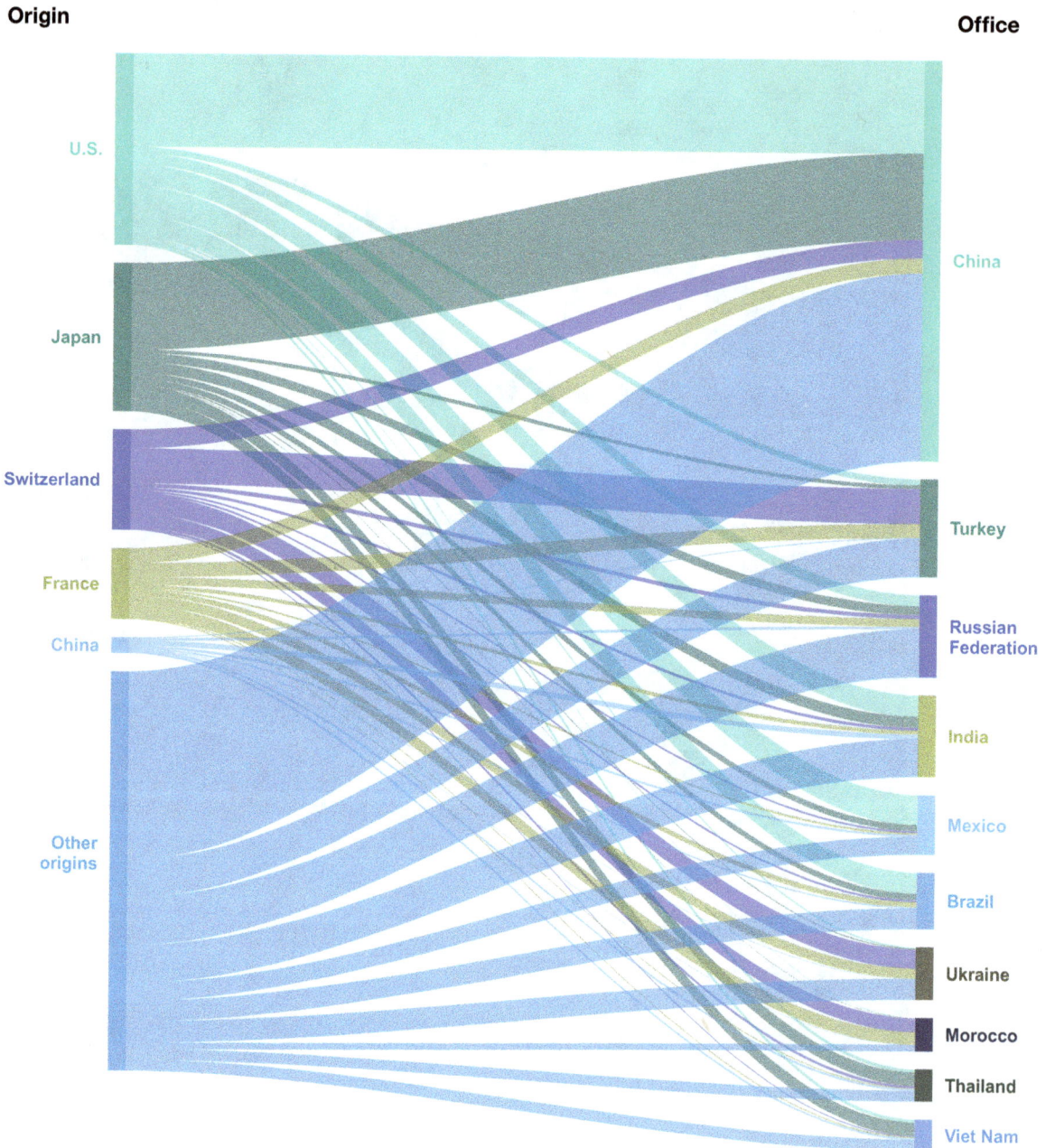

Origins: U.S., Japan, Switzerland, France, China, Other origins

Offices: China, Turkey, Russian Federation, India, Mexico, Brazil, Ukraine, Morocco, Thailand, Viet Nam

Note: Data are based on absolute count, not equivalent count.
Source: WIPO Statistics Database, September 2018.

Application design counts by Locarno class and industry sector

C22. Application design counts by Locarno class, 2017

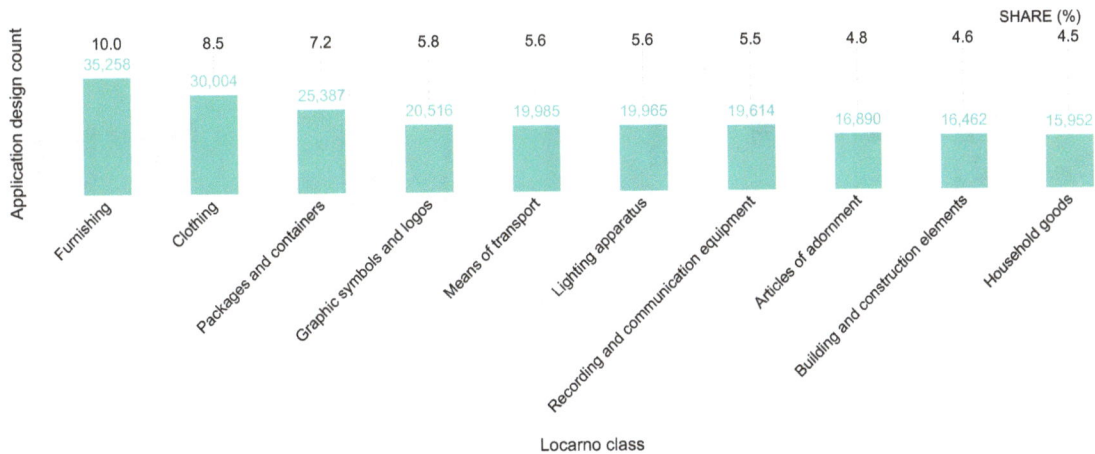

SHARE (%)

Application design count	10.0	8.5	7.2	5.8	5.6	5.6	5.5	4.8	4.6	4.5

| 35,258 | 30,004 | 25,387 | 20,516 | 19,985 | 19,965 | 19,614 | 16,890 | 16,462 | 15,952 |

Furnishing | Clothing | Packages and containers | Graphic symbols and logos | Means of transport | Lighting apparatus | Recording and communication equipment | Articles of adornment | Building and construction elements | Household goods

Locarno class

Note: See annex C for class numbers. These figures are based on data from 107 IP offices. Data for several large offices are not available or are incomplete, including the offices of China, Japan and the U.S.

Source: WIPO Statistics Database, September 2018.

Industrial designs

C23. Distribution of application design counts by the top three sectors and for the top 10 offices, 2017

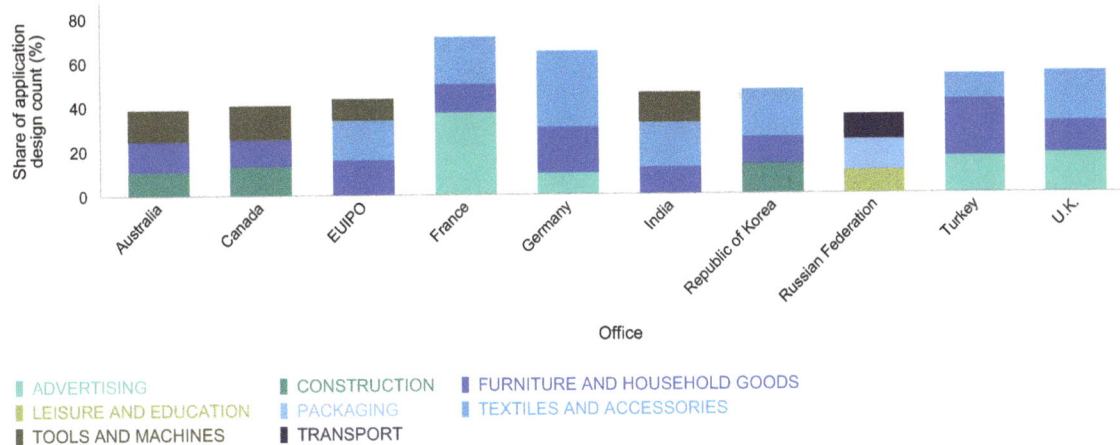

Share of application design count (%)

80
60
40
20
0

Australia | Canada | EUIPO | France | Germany | India | Republic of Korea | Russian Federation | Turkey | U.K.

Office

- ▍ ADVERTISING
- ▍ LEISURE AND EDUCATION
- ▍ TOOLS AND MACHINES
- ▍ CONSTRUCTION
- ▍ PACKAGING
- ▍ TRANSPORT
- ▍ FURNITURE AND HOUSEHOLD GOODS
- ▍ TEXTILES AND ACCESSORIES

Note: EUIPO is the European Union Intellectual Property Office. A concordance table produced by the Organisation for Economic Co-operation and Development (OECD) was used to convert the 32 classes into 12 industry sectors (see annex C for definitions). The top three sectors and top 10 offices were selected based on their 2017 totals. Data for several large offices are not available or are incomplete, including the offices of China, Japan and the U.S.

Source: WIPO Statistics Database, September 2018.

C24. Distribution of application design counts by the top three sectors for the top 10 origins, 2017

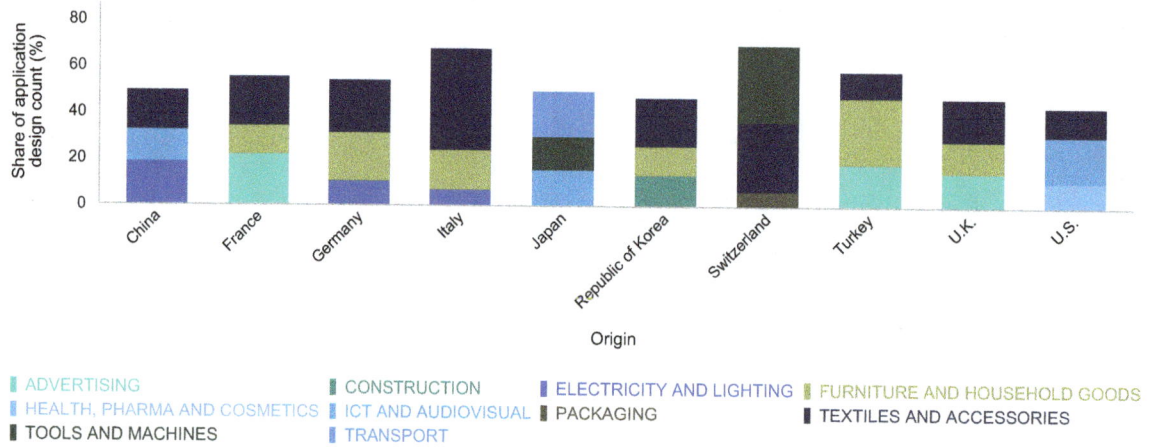

Legend:
- ADVERTISING
- CONSTRUCTION
- ELECTRICITY AND LIGHTING
- FURNITURE AND HOUSEHOLD GOODS
- HEALTH, PHARMA AND COSMETICS
- ICT AND AUDIOVISUAL
- PACKAGING
- TEXTILES AND ACCESSORIES
- TOOLS AND MACHINES
- TRANSPORT

Note: A concordance table produced by the Organisation for Economic Co-operation and Development (OECD) was used to convert the 32 classes into 12 industry sectors (see annex C for definitions). These figures are based on data from 107 IP offices. Data for several large offices are not available or are incomplete, including the offices of China, Japan and the U.S.

Source: WIPO Statistics Database, September 2018.

Industrial designs

Application design count in relation to GDP and population

C25. Resident application design count per USD 100 billion of GDP for the top 20 origins, 2007 and 2017

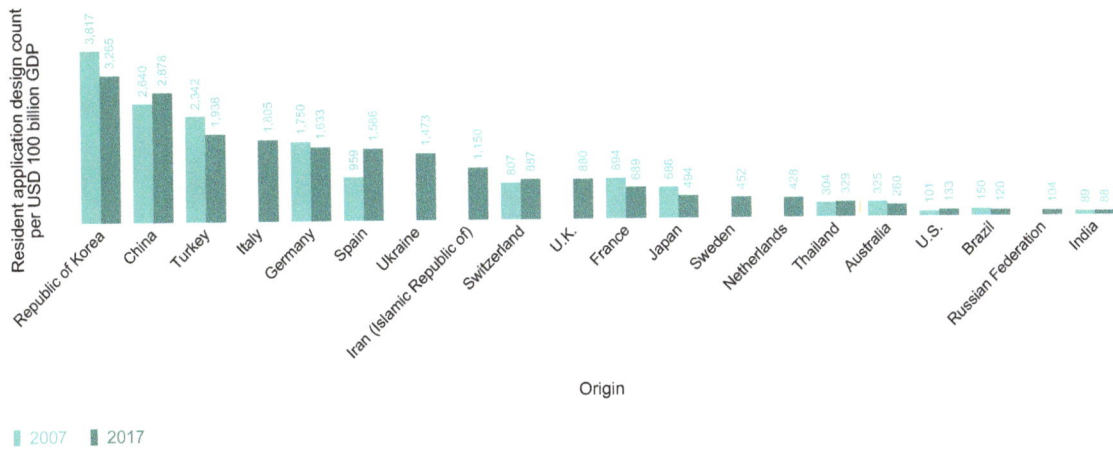

Resident application design count per USD 100 billion GDP

Republic of Korea: 3,817 (2007), 3,255 (2017)
China: 2,640 (2007), 2,676 (2017)
Turkey: 2,242 (2007), 1,936 (2017)
Italy: 1,805 (2017)
Germany: 1,750 (2007), 1,633 (2017)
Spain: 959 (2007), 1,586 (2017)
Ukraine: 1,473 (2017)
Iran (Islamic Republic of): 1,150 (2017)
Switzerland: 807 (2007), 987 (2017)
U.K.: 880 (2017)
France: 834 (2007), 839 (2017)
Japan: 686 (2007), 494 (2017)
Sweden: 452 (2017)
Netherlands: 428 (2017)
Thailand: 304 (2007), 329 (2017)
Australia: 325 (2007), 280 (2017)
U.S.: 101 (2007), 133 (2017)
Brazil: 150 (2007), 120 (2017)
Russian Federation: 104 (2017)
India: 89 (2007), 68 (2017)

Origin

■ 2007   ■ 2017

Note: GDP data are in constant 2011 US PPP dollars. Origins were selected based on the top 20 origins list in terms of application design count.
Sources: WIPO Statistics Database and World Bank, September 2018.

C26. Resident application design count per million population for the top 20 origins, 2007 and 2017

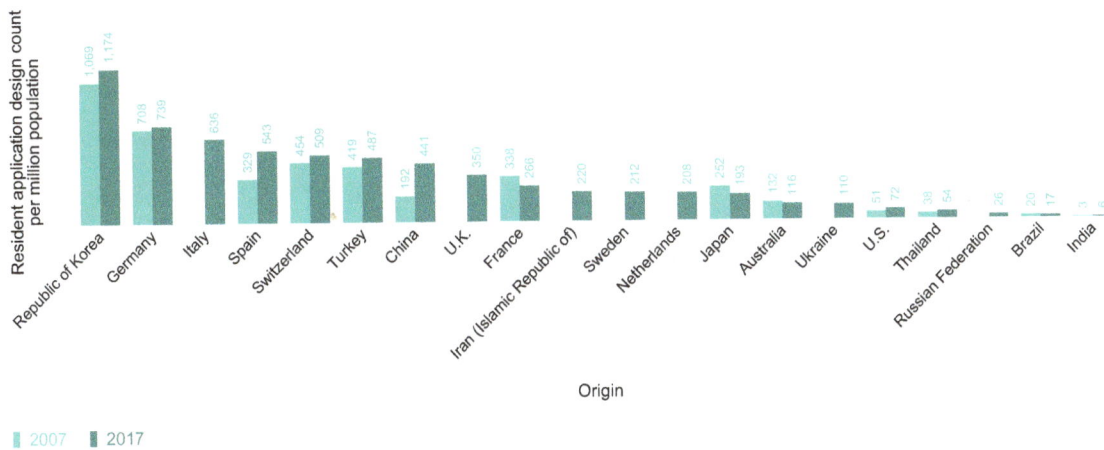

Resident application design count per million population

Republic of Korea: 1,069 (2007), 1,174 (2017)
Germany: 708 (2007), 709 (2017)
Italy: 636 (2017)
Spain: 329 (2007), 543 (2017)
Switzerland: 454 (2007), 509 (2017)
Turkey: 419 (2007), 487 (2017)
China: 192 (2007), 441 (2017)
U.K.: 350 (2017)
France: 336 (2007), 266 (2017)
Iran (Islamic Republic of): 220 (2017)
Sweden: 212 (2017)
Netherlands: 208 (2017)
Japan: 262 (2007), 193 (2017)
Australia: 112 (2007), 116 (2017)
Ukraine: 110 (2017)
U.S.: 61 (2007), 72 (2017)
Thailand: 38 (2007), 54 (2017)
Russian Federation: 26 (2017)
Brazil: 20 (2007), 17 (2017)
India: 3 (2007), 6 (2017)

Origin

■ 2007   ■ 2017

Note: Origins were selected based on the top 20 origins list in terms of application design count.
Sources: WIPO Statistics Database and World Bank, September 2018.

Industrial design registrations in force

C27. Trend in industrial design registrations in force worldwide, 2010–2017

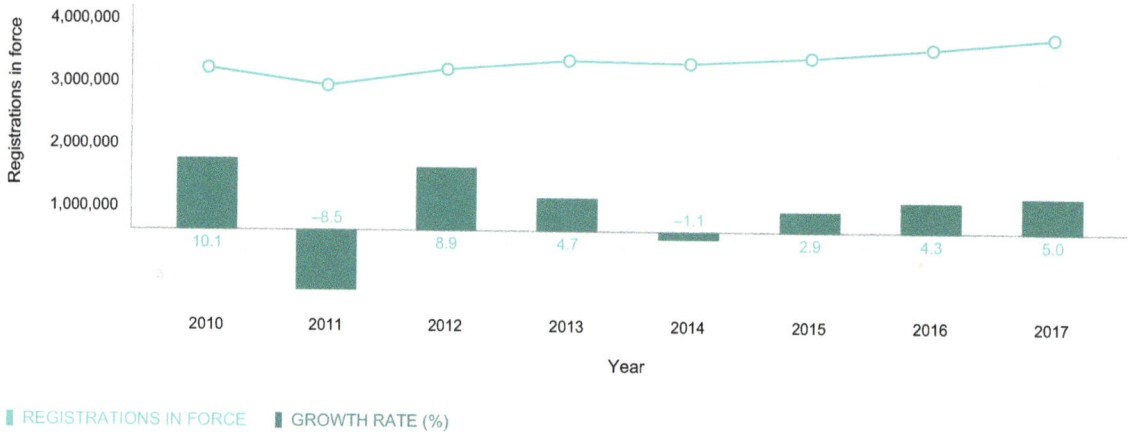

■ REGISTRATIONS IN FORCE   ■ GROWTH RATE (%)

Note: WIPO estimates cover 113 IP offices and include direct national and regional applications as well as designations received via the Hague System. Data refer to the number of industrial design registrations in force and not the number of designs contained in registrations in force.

Source: WIPO Statistics Database, September 2018.

C28. Industrial design registrations in force for the top 20 offices, 2017

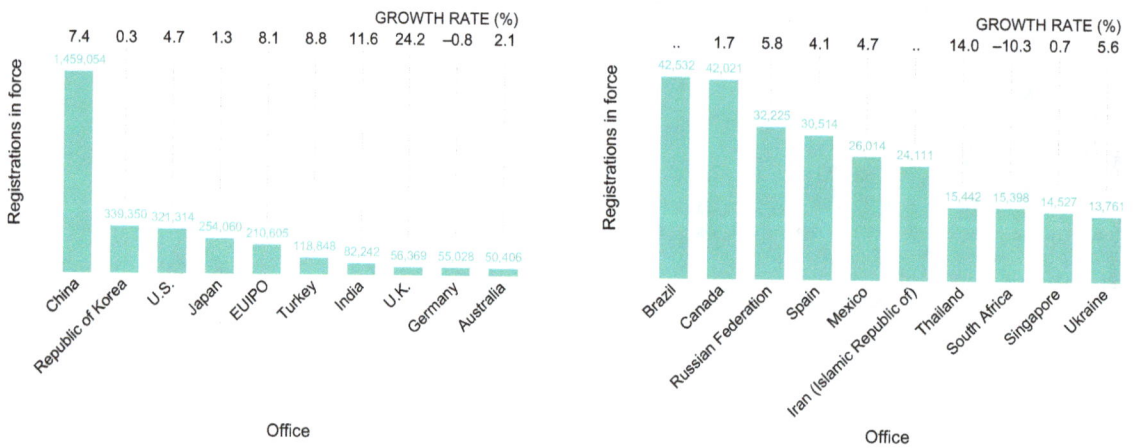

.. indicates not available.

Note: EUIPO is the European Union Intellectual Property Office. Data refer to the number of industrial design registrations in force and not the number of designs contained in registrations in force. Registrations in force data are not available for France and Italy.

Source: WIPO Statistics Database, September 2018.

C29. Industrial design registrations in force in 2017 as a percentage of total registrations

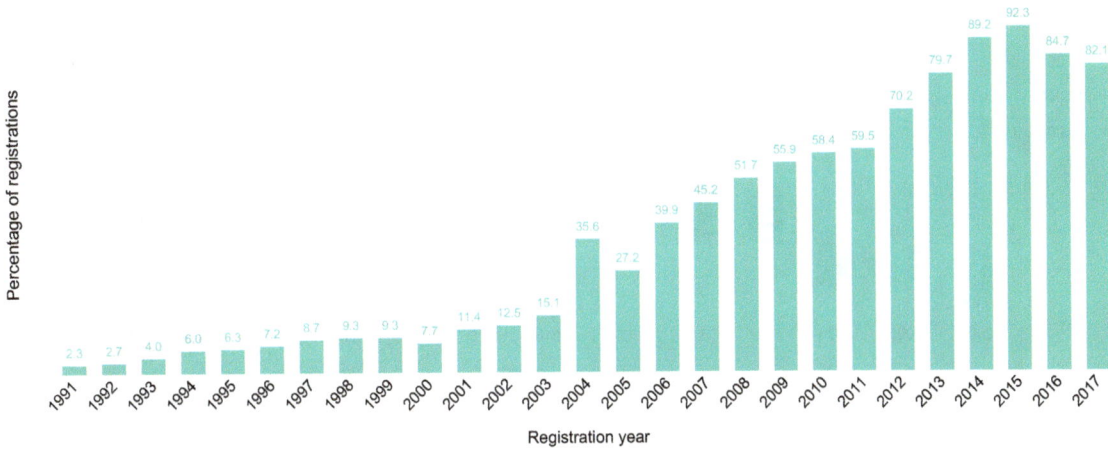

Note: Percentages are calculated using the number of industrial designs registered in year *t* and in force in 2017 divided by the total number of industrial designs registered in year *t*. The graph is based on data from 77 offices (including most large offices, with the exception of France, Italy and Japan) for which a breakdown of industrial design registrations in force by year of registration was available.

Source: WIPO Statistics Database, September 2018.

C30. Average age of industrial design registrations in force at selected offices, 2012 and 2017

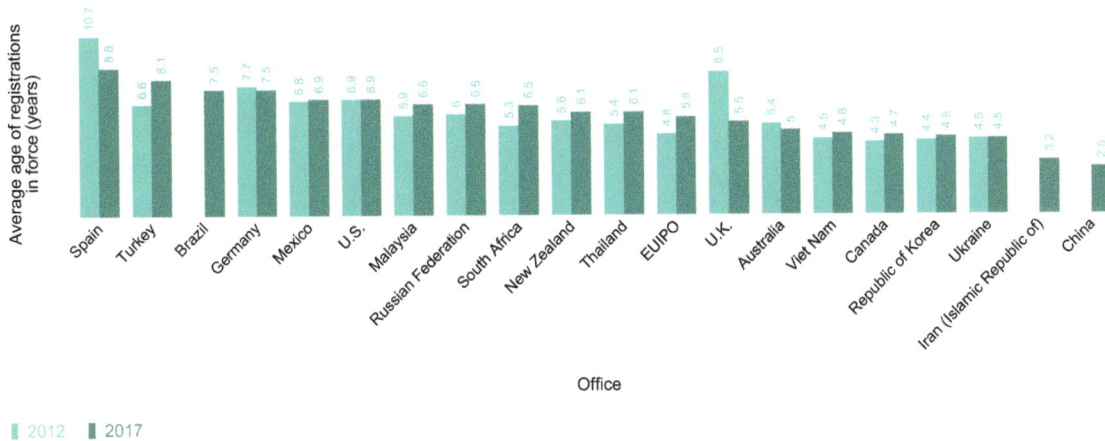

■ 2012 ■ 2017

Note: EUIPO is the European Union Intellectual Property Office.

Source: WIPO Statistics Database, September 2018.

Industrial design applications through the Hague System

C31. Trend in designs contained in Hague international applications, 2004–2017

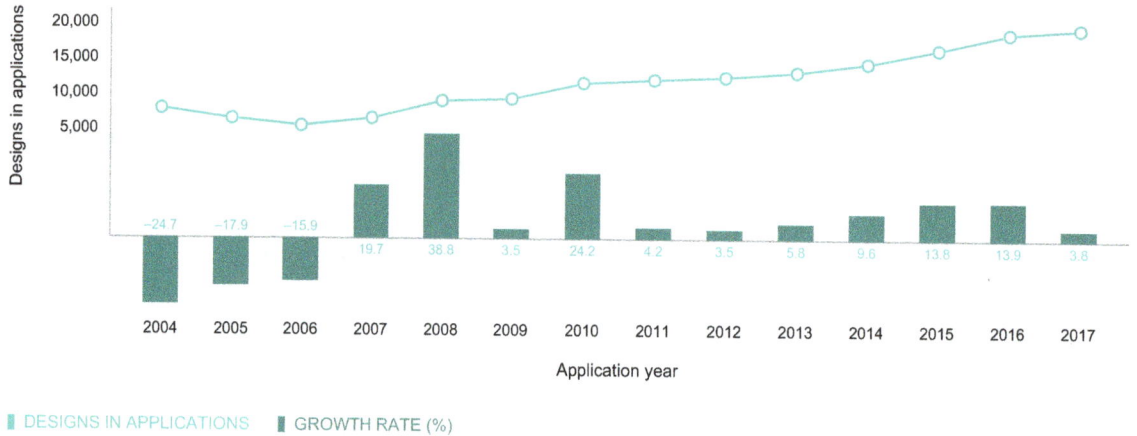

DESIGNS IN APPLICATIONS   GROWTH RATE (%)

Source: WIPO Statistics Database, September 2018.

C32. Designs contained in Hague international applications by origin, 2017

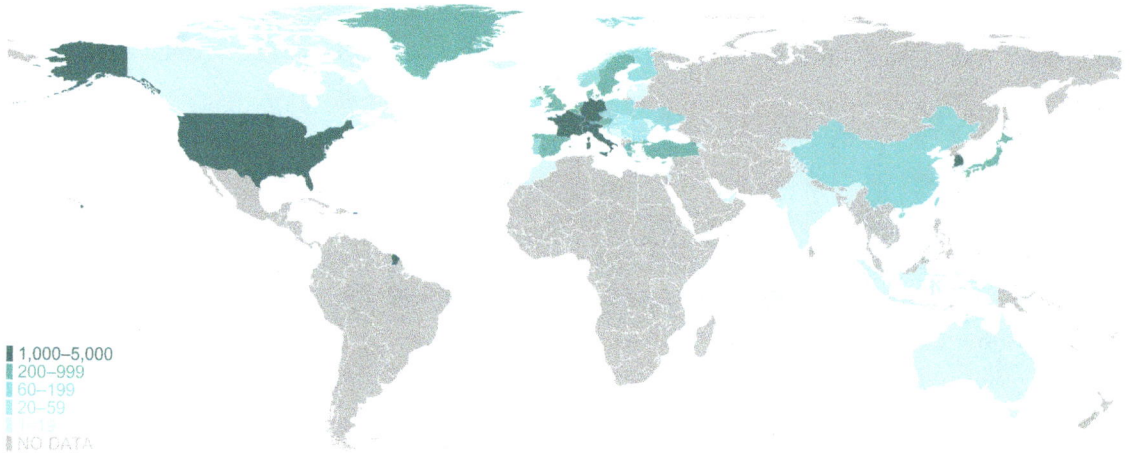

1,000–5,000
200–999
60–199
20–59
NO DATA

Note: Applicants residing in a non-member country can file applications for international registrations if they have a real and effective industrial or commercial establishment within the jurisdiction of a Hague member.

Source: WIPO Statistics Database, September 2018.

C33. Designs contained in Hague international applications for the top 20 origins, 2017

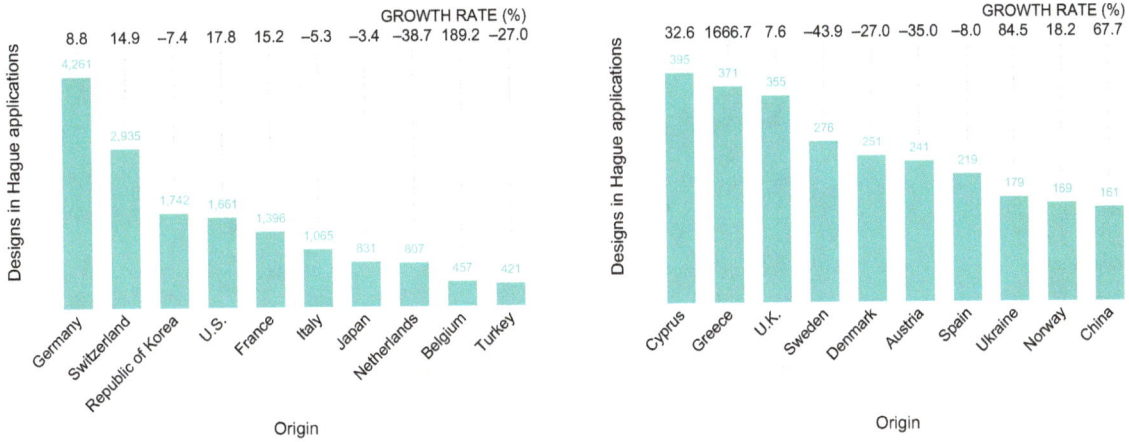

GROWTH RATE (%)

8.8 14.9 −7.4 17.8 15.2 −5.3 −3.4 −38.7 189.2 −27.0

Designs in Hague applications

- Germany 4,261
- Switzerland 2,935
- Republic of Korea 1,742
- U.S. 1,661
- France 1,396
- Italy 1,065
- Japan 831
- Netherlands 897
- Belgium 457
- Turkey 421

Origin

GROWTH RATE (%)

32.6 1666.7 7.6 −43.9 −27.0 −35.0 −8.0 84.5 18.2 67.7

Designs in Hague applications

- Cyprus 395
- Greece 371
- U.K. 355
- Sweden 276
- Denmark 251
- Austria 241
- Spain 219
- Ukraine 179
- Norway 169
- China 161

Origin

Note: Applicants residing in a non-member country can file applications for international registrations if they have a real and effective industrial or commercial establishment within the jurisdiction of a Hague member. The top 20 origins were selected based on the number of designs contained in applications filed in 2017.

Source: WIPO Statistics Database, September 2018.

C34. Designs contained in designations in Hague international applications for the top 20 designated Hague members, 2017

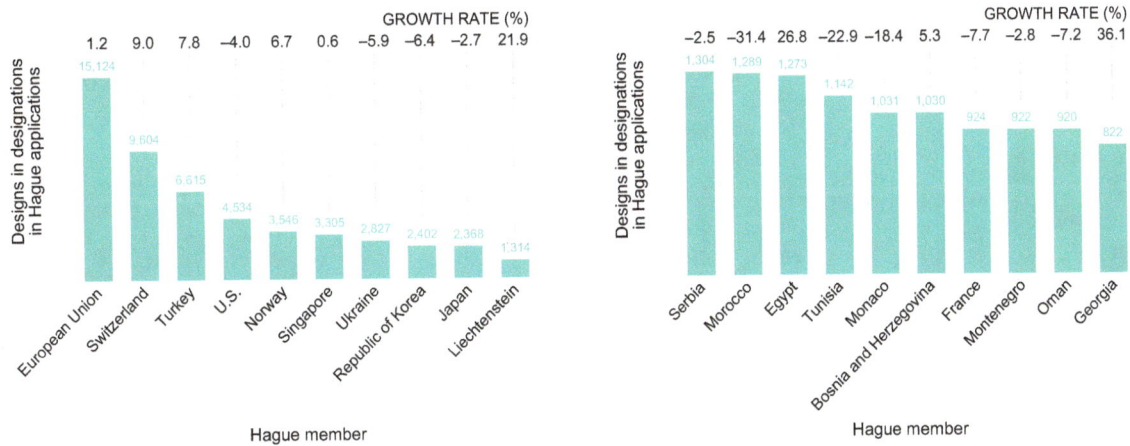

GROWTH RATE (%)

1.2 9.0 7.8 −4.0 6.7 0.6 −5.9 −6.4 −2.7 21.9

Designs in designations in Hague applications

- European Union 15,124
- Switzerland 9,604
- Turkey 6,615
- U.S. 4,534
- Norway 3,546
- Singapore 3,305
- Ukraine 2,827
- Republic of Korea 2,402
- Japan 2,368
- Liechtenstein 1,314

Hague member

GROWTH RATE (%)

−2.5 −31.4 26.8 −22.9 −18.4 5.3 −7.7 −2.8 −7.2 36.1

Designs in designations in Hague applications

- Serbia 1,304
- Morocco 1,289
- Egypt 1,273
- Tunisia 1,142
- Monaco 1,031
- Bosnia and Herzegovina 1,030
- France 924
- Montenegro 922
- Oman 920
- Georgia 822

Hague member

Source: WIPO Statistics Database, September 2018.

Statistical tables

C35. Industrial design applications by office and origin, 2017

Name	Application design count by office			Application design count by origin	Equivalent application design count by origin	Hague international application design count	
	Total	Resident	Non-resident	Total [a]	Total [a]	Origin [c]	Designated Hague member
Afghanistan (b)	..	..	..	11	11	..	n.a.
African Intellectual Property Organization	933	317	616	n.a.	n.a.	n.a.	582
African Regional Intellectual Property Organization	90	20	70	n.a.	n.a.	n.a.	n.a.
Albania (b)	..	..	..	18	45	..	814
Algeria (b)	..	..	..	11	38	..	n.a.
Andorra (b)	..	..	..	1	1	..	n.a.
Argentina	1,649	972	677	1,040	1,148	..	n.a.
Armenia	638	54	584	64	118	3	641
Australia	7,708	2,854	4,854	4,804	18,090	4	n.a.
Austria (b)	..	..	..	3,122	63,710	241	n.a.
Azerbaijan (b)	..	..	..	..	..	..	774
Bahamas (b)	..	..	..	8	8	..	n.a.
Bahrain	79	26	53	26	26	..	n.a.
Bangladesh	1,707	1,577	130	1,583	1,583	..	n.a.
Barbados	1	1	0	330	1,572	..	n.a.
Belarus	583	177	406	306	1,143	..	n.a.
Belgium	n.a.	n.a.	n.a.	1,921	29,966	457	n.a.
Belize (b)	..	..	..	4	112	..	349
Benelux Office for Intellectual Property	1,469	954	515	n.a.	n.a.	n.a.	514
Benin (b,d)	n.a.	n.a.	n.a.	4	68	..	156
Bermuda (b)	..	..	..	9	198	..	n.a.
Bolivia (Plurinational State of)	59	16	43	16	16	..	n.a.
Bosnia and Herzegovina	1,126	108	1,018	156	399	8	1,030
Botswana (b)	..	..	..	..	..	..	237
Brazil	6,000	3,532	2,468	3,914	7,235	..	n.a.
Brunei Darussalam	265	1	264	1	1	..	250
Bulgaria	897	631	266	1,400	17,816	41	239
Burkina Faso (b,d)	n.a.	n.a.	n.a.	18	306	..	n.a.
Cambodia (b)	..	..	..	..	..	..	212
Cameroon (b,d)	n.a.	n.a.	n.a.	27	459	..	n.a.
Canada	6,533	815	5,718	2,564	14,012	4	n.a.
Central African Republic (b,d)	n.a.	n.a.	n.a.	1	17	..	n.a.
Chile	438	82	356	146	254	..	n.a.
China	628,658	610,817	17,841	627,666	857,753	161	n.a.
China, Hong Kong SAR	4,816	1,216	3,600	3,280	36,490	1	n.a.
China, Macao SAR	193	17	176	163	1,243	..	n.a.
Colombia	556	259	297	323	377	..	n.a.
Cook Islands (b)	..	..	..	13	13	..	n.a.
Costa Rica	52	5	47	19	19	..	n.a.
Côte d'Ivoire (b,d)	n.a.	n.a.	n.a.	145	2,465	..	171
Croatia	1,041	375	666	827	4,265	34	632
Cuba	12	6	6	6	6	..	n.a.
Cyprus	58	58	0	626	1,976	395	n.a.
Czech Republic	855	782	73	2,776	48,028	151	n.a.
Democratic People's Republic of Korea (b)	..	..	..	5	32	..	245

Name	Application design count by office			Application design count by origin	Equivalent application design count by origin	Hague international application design count	
	Total	Resident	Non-resident	Total [a]	Total [a]	Origin [c]	Designated Hague member
Denmark	554	138	416	3,039	52,448	251	372
Dominican Republic	35	35	0	41	68	..	n.a.
Ecuador	297	192	105	211	265	..	n.a.
Egypt	3,317	2,063	1,254	2,081	2,324	..	1,273
El Salvador	49	10	39	10	10	..	n.a.
Estonia	320	46	274	371	6,365	13	229
Eswatini (b)	..	..	..	53	53	..	n.a.
European Union Intellectual Property Office	111,021	75,192	35,829	n.a.	n.a.	n.a.	15,124
Finland	495	194	301	1,738	22,641	81	236
France	12,132	11,013	1,119	36,473	226,670	1,396	924
Gabon (b,d)	n.a.	n.a.	n.a.	4	52	..	141
Georgia	1,193	472	721	504	504	..	822
Germany	45,803	38,809	6,994	74,348	676,139	4,261	802
Ghana	963	735	228	735	735	..	250
Greece	1,424	829	595	1,123	7,657	371	515
Guatemala	245	10	235	11	11	..	n.a.
Guinea (b,d)	n.a.	n.a.	n.a.	48	816	..	n.a.
Guinea-Bissau (b,d)	n.a.	n.a.	n.a.	7	119	..	n.a.
Honduras	24	4	20	4	4	..	n.a.
Hungary	917	682	235	996	7,341	30	211
Iceland	597	15	582	26	107	1	574
India	11,117	7,534	3,583	8,007	10,253	4	n.a.
Indonesia	3,641	2,319	1,322	2,397	2,694	1	n.a.
Iran (Islamic Republic of)	17,978	17,818	160	17,831	17,885	..	n.a.
Iraq (b)	..	..	..	6	33	..	n.a.
Ireland	155	125	30	714	10,812	20	n.a.
Israel	1,656	1,075	581	1,988	10,358	1	n.a.
Italy	30,925	28,892	2,033	45,599	304,664	1,065	456
Jamaica	140	128	12	131	131	..	n.a.
Japan	32,457	24,438	8,019	42,292	138,389	831	2,368
Jordan	103	71	32	89	89	..	n.a.
Kazakhstan	203	105	98	111	111	..	n.a.
Kenya	148	141	7	141	141	..	n.a.
Kuwait (b)	..	..	..	3	3	..	n.a.
Kyrgyzstan	490	11	479	15	42	1	456
Latvia	355	141	214	197	1,520	1	210
Lebanon (b)	..	..	..	42	1,014	..	n.a.
Liberia (b)	..	..	..	4	4	..	n.a.
Liechtenstein	1,311	48	1,263	528	6,603	87	1,314
Lithuania	794	204	590	374	3,484	13	546
Luxembourg	n.a.	n.a.	n.a.	691	7,765	97	n.a.
Madagascar	186	163	23	163	163	..	n.a.
Malaysia	1,814	517	1,297	714	1,011	..	n.a.
Mali (b,d)	n.a.	n.a.	n.a.	11	155	..	136
Malta (b)	..	..	..	231	5,091	2	n.a.
Marshall Islands (b)	..	..	..	6	168	..	n.a.
Mauritius (b)	..	..	..	12	82	..	n.a.

Industrial designs

Industrial designs

Name	Application design count by office			Application design count by origin	Equivalent application design count by origin	Hague international application design count	
	Total	Resident	Non-resident	Total [a]	Total [a]	Origin [c]	Designated Hague member
Mexico	4,233	1,635	2,598	1,912	2,803	..	n.a.
Monaco	1,173	84	1,089	218	2,837	4	1,031
Mongolia	1,251	711	540	711	711	..	542
Montenegro (b)	..	..	..	4	31	1	922
Morocco	5,374	3,714	1,660	3,722	3,772	3	1,289
Namibia (b)	..	..	..	8	8	..	278
Nepal	40	15	25	15	15	..	n.a.
Netherlands	n.a.	n.a.	n.a.	6,318	85,180	807	n.a.
New Zealand	1,291	343	948	958	4,711	..	n.a.
Niger (b,d)	n.a.	n.a.	n.a.	..	..	..	133
Nigeria (b)	..	..	..	6	6	..	n.a.
Norway	4,521	582	3,939	1,160	8,142	169	3,546
Oman (b)	..	..	..	..	..	..	920
Pakistan	490	387	103	396	423	..	n.a.
Panama	63	3	60	17	71	..	n.a.
Peru	349	92	257	93	93	..	n.a.
Philippines	1,417	751	666	799	907	..	n.a.
Poland (b)	..	..	..	5,167	125,877	142	289
Portugal	1,663	1,450	213	2,370	24,281	80	n.a.
Qatar (b)	..	..	..	77	77	5	n.a.
Republic of Korea	67,357	60,397	6,960	69,060	118,209	1,742	2,402
Republic of Moldova	1,011	290	721	352	892	2	791
Romania	1,147	666	481	1,269	16,686	45	423
Russian Federation	7,390	3,789	3,601	4,238	6,398	..	n.a.
Rwanda (b)	..	..	..	..	..	..	239
Saint Kitts and Nevis (b)	..	..	..	1	28	..	n.a.
Samoa (b)	..	..	..	3	3	..	n.a.
San Marino (b)	..	..	..	1,225	1,306	..	n.a.
Sao Tome and Principe (b)	..	..	..	..	..	..	181
Saudi Arabia	1,001	461	540	551	632	..	n.a.
Senegal (b,d)	n.a.	n.a.	n.a.	45	765	..	171
Serbia	1,389	207	1,182	524	2,477	57	1,304
Seychelles (b)	..	..	..	3	30	..	n.a.
Singapore	4,917	606	4,311	1,326	4,690	13	3,305
Slovakia	465	329	136	615	7,014	59	n.a.
Slovenia (b)	..	..	..	658	6,693	120	698
South Africa	2,126	1,012	1,114	1,313	3,721	..	n.a.
Spain	22,628	21,845	783	27,757	121,387	219	474
Sri Lanka	336	287	49	323	485	..	n.a.
Sudan	545	488	57	488	488	..	n.a.
Suriname (b)	..	..	..	..	..	..	163
Sweden	615	551	64	4,092	46,887	276	n.a.
Switzerland	13,114	4,313	8,801	24,810	162,862	2,935	9,604
Syrian Arab Republic	759	450	309	504	504	..	245
Tajikistan (b)	..	..	..	..	..	..	299
Thailand	5,122	3,698	1,424	3,981	5,817	..	n.a.
The former Yugoslav Republic of Macedonia	1,025	99	926	105	159	..	1,049

Name	Application design count by office			Application design count by origin	Equivalent application design count by origin	Hague international application design count	
	Total	Resident	Non-resident	Total [a]	Total [a]	Origin [c]	Designated Hague member
Togo (b,d)	n.a.	n.a.	n.a.	10	170	..	n.a.
Trinidad and Tobago	300	294	6	313	313	..	n.a.
Tunisia	1,381	150	1,231	152	152	..	1,142
Turkey	46,875	39,321	7,554	41,137	56,737	421	6,615
Turkmenistan (b)	..	..	..	..	..	..	243
Ukraine	8,346	4,942	3,404	5,722	10,713	179	2,827
United Arab Emirates (b)	..	..	..	157	778	2	n.a.
United Kingdom	19,269	16,665	2,604	29,199	202,534	355	n.a.
United Republic of Tanzania (b)	..	..	..	3	3	..	n.a.
United States of America	45,881	23,568	22,313	57,576	353,707	1,661	4,534
Uruguay	115	53	62	55	55	..	n.a.
Uzbekistan	343	321	22	326	326	..	n.a.
Viet Nam	3,183	1,763	1,420	1,887	2,589	..	n.a.
Yemen	27	24	3	24	24	..	n.a.
Zambia	30	30	0	30	30	..	n.a.
Zimbabwe (b)	..	..	..	1	1	..	n.a.
Others/Unknown	..	..	..	30,269	59,487	105	n.a.
Total (2017 estimates)	**1,242,100**	**1,040,000**	**202,100**	**1,242,100**	**n.a.**	**19,429**	**79,464**

(a) Design count by origin data are incomplete because some offices do not report the origin of applications.

(b) Only Hague designation data are available and/or the office has not reported the origin of applications, so design count by office and origin data may be incomplete.

(c) Origin is defined as the country of the stated address of residence of the first named applicant in an international application.

(d) The African Intellectual Property Organization (OAPI) is the competent office for processing applications.

n.a. indicates not applicable.

.. indicates not available.

Source: WIPO Statistics Database, September 2018.

Industrial designs

C36. Industrial design registrations by office and origin, and industrial designs in force, 2017

Name	Registration design count by office			Registration design count by origin	Equivalent registration design count by origin	Hague international registration design count	In force by office
	Total	Resident	Non-resident	Total [a]	Total [a]	Origin [c]	Total
Afghanistan (b)	..	..	..	1	1	..	..
African Intellectual Property Organization	989	347	642	n.a.	n.a.	n.a.	..
African Regional Intellectual Property Organization (b)	..	..	..	n.a.	n.a.	n.a.	812
Albania	778	5	773	16	70	1	14
Algeria (b)	..	..	..	7	34	..	..
Argentina	1,554	851	703	889	1,024	..	..
Armenia	576	31	545	34	88	..	86
Australia	7,356	2,572	4,784	4,123	15,641	5	50,406
Austria (b)	..	..	..	3,533	57,886	246	9,490
Azerbaijan (b)	..	..	..	..	..	..	..
Bahamas (b)	..	..	..	12	39	..	..
Bahrain	147	37	110	38	38	..	244
Bangladesh	829	701	128	705	705	..	..
Barbados (b)	..	..	..	274	1,462	..	..
Belarus	542	140	402	257	905	..	1,498
Belgium	n.a.	n.a.	n.a.	1,783	30,758	407	n.a.
Belize (b)	..	..	..	9	171	..	..
Benelux Office for Intellectual Property	1,420	888	532	n.a.	n.a.	n.a.	5,387
Benin (b,d)	n.a.	n.a.	n.a.	4	68	..	..
Bermuda (b)	..	..	..	8	197	..	..
Bolivia (Plurinational State of)	79	33	46	36	36	..	321
Bosnia and Herzegovina	1,080	56	1,024	97	340	10	410
Botswana (b)	..	..	..	..	..	..	376
Brazil	6,220	3,134	3,086	3,543	7,971	..	42,532
Brunei Darussalam	265	1	264	1	1	..	..
Bulgaria	823	552	271	1,301	17,177	28	2,208
Burkina Faso (b,d)	n.a.	n.a.	n.a.	13	221	..	..
Cambodia (b)	..	..	..	..	..	..	..
Cameroon (b,d)	n.a.	n.a.	n.a.	43	731	..	..
Canada	5,185	692	4,493	2,262	15,195	4	42,021
Central African Republic (b,d)	n.a.	n.a.	n.a.	1	17	..	..
Chile	712	62	650	129	210	..	2,802
China	442,996	426,442	16,554	439,138	662,091	72	1,459,054
China, Hong Kong SAR	4,604	1,127	3,477	2,819	34,436	1	..
China, Macao SAR	289	34	255	146	1,874	..	1,126
Colombia	555	193	362	226	280	..	4,173
Congo (b,d)	n.a.	n.a.	n.a.	4	68	..	..
Cook Islands (b)	..	..	..	2	2	..	..
Costa Rica	50	13	37	14	14	..	670
Côte d'Ivoire (b,d)	n.a.	n.a.	n.a.	164	2,788	..	..
Croatia	1,010	345	665	734	3,146	27	4,346
Cuba	9	8	1	8	8	..	48
Cyprus	52	52	0	434	1,622	542	60
Czech Republic	661	508	153	2,458	45,631	141	3,119
Democratic People's Republic of Korea (b)	..	..	..	10	37	..	..

Name	Registration design count by office			Registration design count by origin	Equivalent registration design count by origin	Hague international registration design count	In force by office
	Total	Resident	Non-resident	Total (a)	Total (a)	Origin (c)	Total
Democratic Republic of the Congo (b)	..	..	..	1	1	..	..
Denmark	510	95	415	2,795	50,721	213	1,177
Dominican Republic	18	18	0	24	51	..	14
Ecuador	88	44	44	49	76	..	1,187
Egypt	1,764	552	1,212	552	552	..	..
El Salvador	25	5	20	6	6	..	597
Estonia (b)	..	..	..	334	6,141	15	1,450
Eswatini (b)	..	..	..	63	63	..	..
European Union Intellectual Property Office	109,109	73,544	35,565	n.a.	n.a.	n.a.	210,605
Finland	481	153	328	1,514	21,125	95	2,127
France (b)	..	..	..	24,488	211,180	1,310	..
Gabon (b,d)	n.a.	n.a.	n.a.	3	51	..	..
Georgia	922	210	712	247	247	..	295
Germany	47,987	39,792	8,195	74,862	661,022	4,347	55,028
Ghana (b)	..	..	..	..	..	..	..
Greece	1,449	852	597	1,111	6,511	317	1,461
Guatemala	180	10	170	16	16	..	454
Guinea (b,d)	n.a.	n.a.	n.a.	46	782	..	..
Guinea-Bissau (b,d)	n.a.	n.a.	n.a.	5	85	..	..
Honduras	18	2	16	2	2	..	365
Hungary	385	148	237	398	6,230	17	3,780
Iceland	601	19	582	26	134	..	985
India	10,188	6,622	3,566	6,949	8,994	4	82,242
Indonesia (b)	..	..	..	29	326	1	..
Iran (Islamic Republic of)	5,687	5,605	82	5,629	5,656	..	24,111
Iraq (b)	..	..	..	13	310	..	75
Ireland (b)	..	..	..	495	8,865	19	1,140
Israel	1,324	771	553	1,515	9,642	1	..
Italy	29,516	28,598	918	45,220	306,694	1,047	..
Jamaica	146	129	17	130	130	..	1,284
Japan	27,619	21,471	6,148	38,176	133,546	964	254,060
Jordan	88	55	33	69	69	..	1,127
Kazakhstan	129	42	87	42	42	..	..
Kenya	72	60	12	60	60	..	..
Kuwait (b)	..	..	..	2	2	..	..
Kyrgyzstan	472	7	465	9	36	..	97
Latvia	362	148	214	212	1,589	1	391
Lebanon (b)	..	..	..	42	1,014	..	..
Liechtenstein (b)	..	..	..	455	6,422	98	..
Lithuania	694	55	639	210	3,266	14	292
Luxembourg	n.a.	n.a.	n.a.	873	9,347	60	n.a.
Madagascar (b)	..	..	..	..	..	..	1,023
Malaysia	1,379	499	880	645	807	..	13,684
Mali (b,d)	n.a.	n.a.	n.a.	13	173	..	..
Malta (b)	..	..	..	213	5,343	2	..
Marshall Islands (b)	..	..	..	10	172	..	..

Industrial designs

Name	Registration design count by office			Registration design count by origin	Equivalent registration design count by origin	Hague international registration design count	In force by office
	Total	Resident	Non-resident	Total [a]	Total [a]	Origin [c]	Total
Mauritius (b)	..	..	..	17	87	..	..
Mexico	3,042	861	2,181	1,052	1,943	..	26,014
Monaco	1,102	15	1,087	167	3,110	29	343
Mongolia	1,087	547	540	547	547	..	..
Montenegro (b)	..	..	..	3	30	1	..
Morocco	5,772	3,961	1,811	3,968	4,002	1	9,297
Namibia (b)	..	..	..	..	..	..	..
Nepal	11	3	8	7	7	..	..
Netherlands	n.a.	n.a.	n.a.	5,458	81,215	938	n.a.
New Zealand	1,267	299	968	833	4,640	..	11,022
Nicaragua (b)	..	..	..	19	19	..	..
Niger (b,d)	n.a.	n.a.	n.a.	..	..	..	..
Nigeria (b)	..	..	..	7	7	..	..
Norway	4,295	445	3,850	991	7,973	145	9,891
Oman (b)	..	..	..	..	..	..	..
Pakistan	279	192	87	202	310	..	6,460
Panama	88	14	74	40	94	..	588
Paraguay (b)	..	..	..	3	3	..	..
Peru	266	64	202	64	64	..	2,798
Philippines	1,662	1,019	643	1,045	1,207	..	..
Poland (b)	..	..	..	4,984	121,401	174	..
Portugal	1,744	1,625	119	2,520	24,755	52	4,273
Qatar (b)	..	..	..	78	78	5	..
Republic of Korea	49,288	44,052	5,236	53,228	102,349	1,598	339,350
Republic of Moldova	978	248	730	294	834	8	3,269
Romania	1,114	580	534	1,109	14,771	..	3,884
Russian Federation	6,125	2,635	3,490	3,264	5,370	..	32,225
Rwanda (b)	..	..	..	..	..	..	..
Saint Kitts and Nevis (b)	..	..	..	1	28	..	..
Samoa	2	2	0	5	5	..	..
San Marino (b)	..	..	..	214	295	..	..
Sao Tome and Principe (b)	..	..	..	..	..	..	..
Saudi Arabia	921	336	585	426	480	..	4,284
Senegal (b,d)	n.a.	n.a.	n.a.	46	782	..	..
Serbia	1,370	187	1,183	498	2,478	82	6,002
Seychelles (b)	..	..	..	5	5	..	..
Singapore	4,782	511	4,271	1,002	4,285	5	14,527
Slovakia	462	266	196	532	6,364	66	874
Slovenia (b)	..	..	..	562	6,516	119	..
South Africa	1,661	686	975	907	3,342	..	15,398
Spain	22,895	22,113	782	28,149	125,343	206	30,514
Sri Lanka	330	178	152	197	413	..	1,378
Sudan	372	297	75	297	297	..	..
Suriname (b)	..	..	..	..	..	..	..
Sweden	554	500	54	5,013	46,867	224	4,797
Switzerland	12,854	4,213	8,641	23,909	164,310	2,928	9,680
Syrian Arab Republic	226	80	146	143	143	..	137

Name	Registration design count by office			Registration design count by origin	Equivalent registration design count by origin	Hague international registration design count	In force by office
	Total	Resident	Non-resident	Total [a]	Total [a]	Origin [c]	Total
Tajikistan (b)	..	..	..	..	..	..	..
Thailand	3,561	2,092	1,469	2,321	3,752	..	15,442
The former Yugoslav Republic of Macedonia	1,067	123	944	128	182	2	2,426
Togo (b,d)	n.a.	n.a.	n.a.	8	136	..	..
Trinidad and Tobago	85	79	6	80	80	..	118
Tunisia	1,381	150	1,231	159	310	..	..
Turkey	44,995	37,280	7,715	38,939	54,404	451	118,848
Turkmenistan (b)	..	..	..	..	..	..	..
Ukraine	8,627	5,095	3,532	5,815	10,833	159	13,761
United Arab Emirates (b)	..	..	..	135	756	2	..
United Kingdom	17,195	14,826	2,369	25,095	191,956	363	56,369
United States of America	32,483	17,584	14,899	48,829	347,897	1,673	321,314
Uruguay	65	15	50	24	24	..	647
Uzbekistan	268	191	77	192	192	..	523
Venezuela (Bolivarian Republic of) (b)	..	..	..	4	4	..	..
Viet Nam	2,608	1,504	1,104	1,647	2,619	..	11,068
Yemen	13	13	0	16	16	..	46
Zambia	86	84	2	84	84	..	404
Others/Unknown	..	..	..	28,468	54,138	1	..
Total (2017 estimates)	**985,800**	**798,500**	**187,300**	**985,800**	**n.a.**	**19,241**	**3,746,200**

(a) Design count by origin data are incomplete because some offices do not report the origin of registrations.

(b) Only Hague designation data are available and/or the office has not reported the origin of registrations, so design count by office and origin data may be incomplete.

(c) Origin is defined as the country of the stated address of residence of the holder in an international registration.

(d) The African Intellectual Property Organization (OAPI) is the competent office for registering applications.

n.a. indicates not applicable.

.. indicates not available.

Source: WIPO Statistics Database, September 2018.

Industrial designs

Plant varieties

Highlights

Plant variety applications grew at their fastest rate in 15 years

Around 18,490 plant variety applications were filed worldwide in 2017, up 11.7% on 2016 – the largest increase in applications in 15 years (see figure 4.1). The offices of China, the United Kingdom (U.K.), the Community Plant Variety Office of the European Union (CPVO), Viet Nam and Ukraine accounted for most of this growth.

China becomes the top filing office

China became the top filing office in 2017, receiving 4,465 applications. The CPVO received 3,422 applications. This marks the first time in over 23 years that the CPVO was not the top destination for plant variety filings. The CPVO was followed by the national offices of the United States of America (U.S.) (1,557), Ukraine (1,345) and Japan (1,019) (see figure 4.2). Filings in China represent a 52.8% year-on-year growth, driven almost entirely by resident filings. Among the other offices in the top five, the CPVO (+3.7%), Japan (+4.3%) and Ukraine (+5.6%) experienced growth, while the U.S. (−2.9%) was the only top-five office to experience a decline in filings. The growth at the CPVO and in the Ukraine office was driven by resident filings, whereas an increase in non-resident filings drove growth in Japan. The decline in filings in the U.S. was the result of a decrease in non-resident filings, which outweighed the slight year-on-year increase in resident filings.

The combined share of applications received at the top five offices worldwide increased, from around 61% in 2016 to 64% in 2017, due to the large growth experienced by China. This concentration was only partially offset by the U.S. decline.

Eight of the top 10 offices received more applications from residents than from non-residents. Among these offices, China's resident share (89.7%) was the highest. In contrast, Australia and Ukraine received more than half their filings from non-resident applicants.

Offices of high-income economies accounted for the largest proportion (52.2%) of plant variety applications received in 2017, but this figure was down from 72.2% a decade earlier in 2007 (see figure 4.3). Offices in the upper middle-income group, however, saw their combined share increase from 21.9% in 2007 to 36.9% in 2017, mostly driven by the increase in filings in China. The share held by the lower middle-income group likewise increased, from 5.9% in 2007 to 10.7% in 2017, driven by Morocco, Ukraine and Viet Nam.

Offices in Europe received 39.8% of all plant variety applications in 2017 – less than their share a decade earlier (48.1%) (see figure 4.4). Asia saw its share increase from 22.6% in 2007 to 37.0% in 2017, at the expense of a drop of 4.0 percentage points in North America. Shares for Latin America and the Caribbean (LAC) (7.4%), Africa (2.9%) and Oceania (2.7%) decreased slightly due to Asia's rising share.

Applications grew by 11.7%

4.1. Plant variety applications worldwide, 2003–2017

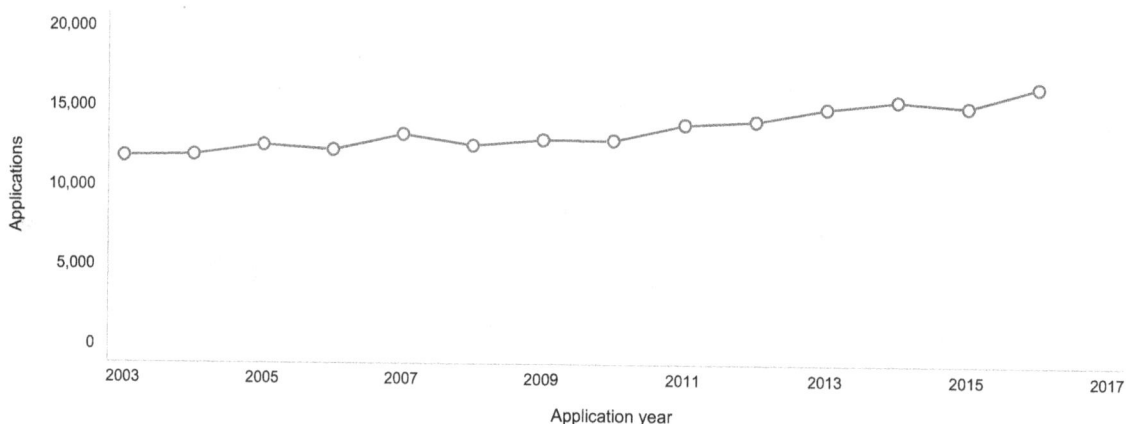

Source: Figure D1.

China surpassed the CPVO as the top destination for plant variety applications

4.2. Plant variety applications for the top 10 offices, 2017

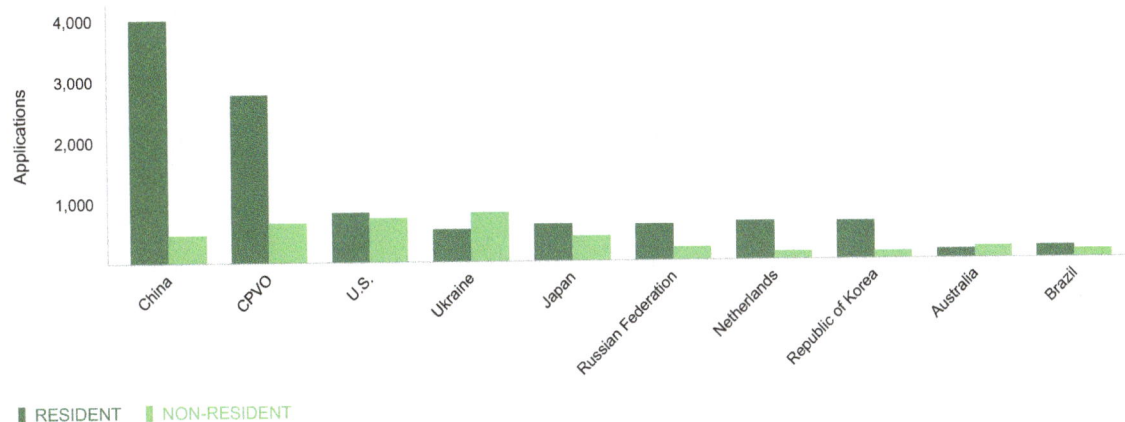

RESIDENT   NON-RESIDENT

Source: Figure D5.

Offices of high-income countries received 52.2% of all applications filed worldwide

4.3. Plant variety applications by income group, 2007 and 2017

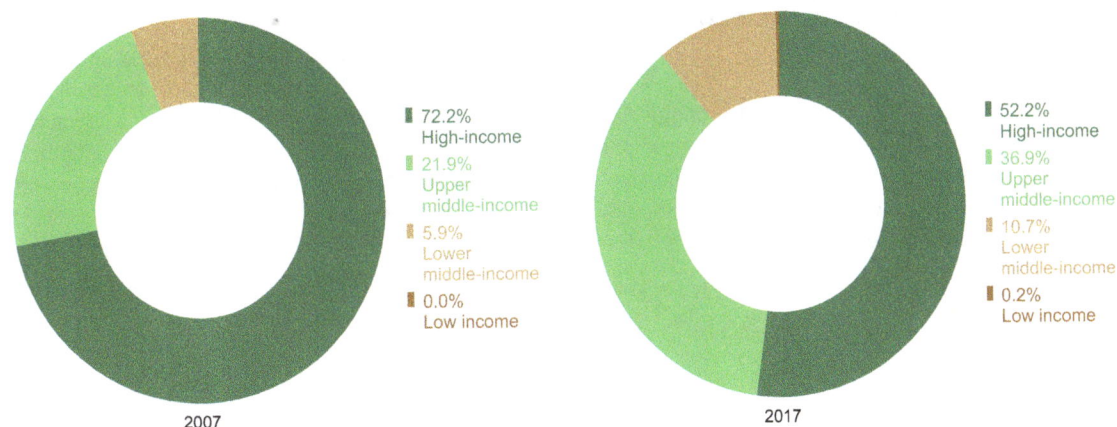

72.2%
High-income

21.9%
Upper
middle-income

5.9%
Lower
middle-income

0.0%
Low income

2007

52.2%
High-income

36.9%
Upper
middle-income

10.7%
Lower
middle-income

0.2%
Low income

2017

Source: Table D3.

Offices located in Europe accounted for 39.8% of all applications

4.4. Plant variety applications by region, 2007 and 2017

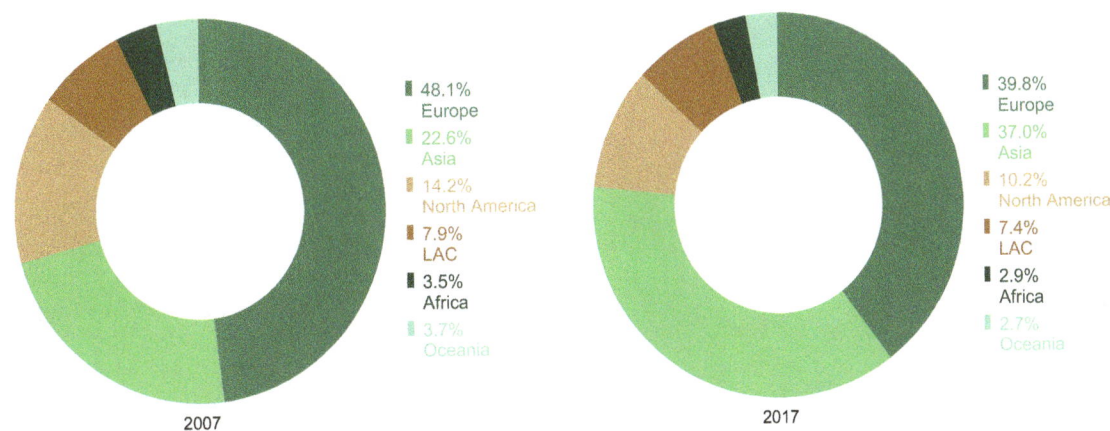

48.1%
Europe

22.6%
Asia

14.2%
North America

7.9%
LAC

3.5%
Africa

3.7%
Oceania

2007

39.8%
Europe

37.0%
Asia

10.2%
North America

7.4%
LAC

2.9%
Africa

2.7%
Oceania

2017

Source: Table D4.

Plant varieties

Applicants from China filed the greatest number of applications worldwide

Applications received by offices from resident and non-resident applicants are referred to as office data, whereas applications filed by applicants at a national/regional office (resident applications) or at a foreign office (applications abroad) are referred to as origin data. Here, plant variety statistics based on the origin of residence are reported in order to complement the picture of activity worldwide. Note that for applicants domiciled in European Union (EU) member states, filing at the CPVO regional office is also regarded as a resident filing.

Applicants from China were the most active applicants in the world in 2017, filing 4,041 plant variety applications. This represents a 48.6% growth in filing activity for Chinese applicants – the fastest growth among the top 10 origins. They were followed by applicants from the Netherlands, who filed 3,320 applications. The U.S. (2,084), France (1,068) and Germany (865) were ranked third, fourth and fifth largest origins, respectively (see figure D10). The Netherlands (+6.1%), the U.S. (+2.4%) and France (+1.7%) all saw growth.

While applicants from four of the top five origins filed most of their applications abroad or at the regional office, only those from China filed almost exclusively at home. Similarly, applicants from Japan, the Republic of Korea, the Russian Federation and Ukraine also filed predominantly at their home offices.

Equivalent count

Origin data are compiled using two different counting methods – absolute counts and equivalent counts. The difference between the two lies in the treatment of regional offices data (the CPVO and the African Intellectual Property Organization (OAPI)). For absolute counts, an application received by a regional office is counted only once. For the equivalent count, a single application filed at a regional office is equivalent to multiple applications. To calculate the number of equivalent applications at a regional office in 2017, each application has been multiplied by the corresponding number of member states for the regional office. For CPVO applications, if the applicant resided in one of the 28 EU member states, the application was counted as one resident filing and 27 filings abroad. If the applicant did not reside in an EU member state, the application was counted as 28 filings abroad. The same methodology applies to OAPI member states.

By equivalent count, applicants from the Netherlands filed the most

Equivalent counts take multiple members of a regional office into account. One would expect to see those country origins whose applicants filed intensively at the CVPO move up the ranking when this counting method is applied. Not surprisingly, European countries and the U.S. topped the list of origins based on equivalent counts (see Map 4.5). Applicants from the Netherlands are currently ranked number one, with 39,743 equivalent

Applicants from the Netherlands are ranked in first position under equivalent count measure

4.5. Equivalent plant variety applications by origin, 2017

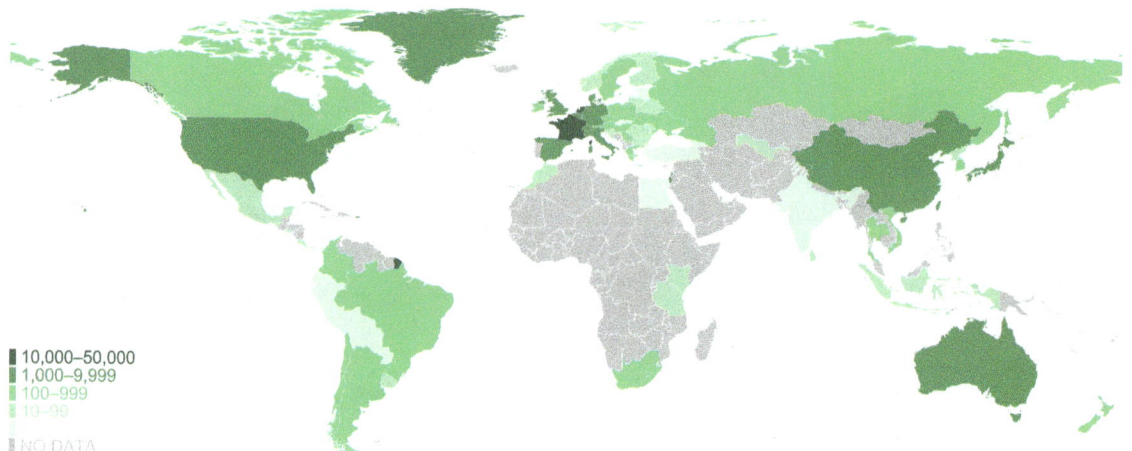

10,000–50,000
1,000–9,999
100–999
10–99
NO DATA

Source: Map D9.

applications filed worldwide. They were followed by applicants from France (13,191), Germany (9,721) and the U.S. (9,520). China (4,237) was the only other non-European country among the top 10 origins, despite the fact that only 5.5% of its applicants' filings were equivalent filings abroad. This is in marked contrast to the Netherlands, for which the share was 95%.

The number of titles issued decreased for the first time in five years

In 2017, the total number of plant variety titles issued decreased for the first time in five years by 3.8%, declining to 12,780 (see figure 4.6). China accounted for most of this contraction, with titles issued decreasing by 22.8%, while still representing the second largest issuing office with 1,646 titles in total. The CPVO, which issued the largest number of titles (2,865), also experienced a slight decline (–3.9%). The CPVO and the Chinese office were followed by the offices of the U.S. (1,604), Ukraine (887) and Japan (812) (see figure D8). The offices of both Japan (–13.7%) and the U.S. (–5.8%) contributed to the overall decline in titles issued in 2017.

The grant process takes time, so fluctuations in volumes of granted plant variety titles may reflect changes in processing capacities or procedural delays.

Plant variety titles issued decreased by 3.8%
4.6. Plant variety titles issued worldwide, 2003–2017

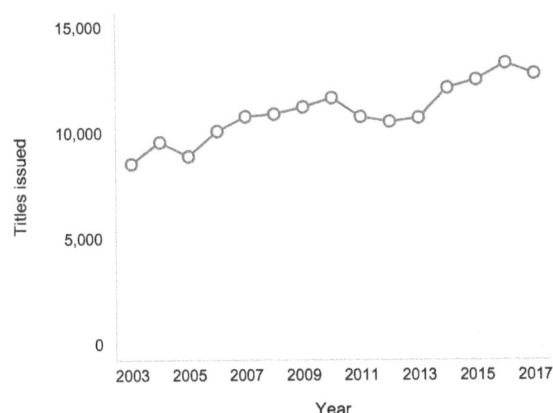

Steady growth in plant variety titles in force

Around 126,150 plant variety titles were in force at the end of 2017, up 6.7% on 2017. The CPVO (25,914) and the U.S. (25,238) were the two offices with the highest numbers of active titles (see figure D15). Other offices maintaining at least 4,000 active titles included Japan (8,490), the Netherlands (8,389), Ukraine (8,127), China (7,723), the Republic of Korea (5,064) and the Russian Federation (5,048).

Plant varieties

Plant varieties statistics

Plant varieties

Plant variety applications and titles issued worldwide

D1. Trend in plant variety applications worldwide, 2003–2017

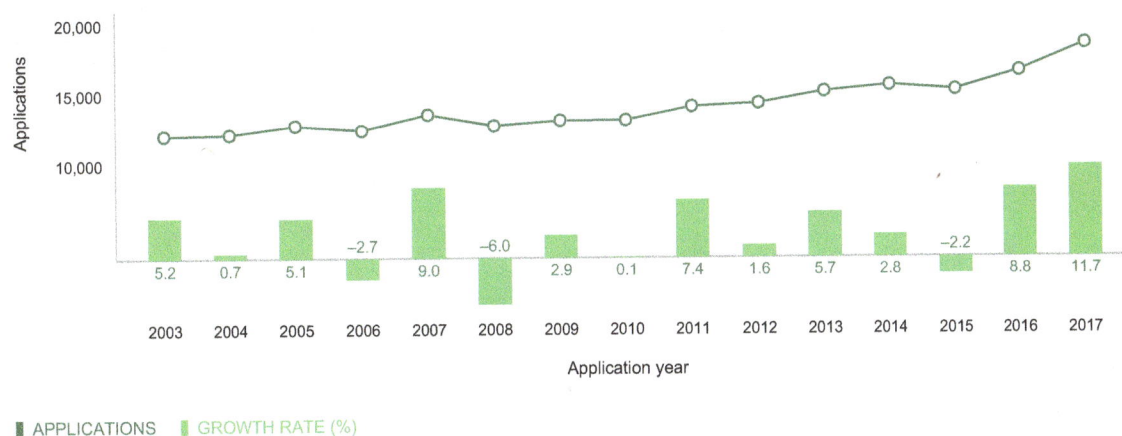

Applications

	2003	2004	2005	2006	2007	2008	2009	2010	2011	2012	2013	2014	2015	2016	2017
	5.2	0.7	5.1	−2.7	9.0	−6.0	2.9	0.1	7.4	1.6	5.7	2.8	−2.2	8.8	11.7

Application year

■ APPLICATIONS   ■ GROWTH RATE (%)

Note: World totals are WIPO estimates using data covering 69 offices.
Source: WIPO Statistics Database, September 2018.

D2. Trend in plant variety titles issued worldwide, 2003–2017

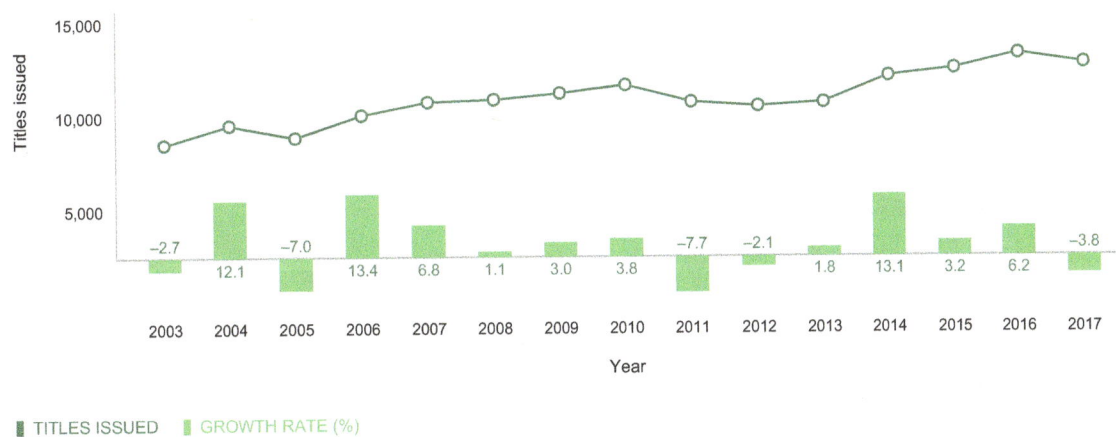

Titles issued

	2003	2004	2005	2006	2007	2008	2009	2010	2011	2012	2013	2014	2015	2016	2017
	−2.7	12.1	−7.0	13.4	6.8	1.1	3.0	3.8	−7.7	−2.1	1.8	13.1	3.2	6.2	−3.8

Year

■ TITLES ISSUED   ■ GROWTH RATE (%)

Note: World totals are WIPO estimates using data covering 69 offices.
Source: WIPO Statistics Database, September 2018.

Plant varieties

Plant variety applications and titles issued by office

D3. Plant variety applications by income group, 2007 and 2017

Income group	Number of applications		Resident share (%)		Share of world total (%)		Average growth (%)
	2007	2017	2007	2017	2007	2017	2007–2017
High-income	9,789	9,650	63.9	67.5	72.2	52.2	−0.1
Upper middle-income	2,969	6,825	68.5	76.9	21.9	36.9	8.7
Lower middle-income	792	1,975	49.1	44.3	5.9	10.7	9.6
Low-income	0	40		86.4		0.2	
World	**13,550**	**18,490**	**64.1**	**68.5**	**100.0**	**100.0**	**3.2**

Note: Totals by income group are WIPO estimates using data covering 69 offices. Each category includes the following number of offices: high-income countries/economies (38), upper middle-income (19), lower middle-income (11) and low-income (1). The EU's Community Plant Variety Office (CPVO) data are allocated to the high-income group because the majority of EU member states are high-income countries. For information on income group classification, see the data description section.

Source: WIPO Statistics Database, September 2018.

D4. Plant variety applications by region, 2007 and 2017

Region	Number of applications		Resident share (%)		Share of world total (%)		Average growth (%)
	2007	2017	2007	2017	2007	2017	2007–2017
Africa	481	540	37.0	22.3	3.5	2.9	1.2
Asia	3,069	6,845	76.6	83.4	22.6	37.0	8.4
Europe	6,512	7,363	74.1	70.1	48.1	39.8	1.2
Latin America and the Caribbean	1,054	1,371	33.0	42.8	7.9	7.4	2.7
North America	1,928	1,880	39.4	48.0	14.2	10.2	−0.3
Oceania	506	491	46.2	39.1	3.7	2.7	−0.3
World	**13,550**	**18,490**	**64.1**	**68.5**	**100.0**	**100.0**	**3.2**

Note: Totals by geographic region are WIPO estimates using data covering 69 offices. Each region includes the following number of offices: Africa (5), Asia (12), Europe (33), Latin America and the Caribbean (14), North America (3) and Oceania (2).

Source: WIPO Statistics Database, September 2018.

D5. Plant variety applications for the top 20 offices, 2017

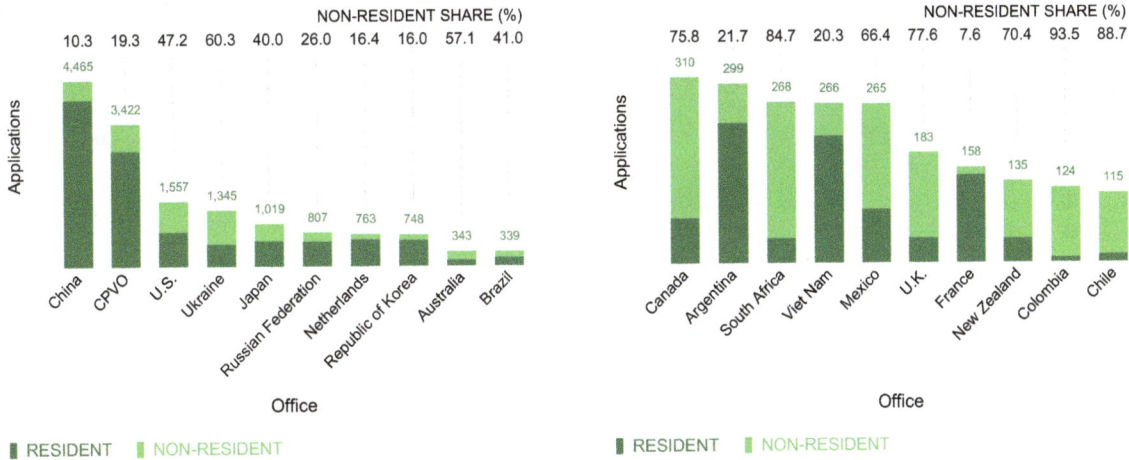

NON-RESIDENT SHARE (%)

| 10.3 | 19.3 | 47.2 | 60.3 | 40.0 | 26.0 | 16.4 | 16.0 | 57.1 | 41.0 |

NON-RESIDENT SHARE (%)

| 75.8 | 21.7 | 84.7 | 20.3 | 66.4 | 77.6 | 7.6 | 70.4 | 93.5 | 88.7 |

■ RESIDENT ■ NON-RESIDENT   ■ RESIDENT ■ NON-RESIDENT

Note: CPVO is the Community Plant Variety Office of the European Union. In general, national offices of CPVO member states receive lower volumes of applications because applicants may apply via the CPVO to seek protection within any CPVO member state.

Source: WIPO Statistics Database, September 2018.

D6. Contribution of resident and non-resident applications to total growth for the top 20 offices, 2016–2017

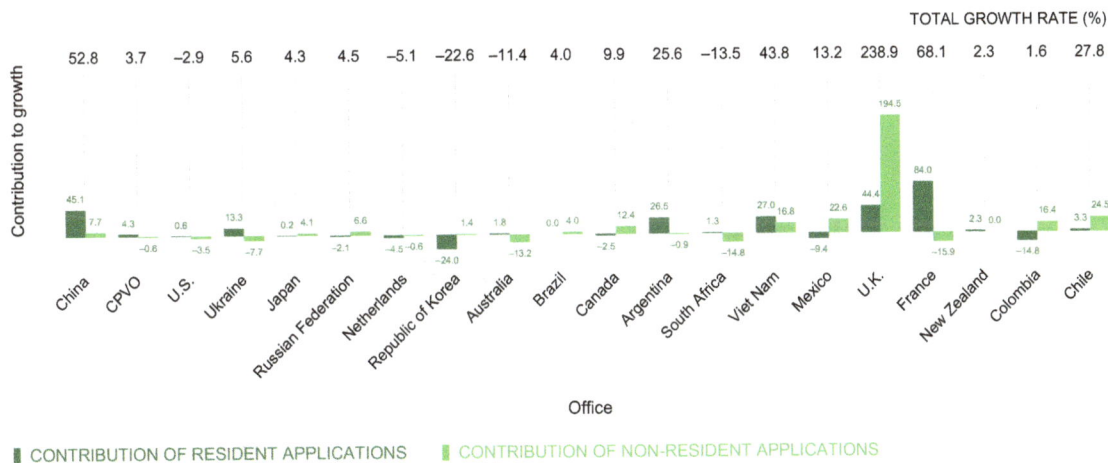

TOTAL GROWTH RATE (%)

| 52.8 | 3.7 | −2.9 | 5.6 | 4.3 | 4.5 | −5.1 | −22.6 | −11.4 | 4.0 | 9.9 | 25.6 | −13.5 | 43.8 | 13.2 | 238.9 | 68.1 | 2.3 | 1.6 | 27.8 |

■ CONTRIBUTION OF RESIDENT APPLICATIONS   ■ CONTRIBUTION OF NON-RESIDENT APPLICATIONS

Note: CPVO is the Community Plant Variety Office of the European Union. This figure shows total growth in plant variety applications, broken down by the respective contributions of resident and non-resident filings. For example, applications in Japan grew by 4.3%, and resident applications contributed 0.2 percentage points to this total growth while non-resident applications accounted for the other 4.1 percentage points.

Source: WIPO Statistics Database, September 2018.

D7. Plant variety applications for offices of selected low- and middle-income countries, 2017

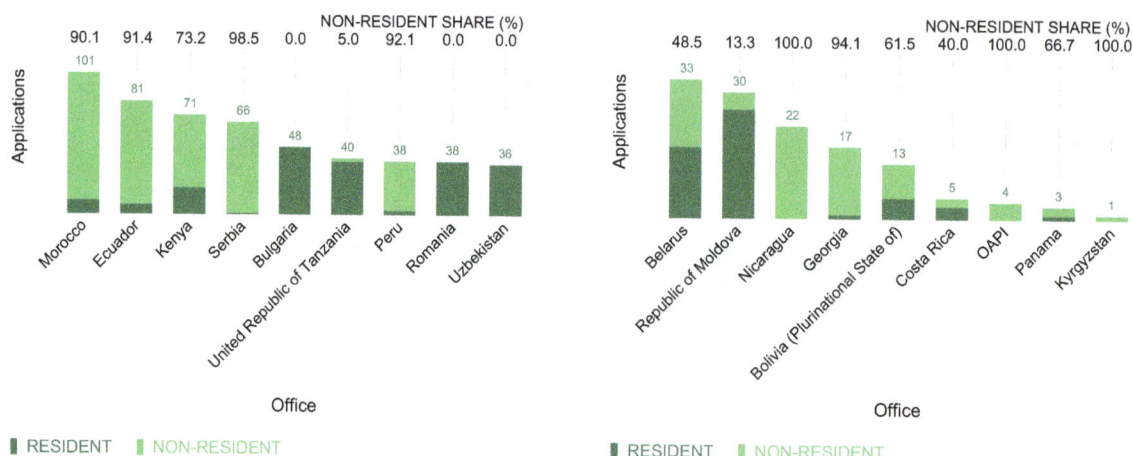

NON-RESIDENT SHARE (%)

90.1 91.4 73.2 98.5 0.0 5.0 92.1 0.0 0.0

Applications: 101 (Morocco), 81 (Ecuador), 71 (Kenya), 66 (Serbia), 48 (Bulgaria), 40 (United Republic of Tanzania), 38 (Peru), 38 (Romania), 36 (Uzbekistan)

NON-RESIDENT SHARE (%)

48.5 13.3 100.0 94.1 61.5 40.0 100.0 66.7 100.0

Applications: 33 (Belarus), 30 (Republic of Moldova), 22 (Nicaragua), 17 (Georgia), 13 (Bolivia (Plurinational State of)), 5 (Costa Rica), 4 (OAPI), 3 (Panama), 1 (Kyrgyzstan)

Office

■ RESIDENT ■ NON-RESIDENT

Note: OAPI is the African Intellectual Property Organization. The selected offices are from different world regions and income groups. Where available, data for all offices are presented in the statistical table at the end of this section.

Source: WIPO Statistics Database, September 2018.

D8. Plant variety titles issued by the top 20 offices, 2017

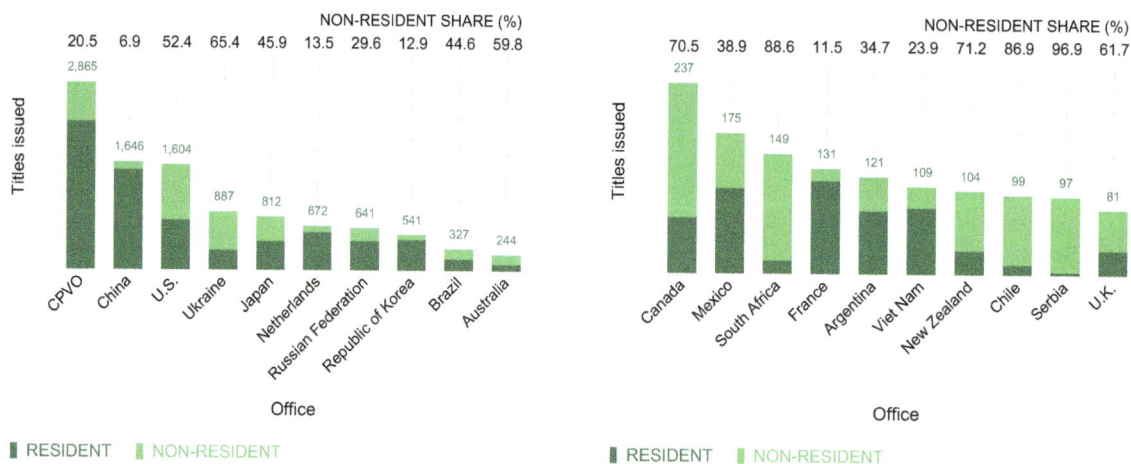

NON-RESIDENT SHARE (%)

20.5 6.9 52.4 65.4 45.9 13.5 29.6 12.9 44.6 59.8

Titles issued: 2,865 (CPVO), 1,646 (China), 1,604 (U.S.), 887 (Ukraine), 812 (Japan), 672 (Netherlands), 641 (Russian Federation), 541 (Republic of Korea), 327 (Brazil), 244 (Australia)

NON-RESIDENT SHARE (%)

70.5 38.9 88.6 11.5 34.7 23.9 71.2 86.9 96.9 61.7

Titles issued: 237 (Canada), 175 (Mexico), 149 (South Africa), 131 (France), 121 (Argentina), 109 (Viet Nam), 104 (New Zealand), 99 (Chile), 97 (Serbia), 81 (U.K.)

Office

■ RESIDENT ■ NON-RESIDENT

Note: CPVO is the Community Plant Variety Office of the European Union. The procedure for issuing titles varies between offices, and differences in the numbers of titles issued between offices depend on factors such as examination capacity and procedural delays, so there is a time lag between application and title issue dates. For this reason, data on applications for a given year should not be compared with data on titles issued for the same year.

Source: WIPO Statistics Database, September 2018.

Plant varieties

Plant variety applications and titles issued by origin

D9. Equivalent plant variety applications by origin, 2017

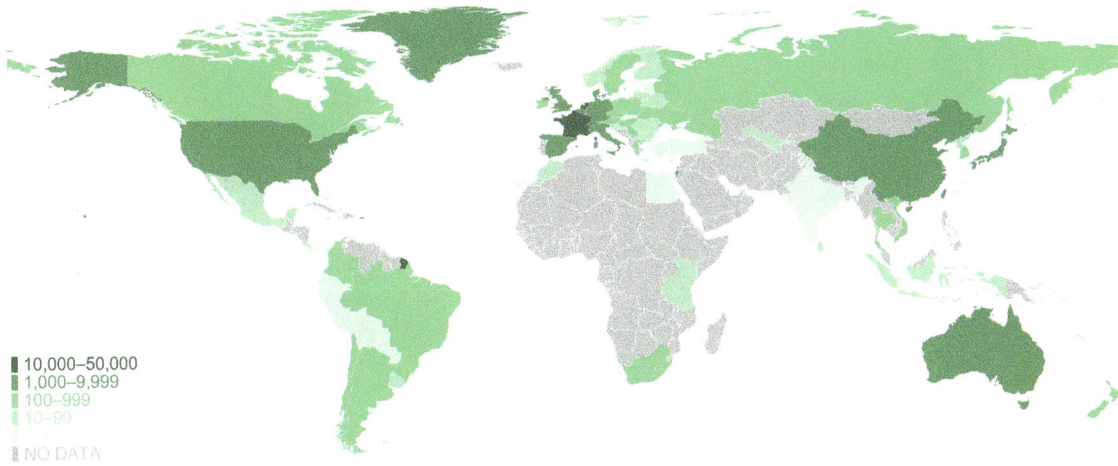

- 10,000–50,000
- 1,000–9,999
- 100–999
- 10–99
- NO DATA

Note: Equivalent plant variety applications by origin include resident applications and applications filed abroad. The origin of an application is determined by the residence of the applicant. Applications filed at regional offices are considered equivalent to multiple applications in the relevant member states. See the glossary for the definition of equivalent application.

Source: WIPO Statistics Database, September 2018.

D10. Plant variety applications for the top 20 origins, 2017

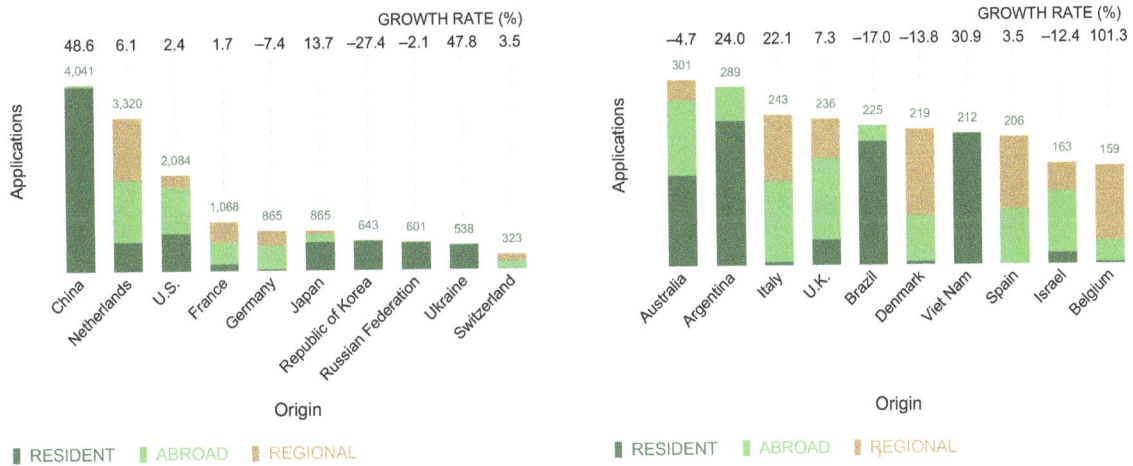

GROWTH RATE (%)

| 48.6 | 6.1 | 2.4 | 1.7 | −7.4 | 13.7 | −27.4 | −2.1 | 47.8 | 3.5 |

| China | Netherlands | U.S. | France | Germany | Japan | Republic of Korea | Russian Federation | Ukraine | Switzerland |
| 4,041 | 3,320 | 2,084 | 1,068 | 865 | 865 | 643 | 601 | 538 | 323 |

GROWTH RATE (%)

| −4.7 | 24.0 | 22.1 | 7.3 | −17.0 | −13.8 | 30.9 | 3.5 | −12.4 | 101.3 |

| Australia | Argentina | Italy | U.K. | Brazil | Denmark | Viet Nam | Spain | Israel | Belgium |
| 301 | 289 | 243 | 236 | 225 | 219 | 212 | 206 | 163 | 159 |

RESIDENT · ABROAD · REGIONAL

Note: Data are based on absolute count, not equivalent count. Applications by origin include resident applications and applications filed abroad. The origin of an application is determined by the residence of the applicant. Regional refers to applications filed at the EU's Community Plant Variety Office.

Source: WIPO Statistics Database, September 2018.

Plant varieties

D11. Plant variety applications abroad for the top 20 origins, 2017

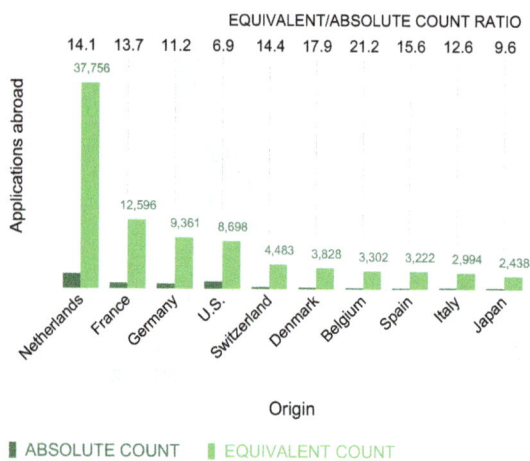

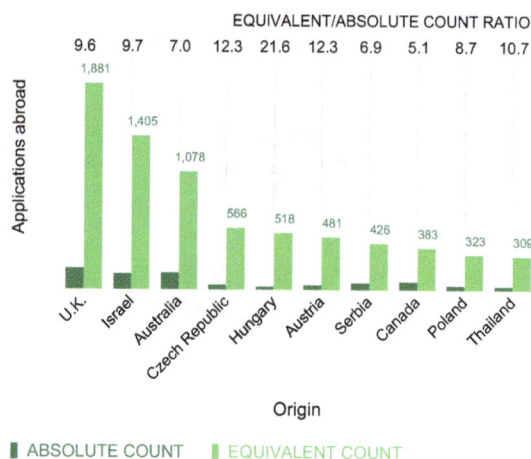

EQUIVALENT/ABSOLUTE COUNT RATIO

14.1	13.7	11.2	6.9	14.4	17.9	21.2	15.6	12.6	9.6

Applications abroad

37,756 — Netherlands
12,596 — France
9,361 — Germany
8,698 — U.S.
4,483 — Switzerland
3,828 — Denmark
3,302 — Belgium
3,222 — Spain
2,994 — Italy
2,438 — Japan

Origin

■ ABSOLUTE COUNT   ■ EQUIVALENT COUNT

EQUIVALENT/ABSOLUTE COUNT RATIO

9.6	9.7	7.0	12.3	21.6	12.3	6.9	5.1	8.7	10.7

Applications abroad

1,881 — U.K.
1,405 — Israel
1,078 — Australia
566 — Czech Republic
518 — Hungary
481 — Austria
426 — Serbia
383 — Canada
323 — Poland
309 — Thailand

Origin

■ ABSOLUTE COUNT   ■ EQUIVALENT COUNT

Note: The origin of an application is determined by the residence of the applicant. Applications filed at regional offices are considered equivalent to multiple applications in the relevant member states. See the glossary for the definition of equivalent applications.

Source: WIPO Statistics Database, September 2018.

D12. Plant variety titles issued for the top 20 origins, 2017

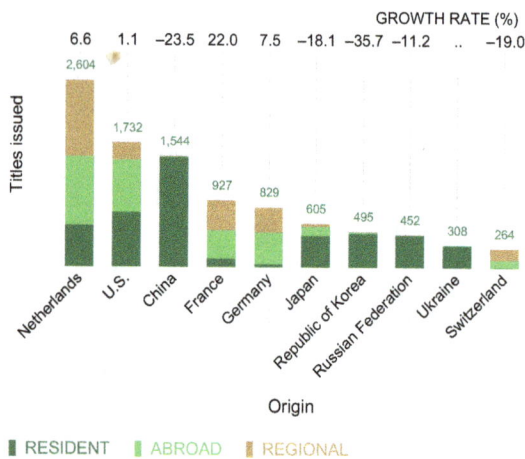

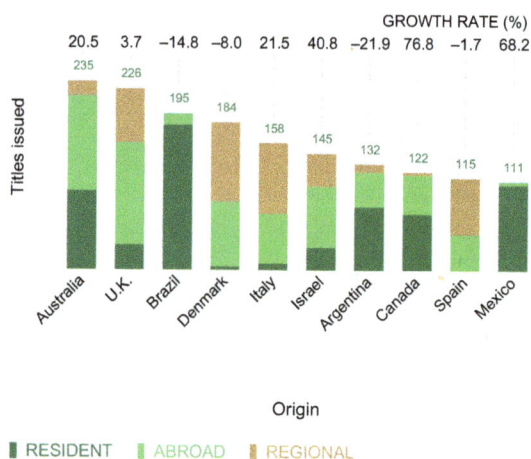

GROWTH RATE (%)

6.6	1.1	−23.5	22.0	7.5	−18.1	−35.7	−11.2	..	−19.0

Titles issued

2,604 — Netherlands
1,732 — U.S.
1,544 — China
927 — France
829 — Germany
605 — Japan
495 — Republic of Korea
452 — Russian Federation
308 — Ukraine
264 — Switzerland

Origin

■ RESIDENT   ■ ABROAD   ■ REGIONAL

GROWTH RATE (%)

20.5	3.7	−14.8	−8.0	21.5	40.8	−21.9	76.8	−1.7	68.2

Titles issued

235 — Australia
226 — U.K.
195 — Brazil
184 — Denmark
158 — Italy
145 — Israel
132 — Argentina
122 — Canada
115 — Spain
111 — Mexico

Origin

■ RESIDENT   ■ ABROAD   ■ REGIONAL

.. indicates not available.

Note: Data are based on absolute count, not equivalent count. The origin of titles issued is determined by the residence of the applicant. Regional refers to titles issued by the Community Plant Variety Office of the European Union.

Source: WIPO Statistics Database, September 2018.

Plant varieties

D13. Plant variety titles issued abroad for the top 20 origins, 2017

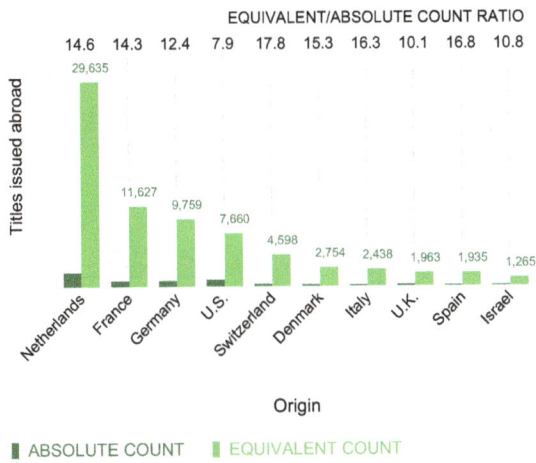

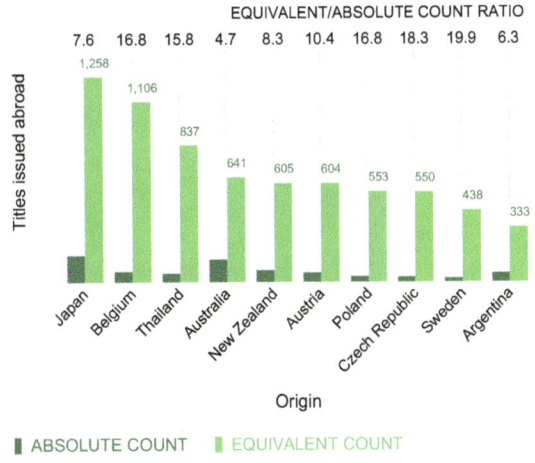

EQUIVALENT/ABSOLUTE COUNT RATIO

| 14.6 | 14.3 | 12.4 | 7.9 | 17.8 | 15.3 | 16.3 | 10.1 | 16.8 | 10.8 |

Titles issued abroad

- Netherlands: 29,635
- France: 11,627
- Germany: 9,759
- U.S.: 7,660
- Switzerland: 4,598
- Denmark: 2,754
- Italy: 2,438
- U.K.: 1,963
- Spain: 1,935
- Israel: 1,265

Origin

EQUIVALENT/ABSOLUTE COUNT RATIO

| 7.6 | 16.8 | 15.8 | 4.7 | 8.3 | 10.4 | 16.8 | 18.3 | 19.9 | 6.3 |

Titles issued abroad

- Japan: 1,258
- Belgium: 1,106
- Thailand: 837
- Australia: 641
- New Zealand: 605
- Austria: 604
- Poland: 553
- Czech Republic: 550
- Sweden: 438
- Argentina: 333

Origin

▮ ABSOLUTE COUNT   ▮ EQUIVALENT COUNT

▮ ABSOLUTE COUNT   ▮ EQUIVALENT COUNT

Note: The origin of titles issued is determined by the residence of the applicant. Titles issued by regional offices are considered equivalent to multiple titles in the relevant member states. See the glossary for the definition of equivalent count.

Source: WIPO Statistics Database, September 2018.

Plant varieties

Plant variety titles in force

D14. Trend in plant variety titles in force worldwide, 2003–2017

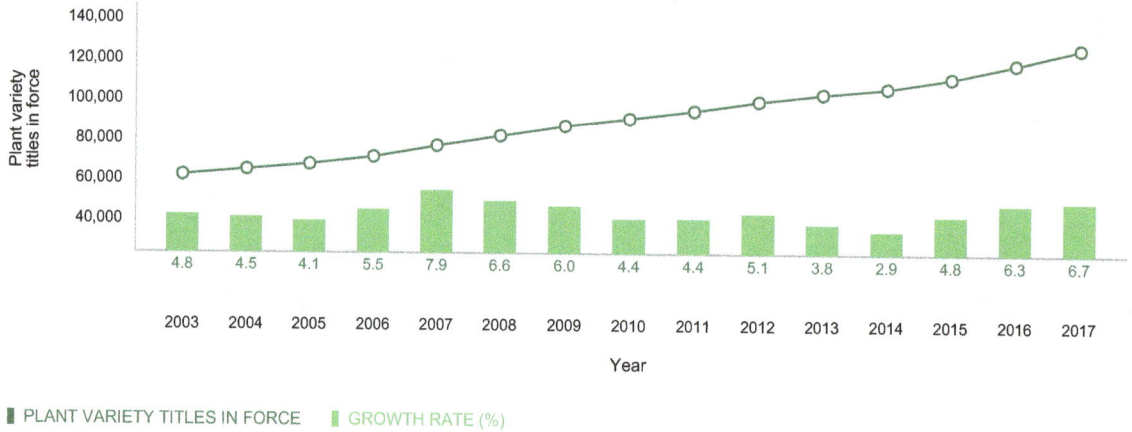

Note: World totals are WIPO estimates using data covering 69 offices.
Source: WIPO Statistics Database, September 2018.

D15. Plant variety titles in force at selected offices, 2017

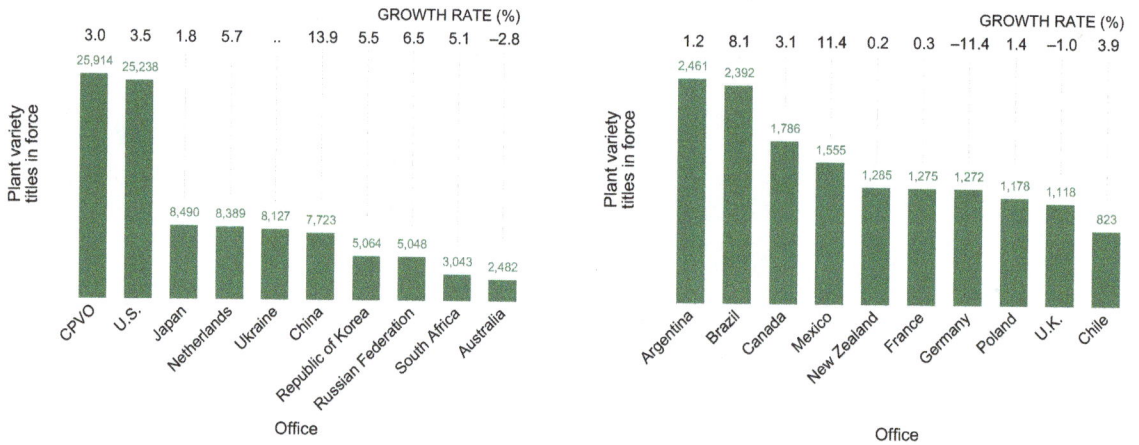

Note: CPVO is the Community Plant Variety Office of the European Union.
Source: WIPO Statistics Database, September 2018.

Statistical table

D16. Plant variety applications and titles issued by office and origin, and plant variety titles in force by office, 2017

Name	Applications by office			Applications by origin	Equivalent applications by origin	Grants by office			Plant variety titles in force
	Total	Resident	Non-resident	Total	Total	Total	Resident	Non-resident	Office
African Intellectual Property Organization	4	0	4	..	..	..	..	..	40
Argentina	299	234	65	289	289	121	79	42	2,461
Australia	343	147	196	301	1,225	244	98	146	2,482
Austria (a)	..	..	..	39	498	1	1	0	18
Belarus	33	17	16	17	17	42	24	18	245
Belgium	3	3	0	159	3,426	1	1	0	43
Bolivia (Plurinational State of)	13	5	8	5	5	13	5	8	62
Brazil	339	200	139	225	225	327	181	146	2,392
Bulgaria	48	48	0	60	60	24	24	0	..
Canada	310	75	235	150	458	237	70	167	1,786
Chile	115	13	102	31	115	99	13	86	823
China	4,465	4,004	461	4,041	4,237	1,646	1,532	114	7,723
Colombia	124	8	116	21	301	73	16	57	548
Community Plant Variety Office	3,422	2,763	659	n.a.	..	2,865	2,277	588	25,914
Costa Rica	5	3	2	8	64	5	1	4	16
Croatia	13	13	0	19	19	3	3	0	54
Czech Republic	57	49	8	95	635	69	53	16	768
Democratic People's Republic of Korea (b)	..	..	..	68	68	..	..	..	..
Denmark	7	5	2	219	3,972	4	4	0	89
Ecuador	81	7	74	8	8	43	0	43	277
Egypt (b)	..	..	..	3	3	..	..	..	..
El Salvador (b)	..	..	..	19	19	..	..	..	..
Estonia	10	2	8	2	2	10	3	7	94
Eswatini (b)	..	..	..	29	29	..	..	..	..
Finland	14	13	1	26	80	14	13	1	192
France	158	146	12	1,068	13,191	131	116	15	1,275
Georgia	17	1	16	1	1	57	21	36	209
Germany	39	32	7	865	9,721	44	40	4	1,272
Greece (b)	..	..	..	5	140	..	..	..	..
Hungary	16	16	0	40	553	16	15	1	155
India (b)	..	..	..	7	7	..	..	..	..
Indonesia (b)	..	..	..	1	29	..	..	..	..
Ireland	1	1	0	22	103	2	2	0	67
Israel	53	18	35	163	1,423	59	28	31	810
Italy	5	5	0	243	3,105	11	8	3	..
Japan	1,019	611	408	865	3,049	812	439	373	8,490
Kenya	71	19	52	25	25	34	0	34	389
Kyrgyzstan	1	0	1	..	..	..	..	..	5
Latvia	1	1	0	1	1	2	2	0	186
Lithuania	18	13	5	13	13	20	14	6	91
Luxembourg (b)	..	..	..	44	125	..	..	..	..
Mauritius (b)	..	..	..	7	7	..	..	..	..
Mexico	265	89	176	97	97	175	107	68	1,555
Monaco (b)	..	..	..	3	3	..	..	..	..
Morocco	101	10	91	10	10	38	10	28	340

Plant varieties

Name	Applications by office			Applications by origin	Equivalent applications by origin	Grants by office			Plant variety titles in force
	Total	Resident	Non-resident	Total	Total	Total	Resident	Non-resident	Office
Netherlands	763	638	125	3,320	39,743	672	581	91	8,389
New Zealand	135	40	95	78	246	104	30	74	1,285
Nicaragua	22	0	22	..	..	3	3	0	13
Norway	19	7	12	10	38	15	10	5	228
Panama	3	1	2	1	1	..	..	..	19
Paraguay (a)	..	..	..	3	3	..	..	..	..
Peru	38	3	35	3	3	68	20	48	165
Poland	110	84	26	121	418	74	66	8	1,178
Portugal (a)	..	..	..	..	..	1	0	1	13
Republic of Korea	748	628	120	643	727	541	471	70	5,064
Republic of Moldova	30	26	4	27	55	17	14	3	188
Romania	38	38	0	50	50	38	38	0	365
Russian Federation	807	597	210	601	629	641	451	190	5,048
Serbia	66	1	65	63	427	97	3	94	341
Singapore	5	0	5	..	..	..	..	..	3
Slovakia	8	7	1	9	9	16	16	0	377
Slovenia (a)	..	..	..	3	57	1	1	0	16
South Africa	268	41	227	82	250	149	17	132	3,043
Spain (a)	..	..	..	206	3,338	..	..	..	..
Sri Lanka (b)	..	..	..	2	58	..	..	..	..
Sweden	4	0	4	13	283	5	1	4	115
Switzerland	75	12	63	323	4,495	54	6	48	680
Thailand (b)	..	..	..	29	309	..	..	..	..
Turkey (a)	..	..	..	5	5	..	..	..	..
Ukraine	1,345	534	811	538	538	887	307	580	8,127
United Kingdom	183	41	142	236	1,985	81	31	50	1,118
United Republic of Tanzania	40	38	2	38	38	38	38	0	111
United States of America (PPA) (c)	1,059	422	637	n.a.	..	1,311	516	795	17,644
United States of America (PVPA)	498	400	98	2,084	9,520	293	248	45	7,594
Uruguay	54	18	36	23	23	52	20	32	588
Uzbekistan	36	36	0	36	36	39	39	0	98
Viet Nam	266	212	54	212	212	109	83	26	359
Others/Unknown	..	..	..	17	353	..	..	..	..
Total (2017 estimates)	**18,490**	**12,700**	**5,790**	**18,490**	**n.a.**	**12,780**	**8,300**	**3,810**	**126,150**

(a) The office did not report data; therefore, applications by origin data may be incomplete.

(b) Is not a member of the International Union for the Protection of New Varieties of Plants (UPOV).

(c) Applications by origin are reported under the U.S. Plant Variety Protection Act (PVPA).

.. indicates not available.

Source: WIPO Statistics Database, September 2018.

Plant varieties

Geographical indications

In 2017, for the first time, WIPO published statistics on geographical indicators (GIs) in force covering data for 54 jurisdictions. Data were collected from national and regional intellectual property (IP) offices and other competent authorities using three questionnaires.

In 2018, WIPO revised the GI questionnaire and invited national/regional authorities to share their latest GIs in force data with WIPO. In total, 82 authorities responded, which is a considerable improvement on the 54 responses that WIPO received in the previous year. Furthermore, a number of authorities reviewed their previous data submissions and revised their data in order to provide a more comprehensive and refined perspective of GIs in force within their jurisdictions.

It is important to note that GIs can be protected through a variety of legal means (e.g., *sui generis* systems, trademark laws, international agreements, other national legal means, etc.). This can make it challenging to obtain a complete picture of all GIs protected in any particular country. WIPO has made substantial efforts to gather data from all sources. Notwithstanding the improvements mentioned above, in many instances it has not been possible to obtain data from every source. Nonetheless, these statistics offer some insight into how this form of IP is used in different parts of the world.

With the support of its member states, WIPO hopes to improve the geographical coverage and completeness of GI statistics in the coming years.

How many GIs are in force worldwide?

Data received from the 82 national/regional authorities that shared their 2017 data with WIPO reveals the existence of approximately 59,500 protected GIs. This figure excludes the 4,932 European Union (EU) GIs in force in each of the EU member states in order to minimize double counting. The 4,932 EU GIs in force are counted once rather than as 4,932 multiplied by 28 member states.

Figure 5.1 shows the total number of GIs in force for each selected national/regional authority, while figure 5.2 reports data on GIs in force for the EU member states. Germany had the largest number of GIs in force (14,073), followed by Austria (8,749), China (8,507), Hungary (6,646), Czech Republic (6,191), Bulgaria (6,096) and Italy (5,977). Apart from Bulgaria and China, there are several middle-income countries with a large number of GIs in force within their respective jurisdictions. For example, there were 4,615 GIs in force in the Republic of Moldova in 2017, 3,415 in Bosnia and Herzegovina and 3,112 in Ukraine. India (305) and Brazil (63) – two of the large middle-income countries – have considerably lower numbers of GIs in force.

GIs in force relating to "wines and spirits" accounted for 57.1% of the 2017 total, followed by agricultural products and foodstuffs (28.2%) (see figure 5.3). Handicrafts accounted for 2.7% of the total. China, Hungary, India and the Islamic Republic of Iran each had more than 100 GIs for handicrafts in force within their jurisdictions.

China had more than 8,500 GIs in force

5.1. Geographical indications in force for selected national/regional authorities, 2017

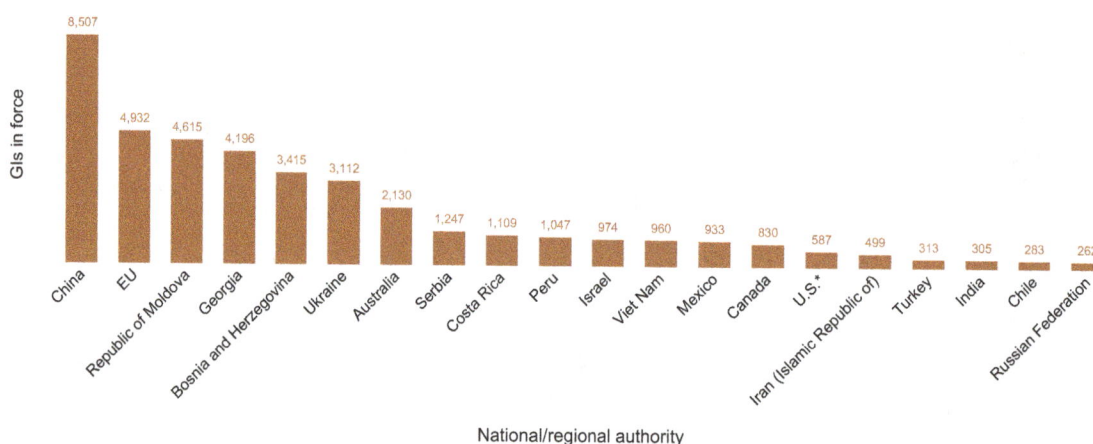

Note: * indicates 2016 data.

Source: WIPO Statistics Database, September 2018.

GIs in force based on national systems accounted for 65% of total GIs in Germany

5.2. Geographical indications in force for EU member states, 2017

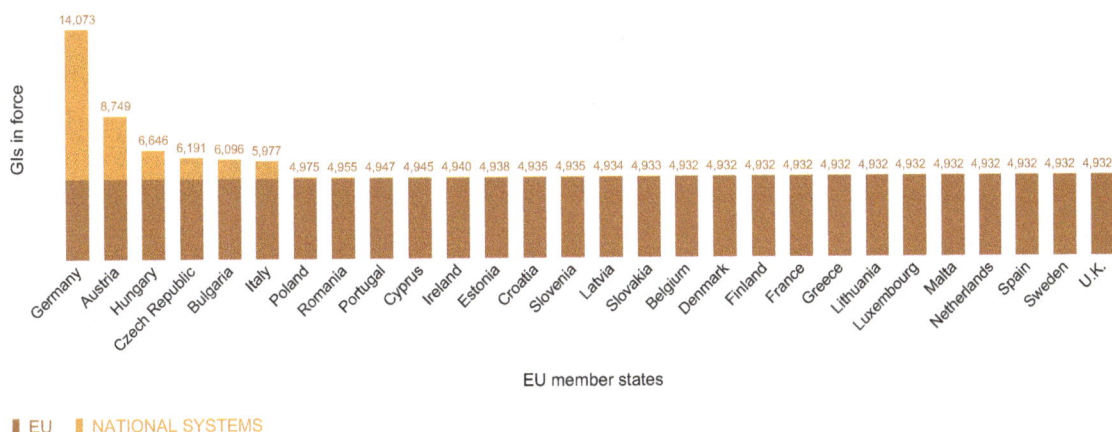

EU member states

■ EU   ■ NATIONAL SYSTEMS

Note: This figure shows the total number of geographical indications in force in the EU member states, broken down by GIs in force based on the EU regional systems and agreements and on national systems. The EU has regional systems for the protection of GIs covering agricultural and foodstuff products, wines and spirits.

Source: WIPO Statistics Database, September 2018.

Wine and spirits accounted for 57.1% of GIs in force

5.3. Geographical indications in force by product categories, 2017

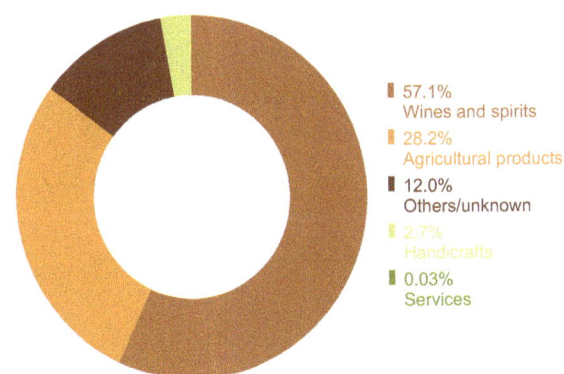

- 57.1% Wines and spirits
- 28.2% Agricultural products
- 12.0% Others/unknown
- 2.7% Handicrafts
- 0.03% Services

Note: GIs in force through the EU regional systems are counted once rather than 28 times as they are in force in all EU member states. This is done to minimize double counting.

Source: WIPO Statistics Database, September 2018.

These figures should be interpreted with caution, however. Not only are the data limited to the 82 countries that shared their 2017 data with WIPO, but the submissions made by many countries were incomplete. The questionnaire underlying the data collection asked for information regarding GIs protected through *sui generis* systems, trademark systems, other national legal means, regional systems and international agreements (including GIs in force under the Lisbon System and the Madrid System). As can be seen from table 5.4, many countries were unable to provide statistics on the number of GIs protected through trademark systems, reflecting the difficulty of identifying such GIs among all trademarks (most commonly collective and certification trademarks) registered. In addition, several countries could not provide data on the number of GIs protected through international agreements. Finally, there is likely to be double-counting of GIs protected through two or more legal means.[1]

Use of the Lisbon System to protect appellations of origin

The Lisbon System consists of 28 member countries, seven of which are European Union members. In 2017, there were 991 appellations of origin in force via the Lisbon System (see figure 5.5). This represents a 3.7% increase on the previous year, which is mostly driven by strong growth from Italy. France remains the largest user of the Lisbon System. It accounted for 51.4% of the 2017 total, followed by Italy (17%), Czech Republic (7.6%), Bulgaria (5.1%) and the Islamic Republic of Iran (4.1%).

[1] In principle, double-counting of the same subject matter protected by different IP rights also occurs in patent, trademark and industrial design statistics. However, the inclusion of GIs covered in trade agreements adds a layer of complexity, as relevant GIs may, in some cases, only have legal effect once registered at the national level.

5.4. Geographical indications in force in 2017

National/regional authority	Total	Sui generis	Trademarks	Other national legal means	Regional system	Agreements	Unknown
Andorra	7	4	2	..	..	1	..
Argentina	107	107	..	..	..	..	..
Armenia (a)	8	..	8	..	..	..	..
Australia	2,130	116	73	..	..	1,941	..
Austria	8,749	..	..	..	3,399	5,350	..
Azerbaijan (a)	18	..	..	..	..	..	18
Bahamas	..	..	..	..	..	..	..
Bangladesh	1	1	..	..	..	..	..
Barbados	..	..	..	..	..	..	..
Belarus	34	32	2	..	..	..	..
Belgium	4,932	..	..	..	3,399	1,533	..
Bosnia and Herzegovina	3,415	13	..	..	..	3,402	..
Brazil	63	63	..	..	..	..	..
Bulgaria	6,096	122	..	..	3,399	2,575	..
Cambodia	2	2	..	..	..	..	..
Canada	830	646	..	..	..	184	..
Chile	283	167	..	..	..	116	..
China	8,507	..	3,906	..	..	..	4,601
China, Hong Kong SAR	43	..	43	..	..	..	..
China, Macao SAR	11	1	10	..	..	..	..
Colombia	151	151	..	..	..	..	..
Costa Rica	1,109	4	..	..	..	1,105	..
Côte d'Ivoire	..	..	..	..	..	..	..
Croatia	4,935	3	..	..	3,399	1,533	..
Cuba	29	25	..	..	..	4	..
Cyprus	4,945	11	2	..	3,399	1,533	..
Czech Republic	6,191	62	..	..	3,399	2,730	..
Denmark	4,932	..	..	..	3,399	1,533	..
Ecuador	52	4	..	..	..	48	..
Estonia	4,938	6	..	..	3,399	1,533	..
European Union	4,932	3,399	..	..	..	1,533	..
Finland	4,932	..	..	..	3,399	1,533	..
France	4,932	..	..	..	3,399	1,533	..
Georgia	4,196	47	..	..	..	4,149	..
Germany	14,073	7,276	1	..	4,508	2,288	..
Greece	4,932	..	..	..	3,399	1,533	..
Guatemala (a)	32	32	..	..	..	..	..
Honduras	135	..	135	..	..	..	..
Hungary	6,646	24	..	..	3,399	3,223	..
Iceland	..	..	..	..	..	..	..
India	305	305	..	..	..	..	..
Iran (Islamic Republic of)	499	499	..	..	..	..	..
Ireland	4,940	8	..	..	3,399	1,533	..
Israel	974	1	..	..	..	973	..
Italy	5,977	..	..	36	3,399	2,542	..
Jamaica	3	2	1	..	..	..	..
Japan	73	58	..	8	..	7	..
Kazakhstan	42	42	..	..	..	..	..
Kenya	5	..	5	..	..	..	..
Latvia	4,934	2	..	..	3,399	1,533	..
Lithuania	4,932	..	..	..	3,399	1,533	..
Luxembourg	4,932	..	..	..	3,399	1,533	..
Malaysia	79	..	..	..	..	..	79
Maldives	..	..	..	..	..	..	..
Malta	4,932	..	..	..	3,399	1,533	..
Mexico	933	15	..	..	..	918	..
Mongolia	2	..	2	..	..	..	..
Morocco	85	36	49	..	..	..	..
Netherlands	4,932	..	..	..	3,399	1,533	..
New Zealand	..	..	..	..	..	..	..
Norway	28	28	..	..	..	..	..
Peru	1,047	10	..	..	..	1,037	..
Philippines	..	..	..	..	..	..	..
Poland	4,975	43	..	..	3,399	1,533	..

National/regional authority	Total	Sui generis	Trademarks	Other national legal means	Regional system	Agreements	Unknown
Portugal	4,947	15	..	..	3,399	1,533	..
Republic of Moldova	4,615	17	..	..	..	4,598	..
Romania	4,955	23	..	..	3,399	1,533	..
Russian Federation	262	165	..	97	..	..	..
Saint Vincent and Grenadines	..	..	..	..	..	..	..
Serbia	1,247	61	3	214	..	969	..
Singapore	..	..	..	..	..	..	..
Slovakia	4,933	1	..	..	3,399	1,533	..
Slovenia	4,935	..	..	3	3,399	1,533	..
Spain	4,932	..	..	..	3,399	1,533	..
Sweden	4,932	..	..	..	3,399	1,533	..
Thailand	13	9	..	..	..	4	..
Togo	..	..	..	..	..	..	..
Trinidad and Tobago	1	1	..	..	..	..	..
Turkey	313	310	..	..	..	3	..
Uganda	..	..	..	..	..	..	..
Ukraine	3,112	22	..	..	..	3,090	..
United Kingdom	4,932	..	..	..	3,399	1,533	..
United States of America (a)	587	..	587	..	..	..	..
Uzbekistan	..	..	..	..	..	..	..
Viet Nam	960	66	894	..	..	..	..
Yemen	..	..	..	..	..	..	..

(a) 2016 data.

.. indicates zero.

Source: WIPO Statistics Database, September 2018.

France remains the largest user of the Lisbon System

5.5. Appellations of origin in force by origin, 2017

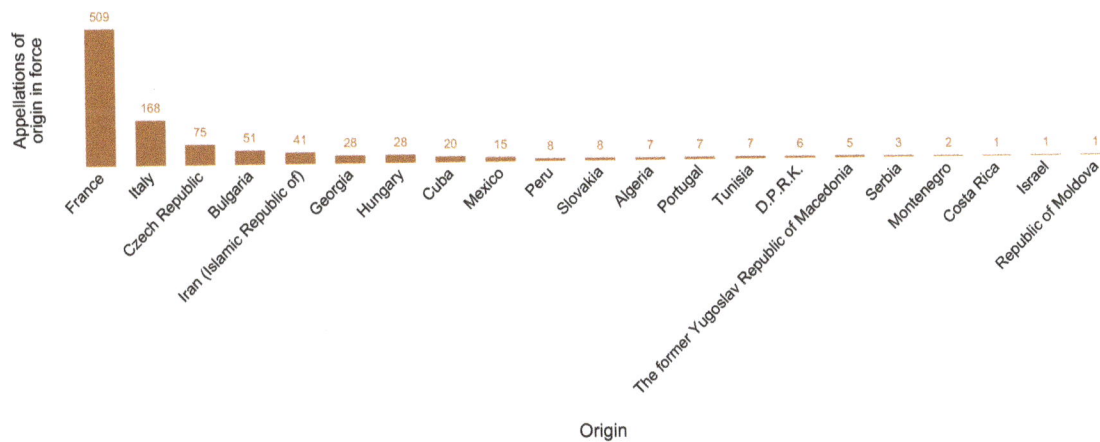

Note: D.P.R.K. is the Democratic People's Republic of Korea

Source: WIPO Statistics Database, September 2018.

Creative economy

Highlights

In 2016, the International Publishers Association (IPA) and the World Intellectual Property Organization (WIPO) joined forces to improve the availability of statistics on global publishing activity. Accordingly, the two organizations launched a pilot survey in 2017, covering three market segments: trade; educational; and scientific, technical and medical (STM) publishing. In total, 35 national publishers' associations and copyright authorities shared their 2016 data.[1]

In April 2018, WIPO refined the guidelines for completing the questionnaire and invited national publishers' associations and copyright authorities to share their 2017 data. In total, 28 associations/authorities complied, while another 10 indicated that they would share their 2017 data when they are available. This section summarizes the statistics received so far. The full set of 2017 statistics will be published at a later date.

It is important to note that, unlike for patents and trademarks, the collection of publishing industry data is not unified under a single public authority within a country. In most countries, national statistical offices or other government agencies do not collect such data, although there are a few exceptions, such as Canada, China and Japan. Data for the publishing industry are compiled by private entities and national publishers' associations (NPAs), among others. The main limitation with NPA data is that not all the publishers within a country are members of the NPA. The share of the total publishing industry represented by NPAs varies between countries. There are also methodological differences – for example, some of the NPAs collect data for printed editions only, while others compile data for both printed and digital editions – which makes it challenging to draw comparisons between countries. Despite the data limitations – i.e., the fact that the data are incomplete, this initiative should be considered as a longer term effort toward the creation of a more comprehensive publishing industry data set. The ultimate objective is to provide, on a regular basis, accurate statistics that are comparable between countries. WIPO will continue to make every effort to improve data comparability and extend country coverage by reaching out to countries that are not in a position to respond to the questionnaire at present.

China's publishing industry revenue reached 202 billion U.S. dollars in 2017

Data on the 2017 revenues generated by the three sectors – trade, educational and STM – are available for 11 countries. Those 11 countries generated USD 248 billion revenue in 2017. China (USD 202.4 billion) reported the largest net revenue, followed by the United States of America (U.S.) (USD 25.9 billion), Germany (USD 5.8 billion) and the United Kingdom (U.K.) (USD 4.7 billion) (see figure 6.1). Trade sector revenue accounted for 50% or more of the total revenue in seven of those same 11 countries – ranging from 69% in France to 50% in the U.K. The educational sector revenue accounted for a high share of total revenue in Yemen (68.2%) and Brazil (62%). The STM sector generated more than a third of total revenue in Belgium (46.1%), Brazil (37.9%) and the U.K. (33.2%).

Net publishing industry revenue, covering 11 countries, amounted to USD 248 billion

6.1. Total net publishing industry revenue (USD million), 2017

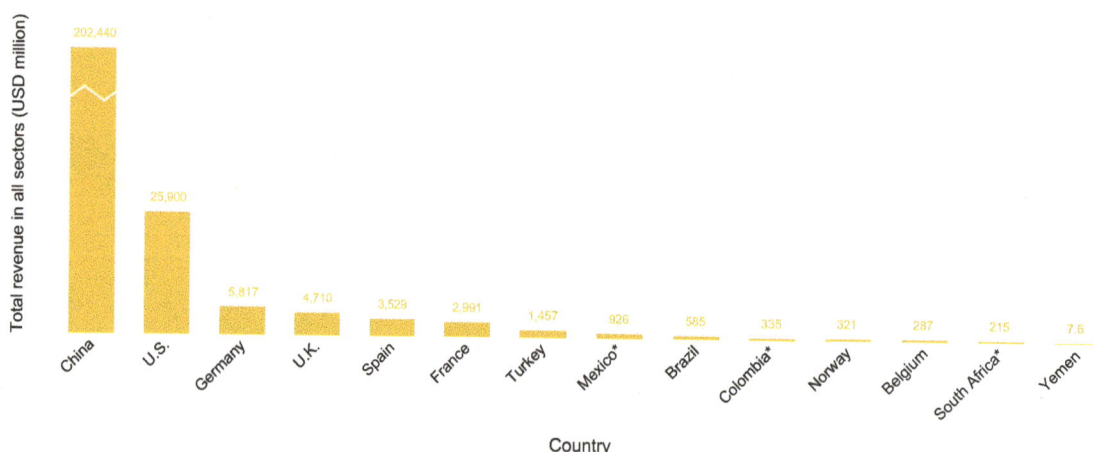

* indicates 2016 data.

Source: Table F17.

Digital editions generated 28.3% of the total trade sector revenue in China

Data on the 2017 revenues generated by the trade sector are available for 18 countries. China, with USD 111.5 billion, reported the largest revenue, followed by the U.S. (USD 16 billion), Japan (USD 8.4 billion), the U.K. (USD 2.4 billion) and France (USD 2.1 billion) (see figure F1).

Data on the 2017 trade sector revenues, broken down into the categories "printed", "digital" and "other formats," are available for 15 countries. The bulk of the trade sector revenue is generated by print editions; digital editions account for around 28.3% of the total in China, 23.5% in Japan, 18.4% in Sweden, 13.2% in Finland and 12.9% in the U.S. (see figure F2). Domestic sales account for the bulk of total revenue for most countries. However, revenue from foreign sales and licensing represents 81.4% of total revenue in Belgium (see figure F3). Revenue from foreign sales is also high in Saudi Arabia (49.4%), the U.K. (31.4%), China (23.4%) and Spain (16.4%).

Foreign sales accounted for 69.8% of total educational sector revenue of the U.K.

Data on the 2017 revenues generated by the educational sector are available for 15 countries. China, with USD 72.8 billion, reported the largest sale and license revenue total, followed by the U.S. (USD 7.6 billion) and Spain (USD 1 billion) (see figure F8). The bulk of the total educational sector revenue is generated by printed editions. Digital editions accounted for 37.8% of the total

in China, 29.6% in Denmark, 9.5% in Finland and 9.1% in Saudi Arabia (see figure F9). The 2017 educational sector revenue, broken down by domestic and foreign sales, is available for nine countries. Domestic sales account for the bulk of the total revenue for all countries except the U.K., for which foreign sales accounted for 69.8% of the total (see figure F10).

China published 65 million titles covering three sectors in 2017

Data on the total number of titles published covering the three sectors are available for 17 countries. China reported a combined total of 65 million published titles in 2017, followed by Japan (2 million), Spain (119,778), France (104,670) and Turkey (104,283) (see figure 6.2). The trade sector accounted for more than half of all titles published in 10 of those countries – ranging from 99.3% in Japan to 55.9% in Turkey. Educational publishing accounted for around half of all titles published in Belarus (50.9%), Yemen (49.3%) and China (43%). The STM sector accounted for almost two-thirds of all titles published in Belgium.

Digital editions accounted for half of the total number of titles published by the trade sector in Japan

Data on the number of titles published by the trade sector are available for 22 countries. China had by far the largest number of titles published in 2017 (12.7 million), followed by Japan (2 million), Italy (130,242) and Spain (82,238) (see figure F4). In total, 13 countries were able

China published 65 million titles, covering the trade, educational and STM sectors

6.2. Total number of titles published, 2017

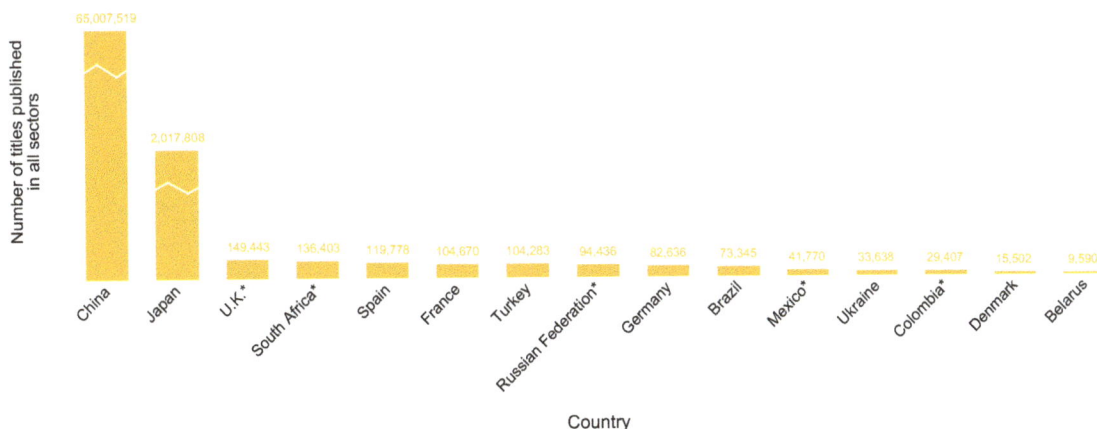

* indicates 2016 data.

Source: Table F18.

to disaggregate the number of titles published by the trade sector between printed editions, digital editions and other formats. Print editions accounted for more than half of the total number of titles published for the trade sector. The share of digital editions was high in Japan (49.9%) and Italy (47.8%) (see figure F5).

Data on the number of titles published by the educational sector are available for 19 countries. China had by far the largest number of titles published (27.9 million), followed by Turkey (35,642) and Brazil (11,060) (see figure F11). The number of titles published by the STM sector was highest in China (24.4 million), followed by Spain (26,656), France (20,246) and Brazil (13,406) (see figure F16).

The U.S. sold 2,693 million copies of published titles in 2017

Eleven countries were able to report data on the total number of copies sold covering the three sectors. The U.S. sold 2,693 million copies in 2017, followed by the U.K. (647 million), Brazil (617 million) and France (430 million) (see figure 6.3). The trade sector accounted for more than 80% of the total copies sold for France, Norway and the U.S. The educational sector had a high share of total copies sold in Yemen (73.3%) and Turkey (48.8%), while the STM sector had a high share in Yemen (16.7%), the Republic of Moldova (14.7%) and Spain (11.5%).

The U.S. sold 2,693 million copies of published titles covering the trade, educational and STM sectors

6.3. Total number of copies sold, 2017

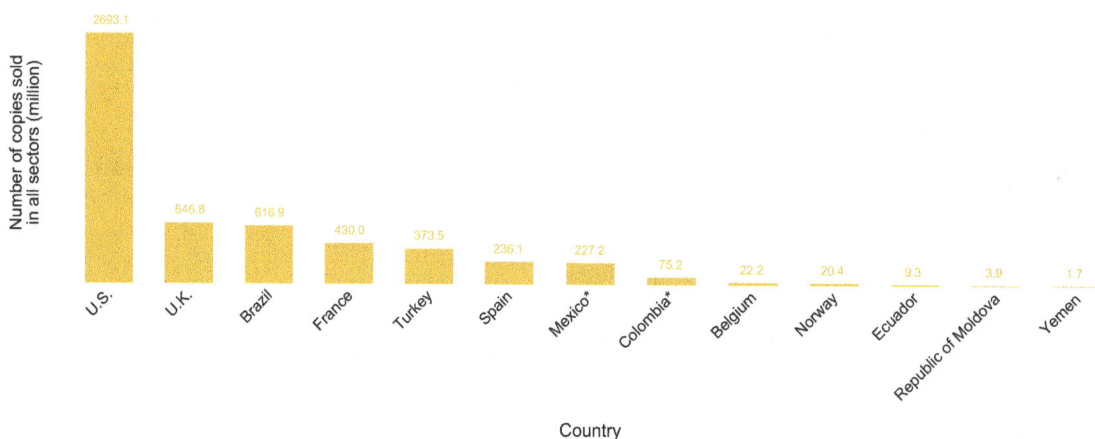

* indicates 2016 data.

Source: Table F19.

1   See IPA and WIPO (2018). *The Global Publishing Industry in 2016*. Geneva.

Creative economy

Creative economy statistics

Creative economy

Trade sector

F1. Trade sector revenue (USD million), 2017

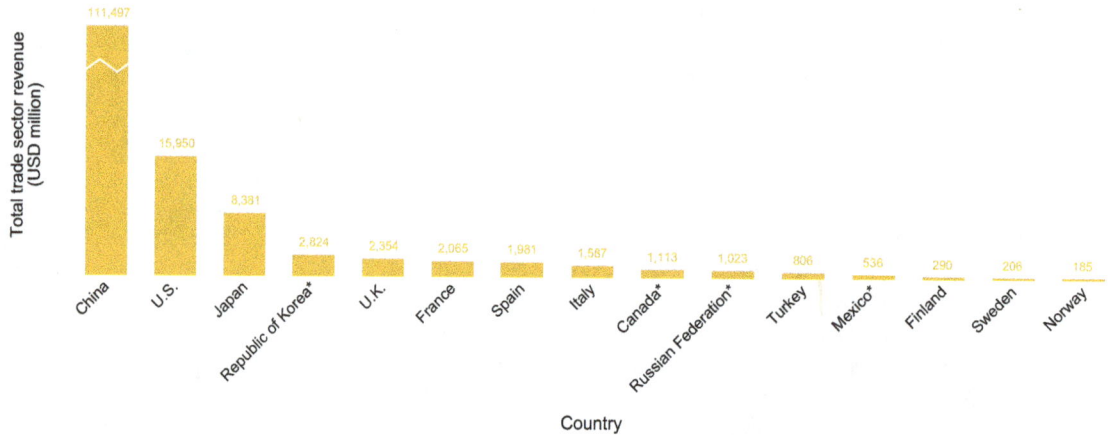

Total trade sector revenue (USD million)

China 111,497
U.S. 15,950
Japan 8,381
Republic of Korea* 2,824
U.K. 2,354
France 2,065
Spain 1,981
Italy 1,587
Canada* 1,113
Russian Federation* 1,023
Turkey 806
Mexico* 536
Finland 290
Sweden 206
Norway 185

Country

* indicates 2016 data.

Note: Caution should be exercised when interpreting the data shown here due to the fact that they are incomplete. The share of the total publishing industry represented by national publishers' associations (NPAs) varies between countries. There are also methodological differences that make it challenging to draw comparisons between countries. For all reported countries, the data source is the NPA, except for Canada (Statistics Canada), China (National Copyright Administration of China) and Japan (Japan Copyright Office).

Source: WIPO Statistics Database, September 2018.

F2. Distribution of the trade sector revenue by format type, 2017

SHARE OF DIGITAL (%)

China	Colombia*	Japan	Sweden	Finland	U.S.	Denmark	U.K.	Saudi Arabia	Italy	Russian Federation*	France	Spain	South Africa*	Mexico*
28.3	24.0	23.5	18.4	13.2	12.9	12.5	12.2	6.2	4.5	3.9	2.3	1.9	1.5	1.2

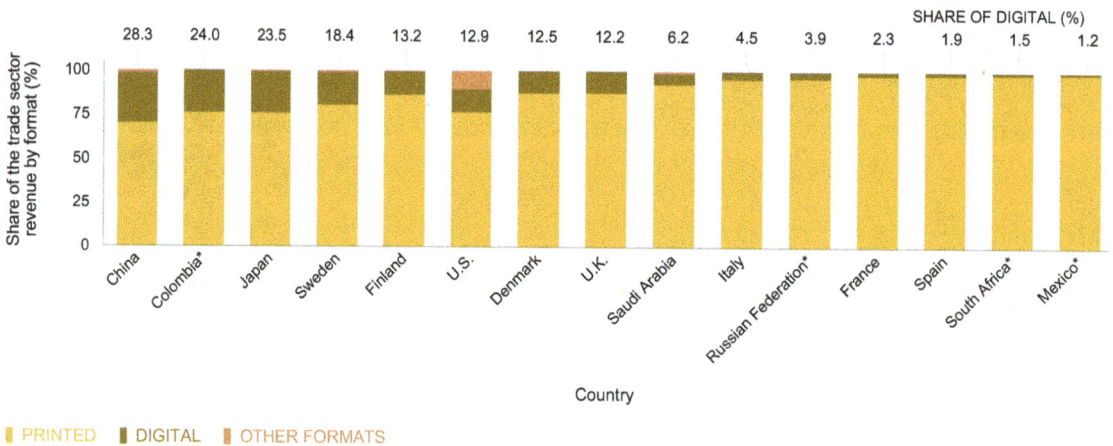

Share of the trade sector revenue by format (%)

Country

▮ PRINTED ▮ DIGITAL ▮ OTHER FORMATS

* indicates 2016 data.

Note: Caution should be exercised when interpreting the data shown here due to the fact that they are incomplete. The share of the total publishing industry represented by national publishers' associations (NPAs) varies between countries. There are also methodological differences that make it challenging to draw comparisons between countries. For all reported countries, the data source is the NPA, except for Canada (Statistics Canada), China (National Copyright Administration of China) and Japan (Japan Copyright Office).

Source: WIPO Statistics Database, September 2018.

Creative economy

F3. Distribution of the trade sector revenue by destination, 2017

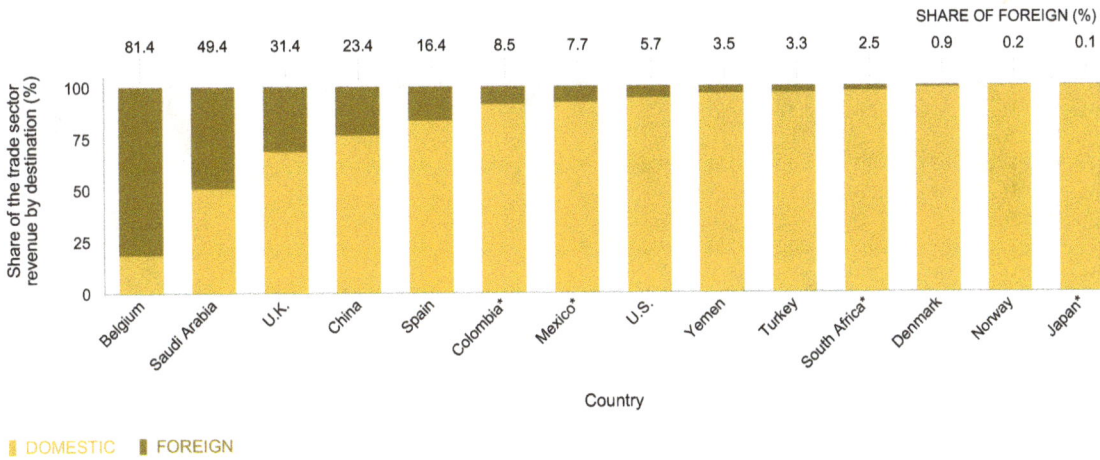

SHARE OF FOREIGN (%)

| 81.4 | 49.4 | 31.4 | 23.4 | 16.4 | 8.5 | 7.7 | 5.7 | 3.5 | 3.3 | 2.5 | 0.9 | 0.2 | 0.1 |

Share of the trade sector revenue by destination (%)

100 / 75 / 50 / 25 / 0

Belgium, Saudi Arabia, U.K., China, Spain, Colombia*, Mexico*, U.S., Yemen, Turkey, South Africa*, Denmark, Norway, Japan*

Country

DOMESTIC **FOREIGN**

* indicates 2016 data.

Note: Caution should be exercised when interpreting the data shown here due to the fact that they are incomplete. The share of the total publishing industry represented by national publishers' associations (NPAs) varies between countries. There are also methodological differences that make it challenging to draw comparisons between countries. For all reported countries, the data source is the NPA, except for Canada (Statistics Canada), China (National Copyright Administration of China) and Japan (Japan Copyright Office).

Source: WIPO Statistics Database, September 2018.

F4. Number of titles published by the trade sector, 2017

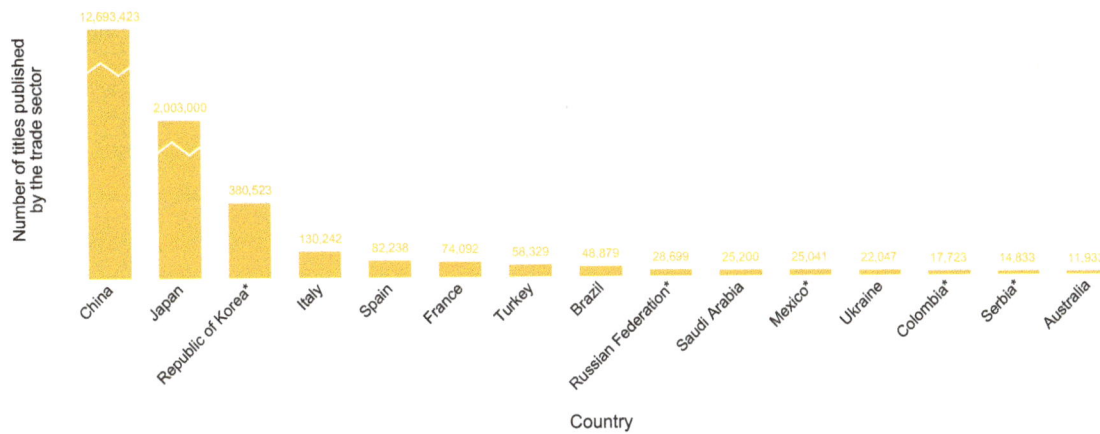

Number of titles published by the trade sector

| 12,693,423 | 2,003,000 | 380,523 | 130,242 | 92,238 | 74,092 | 58,329 | 48,879 | 26,699 | 25,200 | 25,041 | 22,047 | 17,723 | 14,833 | 11,933 |

China, Japan, Republic of Korea*, Italy, Spain, France, Turkey, Brazil, Russian Federation*, Saudi Arabia, Mexico*, Ukraine, Colombia*, Serbia*, Australia

Country

* indicates 2016 data.

Note: Caution should be exercised when interpreting the data shown here due to the fact that they are incomplete. The share of the total publishing industry represented by national publishers' associations (NPAs) varies between countries. There are also methodological differences that make it challenging to draw comparisons between countries. For all reported countries, the data source is the NPA, except for Canada (Statistics Canada), China (National Copyright Administration of China) and Japan (Japan Copyright Office).

Source: WIPO Statistics Database, September 2018.

Creative economy

F5. Distribution of titles published by the trade sector by format, 2017

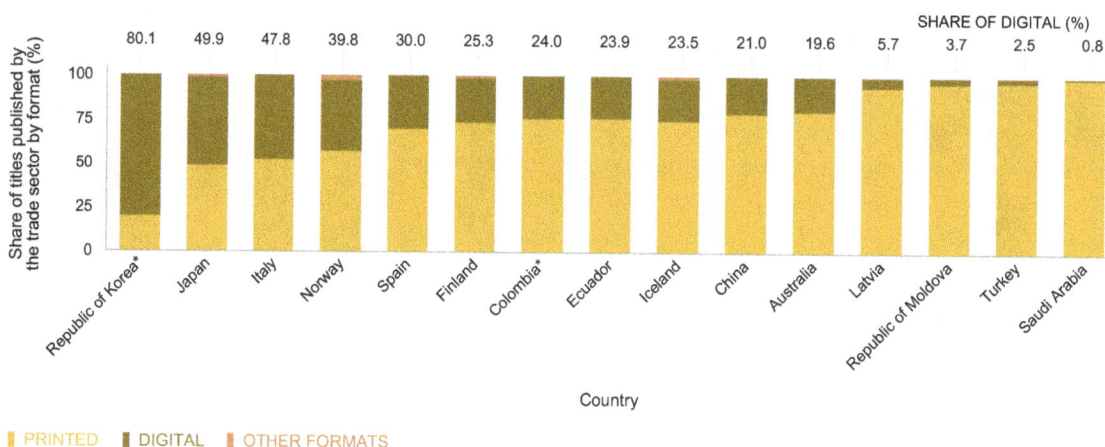

SHARE OF DIGITAL (%)

| 80.1 | 49.9 | 47.8 | 39.8 | 30.0 | 25.3 | 24.0 | 23.9 | 23.5 | 21.0 | 19.6 | 5.7 | 3.7 | 2.5 | 0.8 |

Share of titles published by the trade sector by format (%)

Country

PRINTED   DIGITAL   OTHER FORMATS

* indicates 2016 data.

Note: Caution should be exercised when interpreting the data shown here due to the fact that they are incomplete. The share of the total publishing industry represented by national publishers' associations (NPAs) varies between countries. There are also methodological differences that make it challenging to draw comparisons between countries. For all reported countries, the data source is the NPA, except for Canada (Statistics Canada), China (National Copyright Administration of China) and Japan (Japan Copyright Office).

Source: WIPO Statistics Database, September 2018.

F6. Number of copies sold by the trade sector, 2017

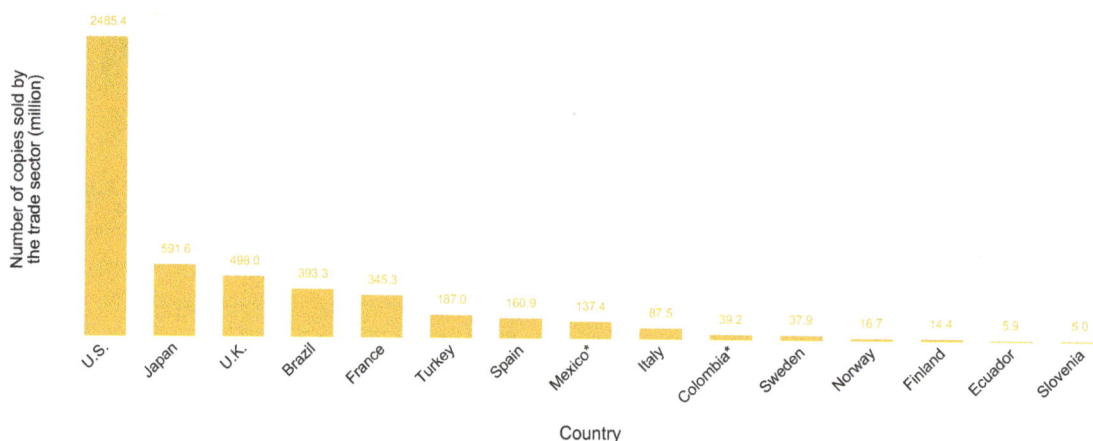

Number of copies sold by the trade sector (million)

2485.4

591.6
498.0
393.3
345.3
187.9
160.9
137.4
87.5
39.2
37.9
16.7
14.4
5.9
5.0

U.S. | Japan | U.K. | Brazil | France | Turkey | Spain | Mexico* | Italy | Colombia* | Sweden | Norway | Finland | Ecuador | Slovenia

Country

* indicates 2016 data.

Note: Caution should be exercised when interpreting the data shown here due to the fact that they are incomplete. The share of the total publishing industry represented by national publishers' associations (NPAs) varies between countries. There are also methodological differences that make it challenging to draw comparisons between countries. For all reported countries, the data source is the NPA, except for Canada (Statistics Canada), China (National Copyright Administration of China) and Japan (Japan Copyright Office).

Source: WIPO Statistics Database, September 2018.

Creative economy

F7. Distribution of copies sold by sales channel for the trade sector, 2017

SHARE OF BRICK/MORTAR (%)

| 22.3 | 41.7 | 41.8 | 59.0 | 60.0 | 77.7 | 77.9 | 82.3 | 99.9 |

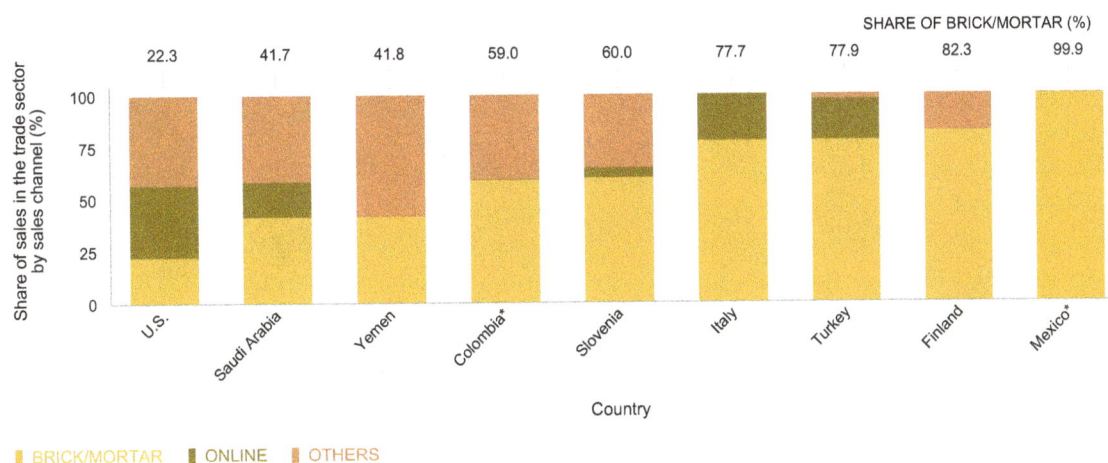

Share of sales in the trade sector by sales channel (%)

Country

U.S. · Saudi Arabia · Yemen · Colombia* · Slovenia · Italy · Turkey · Finland · Mexico*

BRICK/MORTAR   ONLINE   OTHERS

* indicates 2016 data.

Note: Caution should be exercised when interpreting the data shown here due to the fact that they are incomplete. The share of the total publishing industry represented by national publishers' associations (NPAs) varies between countries. There are also methodological differences that make it challenging to draw comparisons between countries. For all reported countries, the data source is the NPA, except for Canada (Statistics Canada), China (National Copyright Administration of China) and Japan (Japan Copyright Office).

Source: WIPO Statistics Database, September 2018.

Educational sector

F8. Educational sector revenue (USD million), 2017

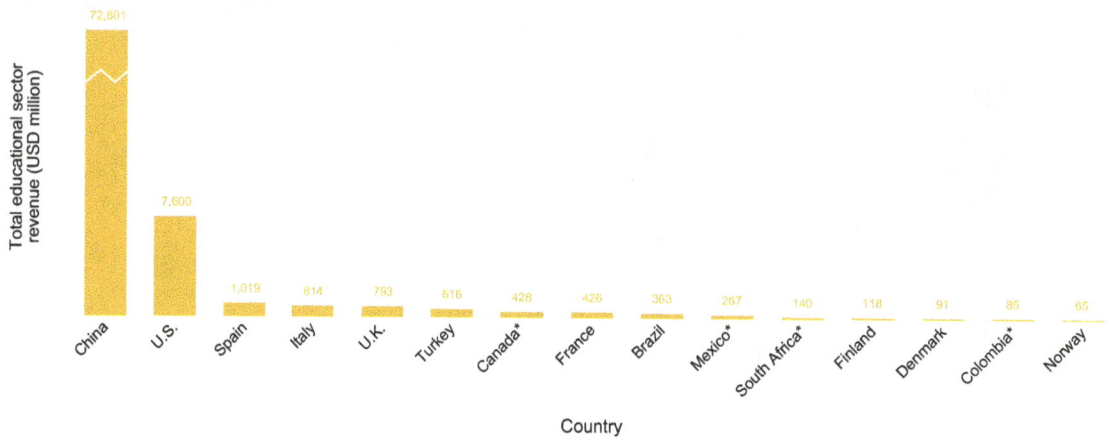

* indicates 2016 data.

Note: Caution should be exercised when interpreting the data shown here due to the fact that they are incomplete. The share of the total publishing industry represented by national publishers' associations (NPAs) varies between countries. There are also methodological differences that make it challenging to draw comparisons between countries. For all reported countries, the data source is the NPA, except for Canada (Statistics Canada), China (National Copyright Administration of China) and Japan (Japan Copyright Office).

Source: WIPO Statistics Database, September 2018.

F9. Distribution of the educational sector revenue by format, 2017

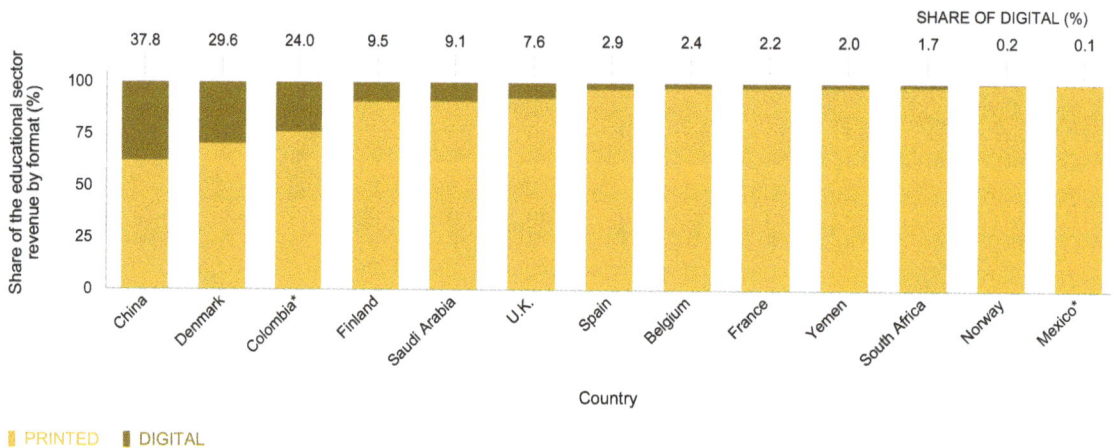

PRINTED DIGITAL

* indicates 2016 data.

Note: Caution should be exercised when interpreting the data shown here due to the fact that they are incomplete. The share of the total publishing industry represented by national publishers' associations (NPAs) varies between countries. There are also methodological differences that make it challenging to draw comparisons between countries. For all reported countries, the data source is the NPA, except for Canada (Statistics Canada), China (National Copyright Administration of China) and Japan (Japan Copyright Office).

Source: WIPO Statistics Database, September 2018.

F10. Distribution of the educational sector revenue by destination, 2017

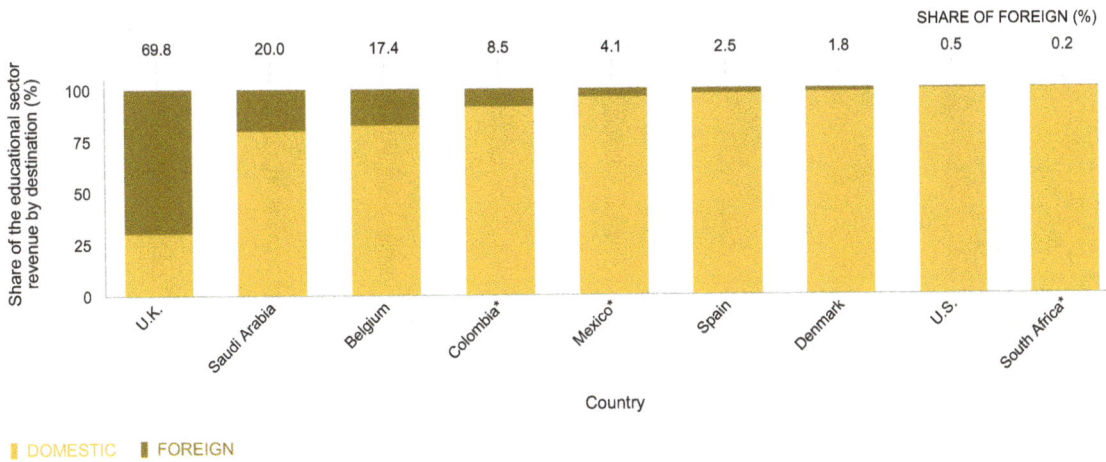

SHARE OF FOREIGN (%)

| 69.8 | 20.0 | 17.4 | 8.5 | 4.1 | 2.5 | 1.8 | 0.5 | 0.2 |

Y-axis: Share of the educational sector revenue by destination (%), scale 0, 25, 50, 75, 100

X-axis (Country): U.K., Saudi Arabia, Belgium, Colombia*, Mexico*, Spain, Denmark, U.S., South Africa*

Legend: DOMESTIC   FOREIGN

* indicates 2016 data.

Note: Caution should be exercised when interpreting the data shown here due to the fact that they are incomplete. The share of the total publishing industry represented by national publishers' associations (NPAs) varies between countries. There are also methodological differences that make it challenging to draw comparisons between countries. For all reported countries, the data source is the NPA, except for Canada (Statistics Canada), China (National Copyright Administration of China) and Japan (Japan Copyright Office).

Source: WIPO Statistics Database, September 2018.

F11. Number of titles published by the educational sector, 2017

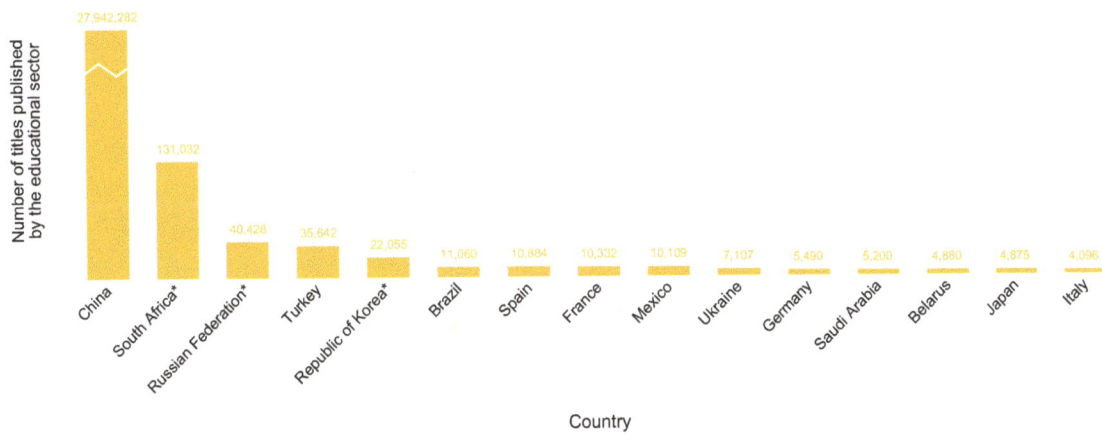

Y-axis: Number of titles published by the educational sector

Bar values:
- China: 27,942,282
- South Africa*: 131,032
- Russian Federation*: 40,428
- Turkey: 35,642
- Republic of Korea*: 22,055
- Brazil: 11,060
- Spain: 10,884
- France: 10,332
- Mexico: 10,109
- Ukraine: 7,107
- Germany: 5,490
- Saudi Arabia: 5,200
- Belarus: 4,880
- Japan: 4,875
- Italy: 4,096

X-axis (Country): China, South Africa*, Russian Federation*, Turkey, Republic of Korea*, Brazil, Spain, France, Mexico, Ukraine, Germany, Saudi Arabia, Belarus, Japan, Italy

* indicates 2016 data.

Note: Caution should be exercised when interpreting the data shown here due to the fact that they are incomplete. The share of the total publishing industry represented by national publishers' associations (NPAs) varies between countries. There are also methodological differences that make it challenging to draw comparisons between countries. For all reported countries, the data source is the NPA, except for Canada (Statistics Canada), China (National Copyright Administration of China) and Japan (Japan Copyright Office).

Source: WIPO Statistics Database, September 2018.

Creative economy

F12. Distribution of titles published by the educational sector by format, 2017

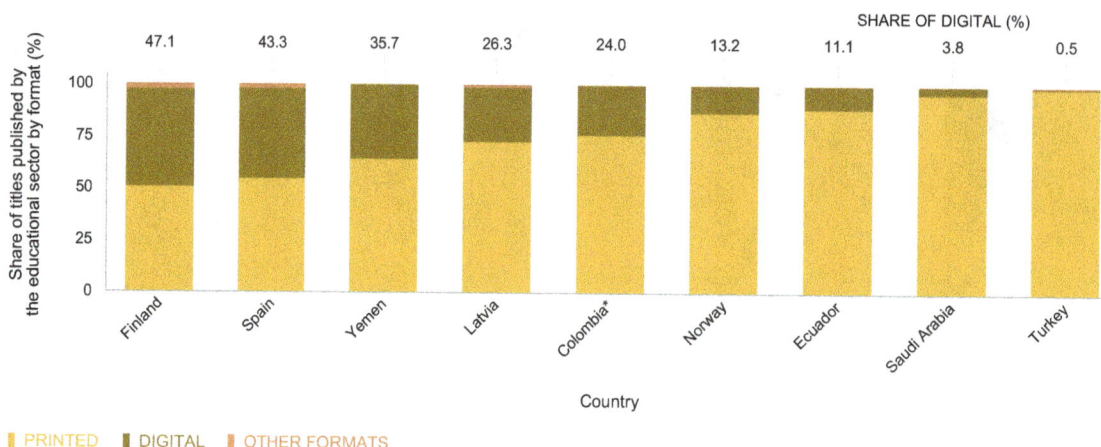

SHARE OF DIGITAL (%)

| 47.1 | 43.3 | 35.7 | 26.3 | 24.0 | 13.2 | 11.1 | 3.8 | 0.5 |

Share of titles published by the educational sector by format (%)

Finland · Spain · Yemen · Latvia · Colombia* · Norway · Ecuador · Saudi Arabia · Turkey

Country

PRINTED **DIGITAL** **OTHER FORMATS**

* indicates 2016 data.

Note: Caution should be exercised when interpreting the data shown here due to the fact that they are incomplete. The share of the total publishing industry represented by national publishers' associations (NPAs) varies between countries. There are also methodological differences that make it challenging to draw comparisons between countries. For all reported countries, the data source is the NPA, except for Canada (Statistics Canada), China (National Copyright Administration of China) and Japan (Japan Copyright Office).

Source: WIPO Statistics Database, September 2018.

F13. Number of copies sold by the educational sector, 2017

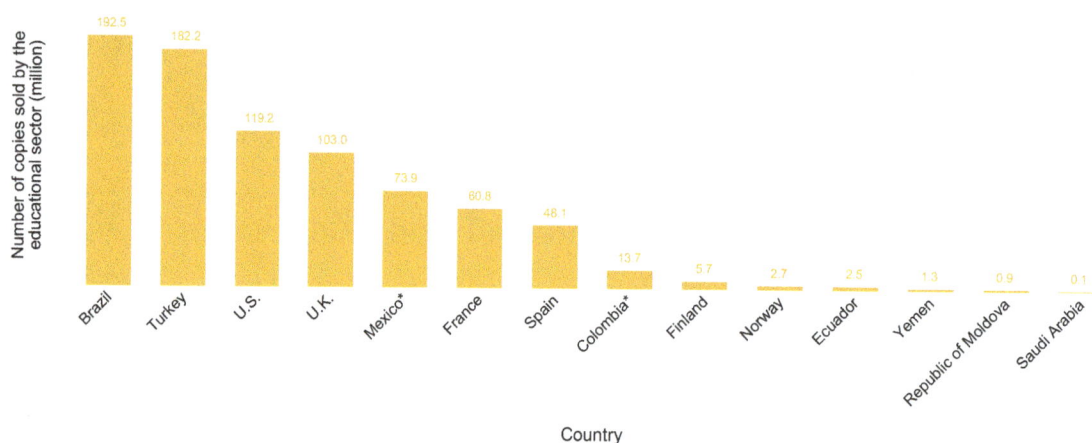

Number of copies sold by the educational sector (million)

| 192.5 | 182.2 | 119.2 | 103.0 | 73.9 | 60.8 | 46.1 | 13.7 | 5.7 | 2.7 | 2.5 | 1.3 | 0.9 | 0.1 |

Brazil · Turkey · U.S. · U.K. · Mexico* · France · Spain · Colombia* · Finland · Norway · Ecuador · Yemen · Republic of Moldova · Saudi Arabia

Country

* indicates 2016 data.

Note: Caution should be exercised when interpreting the data shown here due to the fact that they are incomplete. The share of the total publishing industry represented by national publishers' associations (NPAs) varies between countries. There are also methodological differences that make it challenging to draw comparisons between countries. For all reported countries, the data source is the NPA, except for Canada (Statistics Canada), China (National Copyright Administration of China) and Japan (Japan Copyright Office).

Source: WIPO Statistics Database, September 2018.

Creative economy

F14. Distribution of copies sold by sales channel for the educational sector, 2017

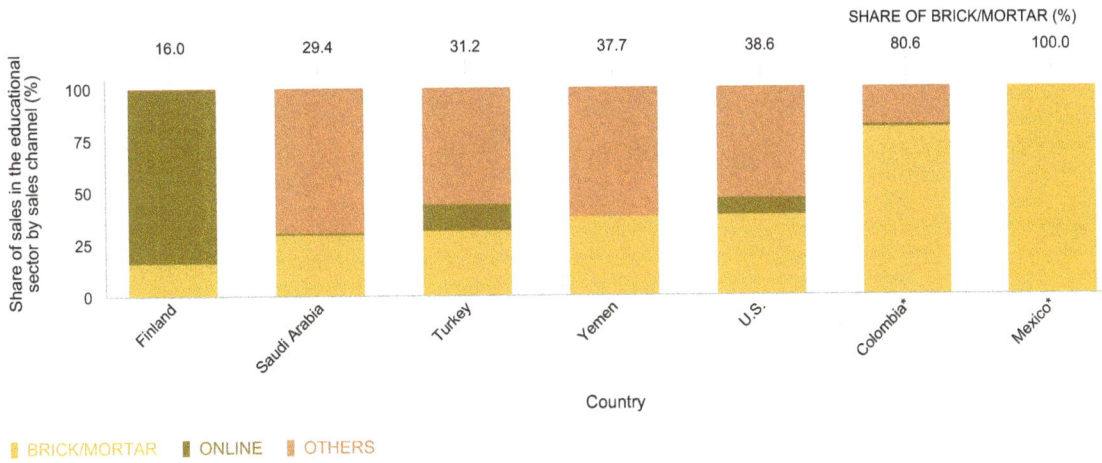

SHARE OF BRICK/MORTAR (%)

| 16.0 | 29.4 | 31.2 | 37.7 | 38.6 | 80.6 | 100.0 |

Share of sales in the educational sector by sales channel (%)

100
75
50
25
0

Finland · Saudi Arabia · Turkey · Yemen · U.S. · Colombia* · Mexico*

Country

■ BRICK/MORTAR   ■ ONLINE   ■ OTHERS

* indicates 2016 data.

Note: Caution should be exercised when interpreting the data shown here due to the fact that they are incomplete. The share of the total publishing industry represented by national publishers' associations (NPAs) varies between countries. There are also methodological differences that make it challenging to draw comparisons between countries. For all reported countries, the data source is the NPA, except for Canada (Statistics Canada), China (National Copyright Administration of China) and Japan (Japan Copyright Office).

Source: WIPO Statistics Database, September 2018.

Creative economy

Scientific, technical and medical (STM) sector

F15. STM sector revenue (USD million), 2017

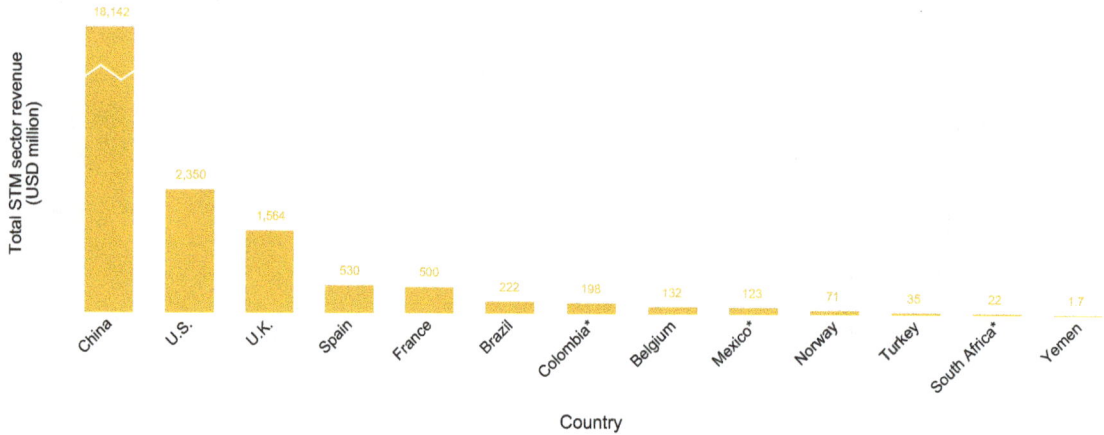

* indicates 2016 data.

Note: Caution should be exercised when interpreting the data shown here due to the fact that they are incomplete. The share of the total publishing industry represented by national publishers' associations varies between countries. There are also methodological differences that make it challenging to draw comparisons between countries. For all reported countries, the data source is the NPA, except for Canada (Statistics Canada), China (National Copyright Administration of China) and Japan (Japan Copyright Office).

Source: WIPO Statistics Database, September 2018.

F16. Number of titles published by the STM sector, 2017

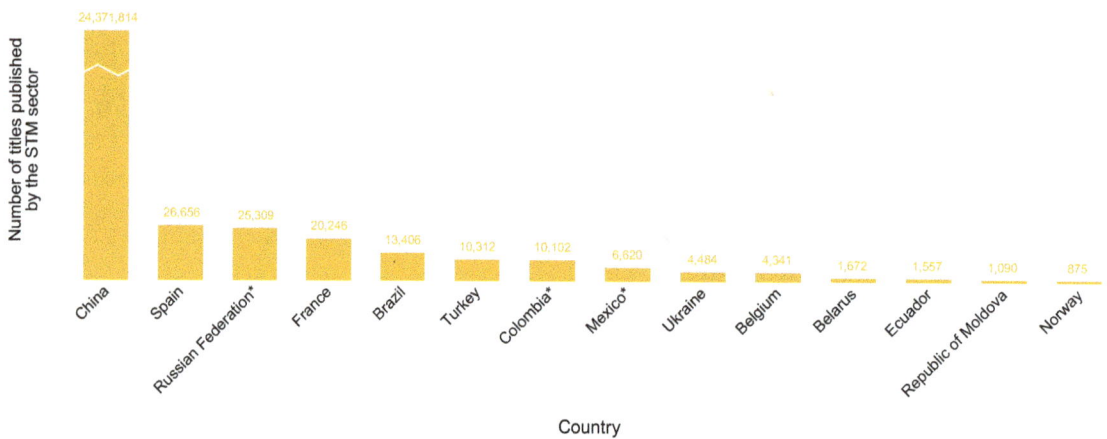

* indicates 2016 data.

Note: Caution should be exercised when interpreting the data shown here due to the fact that they are incomplete. The share of the total publishing industry represented by national publishers' associations (NPAs) varies between countries. There are also methodological differences that make it challenging to draw comparisons between countries. For all reported countries, the data source is the NPA, except for Canada (Statistics Canada), China (National Copyright Administration of China) and Japan (Japan Copyright Office).

Source: WIPO Statistics Database, September 2018.

Creative economy

Statistical tables

F17. Total net publishing industry revenue by sector (USD million), 2017

Country	Total	Trade	Educational	STM
Australia	..	..	..	..
Belarus	..	..	..	..
Belgium	287.4	104.6	50.4	132.4
Brazil	585.2	0.6	362.7	221.9
Canada (a)	..	1,113.5	427.8	..
China	202,440.3	111,497.3	72,801.2	18,141.8
Colombia (a)	335.1	52.6	84.9	197.5
Denmark	..	169.9	91.2	..
Ecuador	..	..	..	..
Finland	..	289.6	118.3	..
France	2,991.2	2,065.0	426.0	500.1
Germany	5,817.1	..	..	..
Iceland	..	29.0	..	..
Italy	..	1,586.7	813.6	..
Japan	..	8,381.1	..	..
Kyrgyzstan	..	..	..	..
Latvia	..	..	..	..
Lithuania (a)	..	..	..	..
Mauritius (a)	..	..	0.0	..
Mexico (a)	925.7	535.7	267.0	123.0
Montenegro	..	..	..	..
Norway	321.0	184.8	65.4	70.7
Peru (a)	..	..	..	..
Republic of Korea (a)	..	2,823.8	..	..
Republic of Moldova	..	..	..	..
Russian Federation (a)	..	1,023.5	..	..
Saudi Arabia	..	16.2	0.6	..
Serbia (a)	..	93.1	..	..
Slovenia	..	76.7	22.5	..
South Africa (a)	215.0	52.7	140.4	21.8
Spain	3,529.1	1,980.7	1,018.5	529.9
Sweden	..	206.3	..	..
Turkey	1,457.0	806.0	616.0	35.0
United Kingdom	4,710.4	2,353.9	792.8	1,563.7
United States of America	25,900.0	15,950.0	7,600.0	2,350.0
Ukraine	..	..	..	..
Yemen	7.6	0.7	5.2	1.7

Note: Caution should be exercised when interpreting the data shown here due to the fact that they are incomplete. The share of the total publishing industry represented by national publishers' associations (NPAs) varies between countries. There are also methodological differences that make it challenging to draw comparisons between countries. For all reported countries, the data source is the NPA, except for Canada (Statistics Canada), China (National Copyright Administration of China) and Japan (Japan Copyright Office). STM is the scientific, technical and medical sector.

(a) indicates 2016 data.

.. indicates not available.

Source: WIPO Statistics Database, September 2018.

F18. Total number of titles published by sector, 2017

Country	Total	Trade	Educational	STM
Australia	..	11,933	..	..
Belarus	9,590	3,038	4,880	1,672
Belgium	6,614	1,652	621	4,341
Brazil	73,345	48,879	11,060	13,406
Canada (a)	..	9,602	3,049	..
China	65,007,519	12,693,423	27,942,282	24,371,814
Colombia (a)	29,407	17,723	1,582	10,102
Denmark	15,502	..	..	..
Ecuador	7,170	4,594	1,019	1,557
Finland	..	6,523	3,654	..
France	104,670	74,092	10,332	20,246
Germany	82,636	..	5,490	..
Iceland	..	1,148	..	..
Italy	..	130,242	4,096	..
Japan	2,017,808	2,003,000	4,875	9,933
Kyrgyzstan	1,895	1,360	338	197
Latvia	2,803	2,323	95	385
Lithuania (a)	3,272	..	..	..
Mauritius (a)	324	246	44	34
Mexico (a)	41,770	25,041	10,109	6,620
Montenegro (a)	..	..	..	10
Norway	6,930	5,797	258	875
Peru (a)	..	6,463	..	..
Republic of Korea (a)	..	380,523	22,055	..
Republic of Moldova	4,513	2,760	663	1,090
Russian Federation (a)	94,436	28,699	40,428	25,309
Saudi Arabia	..	25,200	5,200	..
Serbia	..	..	..	277
Slovenia	..	5,014	..	..
South Africa (a)	136,403	..	..	..
Spain	119,778	82,238	10,884	26,656
Sweden	..	3,419	..	..
Turkey	104,283	58,329	35,642	10,312
United Kingdom (a)	149,443	..	..	..
United States of America	..	..	..	..
Ukraine	33,638	22,047	7,107	4,484
Yemen	1,420	650	700	70

Note: Caution should be exercised when interpreting the data shown here due to the fact that they are incomplete. The share of the total publishing industry represented by national publishers' associations (NPAs) varies between countries. There are also methodological differences that make it challenging to draw comparisons between countries. For all reported countries, the data source is the NPA, except for Canada (Statistics Canada), China (National Copyright Administration of China) and Japan (Japan Copyright Office). STM is the scientific, technical and medical sector.

(a) indicates 2016 data.

.. indicates not available.

Source: WIPO Statistics Database, September 2018.

F19. Total number of copies sold by sector (million), 2017

Country	Total	Trade	Educational	STM
Australia	..	..	..	..
Belarus	..	..	..	..
Belgium	22.2	..	..	..
Brazil	616.9	393.3	192.5	31.1
Canada	..	..	..	..
China	..	..	..	..
Colombia (a)	75.2	39.2	13.7	22.3
Denmark	..	..	..	..
Ecuador	9.3	5.9	2.5	0.9
Finland	..	14.4	5.7	..
France	430.0	345.3	60.8	24.0
Germany	..	..	..	..
Iceland	..	1.4	..	..
Italy	..	87.5	..	..
Japan	..	591.6	..	18.4
Kyrgyzstan	..	..	..	..
Latvia	..	..	..	..
Lithuania	..	..	..	..
Mauritius (a)	..	0.0001	0.02	..
Mexico (a)	227.2	137.4	73.9	15.9
Montenegro	..	..	..	..
Norway	20.4	16.7	2.7	1.0
Peru	..	..	..	..
Republic of Korea	..	..	..	..
Republic of Moldova	3.9	2.5	0.9	0.6
Russian Federation	..	..	..	..
Saudi Arabia	..	1.3	0.1	..
Serbia	..	..	..	..
Slovenia	..	5.0	..	..
South Africa	..	..	..	..
Spain	236.1	160.9	48.1	27.1
Sweden	..	37.9		
Turkey	373.5	187.0	182.2	4.3
United Kingdom	646.5	498.0	103.0	45.5
United States of America	2,693.1	2,485.4	119.2	88.4
Ukraine	..	..	..	..
Yemen	1.7	0.2	1.3	0.3

Note: Caution should be exercised when interpreting the data shown here due to the fact that they are incomplete. The share of the total publishing industry represented by national publishers' associations (NPAs) varies between countries. There are also methodological differences that make it challenging to draw comparisons between countries. For all reported countries, the data source is the NPA, except for Canada (Statistics Canada), China (National Copyright Administration of China) and Japan (Japan Copyright Office). STM is the scientific, technical and medical sector.

(a) indicates 2016 data.

.. indicates not available.

Source: WIPO Statistics Database, September 2018.

Additional information

Data description

Data sources

Intellectual property (IP) data are taken from the WIPO Statistics Database and are based primarily on WIPO's annual IP statistics survey (see below) and on data compiled by WIPO in processing international applications/registrations through the Patent Cooperation Treaty (PCT) and the Madrid and Hague Systems.

Data are available from WIPO's Statistics Data Center at *www.wipo.int/ipstats*.

Patent family and technology data are extracted from the WIPO Statistics Database and from the 2018 spring edition of the European Patent Office's PATSTAT database.

Gross domestic product and population data are from the World Bank's World Development Indicators database.

This report uses the World Bank's income classifications. Economies are classified according to 2017 gross national income per capita, calculated using the World Bank Atlas method. The classifications are low-income (USD 995 or less), lower middle-income (USD 996 to USD 3,895), upper middle-income (USD 3,896 to USD 12,055) and high-income (over USD 12,056).

This report uses United Nations (UN) definitions of regions and sub-regions, although the geographical terms used in the report may differ slightly from those defined by the UN.

WIPO's annual IP statistics surveys

WIPO collects data from national/regional IP offices, other competent authorities and publishers' associations around the world through annual surveys consisting of multiple questionnaires and enters these data into the WIPO Statistics Database. When possible, data published on IP offices' websites or in annual reports are used to supplement questionnaire responses in cases where IP offices/countries do not provide statistics. Continuous efforts are made to improve the quality and availability of IP statistics and to gather data for as many IP offices and countries as possible.

WIPO's long-established regular IP survey covers patents, utility models, trademarks, industrial designs and plant varieties. This survey consists of 28 questionnaires, which are available in English, French and

Spanish at *www.wipo.int/ipstats/en/data_collection/ questionnaire*.

In 2016, WIPO initiated a pilot survey to collect data on GIs in force. In 2017, for the first time, WIPO published statistics on GIs in force covering data for 54 jurisdictions. Data were collected from national and regional IP offices and other competent authorities through three questionnaires. For the 2018 survey, WIPO reduced the number of GI questionnaires from three to one and invited national/regional authorities to share their 2017 data on GIs in force with WIPO. In total, 82 authorities responded, which is a considerable improvement on the 54 responses that WIPO received in 2016.

In 2017, in collaboration with the International Publishers Association (IPA), WIPO launched a new survey of the global publishing industry. A total of 35 national publishers' associations and copyright authorities shared their 2016 data with the IPA and WIPO. The survey only includes published materials (i.e., books, journals, etc.) that have an International Standard Book Number (ISBN), International Standard Serial Number (ISSN) or Digital Object Identifier (DOI). The data collected through this new survey were presented in *The Global Publishing Industry in 2016* (published in April 2018) available to download at *www.wipo.int/ipstats*. In 2018, the publishing industry survey was sent to national publishers' associations and copyright authorities inviting them to share their 2017 data. To date, 28 associations/authorities have shared their 2017 data with the IPA and WIPO.

IP office survey coverage

IP offices are requested to report data by the origin (country or territory) of applications, grants or registrations. However, some offices are unable to provide a detailed breakdown. Instead, these offices report either an aggregate total or a simple breakdown by total resident and total non-resident counts. For this reason, the totals for each origin are underreported. However, the unknown origin shares of the 2017 totals are low – only 0.8% for patent applications, 0.8% for trademark application class counts and 0.7% for application design counts.

IP applications data coverage by IP type

IP type	Number of offices on which 2017 world totals are based	Number of offices for which 2017 data are available	Data coverage (%)
Patents	156	120	99.5
Utility models	75	64	99.9
Trademarks (a)	164	117	97.9
Industrial designs (b)	151	122	99.5
Plant varieties	69	62	97.8

(a) Refers to the number of trademark applications based on class count (that is, the number of classes specified in applications).

(b) Refers to the number of industrial design applications based on design count (that is, the number of designs contained in applications).

Estimating world totals

World totals for applications for, and grants/registrations of, patents, utility models, trademarks, industrial designs and plant varieties are WIPO estimates. Data are not available for all IP offices for every year. Missing data are estimated using methods such as linear extrapolation and averaging adjacent data points. The estimation method used depends on the year and office in question. When an office provides data which are not broken down by origin, WIPO estimates the resident and non-resident counts using the historical shares of that office. Data are available for most of the larger offices; only small shares of world totals are estimated. For example, the estimate of the total number of patent applications worldwide covers 156 offices. Data are available for 120 of them, which account for 99.5% of the estimated world total.

National and international data

Application and grant/registration data include data on both direct filings and filings through WIPO-administered international systems (where applicable). For patents and utility models, data include direct filings at national patent offices as well as PCT national phase entries. For trademarks, data include filings at national and regional offices and designations received by relevant offices through the Madrid System. For industrial designs, data include national and regional applications combined with designations received by relevant offices through the Hague System.

International comparability of indicators

Every effort has been made to compile IP statistics based on the same definitions and to facilitate international comparability. Although data are collected from offices using questionnaires from WIPO's harmonized annual IP survey, national laws and regulations for filing IP applications or for issuing IP rights, as well as statistical reporting practices, may differ between jurisdictions. Due to continual updating of data and the revision of historical statistics, data in this report may differ from data in previous editions and from data available on WIPO's website.

Change in method of counting IP applications by CNIPA

Due to a change in the method by which the National Intellectual Property Administration of the People's Republic of China (CNIPA) calculates the number of patent, utility model and industrial design applica-tions filed, data on the number of such applications filed in China in 2017 are not comparable with data for previous years. Prior to 2017, these data included all applications received; however, from 2017 onwards, they only include applications for which the office has received the necessary application fees. As a result, it is not meaningful to report growth rates in the number of patent, utility model and industrial design applications filed in China in 2017 compared to 2016. Moreover, since China represents such a large share of IP applications globally, it is not meaningful to report growth rates in the number of such applications filed worldwide in 2017 compared to 2016.

CNIPA has reported a growth rate of 14.2% in the number of patent applications filed in 2017 compared to 2016, without any breakdown between resident and non-resident filings. The 14.2% growth rate is calculated based on the new method. Recalculating the number of patent applications filed in China in 2016 according to the new method suggests an estimated growth rate of 5.8% in the number of patent applications filed worldwide in 2017 compared to 2016.

This report provides long-term average growth rates in the number of patent, utility model and industrial design applications, as it is expected that the impact of the change in methodology described above will be relatively limited in the long run.

IP systems at a glance

The patent system

A patent is a set of exclusive rights granted by law to applicants for an invention that meets the standards of novelty, non-obviousness and industrial applicability. It is valid for a limited period (generally 20 years), during which time the patent holder can commercially exploit the invention on an exclusive basis. In return, applicants are obliged to disclose their inventions to the public, so that others skilled in the art may replicate them. The patent system is designed to encourage innovation by providing innovators with time-limited exclusive legal rights, thus enabling them to appropriate the returns from their innovative activity.

The procedures for acquiring patent rights are governed by the rules and regulations of national and regional patent offices. These offices are responsible for issuing patents and the rights are limited to the jurisdiction of the issuing authority. To obtain patent rights, applicants must file an application describing the invention with a national or regional office.

Applicants can also file an international application through the Patent Cooperation Treaty (PCT) System, an international treaty administered by WIPO that facilitates the acquisition of patent rights in multiple jurisdictions. The PCT System simplifies the process of multiple national patent filings by delaying the requirement to file a separate application in each jurisdiction in which protection is sought. However, the decision on whether to grant a patent remains the prerogative of national or regional patent offices and patent rights are limited to the jurisdiction of each patent-granting authority.

The PCT application process begins with the international phase, during which an international search and optional preliminary examination and supplementary international search are performed. It concludes with the national phase, during which national (or regional) patent offices decide on the patentability of an invention according to national law. Further information about the PCT System is available at *www.wipo.int/pct.*

The utility model system

Like a patent, a utility model (UM) confers a set of rights to an invention for a limited period, during which the UM rights holder can commercially exploit their invention on an exclusive basis. The terms and condi-tions for granting a UM differ from those for granting a traditional patent. For example, UMs are issued for a shorter period (6–10 years) and at most offices protection is granted without substantive examination. As with patents, procedures for granting UM rights are governed by the rules and regulations of national intellectual property (IP) offices and rights are limited to the jurisdiction of the issuing authority.

Approximately 75 countries provide protection for UMs. In this report, the term "utility model" refers to UMs and other types of protection similar to UMs, such as innovation patents in Australia and short-term patents in Ireland.

Microorganisms under the Budapest Treaty

The Budapest Treaty on the International Recognition of the Deposit of Microorganisms for the Purposes of Patent Procedure plays an important role in relation to biotechnological inventions. Disclosing an invention is a generally recognized requirement for receiving a patent. When an invention involves microorganisms, national laws in most countries require the applicant to deposit a sample at a designated International Depositary Authority (IDA).

To eliminate the need to deposit a microorganism in every country in which patent protection is sought, the Budapest Treaty provides that depositing a microorgan-ism with any IDA will suffice for the purposes of patent procedures at national patent offices of all contracting states and at regional patent offices that recognize the treaty. An IDA is a scientific institution – typically a "culture collection" – capable of storing microorganisms. Currently, there are 47 IDAs around the world. Further information about the Budapest Treaty is available at *www.wipo.int/treaties/en/registration/budapest.*

The trademark system

A trademark is a distinctive sign that identifies certain goods or services as those produced or provided by a specific person or enterprise. Trademarks can be registered for both goods and services. In the latter case, the term "service mark" is sometimes used. For simplicity, this report uses "trademark" regardless of whether the registration concerns goods or services. The holder of a registered trademark has the exclusive right to use the mark in relation to the goods or services for which it is registered and can block unauthorized use of the trademark, or a confusingly similar mark, to prevent consumers from being misled. Unlike patents, trademark registrations can be maintained indefinitely, provided that the trademark holder pays the required renewal fees.

The procedures for registering trademarks are governed by the rules and regulations of national and regional IP offices. Therefore, trademark rights are limited to the jurisdiction of the authority in which a trademark is registered. Trademark applicants can file an application with the relevant national or regional IP office or an international application through the Madrid System. However, when an applicant files internationally via the Madrid System, the decision to issue a trademark registration remains the prerogative of the national or regional IP office concerned and trademark rights remain limited to the jurisdiction of the authority issuing that registration.

Originally, two treaties administered by WIPO governed the Madrid System for the International Registration of Marks. These treaties are the Madrid Agreement Concerning the International Registration of Marks and the Protocol Relating to the Madrid Agreement, and are jointly referred to as the Madrid System. The Madrid Agreement was concluded in 1891 and the Madrid Protocol came into operation in 1996. With Algeria's accession to the Madrid Protocol in October 2015, the last remaining member to be a party only to the Madrid Agreement joined the Protocol, effectively making Madrid a one-treaty system. The Madrid System offers many advantages to both trademark holders and IP offices compared with the alternative method of obtaining international protection for marks, which is called the Paris or direct route. The Paris route involves filing separate applications in a number of countries or regions using rights established under the Paris Convention for the Protection of Industrial Property. In contrast, the Madrid System allows trademark holders to submit a single application in one language while paying a single set of fees in one currency.

The System also simplifies subsequent management of the trademark, since it is possible to centrally request and record further changes, or to renew the registration through a single procedure. A registration recorded in the International Register yields the same effect as a registration made directly with each designated Contracting Party (Madrid member) if the competent authority of that jurisdiction has not issued a refusal within a specified time limit. Further information about the Madrid System is available at *www.wipo.int/madrid*.

The industrial design system

Industrial designs are applied to a wide variety of industrial products and handicrafts.[1] They refer to the ornamental or aesthetic aspects of a useful article, including compositions of lines or colors or three-dimensional forms that give a special appearance to a product or handicraft. The holder of a registered industrial design has exclusive rights over the design and can prevent unauthorized copying or imitation of the design by others.

The procedures for registering industrial designs are governed by national or regional laws. An industrial design can be protected if it is new or original and rights are limited to the jurisdiction of the issuing authority. Registrations can be obtained by filing an application with a relevant national or regional IP office or by filing an international application through the Hague System. Once a design is registered, the term of protection is generally five years and may be renewed for additional periods of five years up to a total of 15 years in most cases. In some countries, industrial designs are protected through the delivery of a design patent rather than design registration.

The Hague System comprises two international treaties – the Hague Act and the Geneva Act. The System makes it possible for an applicant to register industrial designs in multiple countries by filing a single application with the International Bureau of WIPO, thus simplifying the multinational registration process. Moreover, by allowing the filing of up to 100 different designs per application, the System offers considerable opportunities for efficiency gains. It also streamlines the subsequent management of industrial design registration, since it is possible to record changes or renew a registration through a single procedure. Further information about the Hague System is available at *www.wipo.int/hague*.

Plant variety protection

To obtain protection, a plant breeder must file an individual application with each authority entrusted with granting breeders' rights. A breeder's right is granted only when a variety is new, distinct, uniform and stable, and has a suitable denomination.

In the United States of America (U.S.), two legal frameworks protect new plant varieties: the Plant Patent Act (PPA) and the Plant Variety Protection Act (PVPA). Under the PPA, whoever invents or discovers and asexually reproduces any distinct and new variety of plant – including cultivated sports, mutants, hybrids and newly found seedlings, other than a tuber-propagated plant (in practice, Irish potato and Jerusalem artichoke) or a plant found in an uncultivated state – may obtain a patent. Under the PVPA, the U.S. protects all sexually reproduced plant varieties and tuber-propagated plant varieties, excluding fungi and bacteria.

Protection of geographical indications

A geographical indication (GI) is a sign identifying a good as originating in a specific geographical area and possessing a given quality, reputation or other characteristic that is essentially attributable to that geographical origin. Thus, the main function of a GI is to indicate a connection between that quality, characteristic or reputation of the good and its territory of origin.

World-renowned examples of GIs include Café de Colombia (Colombia), Bordeaux (France), Kampot Pepper (Cambodia), Penja Pepper (Cameroon) and Scotch whisky (U.K.).

GIs are mainly used for agricultural and food products, which typically tend to have a close natural link with their place of origin. There are, however, also many GIs for other kinds of products. The specific qualities of the product may derive from traditional manufacturing skills or from a combination of local know-how and natural resources. Examples of such GIs include Bohemia Crystal (Czech Republic), Solingen Cutlery (Germany), Isfahan Handmade Carpet (Islamic Republic of Iran), Swiss Watches (Switzerland) and Yangzhou Lacquerware (China).

Although GIs are commonly names of places, under many systems they may consist of non-geographical terms with a traditional geographical connotation. Reblochon (France) and Argane (Morocco) serve as GIs although they are not geographical names.

Geographical indications can only be used by producers whose goods conform to the applicable requirements concerning the area of origin, processing method and typicity of the product. Production sites located outside the area of origin and goods that do not meet the applicable requirements are prevented from using the protected indication.

Appellations of origin

An appellation of origin is a special kind of geographical indication. It generally consists of a geographical name or a traditional denomination which serves to designate a product as originating therein, where the quality or characteristics of the product are due exclusively or essentially to the geographical environment, including natural and human factors, and which have given the good its reputation. The most important difference between appellations of origin and other GIs is that the link with the place of origin should be stronger in the case of an appellation of origin. In other words, appellations of origin are a more restrictive sub-category of GIs.

Protection of GIs

At the national and regional levels, GIs are protected through a variety of legal means. These include *sui generis* systems – laws specifically designed to protect geographical indications,[2] often based on a registration procedure. *Sui generis* systems generally provide protection against any direct and indirect commercial use of the GI as well as against its imitation. *Sui generis* systems for GI protection are used in many countries and also by two regional intergovernmental organizations: the African Intellectual Property Organization (OAPI) and the European Union (EU).

GIs are also protected on the basis of trademark law, commonly through the use of collective and certification marks. Because trademarks incorporating geographical terms are typically not recorded by IP offices as a separate category of trademarks, and because not all trademarks incorporating geographical terms can be considered to be GIs, it may be difficult to determine the exact number of registered GIs within those jurisdictions. It is also worth noting that GI protection via trademark and *sui generis* systems are not mutually exclusive but often coexist, under many legal frameworks, and are available to the benefit of GI holders.

Finally, GIs are typically also protected under unfair competition regulation, consumer protection laws and administrative and judicial decisions, as well as under specific laws or decrees recognizing individual GIs.

The effects of a GI right obtained in a particular jurisdiction are limited to the territory of that jurisdiction. Thus, where a right over a GI is obtained in one jurisdiction, it is protected there but not abroad. In order to obtain protection in a foreign jurisdiction, GI holders must, in principle, seek protection under the relevant national laws prevailing in the jurisdiction in question. However, international agreements can facilitate the acquisition of GI rights abroad. In particular, many bilateral and regional trade agreements have incorporated lists of GIs that are to be protected in the relevant parties to the agreement. The listed GIs may relate to existing or subsequent registrations of GI rights, but protection may also emanate from the trade agreements themselves.

Another way of obtaining protection for GIs abroad is through two international registration systems administered by WIPO: the Lisbon System and the Madrid System.

The Lisbon System

The Lisbon System was established in 1958 to facilitate the international protection of appellations of origin through a single registration procedure.[3] Registration with the WIPO International Bureau ensures protection in all Lisbon contracting parties, without the need for renewal and as long as the appellation of origin remains protected in its contracting party of origin. However, the decision on whether to protect a newly registered appellation of origin at the national level remains the prerogative of each contracting party and each Lisbon member can refuse protection based on any ground within one year of being notified of a new appellation of origin by the WIPO International Bureau. The Lisbon System is flexible with regard to the means by which countries may provide protection for the registered appellation of origin (e.g., *sui generis* systems, trademark laws or specific ad hoc decrees, as well as judicial and administrative decisions).

Globally-renowned examples of appellations of origin protected under the Lisbon System include Tequila (Mexico), Chianti for wines (Italy), Habanos for cigars (Cuba) and handicrafts such as Chulucanas for ceramics (Peru), Herend for porcelain (Hungary) and Kraslice musical instruments (Czech Republic). The scope of the System extends to non-geographical traditional names, such as Reblochon (France) and Vinho Verde (Portugal).

In 2015, with the adoption of the Geneva Act of the Lisbon Agreement on Appellations of Origin and Geographical Indications, which will enter into force after five ratifications or accessions, Lisbon contracting parties modernized the System to attract a wider membership, while preserving its principles and objectives. The Geneva Act formally extends the scope of the Lisbon System to the general category of geographical indications in addition to appellations of origin. The new Act also opens the Lisbon System to accession by intergovernmental organizations such as the EU and OAPI.

Protection of GIs abroad through the Madrid System

GIs can also be protected in several countries as trademarks (most commonly collective and certification marks) through the Madrid System, an international registration system legally governed by the Madrid Agreement (1891) and the Madrid Protocol (1989) and administered by WIPO.[4] Famous examples of collective and certification marks registered under the Madrid System include Napa Valley for wine (U.S.) and Parmigiano Reggiano for cheese (Italy). As at June 2017, there were more than 1,200 collective and certification marks registered under the Madrid System. However, collective and certification marks protecting GIs are not separately recorded, so it is difficult to determine their exact number.

1   The products and handicrafts to which industrial designs are applied range from technical and medical instruments to watches, jewelry and other luxury items, and from housewares, electrical appliances, vehicles and construction materials to textile designs and leisure goods.

2   The terminology used at national and regional levels to refer to *sui generis* rights over GIs is not uniform. Different terms, such as appellations of origin, controlled appellations of origin, protected designations of origin, protected geographical indications, (qualified) indications of source or simply geographical indications are used in different legislations. Despite the different terminology, however, the common denominator remains the link between the specific quality, characteristics or reputation of the product and its territory of origin. For simplicity, the present text generally uses "geographical indication (GI)" regardless of the different national and regional terminology.

3   The Lisbon System is administered by WIPO and comprises the Lisbon Agreement for the Protection of Appellations of Origin and their International Registration (1958), as revised at Stockholm in 1967 and amended in 1979, and the Geneva Act of the Lisbon Agreement on Appellations of Origin and Geographical Indications (2015), which has not yet entered into force.

4   For more information about the Madrid System, please see the *Madrid Yearly Review 2018*.

Glossary

This glossary provides definitions of key technical terms and concepts. Many of these terms are defined generically (for example, "application") but apply to several or all of the various forms of intellectual property (IP) covered in this report.

Applicant

An individual or other legal entity that files an application for a patent, utility model, trademark or industrial design. There may be more than one applicant in an application. For the statistics in this publication, the name of the first named applicant is used to determine the origin of the application.

Application

The procedure for requesting IP rights at an office, which then examines the application and decides whether to grant protection. Also refers to a set of documents submitted to an office by the applicant.

Application abroad

For statistical purposes, an application filed by a resident of a given state or jurisdiction with the IP office of another state or jurisdiction. For example, an application filed by an applicant domiciled in France with the Japan Patent Office (JPO) is considered an application abroad from the perspective of France. This differs from a "non-resident application," which describes an application filed by a resident of a foreign state or jurisdiction from the perspective of the office receiving the application: the example above would be a non-resident application from the JPO's point of view.

Application date

The date on which the IP office receives an application that meets the minimum requirements. Also referred to as the filing date.

Budapest Treaty

Disclosure of an invention is a requirement for granting a patent. Normally, an invention is disclosed by means of a written description. Where an invention involves a microorganism or the use of a microorganism, disclosure is not always possible in writing but can sometimes only be effected by depositing a sample of the microorganism with a specialized institution. To eliminate the need to deposit a microorganism in each country in which patent protection is sought, the Budapest Treaty provides that the deposit of a microorganism with any International Depositary Authority (IDA) suffices for the purposes of patent procedure at the national patent offices of all contracting states and at any regional patent office that recognizes the treaty.

Certification trademark

Certification marks are usually given for compliance with defined standards but are not confined to any membership. They may be used by anyone who can certify that the products involved meet certain established standards. In many countries, the main difference between collective marks and certification marks is that collective marks may only be used by a specific group of enterprises, for example, members of an association, while certification marks may be used by anybody who complies with the standards defined by the owner of the certification mark.

Class

May refer to the classes defined in either the Locarno Classification or the Nice Classification. Classes indicate the categories of goods and services (where applicable) for which industrial design or trademark protection is requested. See "Locarno Classification" and "Nice Classification."

Class count

The number of classes specified in a trademark application or registration. In the international trademark system and at certain national and regional offices, an applicant can file a trademark application that specifies one or more of the 45 goods and services classes of the Nice Classification. Offices use a single- or multi-class filing system. For example, the offices of Japan, the Republic of Korea and the United States of America (U.S.), as well as many European IP offices, have multi-class filing systems. The offices of Brazil, Mexico and South Africa follow a single-class filing system, requiring a separate application for each class in which an applicant seeks trademark protection. To capture the differences in application and registration numbers across offices, it is useful to compare their respective application and registration class counts.

Collective trademark

Collective marks are usually defined as signs which distinguish the geographical origin, material, mode of manufacture or other common characteristics of goods or services of different enterprises using the collective mark. The owner may be either an association of which those enterprises are members or any other entity, including a public institution or a cooperative.

Community Plant Variety Office (CPVO) of the European Union (EU)

An EU agency that manages a system of plant variety rights covering all EU member states.

Design count

The number of designs contained in an industrial design application or registration. Under the Hague System for the International Registration of Industrial Designs, it is possible for an applicant to obtain protection for up to 100 industrial designs for products belonging to one and the same class by filing a single application. Some national or regional IP offices allow applications to contain more than one design for the same product or within the same class, while others allow only one design per application. In order to capture the differences in application and registration numbers across offices, it is useful to compare their respective application and registration design counts.

Designation

The request in an international application or registration by which the applicant/international registration holder specifies the jurisdiction(s) in which they seek to protect their industrial designs (Hague System) or trademarks (Madrid System).

Direct filing

See "National route."

Equivalent application

Applications at regional offices are equivalent to multiple applications, one in each of the states that is a member of those offices. To calculate the number of equivalent applications for the Benelux Office for Intellectual Property (BOIP), the Eurasian Patent Organization (EAPO), the African Intellectual Property Organization (OAPI), the Patent Office of the Cooperation Council for the Arab States of the Gulf (GCC Patent Office) and the European Union Intellectual Property Office (EUIPO), each application is multiplied by the corresponding number of member states. For European Patent Office (EPO) and African Regional Intellectual Property Organization (ARIPO) data, each application is counted as one application abroad if the applicant does not reside in a member state or as one resident application and one application abroad if the applicant resides in a member state. The equivalent application concept is used for reporting data by origin.

Equivalent grant (registration)

Grants (registrations) at regional offices are equivalent to multiple grants (registrations), one in each of the states that is a member of those offices. To calculate the number of equivalent grants (registrations) for BOIP, EAPO, the EUIPO, the GCC Patent Office or OAPI, each grant (registration) is multiplied by the corresponding number of member states. For EPO and ARIPO data, each grant is counted as one grant abroad if the applicant does not reside in a member state or as one resident grant and one grant abroad if the applicant resides in a member state. The equivalent grant (registration) concept is used for reporting data by origin.

European Patent Office (EPO)

The EPO is the regional patent office created under the European Patent Convention (EPC), in charge of granting European patents for EPC member states. Under Patent Cooperation Treaty (PCT) procedures, the EPO acts as a receiving office, an International Searching Authority and an International Preliminary Examining Authority.

European Union Intellectual Property Office (EUIPO)

The EUIPO is the office responsible for managing the EU trademark and the registered community design. The validity of these two intellectual property rights extends across the jurisdictions of the EU's 28 member states.

Filing

See "Application."

Foreign-oriented patent families

A special subset of patent families that comprises foreign-oriented patent families: this includes only patent families that have at least one filing office which differs from the office of the applicant's country of origin. Some foreign-oriented patent families include only one filing office, because applicants may choose to file directly with a foreign office. For example, if a Canadian applicant files a patent application directly with the United States Patent and Trademark Office (USPTO) without previously filing with the patent office of Canada, that application and applications filed subsequently with the USPTO will form a foreign-oriented patent family.

Geographical indication

A geographical indication (GI) is a sign identifying a good as originating in a specific geographical area and possessing a given quality, reputation or other characteristic that is essentially attributable to that geographical origin. Thus, the main function of a GI is to indicate a connection between that quality, characteristic or reputation of the good and its territory of origin.

Grant

A set of exclusive rights legally accorded to the applicant when a patent or utility model is granted or issued.

Gross domestic product (GDP)

The total unduplicated output of economic goods and services produced within a country as measured in monetary terms.

Hague international application

An application for the international registration of an industrial design filed under the WIPO-administered Hague System.

Hague international registration

An international registration issued via the Hague System, which facilitates the acquisition of industrial design rights in multiple jurisdictions. An application for international registration of an industrial design leads to its recording in the International Register and the publication of the registration in the *International Designs Bulletin*. If the registration is not refused by the IP office of a designated Hague member, the international registration will have the same effect as a registration made in that jurisdiction.

Hague member (Contracting Party)

A state or intergovernmental organization that is a member of the Hague System. Includes any state or intergovernmental organization which is party to the Geneva Act of 1999 and/or the Hague Act of 1960. Entitlement to file an international application under the Hague Agreement is limited to natural persons or legal entities having a real and effective industrial or commercial establishment, or a domicile, in at least one of the Contracting Parties to the Agreement, or being a national of one of those Contracting Parties or of a member state of an intergovernmental organization that is a Contracting Party. In addition – but only under the 1999 Act – an international application may be filed on the basis of habitual residence in the jurisdiction of a Contracting Party.

Hague route

An alternative to the Paris route (i.e., the direct national or regional route), the Hague route enables an application for international registration of industrial designs to be filed using the Hague System.

Hague System

The abbreviated form of the Hague System for the International Registration of Industrial Designs. This System comprises two international treaties: the Hague Act of 1960 and the Geneva Act of 1999. The Hague System makes it possible for an applicant to register up to 100 industrial designs in multiple jurisdictions by filing a single application with the International Bureau of WIPO. It simplifies multinational registration by reducing the requirement to file separate applications with each IP office. The System also simplifies the subsequent management of the industrial design, since it is possible to record changes or renew a registration through a single procedural step.

In force

Refers to IP rights that are currently valid or, in the case of trademarks, active. To remain in force, IP protection must be maintained.

Industrial design

Industrial designs are applied to a wide variety of industrial products and handicrafts. They refer to the ornamental or aesthetic aspects of a useful article, including compositions of lines or colors or any three-dimensional forms that give a special appearance to a product or handicraft. The holder of a registered industrial design has exclusive rights against unauthorized copying or imitation of the design by third parties. Industrial design registrations are valid for a limited period. The term of protection is usually 15 years in most jurisdictions. However, differences in legislation exist, notably in China (which provides for a 10-year term from the application date).

Intellectual property (IP)

Refers to creations of the mind: inventions, literary and artistic works, and symbols, names, images and designs used in commerce. IP is divided into two categories: industrial property – which includes patents, utility models, trademarks, industrial designs and geographical indications of source – and copyright, which includes literary and artistic works (such as novels, poems, plays, films), musical works, artistic works (such as drawings, paintings, photographs and sculptures) and architectural designs. Rights related to copyright include those of performing artists in their performances, those of producers of sound recordings in their recordings and those of broadcasters in their radio and television programs.

International Depositary Authority (IDA)

A scientific institution – typically a culture collection – capable of storing microorganisms that has acquired the status of an International Depositary Authority under the Budapest Treaty and provides for the receipt, acceptance and storage of microorganisms and the furnishing of samples thereof. Currently, 47 such authorities exist around the world.

International Patent Classification (IPC)

An internationally recognized patent classification system, the IPC has a hierarchical structure of language-independent symbols and is divided into sections, classes, sub-classes and groups. IPC symbols are assigned according to the technical features in patent applications. A patent application that relates to multiple technical features can be assigned several IPC symbols.

International Union for the Protection of New Varieties of Plants (UPOV)

An intergovernmental organization established by the International Convention for the Protection of New Varieties of Plants (the UPOV Convention), which was adopted on December 2, 1961. UPOV provides and promotes an effective system of plant variety protection with the aim of encouraging the development of new varieties of plants for the benefit of society.

Invention

A new solution to a technical problem. To qualify for patent protection, the invention must be novel, involve an inventive step and be industrially applicable, as judged by a person skilled in the art.

Lisbon System

The Lisbon System was established in 1958 to facilitate the international protection of appellations of origin through a single registration procedure. Registration with the WIPO International Bureau ensures protection in all Lisbon contracting parties, without need for renewal and as long as the appellation of origin remains protected in its contracting party of origin. However, the decision on whether to protect a newly registered appellation of origin at the national level remains the prerogative of each contracting party, and each Lisbon member can refuse protection based on any ground within one year of being notified of a new appellation of origin by the WIPO International Bureau. The Lisbon System is flexible with regard to the means by which countries may provide protection for the registered appellation of origin (e.g., *sui generis* systems, trademark laws or specific ad hoc decrees, as well as judicial and administrative decisions).

Locarno Classification

The abbreviated form of the International Classification for Industrial Designs under the Locarno Agreement, used for registering industrial designs. The Locarno Classification consists of 32 classes and their respective subclasses with explanatory notes plus an alphabetical list of the goods in which industrial designs are incorporated and an indication of the classes and subclasses into which they fall.

Madrid international application

An application for international registration under the Madrid System, which is a request for protection of a trademark in one or more Madrid members' jurisdictions. An international application must be based on a basic mark – prior application or registration of a mark in a Madrid member.

Madrid international registration

An application for international registration of a mark leads to its recording in the International Register and the publication of the international registration in the *WIPO Gazette of International Marks*. If the international registration is not refused protection by a designated Madrid member, it will have the same effect as a national or regional trademark registration made under the law applicable in that Madrid member's jurisdiction.

Madrid member (Contracting Party)

A state or intergovernmental organization – for example the European Union (EU) or the African Intellectual Property Organization (OAPI) – that is party to the Madrid Agreement and/or the Madrid Protocol.

Madrid route

The Madrid route (the Madrid System) is an alternative to the direct national or regional route (also called the Paris route).

Madrid System

An abbreviation describing two procedural treaties for the international registration of trademarks; namely, the Madrid Agreement for the International Registration of Marks and the Protocol relating to that Agreement. The Madrid System is administered by the International Bureau of WIPO.

Maintenance

An act by the applicant to keep an IP grant/registration valid (in force), primarily by paying the required fee to the IP office of the state or jurisdiction providing protection. That fee is also known as a "maintenance fee." A trademark can be maintained indefinitely by paying renewal fees; however, patents, utility models and industrial designs can be maintained for only a limited number of years.

Microorganism deposit

The transmittal of a microorganism to an International Depositary Authority (IDA), which receives and accepts it, the storage of such a microorganism by the IDA, or both transmittal and storage.

National phase under the PCT

The phase that follows the international phase of the PCT procedure and that consists of the entry and processing of the international application in the individual countries or regions in which the applicant seeks protection for an invention.

National route

Applications for IP protection filed directly with the national office of, or acting for, the relevant state or jurisdiction (see also "Hague route," "Madrid route" and "PCT route"). The national route is also called the "direct route" or "Paris route."

Nice Classification

The abbreviated form of the International Classification of Goods and Services for the Purposes of Registering Marks, an international classification established under the Nice Agreement. The Nice Classification consists of 45 classes, which are divided into 34 classes for goods and 11 for services. (See "Class.")

Non-resident

For statistical purposes, a "non-resident" application refers to an application filed with the IP office of, or acting for, a state or jurisdiction in which the first named applicant in the application is not domiciled. For example, an application filed with the Japan Patent Office (JPO) by an applicant residing in France is considered to be a non-resident application from the perspective of the JPO. Non-resident applications are sometimes referred to as foreign applications. A non-resident grant or registration is an IP right issued on the basis of a non-resident application.

Origin (country or region)

For statistical purposes, the origin of an application means the country or territory of residence of the first named applicant in the application. In some cases (notably in the U.S.), the country of origin is determined by the residence of the assignee rather than that of the applicant.

Paris Convention

The Paris Convention for the Protection of Industrial Property, signed on March 20, 1883, is one of the most important treaties, as it establishes general principles applicable to all IP rights. It establishes the "right of priority" that enables an IP applicant, when filing an application in countries other than the original country of filing, to claim priority of an earlier application filed up to 12 months previously for patents and utility models, and up to six months previously for trademarks and industrial designs.

Paris route

An alternative to the Hague, Madrid or PCT routes, the Paris route (also called the "direct route" or "national route") enables individual IP applications to be filed directly with an IP office of a country/territory that is a signatory to the Paris Convention.

Patent

A set of exclusive rights granted by law to applicants for inventions that are new, non-obvious and commercially applicable. A patent is valid for a limited period of time (generally 20 years), during which patent holders can commercially exploit their inventions on an exclusive basis. In return, applicants are obliged to disclose their inventions to the public in a manner that enables others skilled in the art to replicate the invention. The patent system is designed to encourage innovation by providing innovators with time-limited exclusive legal rights, thus enabling them to appropriate the returns from their innovative activity.

Patent Cooperation Treaty (PCT)

An international treaty administered by WIPO, the PCT allows applicants to seek patent protection for an invention simultaneously in a large number of countries (PCT contracting states) by filing a single PCT international application. The granting of patents, which remains under the control of national or regional patent offices, is carried out in what is called the "national phase" or "regional phase."

Patent family

Applicants often file patent applications in multiple jurisdictions, so some inventions are recorded more than once. To take this into account, WIPO has indicators related to patent families, defined as patent applications interlinked by one or more of: priority claim, Patent Cooperation Treaty national phase entry, continuation, continuation-in-part, internal priority and addition or division. WIPO's patent family definition includes only those associated with patent applications for inventions and excludes patent families associated with utility model applications.

PCT application

A patent application filed through the WIPO-administered PCT, also known as an international application.

PCT-patent prosecution highway (PCT-PPH) pilots

A number of bilateral agreements signed between patent offices that enable applicants to request an accelerated examination procedure because of positive patentability findings made by the international searching and/or international preliminary examining authority, in the written opinion by an International Searching Authority, the written opinion of an International Preliminary Examining Authority or the international preliminary report on patentability.

PCT route

A patent application filed through the WIPO-administered PCT, also known as an international application.

PCT System

The PCT, an international treaty administered by WIPO, facilitates the acquisition of patent rights in a large number of jurisdictions. The PCT System simplifies the process of multiple national patent filings by reducing the requirement to file a separate application in each jurisdiction. However, the decision on whether to grant patent rights remains in the hands of national and regional patent offices, and patent rights remain limited to the jurisdiction of the patent-granting authority. The PCT application process starts with the international phase, during which an international search and, possibly, a preliminary examination are performed, and concludes with the national phase, during which a national or regional patent office decides on the patentability of an invention according to national law.

Additional information

Pending patent application

In general, this refers to a patent application filed with a patent office for which no patent has yet been granted or refused, and for which the application has not been withdrawn. In jurisdictions where a request for examination is required to start the examination process, a pending application may refer to an application for which a request for examination has been received or one for which no patent has been granted or refused, and for which the application has not been withdrawn.

Plant Patent Act (PPA) of the U.S.

Under the law commonly known as the "Plant Patent Act," whoever invents or discovers and asexually reproduces any distinct and new variety of plant, including cultivated sports, mutants, hybrids and newly found seedlings, other than a tuber-propagated plant or a plant found in an uncultivated state, may obtain a patent therefor.

Plant variety

According to the UPOV Convention, plant variety means a plant grouping within a single botanical taxon of the lowest known rank which, irrespective of whether the conditions for the granting of a breeder's right are fully met, can be defined by the expression of the characteristics resulting from a given genotype or combination of genotypes, distinguished from any other plant grouping by the expression of at least one of the said characteristics and considered as a unit with regard to its suitability for being propagated unchanged.

Plant variety grant

Under the UPOV Convention, the breeder's right is granted (title of protection is issued) only when the variety is new, distinct, uniform, stable and has a suitable denomination.

Plant Variety Protection Act (PVPA) of the U.S.

Under the PVPA, the U.S. protects all sexually reproduced plant varieties and tuber-propagated plant varieties, excluding fungi and bacteria.

Prior art

All information disclosed to the public about an invention, in any form, before a given date. Information on prior art can assist in determining whether the claimed invention is new and involves an inventive step (i.e., is non-obvious) for the purposes of international searches and international preliminary examination.

Priority date

The filing date of the application on the basis of which priority is claimed. (See "Paris Convention.")

Publication date

The date on which an IP application is disclosed to the public. On that date, the subject matter of the application becomes prior art.

Regional application/grant (registration)

An application filed with or granted (registered) by an IP office having regional jurisdiction over more than one country. There are currently seven regional offices: the African Intellectual Property Organization (OAPI), the African Regional Intellectual Property Organization (ARIPO), the Benelux Office for Intellectual Property (BOIP), the Eurasian Patent Organization (EAPO), the European Patent Office (EPO), the European Union Intellectual Property Office (EUIPO) and the Patent Office of the Cooperation Council for the Arab States of the Gulf (GCC Patent Office).

Registered Community design

A registration issued by the EUIPO based on a single application filed directly with the office by an applicant seeking protection within the EU as a whole.

Registration

An exclusive set of rights legally accorded to the applicant when an industrial design or trademark is registered or issued. See "Industrial design" or "Trademark." Registrations are issued to applicants to make use of and exploit their industrial designs or trademarks for a limited period of time and can, in some cases (particularly in the case of trademarks), be renewed indefinitely.

Renewal

The process by which the protection of an IP right is maintained (kept in force). This usually consists of paying renewal fees to an IP office at regular intervals. If renewal fees are not paid, the registration may lapse. See also "Maintenance."

Resident

For statistical purposes, a resident application refers to an application filed with the IP office of, or acting for, the state or jurisdiction in which the first named applicant in the application has residence. For example, an application filed with the JPO by a resident of Japan is considered a resident application from the perspective of the JPO. Resident applications are sometimes referred to as "domestic applications." A resident grant/registration is an IP right issued on the basis of a resident application.

Trademark

A sign used to distinguish the goods or services of one undertaking from those of others. A trademark may consist of words and combinations of words (for instance, names or slogans), logos, figures and images, letters, numbers, sounds, or, in rare instances, smells or moving images, or a combination thereof. The procedures for registering trademarks are governed by the legislation and procedures of national and regional IP offices and WIPO. Trademark rights are limited to the jurisdiction of the IP office that registers the trademark. Trademarks can be registered by filing an application at the relevant national or regional office(s), or by filing an international application through the Madrid System.

Utility model

A special form of patent right granted by a state or jurisdiction to an inventor or the inventor's assignee for a fixed period of time. The terms and conditions for granting a utility model are slightly different from those for normal patents (including a shorter term of protection and less stringent patentability requirements). The term can also describe what are known in certain countries as "petty patents," "short-term patents" or "innovation patents."

World Intellectual Property Organization (WIPO)

A United Nations specialized agency dedicated to the promotion of innovation and creativity for the economic, social and cultural development of all countries through a balanced and effective international IP system. WIPO was established in 1967 with a mandate to promote the protection of IP throughout the world through cooperation between states and in collaboration with other international organizations.

Abbreviations

AIA	America Invents Act
ARIPO	African Regional Intellectual Property Organization
BAILII	British and Irish Legal Information Institute
BOIP	Benelux Office for Intellectual Property
CAFC	Court of Appeals for the Federal Circuit
CNIPA	National Intellectual Property Administration of the People's Republic of China
CPVO	Community Plant Variety Office of the European Union
DPMA	Deutsche Patent- und Markenamt
EAPO	Eurasian Patent Organization
EPO	European Patent Office
EU	European Union
EUIPO	European Union Intellectual Property Office
GCC Patent Office	Patent Office of the Cooperation Council for the Arab States of the Gulf
GDP	gross domestic product
GI	geographical indication
IDA	International Depositary Authority
IP	intellectual property
IPA	International Publishers Association
IPC	International Patent Classification
IPEC	Intellectual Property Enterprise Court
IPR	*inter partes* review
ITC	International Trade Commission
JPO	Japan Patent Office
KIPO	Korean Intellectual Property Office
NPA	national publishers' association
OAPI	African Intellectual Property Organization
PACER	Public Access to Court Electronic Records
PAEs	patent assertion entities
PCT	Patent Cooperation Treaty
PHC	Patents Court (England and Wales)
PPA	Plant Patent Act of the United States of America
PTAB	Patent Trial and Appeal Board
PVPA	Plant Variety Protection Act of the United States of America
R&D	research and development
STM	scientific, technical and medical
U.K.	United Kingdom
UM	utility model
UN	United Nations
UPOV	International Union for the Protection of New Varieties of Plants
U.S.	United States of America
USPTO	United States Patent and Trademark Office
WIPO	World Intellectual Property Organization

Annexes

Annex A. Definitions for selected energy-related technology fields

Energy-related technologies	International patent classification (IPC) symbols
Solar energy technology	E04D 1/30, E04D 13/18, F24J 2/00, F24J 2/02, F24J 2/04, F24J 2/05, F24J 2/06, F24J 2/07, F24J 2/08, F24J 2/10, F24J 2/12, F24J 2/13, F24J 2/14, F24J 2/15, F24J 2/16, F24J 2/18, F24J 2/23, F24J 2/24, F24J 2/36, F24J 2/38, F24J 2/42, F24J 2/46, F03G 6/06, G02B 5/10, H01L 31/052, H01L 31/04, H01L 31/042, H01L 31/18, G02F 1/136, G05F 1/67, H01L 25/00, H01L 31/00, H01L 31/048, H01L 33/00, H02J 7/35, H02N 6/00
Fuel cell technology	H01M 4/00, H01M 4/86, H01M 4/88, H01M 4/90, H01M 8/00, H01M 8/02, H01M 8/04, H01M 8/06, H01M 8/08, H01M 8/10, H01M 8/12, H01M 8/14, H01M 8/16, H01M 8/18, H01M 8/20, H01M 8/22, H01M 8/24
Wind energy	F03D 1/00, F03D 3/00, F03D 5/00, F03D 7/00, F03D 9/00, F03D 11/00, B60L 8/00
Geothermal energy	F24J 3/08, F03G 4/00, F03G 7/05

Note: For definitions of IPC symbols, see *www.wipo.int/classifications/ipc*. The correspondence between IPC symbols and technology fields is not always clear-cut, and so it is difficult to capture all patents in a specific technology field. Nonetheless, the IPC-based definitions of the four technologies presented above are likely to capture the vast majority of related patents.
Source: WIPO.

Annex B. Composition of industry sectors by Nice goods and services classes

Industry sector	Abbreviation (where applicable)	Nice classes
Agricultural products and services	Agriculture	29, 30, 31, 32, 33, 43
Management, communications, real estate and financial services	Business services	35, 36
Chemicals	..	1, 2, 4
Textiles – clothing and accessories	Clothing	14, 18, 22, 23, 24, 25, 26, 27, 34
Construction, infrastructure	Construction	6, 17, 19, 37, 40
Pharmaceuticals, health, cosmetics	Health	3, 5, 10, 44
Household equipment	..	8, 11, 20, 21
Leisure, education, training	Leisure & Education	13, 15, 16, 28, 41
Scientific research, information and communication technology	Research & Technology	9, 38, 42, 45
Transportation and logistics	Transportation	7, 12, 39

Source: Edital®.

Annex C. Industry sectors by Locarno classes

Sector	Locarno classes
Advertising	20, 32
Agricultural products and food preparation	1, 27, 31
Construction	23, 25, 29
Electricity and lighting	13, 26
Furniture and household goods	6, 7, 30
Health, pharma and cosmetics	24, 28
ICT and audiovisual	14, 16, 18
Leisure and education	17, 19, 21, 22
Packaging	9
Textiles and accessories	2, 3, 5, 11
Tools and machines	4, 8, 10, 15
Transport	12

Source: Organisation for Economic Co-operation and Development (OECD).

www.ingramcontent.com/pod-product-compliance
Lightning Source LLC
Chambersburg PA
CBHW082310210326
41599CB00030B/5755